Heritage Visitor Attractions

An Operations Management Perspective

Edited by

Anna Leask and Ian Yeoman

CONTINUUM

London ♦ New York

Continuum
The Tower Building, 11 York Road, London, SE1 7NX
www.continuumbooks.com
370 Lexington Avenue, New York, NY 10017-6503

First published 1999

Reprinted 1999, 2002

British Library Cataloguing-in-Publication Data
A catalogue record for this book is available from the British Library.

ISBN 0-304-70291-9 hb
0-8264-6061-5 pb

Designed and typeset by Kenneth Burnley at Irby, Wirral, Cheshire.
Printed and bound in Great Britain by Bookcraft, Midsomer Norton, Bath.

Contents

CONTENTS

An Answer Book is available on request from the
publishers to lecturers who intend to adopt this text.

Foreword

Think of what could have been lost. An historic crossroads at the base of the Pyrenees, hard by the River Aude. A walled city built up over centuries. The focal point of the Albigensian heresy and the centrepiece of a siege by Pope Innocent III in 1209. An object of the wrath of the Black Prince in 1355. But by the dawn of the nineteenth century, it was a slum, rapidly deteriorating. In 1850, permission was given to the local populace to take its stones, as if it were a quarry.

Carcassonne: now one of the medieval marvels through which visitors can glance back and imagine what life was like 700 years ago and more. One can almost imagine the ghost of Errol Flynn cavorting on the ramparts, ready to pour boiling oil on the attacking forces. And yet, it is only due to the actions of a local scholar, Jean-Pierre Cros-Mayrevielle; the author of *Carmen*, Prosper Merimee; and the renowned architect, E. E. Viollet-le-Duc, that we can enjoy this thrilling site. They saved the fortress city for our generation.

But will we save it for the generations that are to follow us? The answer lies not only in our commitment to historic restoration but also in our financial capability to sustain the costs of maintenance and repair. These costs can be heavy. If visitor attractions such as Carcassonne are to be sustained, they must be well managed, not only to assure that they are well cared for, but also to assure a steady revenue stream.

The quickest way to ruin that I know is a badly run operation. A poorly run operation can drain the life out of companies – waste, high costs, low morale, disregard for the consumer. This is a book about operations. Specifically, it deals with heritage visitor attractions such as Carcassonne. In so doing, it draws upon many very useful case study examples. It is medicine for those weakly managed heritage visitor attractions that might otherwise die a slow death.

Addressing operations for heritage visitor attractions (HVAs) is important. The relatively easy entry and exit of many types of service firms, because of the typically low barriers to entry and exit that prevail in most service operations, do not apply with the same force when it comes to heritage visitor attractions. HVAs typically cannot be easily duplicated, or relocated. Indeed, they often have to be especially cared for against the onslaught of the tourist crowds, and at substantial cost. Modern attractions can be built specifically to handle huge numbers, but even a hitherto impregnable castle may not be able to withstand a continual siege of visitors. In addition, a poorly run HVA cannot easily be compensated for by superb operations elsewhere. Rather, poorly run HVAs represent a dead-weight loss to the economy. In such situations, people would have come and would have enjoyed themselves – and would have spent the money – but they did not, and one cannot re-capture the visitor-day that was lost as a result. We are all the poorer for this.

What we need to do is to enliven and enrich what has been termed the 'service encounter', the moments when the customer comes into contact with the service being delivered. With HVAs, this service encounter can be an extended one, with special characteristics, but it still demands an understanding of three attributes of service businesses that surround and support the service encounter: the service task, service standards, and the service delivery system:

- Service task: why the service exists in the marketplace and what the customer truly values about it *vis-à-vis* the competition.
- Service standards: the operational definition of what effective service provision to the customer is.
- Service delivery system: how the service is produced and how it is controlled for quality, cost, and customer satisfaction.

The various chapters in this book, no matter what their titles, deal with one or more of these aspects of service management. Moreover, in the best-managed HVAs, the service task, standards, and delivery system are not only well understood but they are consistent with one another and thus ably support one another. Without such understanding, one risks the kind of problems that struck the Disney company with the 1992 launch of the Euro Disney theme park attraction.

HVAs and their operations deserve our attention so that they can satisfy their customers more fully and, in the process, keep earning necessary profits. The research and commentary in these pages are devoted to this task. Buy your ticket and enjoy walking about.

Roger W. Schmenner
Kelley School of Business, Indiana University

Introduction

DEFINING OPERATIONS MANAGEMENT FOR HERITAGE VISITOR ATTRACTIONS

The characteristics of heritage visitor attractions (HVAs) are unique, as no standard model of operations management fits their characteristics. These characteristics, or uniqueness, include an experience-based product, intangibility, high fixed costs, varying customer willingness to pay for the product, education role, inability to inventory, service production / consumption often together and a variety of outside influences.

HVAs vary enormously in type and form, ranging from small-scale, locally based properties to large key attractions that form the basis of a country's tourism product. Management issues relating to this range are often surprisingly similar, working within an increasingly competitive environment, with decreasing resources and ongoing conflict between conserving the heritage and allowing access to visitors.

The operations function of the heritage visitor attraction is the arrangement of resources which is devoted to production of the HVA experience. Operations managers are the staff at HVAs responsible for managing the resources that comprise the operations function. Operations management is the term which is used for the activities, decisions and responsibilities of operations managers. Service operations management is a redefined term appropriate for operations management in the service industry. In HVAs it relates to the movement and management of visitors from input to output within an HVA. An HVA is a service delivery system, which is the equivalent of the production and distribution system in manufacturing, but is often very different in character. The service delivery system is the interface between organization and visitor, therefore the HVA operations manager is concerned with design of the service concept, improvement, capacity management, and the strategy of operations management. Therefore the purpose of this book is to produce a model of operations management appropriate to HVAs.

To begin with, the Editors have drawn upon Roger Schmenner's model of service operations management (*Service Operations Management*, Englewood Cliffs, NJ: Prentice-Hall, 1995), as a basis to design a model of HVAs. This model enables the operations manager to think in the terms of service processes, features and operations management. It is helpful to view these HVAs within this context that contrasts labour intensity on one hand, with the degree of customization of the HVA for the visitor on the other. HVAs can be classified in the terms of Factory, Shop, Mass or Professional experience. Once the operations manager has established the foundation of where HVAs are, decisions can be made on how to manage, improve and change the HVA experience. Schmenner draws upon a features approach of service, process, customer, labour and management as a decision-making formula for discussion. This discussion enables the operations manager to enhance the operations process within HVAs moving from one style of service to another if required.

Given the importance of focused operations and changing environment in the HVAs, understanding the nature of operations management and the characteristics of HVAs leads to a tailored model of operations management that is presented in this book.

The nature of operations management for HVAs is presented in Figure 1 (page xi). Section 1 combines the characteristics of HVAs and the principles of operations management. Sue Millar, in Chapter 1, provides the reader with an overview of the HVA sector, a comprehensive classification model that distinguishes HVAs from Schmenner's classification matrix. Liz Sharples and colleagues build upon that classification of HVAs into a model of operations management unique to the HVA sector. This model is based upon service, process, customer and management features. The chapter expands into the challenges of operations management for the different styles of HVAs.

Section 2 deals with the design of HVAs. Tim Caulton, in Chapter 3, describes the concept development of HVAs from a marketing and operations perspective. The chapter deals with the process of developing a new HVA and what is recognized as best practice. Christina Goulding, in Chapter 4, provides a broad overview of the principles of interpretation methods with the industry, focusing on the visitor experience and management responsibilities in interpretation. Myra Shackley, in Chapter 5, introduces the student to the principles of visitor management process. This follows a flow process scenario of: before the visit, during the visit, and measuring performance. Chapter 6, by Marion Bennett, explains the interface between technology and the HVA experience, concentrating on the role of interpretation. Chapter 7 deals with job design and work organization, specifically applied to managing volunteers. Margaret Graham and her colleagues provide a framework that is unique to HVAs. Paul Reynolds, in Chapter 8, discusses the balance between product and design process in HVAs.

Once the HVA has been designed, operations management are concerned with

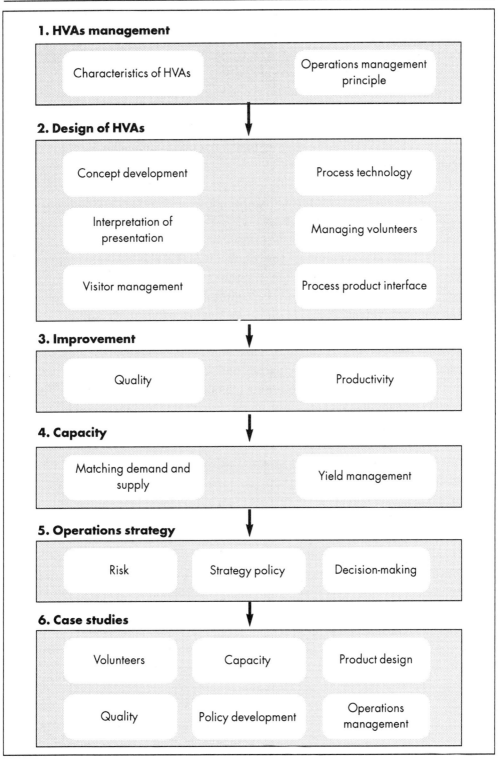

Figure 1: Operations management for HVAs.

maintaining and improvement. Section 3 deals with this process, starting with Nick Johns' discussion regarding the importance of quality. Chapter 9 explains definitions of quality, measurement, maintenance and improvement. John Heap, in Chapter 10, extends theses concepts through productivity.

Section 4 deals with the management of capacity within HVAs. Gerald Barlow, in Chapter 11, deals with the process of matching demand and supply. The reader is provided with an overview of capacity management strategies that are appropriate to HVAs, providing a very useful chapter for the operations manager. Ian Yeoman and Anna Leask discuss the application of yield management from the hospitality and airline industry to HVAs in Chapter 12.

Section 5 deals with the interface of operations and strategy. In Chapter 13, Neil McGregor discusses the balance between preserving the HVA and the need for revenue, through consideration of the consequences of such a strategy. In Chapter 14, Phyllis Laybourn examines the decision-making process of operations management within the context of HVAs, thus providing the reader with a sound understanding of the cognitive and behavioural aspects of decision-making. In Chapter 15, Ros Derrett looks at the relationship of strategy and policy. Ros integrates marketing, human resource and operations management into one model.

Section 6 deals with a range of case studies based upon the principles of operations management. Tony Ingold and colleagues, in Chapter 16, use Schmenner's model to explain operations management practices at Ray's Farm. In Chapter 17, Graham Black provides an overview of the development of the Thackray Medical Museum in Leeds, covering the aspects of interpretation, visitor management, marketing and educational needs.

Jennifer Graham and David Morrison discuss the constraints of capacity applied to Santa Train Special operated by SRPS in Chapter 18. Leo Jago and Margaret Deery in Chapter 19 provide an interesting case study about the relationships of volunteers and paid employees at Nugget Hill Gold Mine Village, Australia. Eric Laws, in Chapter 20, explains the process of service quality blueprinting for enhancing quality at Leeds Castle. This is then followed by Chapter 21, where Alf Hatton overviews Coventry City Council's policy on museum management, with the need for change being considered in terms of developing policy and organizational culture.

The aim of the book is to provide operations managers, students and those with an interest in HVAs with a precise and unique body of knowledge that will result in a better understanding of the operations management process in HVAs.

ANNA LEASK AND IAN YEOMAN
Hospitality & Tourism Management Group
Napier University Business School, Edinburgh
April 1998

Notes on the Contributors

Anna E. Leask is a lecturer in tourism management at Napier University, Edinburgh. She studied at the University of Aberdeen, graduating with an Honours Degree in Geography, after which she graduated from the University of Strathclyde with an MSc in Hotel Administration with Tourism. This was followed by management posts in a variety of properties including Swallow Hotels, Glasgow Royal Concert Hall, before taking up lecturing. She is currently involved in a number of research and consultancy projects in tourism, particularly in the area of heritage management.

Ian Yeoman is a graduate of Sheffield City Polytechnic with a first degree in Catering Systems. After graduation, Ian pursued a career with Forte Hotels, holding several Operations Management posts. Ian is now a lecturer in Service Operations Management at Napier University. Ian has authored and edited a range of journals and books including *Yield Management: Strategies for the Service Industry*. Ian is studying a PhD in Soft Operational Research Techniques due to be completed in 2000. Ian was awarded the Mike Simpson Citation from the Operational Research Society in 1994.

Gerald L. Barlow is a Senior Lecturer in Operations Management in the Department of Business at the University of Central England. He has recently written four chapters for different operations management and quality textbooks. He is currently undertaking a major research contract investigating the issues surrounding 'Break-Out' and business growth, within the SME sector of the restaurant trade. Prior to entering an academic career he was an operations manager for an international group of hotels based in London.

Dr Marion M. Bennett is currently a lecturer in tourism and marketing at the School of Management Studies for the Service Sector, University of Surrey. Prior to joining Surrey in 1995, she spent four years as a lecturer in tourism at the University of Strathclyde. Her PhD, which she obtained from the University of Reading, is on the role of information technology in the travel agency. She also has a First Class Honours Degree (BA) in Geography from the University of Nottingham, together with the Edwards' Prize for Human Geography and an Exhibition. Commercial experience was gained at American Express where she was a marketing executive following completion of the Graduate Development Programme. She has had articles published in a wide range of journals as well as a book published in 1996 co-authored with A. V. Seaton and entitled *Marketing Tourism Products*. Research interests centre on information technology and distribution, heritage, airlines and strategic alliances.

Graham Black is subject leader in Heritage Studies at the Nottingham Trent University. He began his career as a field archaeologist before moving into museum work. He became Senior Curator with Nottingham Museum Service before leaving to become a consultant Heritage Interpreter in 1988. Since then he has been responsible for a number of award-winning exhibitions, most recently the Galleries of Justice in Nottingham, which received the Gulbenkian Prize in 1996, and Thackray Medical Museum in Leeds which received the Special Judges Prize in the Interpret Britain Awards in 1997. His research centres on the practice of heritage interpretation and he continues to combine academic work with his career in exhibition development.

Tim Caulton has been involved in the development and management of several museums since 1982, including Eureka! The Museum for Children, from 1990 to 1993. He is course tutor on the MA in Arts and Heritage Management programme at Sheffield University, and is author of *Hands-on Exhibitions: Managing Interactive Museums and Science Centres.*

Margaret A. Deery is a lecturer in human resource management also at Victoria University. Her research interests include volunteer satisfaction and turnover culture in the hospitality industry.

Ros Derrett is on the academic staff at the School of Tourism and Hospitality Management. She delivers units in Special Interest Tourism, Recreation and Tourism Planning, Tourism Environments and Marketing in the Hospitality and Tourism industry at undergraduate and postgraduate level. Prior to taking up her position at Southern Cross University, Ros worked extensively in education, community cultural development, arts administration and planning in Australia and other countries. She has had extensive experience in marketing and media for public and commercial enterprises. She developed a regional community-based arts centre providing multiple cultural services. Ros's advocacy of appropriate regional development has led to her involvement in policy and planning for cultural tourism, indigenous cultural enterprise development and collaborative marketing projects.

Malcolm Foley is Assistant Head of the Department of Hospitality, Tourism and Leisure Management, and Reader in Leisure Management at Glasgow Caledonian University. His main research interests include the changing nature of management in public sector recreation and the 'new' public management in the leisure industries. His recent work includes studies of the impact of pricing at museums and galleries, the role of exercise referral schemes in sport and recreation management and the development of strategies to influence recreational user behaviour in the Scottish countryside.

Dr Christina Goulding is a Principal Lecturer in Marketing at the University of Wolverhampton Business School. She holds a PhD in the area of consumer experiences and representations of the past. Her current research interests and publications are primarily in the field of consumer behaviour and qualitative research methodologies.

Jennifer J. Graham is a Teaching Fellow at Napier University. She is responsible for industrial links and the development of work-based learning and live projects with students in hospitality and tourism. The focus of her current research is in developing and assessing student teamwork and core transferable skills, and involving employers in the assessment of students.

Margaret Graham is undertaking doctoral research into museum volunteering and teaches leisure operations to undergraduates and postgraduates at the Department of

Hospitality, Leisure and Tourism at Glasgow Caledonian University. She has a BA (Hons) in History and Sociology with work experience in industry, education, the voluntary sector and more recently held the post of assistant curator in a small independent museum.

Alf Hatton is a management consultant, and former Senior Lecturer in Heritage Studies, Nottingham Trent; lecturer in heritage management at Ironbridge Institute (Birmingham University), and founder lecturer in museum studies, Institute of Archaeology, University College, London. Management posts in heritage: Museums Officer, Monmouth District, Curator of Ipswich Museums & Galleries, and Museums Service Manager, Coventry. Previous research: museum performance indicators, organizational culture development and audit. Current research: strategic thinking in heritage.

John Heap is Director of Learning and Information Services at Leeds Metropolitan University, a member of the International Advisory Council of the World Confederation of Productivity Science, a Fellow of the World Academy of Productivity Science, a member of the Council of Management of the Institute of Management Services, and Chair of the British Standards Institution Committee on Management Services.

Bill Hughes is Senior Lecturer in Sociology in the Department of Social Sciences at Glasgow Caledonian University. He has a BA (Hons) from the University of Stirling (awarded 1979) and a PhD from the University of Aberdeen (awarded 1985). His research interests are in the sociology of the body, the sociology of health, illness and medicine, and contemporary sociological theory. His teaching duties and publications reflect these interests.

Anthony Ingold is Reader and Director of Research at Birmingham College of Food, Tourism & Creative Studies. Tony initially trained as a medical microbiologist, then diversified to take a more general interest in applications of research methodologies, notably to a variety of problems encountered in the service industries. Recently, Tony has worked with Land Rover and British Midland Airways, on development of yield management decision support systems. He has co-authored a book on yield mangement, additionally contributing two chapters. Tony has contributed to five books and published 49 research papers to date, with seven more in preparation.

Leo K. Jago is a Senior Lecturer in Tourism and Marketing at Victoria University in Melbourne. His research interests include volunteer motivation, special events and consumer motivation.

Dr Nick Johns is Reader at the Research Centre, City College, Norwich. His interests include both operational and marketing aspects of service quality. Nick is co-author of *Research Methods for Service Industry Management* published by Cassell (1998), and has written and contributed to many textbooks as well as academlc and practitioner periodicals. He is an Associate Editor of the *International Journal of Contemporary Hospitality Management* and a frequent reviewer of papers in the service quality area.

Eric Laws now lectures and researches tourism and service quality in the Faculty of Business at Queensland University of Technology, Brisbane. He has previously held appointments in several British universities, most recently at Napier University, Edinburgh. He is now the Director of the Queensland International Business Research Concentration at QUT.

Phyllis K. Laybourn is a lecturer in psychology at Napier University, Edinburgh. She completed her degree and PhD at the University of Dundee and thereafter took up a post-doctoral research post in the University of Oxford. She currently balances her research interests in cognitive psychology (the areas of decision-making and perception) with an active interest in innovations in teaching and learning in higher education.

Professor David Litteljohn has been Director of Research in the Department of Hospitality, Tourism and Leisure Management at Glasgow Caledonian University since May 1994. He has worked for both public and private sector organizations in hospitality and tourism. His research interests cover international industry trends in tourism markets and tourism organizations.

Neil C. McGregor is a lecturer in applied economics and tourism at the University of Abertay, Dundee. He was previously an ESRC Management Teaching Fellow at Loughborough University Business School after graduating with a BA(Hons) Economics and an MSc in Finance, both from the University of Stirling. He has acted as a consultant on a range of projects for economic development agencies in Scotland and is a registered environmental auditor. Research interests include sustainable tourism development and environmental management.

Sue Millar is Head of the University of Greenwich Business School. Her career has alternated between the heritage and university sectors. As Head of Interpretation and Education, National Maritime Museum, Greenwich, she created innovative life-long learning provision including a maritime interactive gallery. As a pioneer of professional postgraduate management programmes she developed the Masters in Heritage Management, Ironbridge Institute, and currently MAs in Museum, Heritage Arts and Cultural Tourism Management. Publications include *Volunteers in Museums and Heritage Organisations: Policy Planning and Management* (1991).

David J. Morrison is a chartered electrical engineer with a BSc Honours Degree from Glasgow University and a MSc from Heriot-Watt University. He has been the Volunteer Marketing Manager at the Bo'ness and Kinneil Railway since 1993.

Paul Reynolds is currently Associate Professor at Southern Cross University at Coffs Harbour Campus. He has over sixteen years' experience in training and development in the tourism and hospitality field in both South East Asia and Australia and has lectured in hospitality management, quality improvement and service industry management for the past ten years. Paul has extensive knowledge in advising and implementing tourism plans in local areas of China, Hong Kong, Vietnam and UK and has helped companies such as the Peninsula Group, Shangri-La, Accor and Beaufort in training and developing staff in several countries. Research interests include customer satisfaction and value chain assessment in tourism.

Myra Shackley is Professor of Culture Resource Management at Nottingham Trent University and directs their Centre for Tourism and Visitor Management. Her research interests lie mainly in the management of visitors to historic sites and protected areas, with a particular emphasis on the Developing World. Her most recent book is *Visitor Management: Case Studies from World Heritage Sites* (Butterworth-Heinemann 1998).

Liz Sharples is a Senior Lecturer in the School of Leisure and Food Management at Sheffield Hallam University. She has worked as a Duty Manager with a major hotel chain and as a Catering Manager in charge of a multi-site operation. Her research interests include Environmental Policy within Catering Operations and Catering for Visitors at Tourist Destinations. She is currently involved with the development of a catering concept for a new museum, the National Centre for Popular Music, to be opened in Sheffield.

CHAPTER 1

An Overview of the Sector

Sue Millar

A competitive attraction for the 21st century will require a unique combination of courageous creativity and management skills of the highest order. Educative and entertaining, partnerships, multi-media, active visitor participation, quality and value for money are the buzz words as we move to the Millennium.

(Cameron 1995)

The stark realization that heritage visitor attractions provide the focus for the heritage industry's involvement in a global tourist industry that is forecast to double in size by the year 2005, contrasts dramatically with the knowledge that the professional management of heritage attractions, in terms of operations management, is in its infancy. This is true of attractions management in general. 'It is rare to find people specifically called operations managers. More often the role is part of a wider brief, or the job is split between several staff' (Swarbrooke 1995). Recognition that the future success of tourism depends upon the way it is handled at its destination has particular significance in the context of heritage resources and their management, both within the United Kingdom, elsewhere in Europe and among the developing economies of the world.

This chapter offers an exploration and analysis of the issues, debates and developments within the heritage sector in the context of the operations management of HVAs and in relation to the Schmenner (1995) Operations Management matrix. The complexities surrounding definitions of the Heritage Industry and heritage visitor attractions are addressed and a new classification for HVAs is introduced. An examination of the current market environment and visitor profile for HVAs illustrates the fundamental importance of effective operations management to the future success of heritage visitor attractions in the twenty-first century.

THE HERITAGE INDUSTRY – TOWARDS A DEFINITION

In the United Kingdom the fear expressed in the late 1980s, that the commodification of heritage was leading to the prospect of Britain becoming 'one big open air museum', in many respects has become a reality ten years later (Hewison 1987). Heritage can be visited at an increasingly wide range and number of site-specific Heritage Attractions – museums, historic houses, country parks, historic gardens, nature reserves, archaeological sites, heritage centres and heritage theme parks – but also during the course of everyday life. A call at the bank, a walk in the park or along the river bank can often be described as a *heritage experience*. Heritage has become a focus for economic regeneration projects across Europe, usually in run-down inner-city areas. The Lowry Centre at Salford Quays and the Royal Armouries in Leeds are two recent examples in the North of England. Heritage can also be bought. The retail sector of the heritage business is booming. *Museum Company* retail outlets are to be found in shopping malls across the United States as well as Canada and Japan : two have now arrived in Greater London. A tour of the Louvre is available not only in Paris but by courtesy of a CD-rom, sitting at a desk.

The growing multiplicity of meanings embraced within the term 'heritage' and parallel recognition of the economic importance of the service sector as a whole continue to bring heritage centre-stage. Whether imagined or real, heritage connotations imply quality, security and an aura of confidence. Increasing levels of car ownership have made the countryside accessible for retirement homes as well as day trips and holidays. Idealized heritage landscapes are the sought-after valued environments. Again Hewison sounds a warning note: 'The landscape that we see is not out there: it is in our heads, filtered by our cultural perceptions, structured by our psychological needs' (Hewison 1992). Heritage is part of the fabric of people's lives, consciously or unconsciously accommodating aspirations and providing symbols of continuity, icons of identity and places for pleasure, enjoyment and enlightenment in the fast-changing world of global communications.

In short, over the past decade heritage has been employed 'to describe virtually anything by which some link, however tenuous, can be made with the past' (Johnson and Thomas 1995). It is axiomatic that precise definitions are difficult. Ashworth and Tunbridge (1996) have identified five commonly understood meanings:

- Heritage places – objects, buildings, sites, towns, districts, regions.
- Memories – collective and individual.
- Cultural and artistic production.
- Heritage landscapes and heritage flora and fauna.
- The heritage industry – selling goods and services with a heritage component.

The clarity is welcome but a definition of the heritage industry separating the service encounter away from the resources on which it depends is inappropriate. The heritage industry is inter-related and interwoven with, and indeed part of, the cultural industries in general and the burgeoning conservation businesses in particular. The multi-faceted heritage industry is big business. Later in this chapter the operations management of heritage visitor attractions will be examined within this overarching framework.

The heritage industry, broadly defined, draws on the past for the benefit of the present and future whether in the form of ideas, images, stories, plays, traditions, buildings, artefacts or landscapes. In its raw state heritage is simply the natural, cultural and built environment of an area. Philosophically, the present centred nature of heritage means that a cycle of renewal, change and transformation is inherent in the heritage concept for conservation bodies, commercial operators and consumers alike. Heritage is as much a dynamic concept – a springboard for future action – as a catalyst for nostalgia. Continuities can be maintained only through discovery and rediscovery, invention and reinvention, positioning and repositioning. Heritage is culturally constructed and so provides the flexibility and opportunities for development required by heritage organizations and heritage managers. Malleable enough to be used by significant groups at international, national and local levels in the public, private and voluntary sectors to support the interpretation and presentation of a particular point of view, heritage nevertheless remains an enigma.

Ultimately the heritage experience is distinctive and unique to the individual. Nowhere is this shown more poignantly than in the designer-led Holocaust Memorial to the Jewish people, Yad Vashem in Israel, where a single candle burns with six million mirror images leaving room for individual reflection. At the opposite end of the spectrum, heritage has become a source of fun and boisterous relaxation. Themed participatory experiences such as medieval or Tudor banquets, or the Wild West in Frontierland, provide the opportunity to live, for a few hours at least, a fantasy of uniform uniqueness. Recognition of the continuing expansion, fluidity of meaning and different applications of notions of heritage into the twenty-first century is important from the point of view of answering the question: 'What is a heritage visitor attraction?' and locating HVAs in their market and operational context.

HERITAGE VISITOR ATTRACTIONS – TOWARDS A CLASSIFICATION

Heritage visitor attractions defy a commonly accepted definition or agreed typology. Three different perspectives are identifiable – the *outside* commentator/observer of the heritage product; the *outside/inside* protagonist of the tourism product, and the *inside* exponent of conservation. From the point of view of the heritage manager, none of the existing typologies are sufficient on their own in providing supportive diagnostic tools. Therefore a new model is put forward here to further the debate.

The commentator's stance is taken by Prentice. The immense variety of heritage visitor attractions is emphasized. 'The heterogeneity of present-day heritage is mirrored in the heterogeneity of heritage attractions, that is sites, themes and areas promoted as heritage products for consumption by tourists and day trippers visiting from home' (Prentice 1993). Eclectic and detailed (despite aiming to be concise and manageable) his typology of 23 subject-based heritage attractions with many subdivisions is designed to explore the production of heritage within an integrated European model. Major categories of attractions include, among others, natural history, craft centres, performing arts, transport, military, stately and ancestral homes, towns, countryside, seaside resorts, festivals and pageants, socio-cultural and field sports. Prentice's definition of a heritage attraction is broad – 'a site, theme, or area which attracts visitors' – but he points out that the attraction may not itself be attractive, and cites as examples his inclusion of field sports and genocide monuments. Interesting and useful for an analysis of supply and demand patterns, the typology is of limited value in HVA management on the ground.

The tourism perspective places heritage visitor attractions firmly within the overall category of visitor attractions. Recognition of the importance of attractions to tourism is increasing. Visitor attractions are 'the most important component of the tourism system' and the 'core of the tourism product' argues Swarbrooke (1995). He takes a broad view of visitor attractions – a large number are also heritage visitor attractions – but, unlike Prentice, distinguishes between attractions and destinations.

> Attractions are generally single units, individual sites or very small, easily delimited geographical areas based on a single key feature. Destinations are larger areas that include a number of individual attractions together with the support services required by tourists.

In his typology visitor attractions are divided into four types – natural; man-made but not originally designed primarily to attract visitors; man-made and purpose-built to attract tourists; and special events. The category *natural* can be equated with a *destination* rather than an *attraction* according to his own definition (Table 1.1). An understandable tension exists between the macro and micro focus on visitor attractions either as destinations or as single units in terms of the tourism product.

Definitional simplicity is appealing but flawed. The tourist boards in the UK identify five major categories of visitor attractions: historic properties, gardens, museums and art galleries, wildlife attractions, and 'other' attractions such as country parks and steam railways. Further subdivisions include farms, leisure parks, workplaces and visitor centres (Hanna 1997ab). Their current working definition is adapted from an earlier version used by the Scottish Tourist Board.

4

Table 1.1: Four categories of attraction.

Natural	Man-made but not originally designed primarily to attract visitors	Man-made and purpose-built to attract tourists	Special events
Beaches. Caves. Rock faces. Rivers and lakes. Forests. Wildlife: flora and fauna.	Cathedrals and churches. Stately homes and historic houses. Archaeological sites and ancient monuments. Historic gardens. Industrial archaeology sites. Steam railways. Reservoirs.	Amusement parks. Theme parks. Open-air museums. Heritage centres. Country parks. Marinas. Exhibition centres. Garden centres. Craft centres. Factory tours and shops. Working farms open to the public. Safari parks. Entertainment complexes. Casinos. Health spas. Leisure centres. Picnic sites. Museums and galleries. Leisure retail complexes. Waterfront developments.	Sporting events: watching and participating. Arts festivals. Markets and fairs. Traditional customs and folklore events. Historical anniversaries. Religious events.

The attraction must be a permanently established excursion destination, a primary purpose of which is to allow public access for entertainment, interest or education; rather than being primarily a retail outlet or a venue for sporting, theatrical, or film performances.

In addition, 'the attraction must be a single business, under a single management' (Hanna 1997a).

The tourist boards' statement explicitly omits venues for sporting, theatrical or film performances. Yet even if this is convenient, it is not true. Many theatrical performances take place in historic theatres. Sporting events such as polo are not only visitor attractions, but also heritage visitor attractions. Events can be seen as a separate category (Swarbrooke 1995) but from the management point of view this is problematic. Festivals and pageants usually take place within the boundaries of an historic town or heritage site. Decisions need to be taken based on a holistic view of an event in the context of the operation of an existing visitor attraction. The concept of the vertical integration and layering of the destination, site and event, each in their own right an HVA, is the essential starting-point.

Differences in the missions of organizations that have become HVAs are critical to their strategic planning and day-to-day operations. The difference between ecclesiastical sites – churches and cathedrals – and museums and galleries as heritage visitor attractions relates to their different organizational goals rather than, in many cases, their physical infrastructure. They are, first, places of worship and, second, heritage visitor attractions. In contrast, heritage theme parks and heritage centres that use the people and stories of the past, free of the constraints of the physical remains – the *tangible heritage* – have the greatest opportunity to create, control and promote the visitor experience as purpose-made visitor attractions.

What turns a tract of land, monument, park, historic house or coastline into a heritage attraction is often the attitude of the public. An attraction has to be recognized as an attraction by the visitors themselves. The role of the visitor in determining what should and should not be a heritage visitor attraction – encouraged by custom, tradition, fashion or marketing and promotional initiatives – must be juxtaposed with the role of public and private providers (identified in Figure 1.2) in consciously creating a heritage visitor attraction (Walsh-Heron and Stevens 1990). Consumer demand for high standards of facilities world-wide and increasingly distinctive heritage attractions with *rarity value* is potentially conflicting.

The conservationist perspective presents an interesting contrast in terms of a typology (Table 1.2). There is an emphasis on national and international standards primarily in the care of the artefacts, buildings or landscapes for present and future generations. The visitor experience is a very important parallel but secondary concern. In fact, the language is key. Phrases such as public access, public services, public resources and public enjoyment are used rather than *visitors* or indeed *customers*. In the UK the Heritage Lottery Fund is a prime mover, not only in deciding what particular 'items or property' are of local, regional and national importance, but also in clarifying what is to be understood by *the heritage*. The guidelines state:

> You must be able to demonstrate the heritage importance of the asset. Proposals for development and improvement should always be led by conservation considerations. Applicants need to show that their project will help to acquire, maintain, preserve, or enhance through improved access or display, the public's enjoyment or knowledge of one or more of the following types of heritage property: land and countryside; historic buildings and sites, including townscapes, urban parks and places of worship; museums and collections; archives and special libraries; industrial, transport and maritime heritage.
>
> (HLF 1997)

Museums in the UK have a Registration Scheme run by the Museums and Galleries Commission operating to strict criteria (MGC 1995a). The scheme

Table 1.2: Major government agencies/voluntary bodies.

Government agencies	Classification	Number
MGC	Registered museums	1,759
EH	Ancient monuments	15,400
	Listed buildings	450,000
	Conservation areas	9,000
	Historic properties*	409
HS	Ancient monuments	6,800
	Listed buildings	43,347
	Conservation areas	602
	Historic properties	300
CC	National Parks	10
	Areas of Outstanding	
	Natural Beauty (AONB)	41
	Heritage Coast	1,525 km
	Community Forests	12
	National Trails	12
EN	Nature Reserves	194
	Sites of Special	
	Scientific Interest (SSSIs)	4,007

Scottish Natural Heritage[+]

Voluntary bodies		
National Trust	Historic buildings**	300; also 240,000 hectares of coast and countryside
National Trust for Scotland	Historic buildings	122; also 188,000 hectares of coast and countryside

*	Historic properties: earthworks, dolmen, henges (inluding Stonehenge), stone circles, Roman remains, medieval castles, abbeys, houses and gardens.
**	Historic houses, castles, other buildings, mills/industrial archaeology, churches/chapels, prehistoric/Roman sites, farms.
+	Sister organization to both the Countryside Commission and English Nature. Transitional stage of development.
MGC	Museums and Galleries Commission (UK)
EH	English Heritage
HS	Historic Scotland
CC	Countryside Commission
EN	English Nature
NT	National Trust (England, Wales and Northern Ireland)

'encourages all museums and galleries to achieve approved standards in museum management, collections care and public services'. It is designed 'to foster confidence in museums as repositories of our common heritage and managers of public resources'. Some steam railways and historic houses are included but those organizations called *museums*, that either have loan collections or no collections at all and could be classified as HVAs, are excluded. Museums can be autonomous places of formal education and research and may or may not be classified as heritage visitor attractions. Public access is strictly limited to many university museums. English Heritage, the government agency responsible for the built environment, directly or indirectly supports the infrastructure for many towns, villages and buildings in landscapes that have become heritage visitor attractions. Where possible, this organization operates its historic properties both as resources for formal learning and as HVAs. The National Trust (England, Wales and Northern Ireland), as the largest voluntary conservation body in Europe, is in charge of tracts of countryside and coastline, houses, gardens and farms. The vast majority are open to visitors. The balance of *sense* and *sensibility* is maintained by:

> . . . finding ways of integrating visitor management with the whole management plan for each property in such a way that the two cardinal aims are met:
> (i) the particular *genus loci* of the place is wholly respected; and
> (ii) that excellence is achieved in the quality of the experience for visitors, whatever activity they engage in.
>
> (Stirling 1995a)

A new classification for HVAs has been developed to support strategic planning and management initiatives. Whilst accepting the broadest definition that the UK and indeed most of the world can be seen as one large heritage attraction, the classification is specific and based on the assumption that certain urban and rural areas as well as individual sites should be classed as heritage visitor attractions. Both types of resource – heritage areas and heritage sites – require careful management, a topic that will be returned to later. However, a new category is introduced, 'Living Heritage'. This is not re-enactment or costumed interpretation but the traditions and ways of life of people living in the place that can be enhanced to become heritage visitor attractions as well as serving the mutual needs of the local community. The overall classification model in Table 1.3 shifts from the macro to the micro within three main categories: *built* heritage, *natural* heritage and *living* heritage. The generic resources listed within the three sections are not immutable. Forest, for example, is placed in the section *natural heritage site* but, it could be argued, would be better placed under *natural heritage area*. The size of forests varies enormously. National Parks are really mixed resources with historic buildings (built heritage) and

Table 1.3: Generic classification of HVAs.

	'Built' heritage	'Natural' heritage	'Living' heritage
Nation/Region	Cities	Landscape/sea	People
Area	Historic towns Seaside resorts Conservation areas	National Parks Heritage coastline AONBs	Traditional food Festivals Markets
Site	Museums Art galleries Historic buildings Historic sites/monuments Heritage centres Heritage theme parks Transport	Town and country parks Botanic gardens Historic gardens Nature reserves Countryside centres Country parks Forest	Public houses/cafes Craft centres Farms

Table 1.4: Hastings – The Stade – classification of HVAs.

	'Built' heritage	'Natural' heritage	'Living' heritage
Site	The Fishermen's Museum The Shipwreck Heritage Centre Hastings Sea Life Centre The Netshops East Cliff Railway The old boats RNLI Station Historic buildings housing	Country park	The fishing The boat repair man The garage The local community Fish and chips Seafood stalls The wet fish Fish market
Area	Historic fishing beach	The coastline The cliffs The sea The beach	

farms (living heritage). Their focus in the context of a heritage visitor attraction, however, is as a natural resource. The model can be sliced vertically or horizontally and inversed. An example of how the classification system works in practice is shown in Tables 1.4 and 1.5 in relation to the area known as The Stade and the whole resort of the seaside town of Hastings, East Sussex.

HERITAGE VISITOR ATTRACTIONS – THE MARKET ENVIRONMENT

Visits to all area-based heritage visitor attractions and over a third of site-based HVAs are free of charge. The price paid for free visits to heritage attractions can be very high. Those parts of the countryside such as the Lake District and towns like Totnes

Table 1.5: Hastings – seaside resort – classification of HVAs.

	'Built' heritage	'Natural' heritage	'Living' heritage
Site	St Mary in the Castle	Hastings Country Park	Fishing and associated industries
	East Cliff House		The Flower Makers Museum
	Beauport Park		Local cuisine
	Hastings Museum and Art Gallery		Wet fish
	Fishermen's Museum		Local community
	Old Town Hall Museum of Local History		
	The Netshops, old boats at The Stade		
	Shipwreck Heritage Centre		
	RNLI Station		
	The Hastings embroidery display		
	Hastings pier		
	Hastings Castle		
	Smugglers Adventure		
	East and West Cliff Railways		
Area	The Old Town	The coastline	
	Burton St Leonards	The cliffs	
	Town centre	The beach	
	Historic fishing beach	The sea	

in Devon that act as magnets for tourists at peak times have difficulty in sustaining a quality experience. The Lake District Special Planning Board recognizes capacity limits. Strict car parking controls have been introduced. The Italian art cities of Florence and Venice have particular problems of overcrowding. In Florence, Easter 1995, the *Nationale* newspaper proclaimed: 'TRAFFICO CAOS: CITTA INVASA DAI BUS TURISTICO' . 'In no museum, no chapel, no cloister was it possible to move without displacing another person. The crowds seemed dazed, swaying and shuffling past and through one celebrated building after another, camcording the back of the next person's neck' recounted Sir Angus Stirling to the Symposium on World Heritage and Museums in 1995 (Stirling 1995). The only respite – and the only quality experience to be found – was in the high priced Palazzo Riccardi where the numbers looking at the Gozzoli frescoes were limited to fifteen. Experiments with a 'Venice Card' allowing privileged access to selected groups of visitors have been severely criticized as being originated by elitist aesthetes, struggling to regain exclusivity in the determination and enjoyment of culture. Whilst it is possible to sympathize with such fears and query whether charging high admission prices is the answer, the problem is a real one.

Cultural heritage tourism is a growth market for short-stay breaks as well as day trips. It is fuelled by cheaper and cheaper air fares to far-flung places and the increasing trend for people to take more than one holiday a year throughout Western Europe and elsewhere in the developed world. In 1997 there were 22.5 million overseas visitors to England alone, not accounting for Scotland, Wales and Northern Ireland. British residents took 110 million staying trips in England, up 6 per cent on the previous year (ETB 1998). Not only does overcrowding place the quality of the experience in jeopardy – a fundamental pre-requisite for a successful service encounter – but places irreplaceable heritage resources in danger of destruction or just simply wearing out.

A second cost of free access is conservation. The tourist wars are far from subtle and all-invasive. Footpaths in the Lake District, Peak District and in coastal regions require constant attention and renewal. The awareness that the Long Mynd in Shropshire is one of England's last areas of wilderness sits uncomfortably with the cordoning off of a hill next to the car park to enable the land to recover from the erosion caused by too many people climbing to the top. Statues in high-profile public places such as Eros in London's Piccadilly and most recently in Rome have been replaced by replicas. Late in 1997 the trustees of the British Museum briefly decided to think the unthinkable and charge for admission. The new Labour Government in Britain persuaded them to rethink this policy and promised financial support. But the Director is left with the unenviable task of considering controlling access to ensure both the quality of the visitor experience and the conservation needs of the objects on open display. The British Museum has the highest number of visitors of all the non-charging HVAs with 6,228,275 visitors in 1996. Proposals to charge people for climbing Ben Nevis in Scotland were met with an outcry and the scheme was dropped.

The conflict between conservation and access in the heritage industry is likely to augment and reach a crescendo by the Millennium in popular locations at peak times, unless the operational requirements are addressed within a sustainable tourism development policy framework. Up to now tourism and tourists have established an uneasy alliance between communities, conservationists and politicians. This is becoming increasingly precarious. The economic value of the tourist pound, often the incentive and motivation for conservation initiatives and the development of heritage visitor attractions, has not necessarily been forthcoming. Lord Bradford, in a foreword to the official handbook of Britain, 1997, berated 'the cheaper traveller' to London for bringing no economic benefits and clogging up the streets. He proposed a tourist tax on day trippers arriving in the capital city via the ferry terminals and Eurotunnel. 'They often have their own packed lunch . . . One high-spending US tourist could be worth ten times more in economic value than the coach load coming just for the free attractions' (Ford 1997). An increase in visitor numbers has always been the key criterion for success. Unquestionably, this cannot be the sole criterion for the future. Capacity planning, strategies for enabling access to a quality experience without charges of elitism, the relationship of heritage sites to the area in which they are located, development projects and promotional campaigns are all strongly dependent on market intelligence.

VISITOR PROFILE

Visitor trends at site-based heritage attractions reveal a significant disparity between large attendances at a small number of major attractions and, conversely, small attendance figures at the majority of sites. In 1996 over 60 per cent of historic properties, gardens and museums had fewer than 20,000 visitors. From a total of 5,870 attractions analysed, 31 per cent received fewer than 10,000 visits. Stonehenge, Warwick Castle, Hampton Court Palace and Royal Botanic Gardens Edinburgh each receive over half a million visits annually. The big attractions and national icons for tourism dominate. Alton Towers, Madame Tussauds, the Tower of London, National Gallery and York Minster all had over two million visitors, many of them adding to the congestion of city centres. In fact, 7 per cent of all attractions with more than 200,000 visits including one steam railway, 52 museums, 59 historic properties and at least ten visitor centres, received 57 per cent of the total visits. Out of 43 leisure parks in this category, ten or more could be classified as heritage theme parks. Whereas the average number of visits per attraction was 66,000, for leisure parks the average was as high as 469,000 (Hanna 1997a). The picture for the smaller attractions, including many independent museums in the not-for-profit sector, remains precarious (Middleton 1990). Although the target set for museums by Middleton – just under a 3 per cent growth per annum by the year 2000 with between 85 and 105 million visits – has already been realized (estimated at between 80 to 100 million in 1996), supply continues to outstrip demand in the sector. New museums add to the variety of visitor attractions and heritage resources available but not necessarily their economic viability (Hanna 1997ab; DNH 1996; Davies 1994).

Heritage attractions are in the people business. A knowledge and understanding of the characteristics of current and potential visitors to a heritage attraction is the central pre-requisite to identifying and meeting the needs of the different market segments and providing individual customer satisfaction. Higher levels of educational attainment, greater affluence and more leisure time have extended the ranks of the socio-economic groups ABC1 over the last 20 years. The traditional visitors to built heritage attractions are drawn from these groups. In fact, the social selectivity and homogeneity of visitors across museums, art galleries and historic properties is marked (CSO 1995; Davies 1994; Merriman 1991; DNH 1996). Little deviation is shown, however, across socio-economic groupings ABC1 and C2 and even DE where theme parks are concerned, illustrated by the higher visitor figures mentioned earlier. Groupings C2, D and E are more likely to visit a circus or funfair: they go caravanning, camping, visit a public house, take a drive for pleasure and have a meal in a fast-food restaurant in large numbers, even if in proportionately lower numbers than professional, managerial and skilled workers, who are in any case more affluent. Historically, the open countryside has been attractive to a wider range of social groupings than the built environment where *access* – intellectually and emotionally, as well as physically – is more difficult. Nonetheless, given that those groups classically, if inappropriately, described as from the lower socio-economic groups do visit museums and galleries (10 per cent), exhibitions (8 per cent) and historic buildings (12 per cent), there are opportunities for audience development (CSO 1995). Moreover, the heterogeneity of modern lifestyles makes the rigid application of socio-economic groupings less relevant.

At present, the age group visiting historic houses, castles and other historic properties is predominantly between 45 and 64 years (69 per cent), with museums and galleries attracting a third of their visitors from an age group ten years younger – 35 to 54 years (Hanna 1997a; Davies 1994). Teenagers, young adults and the over-65s are the least well-represented groups among museum visitors, but even these groups provide a quarter of all visitors. Children under 16 are the other significant group, accounting for one-third of the total number of visits (DNH 1996). The important point here, as Davies has pointed out, is that museum and art gallery visiting is an activity enjoyed across all age ranges, albeit peaking in the middle age-groups. He concludes that age itself is not a deterrent to visiting. Demographic trends indicate that by 2021 one in five of the population will be aged 65 or over (ONS 1998). A larger mature population, with growing numbers entering higher education from different ethnic and social backgrounds, provides the opportunity to expand visitor numbers to HVAs in parallel with developing new audiences.

Coming from opposite polarities, overseas tourists and local supporters of heritage attractions have proved reliable and constant visitors for over a decade. Overseas tourists make up a fifth of the annual total of visits to museums and galleries in the UK and this trend shows no signs of diminishing (Davies 1994; Hanna 1997ab). Historic properties with over a third of visits from overseas are heavily reliant upon overseas tourism. In fact, the *built* heritage outstrips the *natural* heritage in this respect. The UK is the fifth-largest market for tourism world-wide: history and tradition are the factors uppermost in the decision-making process. The benefits, however, are not evenly distributed. London, the South East, Edinburgh, Stratford, and now Manchester, are the main beneficiaries.

All heritage attractions across the UK gain significantly from local support in their own geographical area. The committed, loyal, frequent visitors who belong to Friends or Membership organizations offer an established basis for relationship marketing activities. Friends groups also provide advocacy, engage in fund-raising activities and many, although not all, support their favoured organization as volunteers.

In the museum sector alone there are in excess of 100,000 volunteers (Walton 1998). Half this number work 'front of house' providing the highly valued human contact visitors seek (MGC 1997c). At the Tate Gallery in Liverpool 'Young Tate' members have acted successfully as exhibition guides for other young people. The Friends of the National Maritime Museum, Greenwich, commissioned a specially designed table in association with the Education department to enable small groups, especially those with visual impairment or other special needs to sit, touch and talk informally about items from the collection that were originally used on board ship. Some heritage organizations attract members nationally as well as locally on the basis of 'communities of interest'. The National Trust currently has over two and a quarter million members and over 35,000 volunteers, many of whom are room stewards in historic houses.

Research relating to non-visitors to site-based HVAs is limited. 'Leisure agendas' have been identified as central to understanding visiting and non-visiting behaviour in American museums. Non-visitors' 'leisure agendas' include social interaction, active participation and feeling comfortable and at ease with their surroundings (Hood 1983). Recent studies have recognized the heterogeneity of both visitors and non-visitors to heritage attractions (Davies and Prentice 1995; Prentice 1993). Moreover, the pattern of consumer demand from discerning visitors is changing. People are seeking a high-quality activity in terms of a 'natural' and informative experience. The rising popularity of farms, visitor centres, work places, wildlife attractions and steam railways (Figure 1.1) is indicative of this trend predicted by Martin and Mason in 1993. They recognized that economic change, social change and new technology would result in the values of 'the thoughtful consumer' moving in the direction of quality of life.

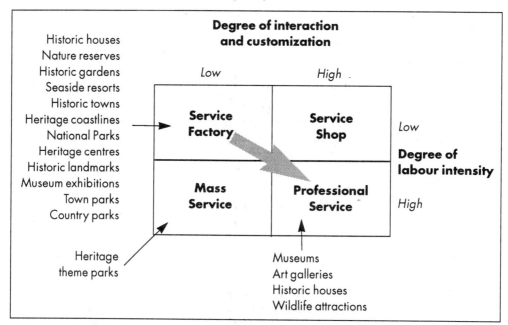

Figure 1.1: Heritage attractions: Schmenner Service Process Matrix.

The intangible and perishable nature of services and the inseparability of the production from the consumption ensures it is more difficult to establish competitive advantage. Promotion is the key to developing that difference. Price is less of an issue. It is arguable, however, that increasingly strategic alliances, co-operative commercial ventures and even mergers and acquisitions are the way forward. If heritage attractions, particularly those of small and medium size, are to maintain the unique qualities that make them interesting and attractive in the first place, develop their potential to provide conduits away from the overcrowded city centres and well-known beauty spots, they will need to focus on the operational requirements of their core business. An individual heritage attraction set up as a separate entity could choose to see itself as a unit within a larger centralized framework, the Regional Tourist Board or Area Museum Council, for example, or remain fully autonomous. There are advantages and disadvantages in both courses of action. The National Trust and English Heritage are able to benefit from economies of scale in establishing common standards of service and facilities across a widely different range of sites in terms of size, layout and location, as well as marketing them in a way that is not available to the small operator. This can be, and often is, at the expense of unblemished uniqueness, but eliminates the possibility of ultimate failure.

OPERATIONS MANAGEMENT

Schmenner's matrix of the different service processes is helpful in determining the nature of the core business (Figure 1.1). The vertical dimension is the degree of labour intensity defined as the ratio of labour cost to capital cost. Capital-intensive services relative to labour costs are located along the upper row. The horizontal dimension measures the degree of customer interaction and customization. Customization is the marketing variable that describes the ability of the customer to affect personally the nature of the service delivered. Four distinct service processes are defined: the Service Factory; the Service Shop; Mass Service; and Professional Service. The application of the Schmenner matrix to heritage visitor attractions reveals why many heritage managers are faced with complex operational choices and challenges. The service factory quartile provides the location for the two main categories of HVA – heritage areas (built and natural) and heritage sites. The need for high capital spend on either conservation or new technology or both, planning management and control of visitor flows, addressing bottlenecks and capacity issues, scheduling service delivery with a small, lower-skilled labour force but access to a range of higher skilled managers, are common characteristics.

Local governments, heritage organizations and heritage businesses have begun to recognize the importance of operations management and the role of the operations manager. There has been a spate of appointments of town centre managers, countryside wardens, front-of-house managers and an operations team, if

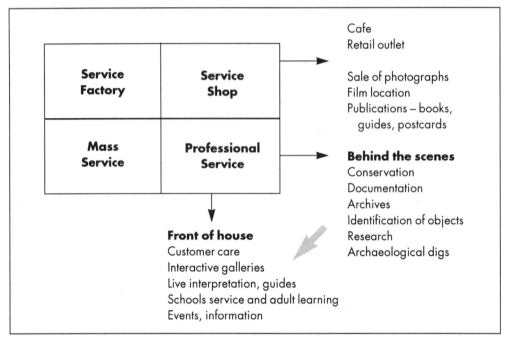

Figure 1.2: Museums and galleries: Schmenner Service Process Matrix.

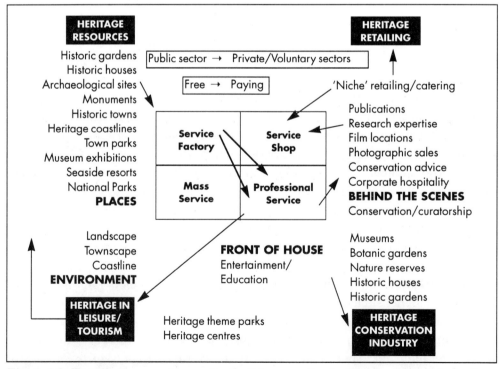

Figure 1.3: Flow diagram superimposed on the Schmenner Service Model as adapted for heritage visitor attractions.

not an operations manager, over the last few years. Congestion in open spaces and urban areas on the one hand and unrealistic competition between site-based HVAs on the other, has brought about a convergence of interests. The advantages of managing areas and sites in a particular geographical region or city to ensure complementarity rather than competition and achieve high standards of service are increasingly acknowledged. Behind the scenes are professional town planners, landscape architects, curators, conservationists, market researchers, interpretative planners, designers and accountants, either employed full-time or on a consultancy basis.

Taking the example of museums and galleries it is apparent that the traditional service factory *front of house* and professional service *behind the scenes* model has broken down over the past twenty years (Figure 1.2). Gone is the image of dusty places with glass cases and either no one to talk to, or impassive custodians and warding staff clinking keys like gaolers. Instead, in addition to the established professional services of curation, conservation, documentation, archives, archaeology and research, a new range of professions has emerged to enhance the visitor experience: interpreters, demonstrators, re-enactors, explainers, guides, stewards, museum and gallery educators, designers, event organizers and, most recently, operations managers. The lead was taken by the independent sector in the 1980s, and the shift to this additional dimension has gathered momentum in the 1990s. Volunteers have become involved in a variety of these roles in many small museums and at heritage sites. The operations manager at the National Maritime Museum, Greenwich, combines policy advice with day-to-day responsibility for two front-of-house managers, one events and one technical manager, communications staff, stewards and cleaners. Concomitant with the development of *the second professional service* has come the development of the service shop with two separate aspects – the first, the provision of niche retail and catering outlets; the second, a customized service based on the site/collection – photographs, corporate hospitality, object identification, books and publications.

If the Schmenner model is taken one stage further and a flow chart is overlaid, the problems and challenges faced by the manager of a heritage attraction can be seen in the context of the heritage industry as a whole (Figure 1.3). Heritage retailing is moving away from the site or location to become a mass service in its own right. Britain's 'unsung boom industry' is calculated to be worth £100 million a year including site-based shops (Atkinson 1996). *Behind the scenes* and *front-of-house* professional services can be found either based on site, at a regional office or delivered by peripatetic consultants with their own small businesses. Catering is mostly offered as a franchise but can be an attraction in its own right. The Victoria & Albert Museum was the first in the field with the slogan *Ace Caf*. At the recently opened reconstructed Globe Theatre the heritage caterers Milburns were tasked to make the restaurant and cafe attractive enough 'to bring people in for food rather

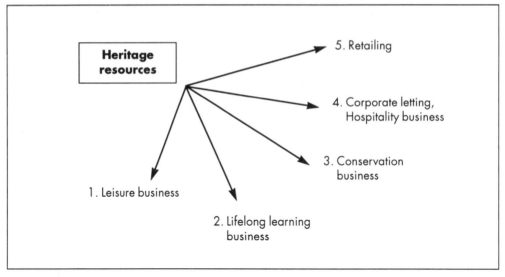

Figure 1.4: Final stage of development of service process matrix into a flow chart showing five separate businesses associated with HVAs.

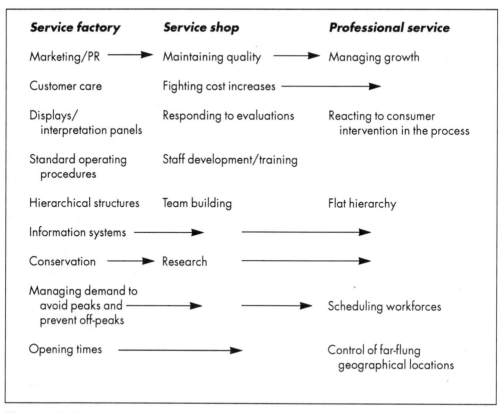

Figure 1.5: Identifying operational issues at HVAs within a service process matrix.

than the theatre' (Clark 1997). In fact, five separate businesses are emerging from the creation and consumption of heritage that will have an overwhelming impact on the development of operations strategies and their implementation at individual HVAs in the future (Figure 1.4).

For the operations manager at a heritage visitor attraction, juggling day-to-day concerns needs to be tempered by a clear understanding of the service process. In order to address the operational issues the manager must first examine what type of service process he or she is involved with and the nature of the challenge. The size, layout and location of a service operation is important for successful income generation. However, for the majority of HVAs these factors cannot be controlled. Charging is the most contentious issue of all, creating an almost insoluble ethical dilemma. The dichotomy between heritage as a community resource and focus for national, regional and local identities that should be freely available for the enlightenment, education and enjoyment of visiting populations from around the world, and heritage as a product for commercial consumption, revolves around the question of admission charges. This is currently a key area of controversy in heritage attractions operations. Earl Spencer overpriced tickets to the recently opened Princess Diana Museum on the Althorp Estate. At £9.50 each, the public considered them to be overly expensive: he was left with 30,000 unsold tickets when they first went on sale. The Shipwreck Heritage Centre in Hastings is considering ending admission charges and providing a donation box instead. The management cost of collecting the fee almost outweighs the income received. The museums in Glasgow, Edinburgh and Birmingham run by the City Councils are free except for special exhibitions. An analysis of the conservation and marketing issues associated with charging and the long term future of HVAs as a quality experience were examined elsewhere. From the operations manager's viewpoint a decision on charging, or otherwise, will be related to the organization's strategic aims and operational objectives (Figure 1.5).

Heritage assets are supported by people as assets whether as trustees, employees, commercial customers, taxpayers, enthusiasts, Friends, volunteers, educationalists or tourists. The range of professional, technical and practical expertise required for the creation and facilitation of the consumption of the heritage product in all its different guises at the HVAs has expanded exponentially over the past decade. The impact of the total or partial reorientation of museums, heritage sites, historic houses, parks and gardens from passively allowing the public entry to proactively encouraging access and participation from all members of the global community has resulted in major growth and a shift of emphasis in staffing needs. The change in the balance of the museum workforce to 60 per cent volunteers (Policy Studies Institute 1998) has coincided not only with swingeing cuts to local authority budgets but consumer demand for front-of-house services. The people management aspect of the operations management role requires the skilful development of teams to maximize the diverse capabilities and talents of individuals. In addition, for most HVAs in the not-for-profit sector this will include the involvement of volunteers and management of part-time staff.

Quality is vital for all HVAs in every aspect of provision – surroundings, service, integrity and genuineness – in order to create an experience of lasting value. Visitor perceptions of the quality of the experience may be entirely dependent on what happens during one short visit rather than an awareness of the facilities and services generally available. Implicit rather than explicit services can be critical. In answer to the question: 'What do we do when the whole world is themed?' Jack Rouse responds:

> Go back to basics and focus on human emotion. Service will be a major issue. Forget the theme. Forget the story. Forget the interactives. Forget the quality. When I am treated rudely or indifferently I am out of there. And I should be.
>
> (Rouse 1998)

Heritage managers have difficult choices to make to ensure both the economic viability and sustainable development of a site or area. The options are many and various: capital investment in new facilities, equipment, conservation or new technology; a dynamic or passive relationship of the site within the area or the area around the site to *living heritage* retail outlets and catering; co-operation rather than competition within an area/region, with strategic alliances to develop the vertical integration of the area, site and events within a comprehensive operations management strategy designed to spread peak demand more evenly and promote off-peak usage introducing a policy of incentives and rationing as necessary. At the day-to-day level the central focus on the quality of the service encounter will remain paramount.

REFERENCES

Ashworth, G. J. and Tunbridge, J. E. (1996) *Dissonant Heritage: The Management of the Past as a Resource in Conflict*, Chichester: John Wiley & Sons.

Atkinson, D. (1996) 'Hundred million pound sector feeds our past to the addicts', *The Guardian*, 3rd January.

Cameron, H. (1995) 'The Royal Armouries Leeds', *Tourism*, 87, Winter.

Central Statistical Office (1995) 'Participation in selected leisure activities away from home by social class, 1993–1994, The Henley Centre', *Social Trends*, 25, London: HMSO.

Clark, S. (1997) 'Encore un foie gras', *Leisure Week*, 9, 5, 23, 21st November.

Davies, A. and Prentice, R. (1995) 'Conceptualizing the latent visitor to heritage attractions', *Tourism Management*, 16, 7, 491–500.

Davies, S. (1994) *By Popular Demand: A Strategic Analysis of the Market Potential for Museums and Art Galleries in the UK*, London: Museums and Galleries Commission.

Department of National Heritage (1996) *People Taking Part*, London: Department of National Heritage, March.

English Tourist Board (1998) *Agenda 2000 – Newsletter*, English Tourist Board, January.

Ford, R. (1997) 'Cheaper tourists clogging our streets', *The Times*, 13th January.

Hanna, M. (1997a) *Sightseeing in the UK 1996*, London: BTA/ETB Research Services.

Hanna, M. (1997b) *Visits to Tourist Attractions*, London: BTA/ETB Research Services.

Heritage Lottery Fund (1997) *Application Pack: Heritage Lottery Fund*, July.

Hewison, R. (1987a) *The Heritage Industry: Britain in a Climate of Decline*, London: Methuen.

Hewison, R. (1992b) 'The future of the pastoral', *Museums Journal*, 92, 9, 30–31, September.

Hood, M.G. (1983a) 'Staying away – why people choose not to visit museums', *Museum News*, 61, 50–57.

Johnson, P. and Thomas, B. (1995) in Herbert, D. (ed.) *Heritage, Tourism and Society*, London: Mansell, 170–190.

Martin, B. and Mason, S. (1993) 'The future for attractions, meeting the needs of new consumers', *Tourism Management*, 14, 1, 34–40, February.

Merriman (1991) *Beyond the Glass Case*, Leicester: Leicester University Press.

MGC (Museums and Galleries Commission) (1995a) *Museums Fit for the Future*, London: MGC.

MGC, Arts Council, Harris Qualitative (1997c) *Children as an Audience for Museums and Galleries*, London: MGC.

Middleton, V. C. (1990) *New Visions for Independent Museums in the UK*, London: AIM.

Office for National Statistics (1998) *Social Trends*, 28, London: HMSO.

Policy Studies Institute (1998) *Cultural Trends*, 28, London: Policy Studies Institute.

Prentice, R. (1993) 'The socio-demographic characteristics of tourists at heritage attractions', in Chapter 3 of *Tourism and Heritage Attractions*, London: Routledge.

Rouse, J. (1998) 'What a feeling !', *Attractions Management*, 19, January.

Schmenner, R. W. (1995) *Service Operations Management*, Englewood Cliffs, NJ: Prentice-Hall.

Stirling, A. (1995) *Sense and Sensibility*, Conference Address: 'After the Millennium, Our Heritage in the 21st Century', World Heritage and Museums Symposium, May.

Swarbrooke, J. (1995) *The Development and Management of Visitor Attractions*, Oxford: Butterworth-Heinemann.

Walsh-Heron, J. and Stevens, T. (1990) *The Management of Visitor Attractions and Events*, London: Prentice-Hall.

Walton, P. (1998) BAFM Heritage Volunteer Training Project Report (unpublished), British Association of Friends of Museums, January.

MODEL QUESTIONS

1. How and why do the characteristics of visitors change in relation to the different types of heritage visitor attractions – theme parks, museums or historic properties?

2. In what areas of their operations do HVAs need to apply standardization? At the same time how can they protect the rarity value of their resources/service?

3. Describe how the service process is changing in museums and analyse why this is happening.

CHAPTER 2

Operations Management

Liz Sharples, Ian Yeoman and Anna Leask

This chapter introduces the reader to the concept of operations management and then suggests a framework from which the relevance of operations management within heritage visitor attractions can be examined. The chapter also looks briefly at the operational challenges faced by managers of heritage visitor attractions.

The chapter includes:

- a definition of the term 'operations management';
- an examination of the nature of service operations management;
- a discussion about the distinction between a 'product' and a 'service';
- an identification of the operations functions within heritage visitor attractions with reference to the Schmenner model of management; to include:
  - service features;
  - process features;
  - customer-orientated features;
  - labour-related features;
  - management features;
- a debate about the current and future challenges to management within the different sectors of heritage visitor attractions.

WHAT IS OPERATIONS MANAGEMENT?

Operations management is defined as the management of resources within an organization with an aim to provide a product or service in the most efficient and effective way possible.

Ray Wild adopts a systems approach to the discipline, defining operations management in the following way:

> operations management is concerned with the design and operation of systems for manufacture, transport, supply, or service.

(Wild 1995)

This is a useful if broad definition, as it introduces the concept of a business as an 'operating system' (sometimes called a productive system) and it also recognizes that different systems have individual aims and objectives.

Any organization such as a heritage attraction exists as an operating system with definite goals and objectives that it strives to achieve. The debate concerning the aim of heritage visitor attractions is a controversial one, with some sites focused totally towards preservation of the heritage in its original state whilst others are geared towards maximum access by the public as a profit-making venture. No doubt the discussion will continue for many years to come, but by adopting the view that all visitor attractions are concerned with providing a quality service of some kind, then it can be appreciated that the design and operation of that system requires efficient and thoughtful management.

The discipline of operations management is relatively new, its roots being traced back to the Industrial Revolution within the UK, with the emergence of the so-called 'Factory System'. In 1776, a Scottish economist called Adam Smith established the principles of 'division of labour' which he published in a book called *The Wealth of Nations* (Smith 1776). Smith's work provided the foundations of work simplification methods which exist in an evolved form in many industries today.

There have been two main areas of development in the field of production/operations management. One significant change has been the expansion of the field into the 'service' sector of the economy as it has been acknowledged that many of the tools and techniques used within the manufacturing field can be used beneficially within many service industries. This move away from a purely manufacturing/production basis has initiated the use of the more general term 'operations management' to describe the discipline.

Another development in operations management has been a 'systems' approach to look at the complex inter-relationships both within a business and with its external environment. This more holistic outward-looking approach will be significant when the management of heritage visitor attractions is considered.

WHAT IS OPERATIONS MANAGEMENT TODAY?

It is important to remember that operations management is a very practical subject, dealing with real people and real issues. Many managers and supervisors, working in organizations around the world, deal with operational issues such as staff scheduling and visitor management as part of their day-to-day job, with very little reference to theories, models, or instruction manuals. Having acknowledged this, a manager cannot always rely on intuition and common sense to solve complex business problems; the most successful businesses being those which adopt a strategic approach to the planning, operation and control of their core activities.

Within the context of a heritage attraction, the operations function could include:

- the concept development/design of the site;
- the presentation/interpretation of the concept;
- the management/control of visitors (visitor management);
- the organization and training of staff;
- the management of the plant – buildings, equipment etc.;
- the management and monitoring of quality issues;
- the matching of supply and demand (capacity management);
- the measurement of visitor satisfaction;
- crisis management;
- risk assessment;
- the management of operating systems such as stock control and ordering.

This list is by no means exhaustive, but we can already start to see that operations management is not a peripheral concern, it is a key function at the heart of every organization. Quite simply, a business relies on efficient management of its operations in order to survive.

THE NATURE OF OPERATIONS MANAGEMENT

Operations as a business function

Operations management is a vital business function alongside other functions such as human resource management, purchasing, marketing and financial management (Finch and Luebbe 1995).

In some organizations these functions may exist in isolation, but in the majority of businesses there is a 'blurring around the edges' of where one function starts and another begins. For example, the development of a new concept for a visitor attraction is closely linked and intertwined with the marketing function.

Finch and Luebbe (1995) also comment on the management of resources as part of this business function:

> the operations function is charged with the management of resources required to produce a product or service, including people, facilities, inventory, processes and systems.

This definition introduces the concept of resources to the discussion, identifying that the careful management of resources is key to the production of a product or service. Without the correct utilization of raw materials, the considered design of the layout and equipment, and the efficient organization of staff, the organizational goals and objectives cannot be met.

Slack, Chambers *et al.* (1995) classify these resources as either:

- *Transformed resources* – the resources that are treated, transformed or converted in some way.
- *Transforming resources* – the resources that act upon the transformed resources.

Transformed resources are usually a mixture of materials, information and customers. In the case of a heritage attraction, key resources that are processed/ changed are the visitor to the site and the heritage itself through careful interpretation.

Transforming resources – there are two types of transforming resources that are common to most operations:

- *Facilities* – site, buildings, equipment, plant, technology.
- *Staff* – who operate, supervise, manage, maintain the operation.

In systems terminology these resources (or 'inputs') are used in varying degrees during a 'transformation process' in order to achieve the desired output. A heritage attraction, for example, focuses on an important element of our past and develops this resource with the help of staff, materials and technology, to provide a unique experience for its visitors.

THE ORGANIZATION AS AN OPERATING/ PRODUCTIVE SYSTEM

Most organizations exist as operating systems of one form or another converting inputs (resources) into outputs which are required by the user/customer, primarily by adding value. Finch and Luebbe (1995) show this 'transformation process' with the aid of a simple systems diagram (Figure 2.1).

Porter (1985) argues that this notion of 'adding value', whilst utilizing a range of resources, allows a company to differentiate itself from its competitors, thus gaining a competitive edge.

Schmenner (1995) develops the idea of offering a quality experience for customers/clients, by highlighting the challenges that managers face when attempting to operate different types of service provision which have differing degrees of staff involvement and customization. His ideas are explored in more detail later in the chapter. It is also important to recognize that an operating system is rarely static.

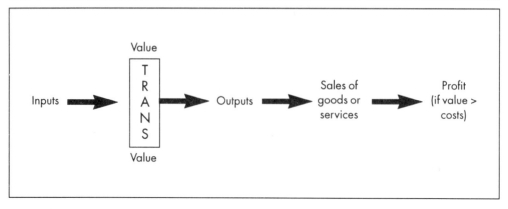

Figure 2.1: Systems view of value-adding transformation process.

Cook and Russell (1980) describe an operating system as 'the mechanism by which goods and services are created', stressing the dynamism of a system which consists of moving parts working together to create the desired product or service. An organization can develop standard procedures in an attempt to offer a quality service, but any business is subject at any time to external and internal influences that can affect the output.

The management of operations

The operations function in any organization is dependent on an individual or a group of people to manage it. Slack and Chambers *et al.* (1995) provide the following definition:

> Operations managers are the staff of the organization who have particular responsibility for managing some or all, of the resources which comprise the operations function.

In a small business, one person may manage the whole of the operations function, but in a large enterprise the operations function may be split into several elements managed by a team of specialist people. In many organizations, the operations managers may be called by some other name, e.g. Site Manager/Duty Manager, but nevertheless will fulfil all or part of the operation's function.

HOW DOES THIS RELATE TO HERITAGE VISITOR ATTRACTIONS?

All categories of heritage visitor attractions, for example folk museums, industrial heritage centres or historic buildings, exist as operating systems of one form or another.

The transformation process is easy to understand for a manufacturing situation. In a factory a bale of cloth can be converted into many pairs of jeans for a chain store, but when visitors look at a heritage attraction, the transformation concept is rarely so straightforward.

Johnson and Thomas (1995) comment that many heritage sites are now subject to a production process by which an original building or land undergoes some kind of transformation with an aim to add value. This may be the upgrading of a stately home, the building of a cafe at a castle, or the provision of interpretative activities, such as historical re-enactments at a museum.

Fierce debate has challenged the scale and nature of these developments however, with worries such as the possible loss of authenticity being voiced.

Another key issue in the management of a heritage attraction is that another important resource/input to the system is the visitor themselves. It could be argued that one of the aims of a heritage attraction may be to 'add value' to people's quality of life by giving them the opportunity to acquire memories, experiences and knowledge to take home. The visitors take nothing 'touchable' away with them apart from perhaps a souvenir or guide book from the gift shop and possibly some mud on their boots!

The notion of adding value has been well proven in the heritage arena. The concept development team responsible for creating the museum experience provided at the Jorvik Centre in York, were successful in providing something novel and exciting which set the Centre apart from its competitors. The Centre has been an unquestionable success. In simple terms, a heritage attraction is concerned with providing a service for its visitors whilst keeping the aims of conservation and possibly profit generation firmly on the agenda.

THE NATURE OF SERVICES

At one time a 'service' was viewed as a supporting feature of a manufacturing industry, but it is now acknowledged that many companies exist as service operations in their own right. Some academics have suggested that it is sometimes easier to define services in a residual way – i.e. by what they are not (Schmenner 1995). We know, for example, that service companies are not involved in the core activities of mining, agriculture or manufacturing, but they are companies who provide some type of benefit or assistance for their customers.

When the word 'service' is used to describe the primary output of a business, it is important to realize that it refers to an activity that has value in its own right.

Services can take many forms: a night out in a high quality restaurant provides psychological benefits at the end of a busy week; a hospital or clinic provides medical care for its patients. Hotels, restaurants, theatres and cinemas are just some of the industry sectors involved in providing services of one type or another. Visitor attractions are also part of this service sector as they provide a number of benefits for their visitors including education, excitement and interest.

The earliest attempts to differentiate between 'goods' and 'services' used a dichotomous approach which consisted of a continuum with pure goods at one end and pure services at the other (Lashley, Lockwood and Taylor 1997). It is now widely accepted that this simplistic approach is not sufficient as most service organizations offer a 'complex bundle' of both tangible and intangible elements, and a service can only be defined as such when the bundle is intangible dominant (Sasser, Olsen and Wyckoff 1978).

To explain this in more simple terms, nearly all goods are accompanied by a 'facilitating service', e.g. the front office in a car salesroom; and almost every service is accompanied by a 'facilitating good', e.g. the shampoo and conditioner used at the hairdresser's (Sasser, Olsen and Wyckoff 1978).

A heritage attraction has primarily an intangible offering and therefore can be classified as a service delivery system. The distinction between goods and services has been explored by many researchers in this field (Zeithaml, Parasuraman and Berry 1985) with an aim to highlight the special characteristics of the two outputs.

It is generally accepted that the characteristics of a service are:

- perishability;
- inseparability of production and consumption;
- tangibility/intangibility;
- heterogeneity.

The following section examines these attributes in more detail.

Perishability

A service provision cannot be stored for future use, or transported easily to another location. If visitors/customers do not turn up at the point of service delivery, then that potential capacity could be lost for ever. This obviously has major implications for a heritage attraction with regard to income generation, as the service cannot be 'stored up' for peak days; capacity management is a key issue for heritage attraction managers, so that both peak and off-peak demands can be accommodated.

Inseparability

Most tangible goods are produced, then transported to a point of distribution where they are sold and subsequently consumed. In many service industries, the services are first sold or requested, then produced and consumed simultaneously through interaction between the customer and the producer (Wright 1995). This concept is demonstrated in a heritage attraction where a visitor pays an entrance fee to a building or site and then experiences the facility in conjunction with other members of the public, through interaction with staff who are manning the operation.

Tangibility/Intangibility

A service such as a heritage attraction may be associated with something physical – a museum, a castle, or an industrial site – but the customers who are buying the service are paying for something 'intangible': a 'feel-good' factor that has no physical attributes. For example, a visitor to a medieval castle may sense a strong feeling of the past, experience excitement when visiting the dungeons and battlements, and enjoy watching their children learn about this period of history. If this visitor has an excellent day out, it is probably because of the intangible nature of what has been provided rather than the associated physical feature, although this is obviously 'key' to the experience.

Heterogeneity

This term refers to the potential for variable, non-standard output in service delivery systems. When two customers buy a certain brand or model of electrical kettle, the standard of those appliances should be identical with little or no variation. This is not the case in service delivery systems where inconsistencies can occur for several reasons:

Occasion

The experience provided by service providers can be significantly different on different occasions. For example, at a heritage attraction the weather may have an important impact on the way that visitors feel about their day out.

Time

The service performed by an individual may vary over time. For example, a tired employee serving ice creams at a heritage attraction on a hot August Bank Holiday may give a less welcoming reception to visitors at the end of the day than he/she did at the opening, despite there being quality control procedures in place.

Customers

Interactions between visitors and providers may vary depending on personality, age and situation. For example, a member of staff may communicate differently with a child, his parents, and his grandparents. [Framework adapted from Zeithaml, Parasuraman and Berry 1985.] Since it is difficult to control this level of variation, particularly when there is a direct interface between customer and employee, there tends to be a greater risk attached to purchasing services than to purchasing goods.

THE SERVICE ENCOUNTER

Muhleman, Oakland and Lockyer (1992) suggest that the presence of customers during the provision of a service can be a 'mixed blessing'. The customers are vital as a resource (an input) to the system, but they also introduce a certain level of unpredictability, in that it is hard to estimate how long they will stay, what their needs will be and how they will behave.

At the centre of this service exchange is the so-called service encounter (Heskett, Sasser and Hart 1990). This is the point at which the customer comes into contact with the part of the organization that provides the service. In a heritage visitor attraction it may be the reception desk, or the member of staff who serves in the gift shop.

Several academics have coined the phrase 'the moment of truth' (Carlzon 1987, Zemke and Schaaf 1989) which is the point in the service encounter when the customer has an opportunity to assess the quality of service provided. This is also sometimes known as 'the critical incident'. The service may meet expectations, exceed expectations or completely fail to meet expectations. Unfortunately, in a service delivery situation, the organization only gets one chance, and poor quality in a particular situation cannot be fixed. It is therefore essential that the number of 'customer defections' is kept to the minimum, as repeat visits and 'word of mouth' advertising are important (Reichald and Sasser 1990).

This management of the employee/customer interaction presents a challenge to the manager of a service operation that is absent in the field of production/manufacturing. Service quality is the 'successful matching of the actual level of desired service with the customer's desired level of service' (Lashley, Lockwood and Taylor 1997). It is essential therefore that the operations manager works closely with the marketing/sales team and the human resources manager to ensure that the service provided meets the customer's needs and expectations.

THE SCHMENNER MODEL

In 1995, Roger W. Schmenner proposed a model which provided a way of categorizing service delivery systems into four main categories, namely, Service Factory, Service Shop, Mass Service, and Professional Service. The grouping takes account of the degree of labour intensity and the degree of customization and interaction.

The background to Schmenner's thinking is in the recognition of the primacy of the service encounter and the three aspects of service that surround it the service task, service standards, and the service delivery system itself.

- *Service task:* This states why the service exists and what the customer values about the service. In clearly stating what the service provides for the customer, it provides clear goals for both management and workforce.

- *Service standards:* These are the measurable standards which define what is an efficient service provision for the customer. They are concerned with the quality of delivery and also the cost-effectiveness.
- *Service delivery system:* This is a specification of how the service is produced including controls for quality, customer satisfaction and cost.

By attempting to identify the key characteristics of different types of service delivery systems with regard to the goals of the organization, the way that the service is delivered and the amount of personal contact that is possible between customer and staff, it is possible to identify the challenges that managers face when co-ordinating a particular service operation. This approach is particularly relevant for heritage visitor attractions, many of which have specific and individual organizational goals but share the need to provide a high-quality visitor experience.

The model suggested by Schmenner takes the form of a matrix and locates organizations dependent upon the degree of *labour intensity* of the process on one hand, with the degree of *interaction and customization* of the service for the consumer on the other (Figure 2.2).

The majority of heritage visitor attractions fit quite easily into the category of 'Service Factory' in that labour intensity is fairly low and they rarely offer the 'one-to-one' professional service that would be offered by a hospital consultant or a solicitor.

For example, a large site such as a medieval castle could be managed with just a handful of staff operating the ticket booth, marshalling visitors around the site and possibly serving refreshments.

Personal contact with the staff is almost seen in this situation as an added bonus and rarely expected, although quality contact with a well-informed member of staff

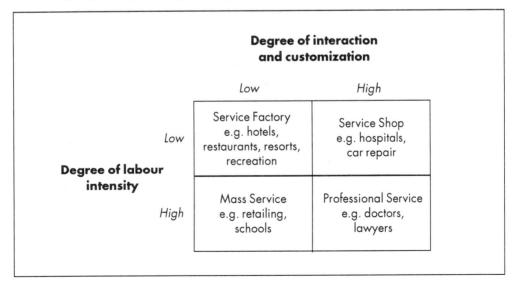

Figure 2.2: The Schmenner (1995) Service Process Matrix.

31

or a volunteer could make the difference between a good experience and a special experience.

Of course this categorization is not quite so simple as it first appears. In many heritage visitor attractions the visitor is expected to gather his/her own information from signage, guidebooks or electronic source, and may have little contact with the site staff.

In the Roman Baths in Bath for example, the introduction of state-of-the-art technology has helped to standardize the quality of visitor information in an organized and structured way, while not increasing staff/visitor contact time (Walter 1996). The operation of a small historic house such as Eyam Hall in Derbyshire, where the owners take pride in showing visitors around is, in contrast, a more personal type of experience.

Schmenner's matrix therefore provides a simple way of categorizing different types of service organization, but it is important to recognize that within each quadrant there is the capacity for considerable variation.

CHALLENGES TO MANAGEMENT

Schmenner (1995) also outlines the challenges that managers face when operating different categories of service provision. A service industry that is highly labour-intensive or highly customized will provide a different set of challenges from one with low involvement (Figure 2.3).

A heritage attraction therefore, as a service factory, has to look carefully at decisions regarding capital investment such as effective use of land, facilities and equipment, and an understanding of the technological advances that could be beneficial. The capacity of the attraction is relatively inflexible, so it is vital to manage the demand in order to smooth peaks and to promote the off-peak times.

The low degree of interaction and customization also implies an important marketing challenge for an attraction manager. As the visitor has limited contact with the staff it is essential that in some way the service offered is made to feel 'warm and exciting' (Schmenner 1995) and this will involve detailed consideration of the layout and physical surroundings which can influence atmosphere. Schmenner (1995) also suggests that in a service factory situation the hierarchy tends to be fairly rigid, and standard operating procedures can often apply. This is certainly the case in some heritage visitor attractions where the visitor is dealt with in a highly organized way with little personal attention.

OPERATIONAL FEATURES OF HERITAGE VISITOR ATTRACTIONS

Schmenner (1995) advocates a systematic way of looking at the features involved in a service delivery system as a method of applying process-related tools, with an aim

Challenges for managers
(low labour intensity)
• Capital decisions
• Technological
• Managing demand to avoid peaks and to promote off-peaks
• Scheduling service delivery

Challenges for managers
(high interaction/ high customization)
• Fighting cost increases
• Maintaining quality
• Reacting to consumer intervention in process
• Managing advancement of people delivering service
• Managing flat hierarchy with loose subordinate superior relationship
• Gaining employee loyalty

Challenges for managers
(low interaction/ low customization)
• Marketing
• Making service warm
• Attention to physical surroundings
• Managing fairly rigid hierarchy with need for standard operating procedures

Service Factory
Low labour intensity/Low interaction and customization

Service Shop
Low labour intensity/High interaction and customization

Mass Service
High labour intensity/Low interaction and customization

Professional Service
High labour intensity/High interaction and customization

Challenges for managers
(high labour intensity)
• Hiring
• Training
• Methods development and control
• Employee welfare
• Scheduling workforces
• Control of far-flung geographical locations
• Start-up of new units
• Managing growth

Figure 2.3: Schmenner's view of challenges for service managers.

of improving the service operation. He examines the service operation under five sets of attributes, namely:

- Service features.
- Process features.
- Customer-orientated features.
- Labour-related features.
- Management features.

An examination of these sets of attributes allows us to take a more in-depth look at the operational challenges of managing a heritage attraction. Table 2.1 outlines these challenges.

Operations management in HVAs provides a greater choice of attractions for visitors, diversification of tourism products and a greater understanding of the service encounter. Managers of HVAs now have a practical tool to assist in the design, maintain and improvement of HVAs. Schmenner's process features matrix can be used as a decision-making tool to move around the matrix, for example, from service factory to professional service. Once the service style is changed, management can address the features element of the matrix. What needs changing? What needs improving? What needs substituting? These questions, imposed through the matrix, provide the operations manager with a powerful decision support tool.

CONCLUSION

The careful management of the operational aspects of a heritage visitor attraction is crucial if the site is to successfully meet its organizational objectives. A holistic integrated approach is required, using the expertise of conservation specialists, concept developers, interpreters and resource managers in the definition of clearly designed plans and policies that are understood by both staff and management. The adoption of specific operational tools can be a key part of this process.

It could be argued that operations management of heritage visitor attractions needs a new recipe; one that is built around the characteristics of service. The ingredients that make up operations management dimensions within Schmenner's matrix need more discussion and development. Therefore subsequent chapters develop some of these ideas through an in-depth examination of the operational aspects of HVAs from initial concept stage to design, interpretation and quality control.

Table 2.1: Issues for the management of an HVA as a service delivery system.

Service features	Implications for a heritage visitor attraction
• A limited mix of services is provided with new services being introduced or performed infrequently. • Price, speed and perceived warmth/excitement are the primary basis of competition.	• The range of services on offer at a HVA are limited and to a large extent are dependent on the 'heritage' that is being presented. There is a need to preserve the heritage stock as a resource, to establish guidelines about the degree of change that is acceptable and to discuss the role of interpretation in marketing the attraction. There is also a need to examine the accessibility of the attraction and the role of supporting services such as catering services and retail outlets. • An integrated approach is required to create a strategic plan for heritage sites such as in the United States National Park Service, which has adopted a multi-disciplinary approach to the problem calling upon the skills of interpreters, archaeologists, architects, designers, and land managers. (USNPS 1990)

Process features	Implications for a heritage visitor attraction
• High capital intensity with equipment often being used as an integral part of the system. The use of equipment and the performance of tasks need to be carefully balanced in order to ensure smooth process functioning. A line flow-like layout is often simplest to operate. • The pattern of process is rigid, with changes to the nature of the processing sometimes being routine and occasionally radical. • Excess capacity is not easy to manage with additions to capacity requiring injections of capital and labour. • Scheduling can sometimes be difficult, especially at peak times but bottlenecks are usually predictable. • The service provision is dependent upon a good flow of materials.	• The location of the attraction is geographically fixed and can rarely be moved (i.e. it is attached to the piece of heritage). This has major implications in terms of capital funding, accessibility and customer demand. • A high volume throughput is generally required to provide return on investment, especially those with high initial capital requirements, e.g. The Granada Studio Tours costing £8 million. (Wooder 1991) • Projects financed by special funding such as Lottery money also need revenue in order to survive. • The use of technology as a means of streamlining the process and providing customer interest requires consideration in order to prevent inappropriate use which could trivialize the heritage. • Seasonality is a key issue within the management of heritage visitor attractions The careful utilization of staff, equipment and other resources is crucial to avoid under-utilization or the inability to cope. • Only 56 per cent of heritage visitor attractions in the UK remain open all year, the remainder close for at least three months. (Stevens 1995)

Table 2.1 (continued)

Customer-orientated features	*Implications for a heritage visitor attraction*
• The attractiveness of the physical surroundings is crucial to the marketing of the service. • The interaction between staff/customer is brief and therefore the opportunity for customizing the service is minimal. • Demand of peaks/non-peaks can sometimes be managed through pricing policy. • Formal quality control systems can be adopted.	• The design and layout of new attractions and the upkeep of existing ones is crucial to the marketing of the site. For example, at the new National Centre for Popular Music in Sheffield, where an award-winning design hopes to assist in the marketing of the site. • The 'service encounter' is key to ensuring that the customer is made to feel that his/her wishes are being met. • The use of innovative pricing policies such as the introduction of season tickets and lifetime tickets targeted at specific sectors of the community needs further development. For example, at the Tullie House Museum in Carlisle, the town's residents are encouraged to purchase a lifetime season ticket allowing unlimited access to the museum for a minimal charge. (Johnson 1993) • The introduction of formal methods to assess the quality of the visitor experience is vital to the success, or otherwise of the attraction. Schemes such as the inspection scheme introduced by the Association of Scottish Visitor Attractions in 1990 are a good first step. (Gaw 1992)

Labour-related features	*Implications for a heritage visitor attraction*
• Pay at a 'service factory' is typically hourly. • Skills levels of staff are not necessarily high. • Additional skills/seniority can lead to advancement.	• The development of comprehensive training programmes for both paid and unpaid staff (volunteers) is essential if the quality of the visitor experience is to be guaranteed and job satisfaction achieved.

Management features	*Implications for a heritage visitor attraction*
• Effective line supervision and trouble-shooting are critical. • The means of control can sometimes be profit-centred but this is not always the case.	• There is a need to establish clear lines of communication between managers, supervisors and staff members to ensure that the goals of that particular attraction are being met. There is a need to establish clear goals and objectives for each attraction in order to avoid conflicting messages to visitors and staff, e.g. profit, conservation, education and/or access for all.

REFERENCES

Carlzon, J. (1987) *Moments of Truth*, New York: Harper & Row.

Cook, T. M. and Russell, R. A. (1980) *Contemporary Operations Management*, New Jersey: Prentice-Hall.

Finch, B. and Luebbe, R. (1995) *Operations Management – Competing in a Changing Environment*, Orlando: The Dryden Press.

Gaw, L. (1992) *The Scottish Experience in Heritage Tourism*, Dublin: Bord Failte.

Heskett, J. L., Sasser, W. E. and Hart, C. W. L. (1990) *Service Breakthrough*, New York: Free Press.

Johnson, P. and Thomas, B. (1995) 'Heritage as business', in Herbert, D. (ed.) *Heritage, Tourism and Society*, London: Mansell.

Johnson, S. (1993) 'Heritage visitor attractions', in Buswell, J. (ed.) *Case Studies in Leisure Management*, London: Longman.

Lashley, C., Lockwood, A. and Taylor, S. (1997) *Aligning Operating Strategies for Service Quality in Hospitality Operations*, paper presented at sixth CHME Hospitality Research Conference.

Muhlemann, A., Oakland, J. and Lockyer, K. (1992) *Production and Operations Management*, London: Pitman.

Porter, M. E. (1985) *Competitive Advantage*, New York: Free Press.

Reicheld, F. and Sasser, W. E. (1990) 'Zero defections: quality comes to services', *Harvard Business Review*, September/October, 105–111.

Sasser, W. E., Olsen, R. P. and Wyckoff, D. D. (1978) *Management of Service Operations, Text, Cases & Readings*, Boston: Allyn and Bacon.

Schmenner, R. W. (1995) *Service Operations Management*, Englewood Cliffs, NJ: Prentice-Hall.

Slack, N. and Chamber, S. *et al.* (1995) *Operations Management*, London: Pitman.

Smith, A. (1776) *An Inquiry into the Nature and Causes of the Wealth of Nations*, London: Strahan and Cadell.

Stevens, T. (1995) 'Heritage as design: a practitioner's perspective', in Herbert, D. (ed.) *Heritage, Tourism and Society*, London: Mansell.

USNPS: The United States National Park Service (1990) *The Interpretive Challenge*, Washington DC: Park Service.

Walter, T. (1996) 'From museum to morgue? Electronic guides in Roman Bath', *Tourism Management*, Vol. 17, 241–5.

Wild, R. (1995) *Essentials of Production and Operations Management*, London: Cassell.

Wooder, S. (1991) *The Handbook of Tourism Products*, London: English Tourist Board.

Wright, L. K. (1995) 'Avoiding services myopia', in Glynn, W. and Barnes, J. (eds) *Understanding Services Management*, Chichester: John Wiley & Sons.

Zeithaml, V. A., Parasuraman, A. and Berry, L. L. (1985) 'Problems and strategies in services marketing', *Journal of Marketing*, Vol. 49, 33–46.

Zemke, R. and Schaaf, D. (1989) *The Service Edge: 101 Companies That Profit from Customer Care*, New York: New American Library.

MODEL QUESTIONS

1. From your readings of Chapters 1 and 2, select four HVAs that you know. Classify those HVAs as Service Factory, Service Shop, Mass Service or Professional Service. Justify your classification.

2. Building upon question 1, what are the challenges for management in the following scenarios:
   - Low labour intensity.
   - High labour intensity.
   - Low interaction/low customization.
   - High interaction/high customization.

3. Design a service comparison matrix for those HVAs using the features of:
   - Service features.
   - Process features.
   - Customer-orientated features.
   - Labour-related features.
   - Management features.

CHAPTER 3

Concept Development

Tim Caulton

INTRODUCTION

This chapter investigates the process of developing heritage visitor attractions from initial concept to implementation of design. The chapter begins by considering the process by which new industrial products are designed, and applies this framework to discuss the development of heritage attractions. The differences in objectives and strategies appropriate for heritage sites are discussed, including the balance between the conservation needs of a heritage site and those of visitors, and the balance between entertainment goals and those of education. It is the relationship between concept development and the service delivery system, particularly the on-going requirement to improve the service encounter, which particularly concerns the operations manager (Schmenner 1995). Concept development impacts upon service delivery in that it affects all aspects of visitor management, from the flow of visitors to productivity issues relating to the use of either staff or new technologies in heritage interpretation. This relationship is introduced in this chapter, but it is developed more fully in subsequent chapters of the book.

Current practice in concept development in the UK heritage industry is identified, with particular reference to the prevailing market conditions in the UK, and especially the effect of the National Lottery. Evidence for this chapter is drawn from a number of heritage sites in the public and independent sectors where the author is a member of the development team, and from interviews conducted with leading heritage designers and exhibition developers.[1]

NEW PRODUCT DEVELOPMENT

In manufacturing industry and the commercial service sector, companies need to develop new products to survive in a competitive marketplace. If companies fail to develop new products, they expose themselves to the great risk of losing sales, and they are vulnerable to changes in consumer tastes, to new technology, or to competition. On the other hand, developing new products is also a risky process:

research suggests that around 75 to 80 per cent of all new products and services are doomed to fail. New products fail for many reasons: an idea may be pushed through at the whim of a manager despite negative market research; the size of the market may be overestimated; the product may be poorly designed; the costs of manufacturing may be higher than expected; the product may be overpriced or promoted ineffectively; or competition may be underestimated (Kotler 1994).

It is because the process of new product development is so risky that sophisticated techniques of concept development and testing are applied in manufacturing industry and the private service sector to minimize risk and enhance the likelihood of commercial success. Figure 3.1 outlines this process.

---

1. Idea generation
To create a large number of new product ideas that meet identified customers' needs and wants.

↓

2. Idea screening
To reduce the number of ideas to an attractive, practical few.

↓

3. Concept development and testing
To refine the idea and test it in the marketplace with target customers.

↓

4. Marketing strategy development
To develop a strategy to introduce and sustain the product in the market.

↓

5. Business analysis
To evaluate the product in terms of its proposed sales, costs and profit projections, and to assess these against corporate objectives.

↓

6. Product development
To developing a cost-effective prototype.

↓

7. Market testing
To evaluate the likely success of the product in the marketplace.

↓

8. Commercialization
To produce and launch the product.

Figure 3.1: The process of new product development in private sector manufacturing and service industries. *Source:* derived from Kotler (1994).

In principle, this process of new product development through the various stages of generating ideas, refining concepts, feasibility analysis, evaluation, construction and launch, applies to any product, service or idea, including the development of new heritage visitor attractions. However, there are differences between the corporate objectives of heritage attractions and those of commercial manufacturing service sector companies, whilst different strategies are needed to realize heritage objectives. Furthermore, industry practice is significantly different in the heritage sector, although competition in the heritage attraction market (particularly influenced by the Heritage Lottery Fund in the UK) is redefining the process. Each of these factors affecting the process of heritage concept development is investigated in subsequent sections, finally leading to a consideration of whether the model is indeed appropriate for the development of heritage visitor attractions.

THEORETICAL PROBLEMS WITH THE APPLICATION OF THE MODEL TO HERITAGE VISITOR ATTRACTIONS

Corporate objectives

The model of new product development described in Figure 3.1 is applicable primarily to commercial organizations with profit-making objectives. Whilst there are some privately-owned stately homes, museums and themed heritage attractions which exist as commercial enterprises, the vast majority of the UK heritage sector is operated by independent organizations with charitable status, or by the public sector at a local or national level. The financial objectives of most public sector or charitable heritage organizations are to maximize income to offset public subsidies or other operating deficits, and many undertake trading activities to generate income to support their heritage responsibilities. However, there is a presumption that commercial activities should enhance the heritage asset, and not provide a financial surplus of income over expenditure to be used for other purposes (Museums Association 1997). Indeed, the legal requirements of charitable status prevent charitable organizations from making a profit, and if any do have a surplus of income over expenditure, this must be ploughed back into the organization.

A museum with profit-making objectives would not be able to gain registration with the Museums and Galleries Commission, and thereafter would not be able to obtain grants from public sources. Furthermore, in the early years of the National Lottery only public, charitable and not-for-profit organizations were eligible to receive grants from the Heritage Lottery Fund (Fitzherbert and Rhoades 1997). The 1997 National Heritage Act enables individuals and private companies with heritage assets to apply for Lottery funding from 1998, although priority will be given to strategic projects co-ordinated by local authorities on behalf of private owners.

If the financial objectives of heritage organizations differ significantly from those of commercial manufacturing and service sector companies, their primary objective is to maintain a heritage site, building or collection for posterity. Whilst it is always possible to change the way a heritage attraction is interpreted and presented to visitors, it is rarely feasible to change the core product itself, which must be protected for future generations. This is the *raison d'être* for the vast majority of heritage organizations, and is therefore the key corporate objective. Schmenner notes that one of the key ways of improving the productivity of the service encounter is by achieving economies of scale (Schmenner 1995). Whilst it is usually in the interests of commercial sector organizations to maximize sales to maximize profits, it is frequently not in the interests of heritage organizations to maximize visitor numbers as this might well destroy the very fabric of the heritage asset itself. There is an inherent conflict between the need to attract visitors to manage a heritage asset as an economically sustainable attraction, and the need to preserve that asset in perpetuity. This presents particular problems to heritage organizations in the public sector, whose main source of income is from local or national tax-payers, as they have a social responsibility to facilitate access by as many tax-payers as possible. For example, it is often very difficult or impossible to improve physical access to historic buildings for people with disabilities without changing the structure of the building, and difficult decisions have to be made. In short, social objectives to tax-payers may well conflict with the heritage objectives of the site.

Conflicting objectives impact upon the service encounter at heritage attractions in many ways, requiring sensitive concept development. Whilst there is a clear need for visitor management strategies to minimize the adverse physical effects of high demand, the position is further complicated by the potential conflict between education and entertainment objectives. Whilst many heritage attractions strive to present a coherent, accurate and popular interpretation of the past, there is a lively academic debate as to whether the whole process of heritage development has commercialized history and misrepresents the past (Hewison 1987; Walsh 1992). In total, heritage visitor attractions often have conflicting financial, heritage, social, educational and entertainment objectives, which necessitate a modified adaptation of models relating to concept development in the commercial sector, and to improving the service encounter in the service industries as a whole.

Market strategies

The process of new product development for commercial companies emphasises the need for a co-ordinated market strategy to meet the corporate goals of the organization. Indeed, it is when the market strategy is weakly developed (for example, if a product is over-priced or poorly promoted) that a new product is most likely to fail. Thus, the successful introduction of a new product requires the implementation of an integrated market strategy utilizing all the tools of the marketing mix. These are commonly known as the 'seven Ps' of product, price, promotion, place, people, process and physical tangibility, and reflect the need for products to be developed which identify and meet the needs of customers. These marketing tools are largely interdependent, and successful product development requires products to be distributed in the right way, in the right places and at the right price. If successful marketing strategies are implemented, the product's launch will be safeguarded and corporate financial goals will be met.

There is no fundamental reason why marketing theory applicable to private manufacturing and service sector companies cannot be applied to not-for-profit heritage organizations, although there are cultural differences which have prevented many heritage organizations from fully embracing a marketing orientation (McLean 1997). The previous section outlined how problems of conflicting objectives for heritage organizations could impact upon the service encounter in areas of visitor management and heritage interpretation. It is clear that heritage attractions demand an adaptation of the marketing mix in many areas, requiring a modification of operations management theory applicable to service industries in general.

This section considers how price, people and place can be tools with limited application in the development of heritage attractions. For example, in the commercial world the restrictions on availability exemplified by a rare product are usually reflected in a high price. However, a heritage site which has to restrict access for conservation reasons is not always able to use price as a marketing tool, particularly if the organization has social responsibilities to tax-payers. Thus, whilst the commercial decision in response to an inability to maximize visitor numbers would be to raise prices to maximize income from a limited number of people, public sector heritage organizations with conflicting short-term social responsibilities and long-term heritage objectives are often unable to respond in this way.

The role of people at heritage attractions also necessitates a modification from service operation theory. Schmenner argues that productivity can be improved when human interactions are minimized, since it is difficult to manage the service encounter consistently when people are involved (Schmenner 1995). Whilst that may well apply to service industries in general, it is less applicable to heritage attractions, where explainers and live interpreters can do much to enhance interpretation.

Similarly, the role of place as a marketing tool in heritage concept development is critical, and differs from its role in the development of commercial products and services. The model of new product development assumes that new products and services can be distributed to all available markets. Thus, the developer of a new tourist attraction should logically choose a site with good access to a substantial population in its catchment area. However, many heritage sites are fixed in place, and have survived precisely because they are in locations away from large centres of population. As such, many can never hope to achieve large numbers of visitors or become sustainable tourist attractions.

Most heritage attractions are based upon one or more of an historic site, an historic building, an historic collection, or an historic theme. There are numerous examples of new heritage attractions being developed in existing tourist honeypots or where there is a large potential catchment area, and of museum collections which have been relocated to improve accessibility (these include, for example, the decentralization of national museums). Overseas, some museums have been developed where there are very large numbers of transient people, such as at motorway service stations (France) or within shopping centres or airports (USA). For all these organizations, place is an important marketing tool. Nevertheless, whilst it is sometimes possible to move a heritage attraction not strongly associated with any particular site to a more accessible location, it is clearly impossible to move an historic site itself, and rarely feasible to move an historic building.

Thus, place – like people and price – is not always a flexible marketing tool in the development of new heritage attractions. The specific – and often conflicting – requirements of heritage attractions mean it is not always possible to implement a coherent marketing strategy appropriate to the requirements of the model for new commercial products, and which maximizes the chances of sustainability in the visitor attraction marketplace.

THE DEVELOPMENT OF HERITAGE VISITOR ATTRACTIONS IN PRACTICE

Traditionally, heritage visitor attractions are product-led rather than visitor-led. For example, in old-fashioned glass showcase museums, new exhibitions were the responsibility of the museum curator, who was typically appointed because of a specialist academic knowledge in the subject matter of the collection. There was no real need for the curator to take too much interest in the needs of visitors, as the care and safety of the collection was the prime responsibility, and revenue from visitors was not essential since the museum received its funding from public sources. If the objectives of the exhibition were stated, they were more likely to relate to the safety and museological significance of artefacts than to the experiences of visitors. Target visitors were rarely defined, and if they were, they would be expressed in vague terms such as 'everyone in the community'. The curator sometimes worked with a museum designer, but the process which produced the scholarly, product-led glass showcase exhibitions typically excluded educationalists.

Traditional exhibition development methods are still significant: a survey has shown that as recently as 1996, only one-third of UK museums have a structured input by educationalists when planning exhibitions and events (Anderson 1997). Competition from other branches of the leisure industry, and especially from hands-on museums and interactive science centres, has resulted in many heritage attractions facing static or declining visitor numbers, alongside declining revenue budgets from public sources (Davies 1995). The outcome is that many traditional museums have been encouraged to redesign exhibitions to maintain or increase their share of the visitor market, and they have recognized that the most effective way of achieving this is to pay more attention to the needs of visitors, and to increase the educational effectiveness of their exhibitions. Thus, many modern heritage attractions, and especially those combining interactive exhibits with historic artefacts, are much more concerned with the experiences of visitors (Caulton 1998).

Research has shown that the visitor experience in museums is influenced not only by their physical surroundings, but also by their prior knowledge and expectations, and by the people attending with them. Thus, the visitor experience is dependent on this interplay of the personal, social and physical contexts of the visit (Falk and Dierking 1992). Since the former are largely beyond the influence of the development team, the primary aim of the development process is to provide a physical environment which will encourage visitors to explore, whatever the social and personal context of the visit. Thus, as well as attending to the conservation needs of artefacts and buildings, the development process also involves:

- the conceptualization of exhibitions;
- writing storylines and exhibit labels appropriate for target audiences;
- designing and building interactive exhibits;
- preparing graphics;
- selecting and arranging artefacts;
- choosing the lighting, colours, and constructional materials to be used in the display;
- generally attending to the physical context of the exhibition.

The development process requires a wide range of specialist skills, including education and interpretation, project management, graphic and 3-D design, interactive and computer software design, lighting and audio-visual design, illustration, scenic painting, joinery, and electrical and mechanical engineering. The process draws upon the skills and knowledge of several key players, but educationalists play a significant role alongside curators and designers in modern heritage attractions. With an increasing emphasis on financial support from external parties, funding partners, sponsors and other stakeholders also have an interest in the content and design of attractions. In addition, in the development of a customer-focused visitor attraction, target visitors should be identified and consulted at the conceptualization stage to ensure that the attraction is both understandable and enjoyable, and meets educational objectives (a process which is repeated at every subsequent stage of development, construction and installation).

There are three main stages of attraction development: project conceptualization and definition, project specification, and project realization. The reality is that few heritage attractions have managers with the skills and experience required in-house to develop a new or revitalized attraction that will survive in an increasingly competitive heritage and leisure marketplace. As a result, heritage visitor attractions are typically developed in a number of alternative ways. The attraction is:

1.   conceived, designed and constructed in-house;
2.   conceived and designed in-house, but constructed by contractors;
3.   conceived in-house, but designed and constructed by contractors;
4.   conceived, designed and constructed by contractors.

Whereas in the past many organizations designed and built all exhibitions in-house, today very few UK heritage attractions develop their own comprehensive skilled exhibition development teams. Indeed, until the advent of the National Lottery, the shortage of capital resources led to a corresponding shortage of exhibition development skills within many organizations. It is more common in the UK today to employ small internal exhibition development teams which draw upon external expertise when it is needed. For example, whereas at one time the Science Museum produced many exhibitions in-house, it now contracts exhibition development and construction to specialist designers and developers. Exhibitions are conceptualized in-house, with clear objectives and methodologies written into the exhibition briefs, but thereafter the Science Museum project manages development, with an emphasis on clear communication with and between contractors to ensure effective exhibits are delivered on time and within budget. A complex array of multi-disciplinary skilled professionals is employed, operating independently, in partnership or within commercial companies, museums, science centres and universities. The process has changed even since the early 1990s: at that time the Science Museum typically employed and co-ordinated a range of specialist contractors, whereas today they are more likely to employ leading design consultants who will themselves sub-contract specialist work.

Many smaller heritage organizations lack the expertise and resources to develop an internal exhibition team, and choose exhibition design companies not simply to design the exhibition, but also to conceptualize the attraction, undertake a feasibility study, write the storylines, procure the exhibits and manage the installation. These companies often incorporate a broad range of experienced people alongside more traditional designers, and they, in turn, recruit any other necessary expertise as and when required. One heritage designer likens his role to that of the conductor of an orchestra, gelling together the various component skills to produce the finished project. He stresses that there are considerable advantages to employing an independent design company: 'Often the client can't see beyond the end of their noses because they are so close to a project and have been for many, many years, and they only have a narrow view of what can be done creatively. It can also give funders a vision – a picture is worth a thousand words' (interview with David Patrick, PLB Design and Consulting, 1997). In short, these large design companies will convert the design and interpretation brief into a completed exhibition. For the client, this process is efficient, and has the advantage of placing all responsibility with the design and development contractors.

However, the process is not without risk or potential difficulty. Although it does not involve the recruitment of in-house staff, it can be expensive since design companies will add a significant fee to all stages of design and construction. Secondly, the intended historical concept may well become distorted, particularly if the original objectives are poorly defined, or if there is little control over the development process. Thirdly, whilst exhibition designers are skilled professionals, they are not necessarily historians, educationalists or exhibition evaluators. Although expertise in these areas may be recruited by the designers, these are specialist skills in their own right which can get excluded from the development process unless the client is careful. One heritage designer claims that organizations which choose to buy in expertise are vulnerable: many of their clients have no experience in the field, and are on a very steep learning curve. The problem facing many organizations is how to minimize the risks involved, and how to ensure that the original concept is turned into an effective attraction.

The key to a successful relationship with contract exhibit developers is to write clear and detailed exhibition briefs, and to send these to a limited number of companies to tender competitively for the work. Tendering for contracts over £100,000 is subject to European Union regulations, but for lesser sums local councils have the authority to set the thresholds above which they require competitive bids (Fraser 1997). Typically, after initial short-listing, around three to six companies are asked to make a full presentation to clients, during which the successful company is selected.

Inexperience in dealing with the exhibition development process by clients can cause problems for the designers. Exhibition designers expect competition, but intensely dislike inadequate briefs, or the requirement to make full presentations along with a large number of competing contractors. One heritage design company has received briefs ranging from three paragraphs to very thick detailed documents. In addition, they are often asked to compete with 60 to 80 other firms bidding for one contract. Some unscrupulous clients go through the tendering process speculatively without the funds to pay for any of the contractors, whilst others have stolen ideas from a range of consultant proposals. It is, as one author has noted, 'an ethical and practical minefield' (Fraser 1997).

Typically, clients for many new heritage attractions are partnerships between different council departments, or between a local authority and English Heritage. This can cause significant problems, since each organization can have its own agenda, and may disagree on the best way forward. Power struggles are common, for example when the heritage requirements of a proposal threaten economic development (few local authorities can afford to set up projects which they have to underwrite permanently, and the underlying reason for many new heritage developments is that there will be indirect economic benefits through tourism or inward investment). A further problem for developers is when individual councillors or officers have their own hobby-horses: one heritage designer described this as the 'dog-with-a-bone mentality', and it can lead to a project taking a direction against market evidence and the advice of consultants (this is cited in the model of new product development as a clear reason for product failure).

In short, whilst many organizations find that it is simpler to write a design brief and award a contract after tender to one company to develop and install a complete heritage attraction, this does not in itself guarantee success. The development process must be monitored at every stage to ensure that conservation, educational, technical and safety considerations are not compromised. The recruitment of an independent project manager and other external advisers may be necessary to oversee production and development, if these skills are not available in-house. This may be less efficient than placing the whole contract in the hands of one company, but it is a sensible strategy which many new projects are employing to ensure that the client maintains control of both the development process and the finished product.

Evaluation studies

The broad principles of modern exhibition design and development have been laid down in a number of key texts (Belcher 1991; Lord and Lord 1991). Most of these focus on the practicalities of the development process at the expense of educational aims, although this has been addressed in a recent compilation (Durbin 1996). In an increasingly competitive leisure market, a focus on the intended activities of the visitor is essential in the development process, and educational and entertainment objectives should feature alongside heritage objectives for the site, building or collection. As each exhibit idea is refined and developed, it is essential that measurable objectives are set for targeted visitors, in terms of physical activities, enjoyment, behaviour, feelings, attitudes and understanding. Research and evaluation are an integral part of the development process, and without specified goals it is impossible to measure the effectiveness of exhibits against expected outcomes. In addition, evaluation helps heritage organizations demonstrate to funding bodies and other stakeholders that stated objectives are being met (Hein 1994).

Evaluation studies for individual sites complement the findings of more general research into public attitudes to history and the heritage industry (Merriman 1991). Increased interest in evaluation studies reflects increasing professionalization, helping heritage attractions to plan and utilize resources efficiently and to target exhibitions effectively (Bicknell 1995). In addition, by concentrating on the visitor experience, evaluation helps to orientate all staff towards the expectations and needs of visitors and away from a product-led approach (Hood 1983). The key to successful evaluation is to employ the right research methods in the right time at the right place, and then to act upon the findings, knowing with confidence that the results represent the views or behaviour of visitors (McManus 1991).

The most important study an organization can undertake is a large-scale survey investigating the socio-economic and demographic characteristics of existing or potential visitors, together with their likes and dislikes. If an attraction can define its audience, this will enable it to undertake smaller-scale evaluation studies subsequently of defined segments (McManus 1991). The usual methodology is to undertake a random sample quantitative questionnaire survey: in general, the more detailed information required concerning small sub-samples, the greater the survey population required to ensure the validity of the results. Visitor research into the characteristics, attitudes and behaviour of existing visitors is simpler than non-visitor research. However, two museum services in London have conducted detailed focus group research into the attitudes of non-visitors to their services, and in particular to identify ways to make their museums more accessible and attractive (Trevelyan 1991; Fisher 1990).

Having identified the characteristics of existing visitors or non-visitors, detailed evaluation of attractions with target visitor groups can take place. Clearly, the earlier in the development process that the evaluation is carried out, the earlier any potential problems can be identified and rectified (see Figure 3.2).

Front-end analysis

Research to identify the attitudes, understanding and misconceptions of identified groups of target visitors to potential exhibitions at the concept stage. This is usually carried out in small focus groups.

Formative evaluation

Research to investigate target visitors' reactions to proposed exhibits at a mock-up stage. This research helps to identify if visitors understand the aims and objectives of the exhibit, if the instructions and labels are clear, if the lighting and ergonomics are appropriate and, indeed, if they actually like the exhibit. The formative process may have to be repeated several times after each modification of the exhibit under trial.

Summative evaluation

Research to investigate how visitors use an exhibition after installation. It is the easiest research to conduct, but leads to the most costly alterations. There are numerous techniques available, including questionnaires, in-depth open-ended interviews, structured interviews, observation or tracking.

Figure 3.2: Evaluation techniques for new heritage visitor attractions.

In short, there are numerous evaluation techniques available to inform the development process. Evaluation should be considered an integral part of the exhibit development programme rather than a one-off activity. The validity of the findings will increase as more research is carried out, and the use of a range of evaluative techniques can be a useful way to triangulate results. Several professional evaluators advocate the use of multiple methodologies to give greater rigour, reliability and depth to evaluative research (Bicknell 1995). At Birmingham Museum's ethnography gallery, Paulette McManus employed no fewer than nine techniques including an exit survey, observation, tracking, analysis of written comments, and research into visitors' long-term memories of the exhibition (Peirson Jones 1993).

Although evaluation studies are increasingly important to ensure the effectiveness of new attractions, not all developments carry them out. A questionnaire survey completed by 74 social history curators in the UK in 1996 identified that whilst 65 per cent of respondents stated that their museums conducted visitor surveys, less than 15 per cent used focus groups or observation studies, and only 18 per cent evaluated proposed exhibits at the design stage (Davies and Caulton 1997). Unless clients specify evaluation studies in the contract, exhibit developers are unlikely to carry them out. One heritage designer questioned in this survey claims that it is the client's responsibility to undertake evaluative research, and whilst they themselves would like to undertake more, in a competitive environment they cannot afford to do so unless it is funded within the contract. The evidence suggests that inexperienced staff on the client side – perhaps operating within very limited resources – frequently rely on the experience of contractors rather than undertaking evaluative research. This is a risky strategy, which may well lead to the development of attractions which are unpopular or misunderstood. For most heritage attractions, the evaluation programme implemented will be a pragmatic response to developing an exhibition with limited resources. However, evaluation is such an important part of exhibit development that it is essential that the heritage attraction either develops in-house skills to oversee the evaluation process, or employs an independent specialist evaluator.

The impact of the National Lottery

The National Lottery, launched in November 1994, raised around £4 billion in less than three years for the five good causes. Even before the impact of the Lottery came into effect, one major survey revealed that whilst demand for visits to UK museums had increased by 9 per cent between 1989 and 1995, this was eclipsed by the growth in the number of heritage attractions (Davies 1995). In 1996, the Heritage Lottery Fund was six times over-subscribed in terms of its annual income (Fitzherbert and Rhoades 1997). Thus, the National Lottery has served to feed an already overcrowded leisure attractions market, in which several museums in 1996–7 failed to meet visitor targets or closed down. Indeed, such is the impact of the National Lottery that many heritage design companies are only working on Lottery-related work (much of which is feasibility studies for heritage attractions which may never be built). One problem that is frequently quoted is that there may simply be an insufficient number of exhibit designers and builders in the UK to meet the demands of Lottery-funded attractions, particularly those being constructed for the millennium. Indeed, one heritage designer predicted that the Millennium Dome in Greenwich alone could swallow up all the best exhibition designers in the UK.

The National Lottery has affected the development of heritage visitor attractions in a number of ways:

1. The increase in funding has encouraged applications from a wide variety of heritage projects, serving to increase competition for visitors.
2. The nature of the UK heritage industry has been redefined, since the Heritage Lottery Fund supports projects which help to preserve or enhance public access to, and enjoyment of: land and countryside; historic buildings and sites (including urban parks and places of worship); museums and collections; archives and special libraries; and industrial, transport and maritime heritage. Specifically excluded from the receipt of funds are visitor attractions not directly related to preserving a collection, building or site (for example, a themed heritage attraction); projects concerned with 'intangible' heritage, such as oral history recording; and education or conservation facilities not directly related to specific heritage sites (Fitzherbert and Rhoades 1997).
3. The exhibition development process has been formalized, with more rigour required in terms of financial and market planning, and exhibition design. Applicants have to demonstrate that the project is financially viable, preserves and enhances the heritage asset, integrates high quality design, is relevant to local, regional and national strategies, and has associated public benefits (such as improved access or improving the quality of the visitor experience). One outcome of this more formal process of heritage attraction development is that many small exhibition design companies increasingly work in temporary partnership with other specialist consultants on a project-by-project basis.

THE DEVELOPMENT OF HERITAGE VISITOR ATTRACTIONS: SOME CONCLUSIONS

There are clear differences between the objectives of commercial organizations developing new products and services, and those of heritage attractions. Indeed, the need both to encourage visitors and to preserve heritage sites, and the need both to educate and to entertain, can result in the development of heritage attractions with conflicting objectives. This impacts upon the service encounter in ways which are not always consistent with service operations management theory. Furthermore, the application of marketing strategies to meet those objectives differs from those available to commercial companies. Nevertheless, the development of new heritage attractions is increasingly following the model of new product development, particularly after the introduction of the National Lottery, which has formalized the development process. Whilst it is true that although the Heritage Lottery Fund requires evidence of community support for projects, the evidence suggests that evaluation studies with target visitor groups are still not yet conducted as readily as one might expect, and certainly not as widespread as in market testing for commercial products. However, as competition for visitors intensifies, it seems inevitable that the developers of heritage visitor attractions will have to demonstrate much more rigour in this area in the future to justify the provision of public funds.

NOTES

1.   Most interviewees are not cited by name, in order to respect the confidentiality of their views.

REFERENCES

Anderson, D. (1997) *A Common Wealth: Museums and Learning in the United Kingdom*, London: Department of National Heritage.
Belcher, M. (1991) *Exhibitions in Museums*, Leicester: Leicester University Press.
Bicknell, S. (1995) 'Here to help: evaluation and effectiveness', in Hooper-Greenhill, E. (ed.) *Museum, Media, Message*, London: Routledge, 281–93.
Caulton, T. (1998) *Hands-on Exhibitions: Managing Interactive Museum Galleries and Science Centres*, London: Routledge.
Davies, S. (1995) *By Popular Demand*, London: Museums and Galleries Commission.
Davies, S. and Caulton, T. (1997), *Social History Curators Group National Research Project*, unpublished research.
Durbin, G. (ed.) (1996) *Developing Museum Exhibitions for Lifelong Learning*, London: Group for Education in Museums.
Falk, J. H. and Dierking, L. D. (1992) *The Museum Experience*, Washington: Whalesback Books.
Fisher, S. (1990) *Bringing History and the Arts to a New Audience: Qualitative Research for the London Borough of Croydon*, unpublished research by the Susie Fisher Group.
Fitzherbert, L. and Rhoades, L. (1997) *1997 National Lottery Yearbook*, London: Directory of Social Change.
Fraser, D. (1997) 'Winning ways', *Museums Journal*, July, 35–6.
Hein, G. (1994), 'Evaluation of programmes and exhibitions', in Hooper-Greenhill, E. (ed.) *The Educational Role of the Museum*, London: Routledge, 281–93.
Hewison, R. (1987) *The Heritage Industry: Britain in a Climate of Decline*, London: Methuen.
Hood, M. (1983) 'Staying away: why people choose not to visit museums', *Museum News*, 61, 4, 50–7.
Kotler, P. (1994) *Marketing Management*, NJ: Prentice-Hall.
Lord, B. and Lord, G. D. (eds) (1991) *Manual of Museum Planning*, London: HMSO.
Merriman, N. (1991) *Beyond the Glass Case: the Past, the Heritage and the Public*, Leicester: Leicester University Press.

McLean, F. (1997) *Marketing the Museum*, London: Routledge.

McManus, P. (1991) 'Towards understanding the needs of visitors', in Lord, B. and Lord, G. D. (eds) (1991) *Manual of Museum Planning*, London: HMSO, 35–51.

Museums Association (1997) *Codes of Ethics and Ethical Guidelines 3: Trading and Commercial Activities*, London: Museums Association.

Peirson Jones, J. (1993) *Gallery 33: a Visitor Study*, Birmingham: Birmingham Museums and Art Gallery.

Schmenner, R. (1995) *Service Operations Management*, Englewood Cliffs, NJ: Prentice-Hall.

Trevelyan, V. (1991) *Dingy Places with Different Kinds of Bits: an Attitudes Survey of London Amongst Non-visitors*, London: London Museums Service.

Walsh, K. (1992) *The Representation of the Past: Museums and Heritage in the Post-modern World*, London: Routledge.

MODEL QUESTIONS AND ANSWERS

1. How does the development of heritage visitor attractions differ from that of new products?

2. How does the design of heritage visitor attractions impact upon service delivery? How does this differ from service industries in general?

3. Survival in the heritage industry has become much more competitive owing to the increase in the number of heritage and leisure attractions. New heritage visitor attractions have to demonstrate that they can survive in the marketplace before they can receive public funds – what do you think will happen to older heritage sites developed when the need to demonstrate economic viability was less intense?

CHAPTER 4

Interpretation and Presentation

Christina Goulding

INTRODUCTION

The nature and characteristics of services pose different challenges for managers given that a service is an act, a process, and a performance. Service delivery occurs through human interaction for most services (Gilmore 1996), and heritage visitor attractions are no exception. As with many services, the heritage product is delivered in a physical environment or site created by the service firm. The physical environment encompasses the land or building area, shape, lighting, and provides a sense of physical and psychological orientation which will impact upon the quality of the experience. The service encounter is the service as seen from the customer's point of view and is most commonly perceived in terms of the interaction between the customer and the firm. Ultimately, the effectiveness of communicating historical information relies on the ability to construct images, convey information, and engage and interact with the visitor either through social exchange, as in the case of living museums, or the more traditional textual and visual methods as found in more orthodox attractions. However, in the late 1990s the heritage sector in Britain is facing a difficult challenge: to reconcile the needs of the market with scholarship in a climate of dwindling financial support. This means broadening appeal and catering not only to the traditional museum public – although this is an important and valued group – but of developing recognition that there are many publics, just as there are many forms of museum and heritage attractions. These publics will differ in what they expect from heritage experiences and they will be selective in the forms of representation that they will choose to visit. It would be foolish to claim that all visitors want re-enactments, living museums or interactive experiences, or conversely that the traditional method of displaying history is the best and only appropriate means to communicate the message.

At the crux of much of the debate is the issue of interpretation: the idea that museums must become more exciting and appealing in how they represent and recreate the past, they must communicate with their visitors, understand their wants and cater to these through stimulating forms of recreations and representations.

However, the idea that heritage resources and museums should value their customers is still a relatively new concept (Cossons 1993). This does not necessarily mean that the integrity of the interpretation needs to be sacrificed in the name of modern consumerism. History and heritage can be made interesting and, it is argued, there are many ways of presenting the past (Myerson 1994).

The focus of this chapter is the issue of interpretation, with a particular emphasis on the consumer experience, a sometimes controversial but challenging endeavour for those engaged in its management. The initial emphasis is placed upon the nature of interpretation which is defined and classified. Having done so, the next part of the chapter attempts to align some of the issues surrounding heritage interpretation and the visitor experience. Following on from this, questions surrounding representations of the past are examined, particularly in relation to meeting the needs of a pluralistic society. Such matters, however, need to be contextualized within a framework based upon an understanding of the relationship between the individual and the resource, which provides the basis for the penultimate section of this chapter. The chapter concludes by highlighting areas of research into visitor behaviour and suggests a number of perspectives which may be used to investigate this fundamental area.

THE NATURE OF INTERPRETATION

The term 'interpretation' is a word that occurs consistently in the debate over the role and nature of the heritage resource, and as such it is important to clarify its use. In theory, interpretation should consist of more than just themes or unconnected historical accounts. It should provide a stimulating and thought-provoking experience. In its literal sense interpretation describes how history, stories, artefacts and re-enactments are presented or 'interpreted' in the medium of the museum or heritage attraction, the degree of information available and the nature and quality of that information. Nonetheless, it must also be pointed out that 'full' interpretation, where everything is laid bare, leaving little to the imagination, does not necessarily equate to 'good' interpretation. Moscardo (1996) refers to the earlier work of Tilden (1977) who defines the term as:

> an activity which aims to reveal meanings and relationships as an art, and revelations based upon information whose aim is not instruction but provocation. (p. 9)

He further maintains that interpretation should connect its topic to: 'something within the personality or experience of the visitors' (Tilden 1977).

Table 4.1 provides a broad classification of the various types of consumer-oriented heritage attractions and museums which can be further differentiated on

Table 4.1: The range of heritage type and interpretation objectives. *Source:* Goulding (1997).

Heritage type and objectives	Examples
1. Fantasy heritage (entertainment, fun)	Robin Hood Experience, Nottingham Dracula Experience, Whitby London Dungeon
2. Museum shopping (consumerism)	Terence Conran's Design Museum The Package, Gloucester Docks
3. Industrial museums (education/entertainment)	Blists Hill, Ironbridge. Black Country Museum, Dudley Beamish North East The Big Pit, Wales Cadbury World, Birmingham
4. Re-enactments (entertainment/education)	Sieges Pageants
5. Nostalgic experiences (nostalgia/entertainment/education)	White Cliffs of Dover Imperial War Museum
6. Orthodox museums (education)	City museums such as Birmingham Museum and Art Gallery
7. Preservation agencies	Castles; houses; ruins; landscapes

the basis of their objectives, their interpretation, and the nature of the customer/service interaction.

These constitute a sample of heritage sites and museums that are becoming, whether through choice or economic necessity, increasingly driven by commercial needs. Nevertheless, regardless of the nature and form of the heritage resource, an understanding of visitor expectations and on-site experiences is becoming more and more important. Failure to account for visitor behaviour in certain cases has resulted in poorly informed management decisions, wasted resources, weak communication, and dissatisfied customers.

HERITAGE INTERPRETATION AND THE VISITOR EXPERIENCE

The question of what influences heritage consumption is one that remains largely ignored or has been subject to partial and sometimes inadequate methodological exploration, a view endorsed by Moscardo (1996) and Masberg and Silverman (1996). Horne (1992) argues that it is a misconception to talk about the public as if they are a homogenous mass. Individuals will negotiate meanings and approach the museum on our own terms. To appreciate this means asking questions about, not only existing but potential markets, with the aim of extending appeal to groups not normally associated with heritage visiting.

It would appear that Britain, as a country, has yet to reach a state where the various groups within society defined by ethnicity, class and gender have equal representation, despite the diversity of contemporary heritage users. However, the museum is a platform that affords the opportunity to gain insights into the forces that shaped the present. Taken as a whole, the experience of the past and the nature of this experience through heritage consumption is largely derived from the form, content, narrative and nature of how the past is 'interpreted'. Stapp (1990) proposes that:

> Perhaps the museum best serves as a barometer for the public about the givens of types of discourse about, and modes of appropriation of cultural goods which ultimately signal a society's view of its past, present, and future.

Whilst recognizing that true authenticity can never be achieved, as much of history itself is so often based on subjective accounts, Haskell (1993) and Russell (1993) propose that heritage conservation and interpretation, has in the past operated partially and prejudicially. Jenkins (1991) discusses the way in which the history 'product' is presented in museums arguing that there is a difference between history as such and ideological history, a view reinforced by Bertens (1995). Such observations are a reflection of Fowler's (1992) proposition that management of the past is conducted on two levels: the physical and the intellectual. The aim of this next section is to explore the boundaries of interpretation in relation to its role, and limitations with regard to issues of learning and elucidation, in keeping with the principles of stimulation and the revelation of meaning. One way to do this is to examine interpretation from a critical perspective in order to highlight the difficulties and challenges facing interpreters. Three areas which have possibly attracted the greatest criticism in relation to how the past is presented and how this impacts on experience, include the interpretation of the history of ethnic groups in Britain, the representation of social class, and the portrayal of gender in museums. Such issues become important when considered in the light of historical representations as a source of cultural pride and identity. Proesler (1990) however, maintains that museums and representations of the past through heritage mediums have three effects; they transform culture, they generate new forms of culture, and they destroy other cultural forms. This process is achieved through the selection, value given, and meaning attached to the objects of display.

REPRESENTATIONS OF THE PAST

Objects in a museum are by their nature in an artificial context. This means that any interpretation surrounding them has to be recognized as a creation of a new reality. Kavanagh (1989) argues that history and social processes are curious affairs with complex ranges of approaches and preconceptions. It therefore does not follow that the social history in the museum is actually addressing the history of society or its cultural configurations and contradictions. Pearce (1989) suggests that it is a museum's job to reflect the community it serves. As such, material objects should be considered in the light of geographical, cultural and economic factors. Hooper-Greenhill (1992) perceives the role of museums as one that actively shapes knowledge through the accumulation of material objects which make it possible to know the world. However, Jenkinson (1989) argues that many remain pitted with yawning gaps that represent major historical silences. West (1990) on a similar note suggests that all too often the past is idealized and packaged, not to invite challenge, but merely to act as a backdrop for the leisure events that attract the paying public. However, even with the inclusion of visitor centres which set the scene and 'fill in' the invisible gaps in order to create a complete picture, artefacts, texts, visual representations and records are not always available to paint a total picture. Whilst appreciating the difficulties faced by interpreters, this does ultimately lead to many groups in society being regarded as 'surplus to requirement' and as such become invisible in the retelling of history.

INTERPRETATION, MEANING AND SOCIAL GROUPS

Garrison (1990) draws attention to the fact that despite the long history of a black presence in Britain, there is still not a single national institution that has accepted responsibility for preserving and documenting their experience. On a similar note, Hasted (1990) and Katriel (1993) argue that while society has become much more multicultural, the tendency is to go along with 'safe' and familiar versions of the past, which usually means those versions which are 'safe' and familiar to the dominant cultural groups.

Garrison (1990) argues that the manner in which, for example, Africa and Africans have been treated in Western historiography has a direct bearing upon how the various ethnic groups in society regard themselves and are regarded by others. Hasted (1990) advocates a proactive policy of inclusion of the contribution that other races have made to building this country. This, she believes, would constitute a step towards developing a positive awareness of cultural diversity as a source of pleasure and pride rather than fear and insecurity.

However, efforts are being made to meet the needs of our pluralistic society.

For example Merriman (1995) discusses the past failure of the London Museum, in common with many others, to adequately represent key areas of historical discourse. In order to take positive action to resolve this problem, the 'Peopling of London' project was launched. This involved participation by minority ethnic groups within the local area and included their contributions to a wide array of cultural presentations including food, dance, theatre and stories. It further aimed to demonstrate that immigration was not a post-war phenomenon, but a previously 'hidden' history. In addition to this, summaries of the exhibition were provided in nine different languages to lend strength to the argument of cultural significance and identity as part of the experience. The result was a greater awareness achieved through communication with local populations and a subsequent increase in interest and visitor numbers from groups who are largely under-represented in museum statistics (Merriman 1995).

Bennett (1988) offers a critique of contemporary industrial museums focusing on Beamish Living Museum in the North East. He argues that all too often displays claiming to represent a true picture of subordinate class culture are revealed under greater scrutiny as being little more than nostalgic and sentimentalized versions of the era. On a similar theme, West's (1988) analysis centred around Blists Hill Living Industrial Museum, Ironbridge, Shropshire. The museum is dedicated to the birthplace of industry; however, rather than demonstrating the processes that would have characterized the period with an emphasis on worker relationships, exploitation and economic conditions, the story is one of retailing. The High Street forms the central focus, and the visitor is kept entertained by actors demonstrating the history of retailing while allowing the consumer to purchase most of the products on display. Consequently the more thought-provoking and unpleasant aspects are often 'overlooked' or ignored.

If there remain doubts about the representation of the class structure in museums, others look to the portrayal of women and their role in the historical process. Chabot (1990) suggests that any discussion of gender in museums seems almost accidental, even in the more orthodox institutions with their stress on unbiased and scholarly interpretation. Gendered language proliferates, with 'man' used as the common metonym where maleness comes to represent all people. Men are shown as hunters, women as nurturers. Men engage in activities that change while women's roles remain the same. Chabot argues that we do not know what gender relationships were like, so why assume – and assume in such a stereotyped manner?

However, it would appear that authenticity does have its price. By presenting an uncoloured interpretation, the museum runs the risk of being regarded as 'political' or 'propagandist'. A tension therefore exists, a dichotomy between portraying 'authentic' conditions on the one hand while attempting to provide the visual and material richness required by the market on the other. It is this question of understanding the requirements of the market that is becoming increasingly central to decision-making policies regarding interpretation management. The following section reflects on the work that has been conducted into understanding the consumers of the heritage experience, and the factors that contribute towards the construction of meaning in the context of interpretation.

UNDERSTANDING THE CONSUMER: VISITOR BEHAVIOUR AND HERITAGE INTERPRETATION

It would be unfair to suggest or imply that museums operate in an uninformed manner regarding their customers. Most museums conduct regular customer surveys that provide information on demographics, spending trends, types of exhibits visited, party composition and length of stay. However, all too often surveys relating to visitor behaviour only serve to replicate the same findings and have rarely advanced an overall understanding of what motivates museum visiting and non-visiting (Merriman 1989). However, outside of the dictate of specific institutions there is a growing body of ethnographic research conducted at museums and heritage sites which aims to explore the nature of the experience from the perspective of the consumers themselves (for example, Kelly 1985; McManus 1989; Delaney 1992; Squire 1994; and Boisvert and Slez 1995).

THE INDIVIDUAL AND THE OBJECT

Until quite recently traditional perceptions of the audience for museums has been divided in terms of, on the one hand, a small 'elite' with 'real' interest in what is on display – connoisseurs, scholars and collectors, while on the other, an undifferentiated, so-called 'general' public (Smith1989). This is exacerbated by the fact that many museums continue to concentrate their research efforts into obtaining data that supports decisions rather than expands understanding of their publics; an observation that Stevens (1989) captures with the metaphor that 'museums use market research rather like a drunk uses a lamppost, for support, not illumination'. However, visitors bring a multiplicity of different attitudes, expectations and experiences to the reading of displays, so that their comprehension of them is 'individualized'. The idea that artefacts have a complex presence which is subject to multiple interpretation has important implications for the way museums and heritage sites think about and present themselves (Smith 1989).

CONSUMER RESEARCH

Fodness (1994) supports this by proposing that most motivational work in the general field of tourist and visitor behaviour does little more than penetrate the surface, consisting of lists of possibilities rather than insightful revelations. This view is substantiated by Stapp, who after an extensive review of the empirical work conducted in the field of museums and their 'publics' concluding that:

> Identifying the public's expectation of and experience in the museum has proceeded on several fronts, disjointedly and haphazardly at best. For the most part prescriptive, rather than descriptive; attempts to ascertain the museums public's attitudes and behaviours have rarely been rigorous.
>
> (Stapp 1990)

Falk, Koran, Dierking and Dreblow (1985) take a more extended view of behavioural analysis. They contend that there are three basic frameworks which may be applied to gain an understanding of the relationship between the visitor and the interpretation offered. These include:

1. *An exhibit perspective:* this maintains that the nature of the exhibit is the dominant motivator and as such is subject to manipulation and control through the degree of participation versus passivity, content, attractiveness and intensity of illumination.
2. *The visitor perspective:* here the view is that visitors come to a museum with an agenda and prior knowledge. The metaphor of the visitor as a shopper is most commonly used with this approach, but the idea of establishing any form of prediction is based on an understanding of the 'goods' on the 'shopping list' and it is one which most museum professionals have tended to ignore.
3. *The 'setting' perspective:* this is an holistic view and one that proposes behaviour is determined by large-scale social and environmental factors rather than by individual differences or the quality of the display. From this perspective the museum must be perceived as a 'behaviour' setting rather than just an entity for education or fun.

Other perspectives on museum visiting include the work of Merriman (1989) and (1991) which has significance in that it addresses not only factors influencing visits to museums, but also highlights reasons why people do not visit.

While motivation studies of museum visiting still remain largely ignored, the area of the heritage experience has possibly yielded more research and evaluation. One common area for investigation is the level of involvement and participation between visitors and exhibits. Eason and Linn (1976) propose that much of the research in museums centres around the effectiveness of participatory exhibits. For example, Boisvert and Slez (1995) used observational methods to assess the impact of museum exhibits. They concluded that attraction levels were highest for exhibits with concrete presentations, while holding power was highest for exhibits which combined both high interaction and concrete presentations. However, Blud (1990) argues that most museums actually ignore the nature of the visit by concentrating too much on the effectiveness of the exhibit. He surmised that visits to museums are perceived as social rather than educational, and therefore it is not merely a case of individual interaction with the exhibit, but the opportunity for social interaction which needs to be considered.

On the theme of group influences and experience, McManus (1989), in her research into communications with and between visitors to the British Museum, concluded that visitors in groups attend to the museum communications as a social unit. The social unit focuses on an exhibition, selectively activating contributions from the text to build conversations. McManus's findings illustrate the experience of interpretation from a socially interactive perspective, but do little to explain the forces driving the individual explorer who actively seeks out the solitude of a little-known heritage site in order to soak up the atmosphere in isolation.

Hodder (1982) looks beyond this to the role and function of 'heritage' consumption arguing that the material things or artefacts are the passive objects of human control. These material symbols are value laden. They do not just indicate status and role, but say something about underlying values and beliefs. Such material symbols are models of, and models for, behaviour.

Moscardo (1996) incorporates psychological explanations to provide a theoretical framework. His theories are based on the work of Langer and Newman (1987) who developed the 'mindfulness'/'mindlessness' distinction. Mindfulness is the product of novelty, surprise, variety and situations that require effort on the part of the individual. Mindlessness on the other hand is a result of over-familiarity or exposure to stimuli which is not perceived as personally relevant (Langer and Newman 1987). Uzzell (1989) and Moscardo (1996) propose that interpretation should produce mindful visitors who are active, interested and capable of questioning and reassessing the situation. Moscardo integrated his theoretical framework with the key findings of museum studies compiled by Bitgood (1988). His conclusions focused on the importance of interaction and control in the experience, the significance of variety, the degree of cognitive orientation, and the usefulness of guided tours and maps to ensure physical orientation.

Goulding's (1997a) research into the nature of motivations behind heritage visiting and the nature of the experience, involved in-depth interviews, observations of on-site visitor behaviour and focused discussion groups. The research was conducted at three separate sites, each of which offered different forms of interpretation. The first site was Blists Hill Living Museum in Shropshire, a reconstructed nineteenth-century village, complete with demonstrators, and could be described as full interpretation. The second site was the Birmingham Museum and Art Gallery, which featured a mixture of static and interactive exhibits. The third site was an English Heritage abbey, with virtually nothing in the way of textual or visual interpretation, a form of uninterpreted heritage where the experience relies heavily on existing knowledge and imagination.

The research revealed that there were a number of interconnected factors that could not be easily isolated. For example, it was found that motivations and experience were constructed and evaluated in accordance with life situations which differed across age and social class and were effected by factors such as the fullness of role repertoire, the quality of existing relationships, and the personal and cultural connection that an individual has towards particular interpretations of the past. Nostalgia was found to be a motivating factor for a number, but again this was a concept that had deeper psychological depth and intensity, depending as much on perceptions of the present as the past (Davis1979) and Goulding (1997b)). In effect, it was virtually impossible to draft a standard picture of a typical heritage visitor, although there was little to suggest any of the passive acceptance of interpretation and historical packaging as described by Hewison (1987).

There were, however, a number of consistent themes which emerged as patterns of behaviour or reactions to various historical stimuli. These suggested that motivations and experiences were interlinked, and although varying in intensity, tended to centre largely around cultural and personal identification and a desire for authenticity of representation. However, the criteria for what constituted authenticity differed depending upon age, education and personal significance; it was in effect a negotiable concept.

Other influences on the experience included the degree of relevant content, educational factors, and the opportunity for social interaction. Additionally, in most cases there was an appreciation of integrated approaches to interpretation which allowed for engagement with the resource and involvement through imaginative problem-solving exercises. The heritage environment was also a significant feature of the visit, and this was evaluated against such factors as a sense of physical and historical orientation, scene-setters, routing and mapping and crowding density levels. These findings indicate the need for a 'total' approach to interpretation, one which considers the experience in its entirety, from start to finish. Some of these issues are illustrated in the following account of visitor behaviour at the Birmingham Museum and Art Gallery's 'Birmingham Exhibition' (Goulding 1997a).

The Birmingham Museum and Art Gallery is a museum associated with the more orthodox form of interpretation. Apart from the art gallery, the museum itself is large offering a variety of exhibits ranging from a history of the city from medieval times to the present day, classical archaeology, a history of gems, to a display entitled 'A Meeting Ground of Cultures'.

The starting-point for analysis naturally enough concerned the entrance to the museum which was located towards the rear of the art gallery and was poorly signed. Once inside, the reception could be described as rather stark and provided very little information regarding current displays. A board was situated to the left of the entrance which was supposed to serve as a map regarding levels and rooms, but proved to be complicated and confusing resulting more in chanced exploration rather than a planned route.

The 'Birmingham Exhibition' was located toward the back of the museum and again was poorly signed which resulted in a low level of attendance. The objective of this display was to present a history of the city dating from medieval times up to the present day. Interpretation was in the form of paintings, objects, text, drawings, newspaper clippings, photographs and diaries.

In brief, this exhibition more than any other at the museum, demonstrated a need for some form of precise and clear map or guide to provide a sense of mental and physical orientation. Visitors who found the room seemed to do so more by accident than purpose, and their demeanour on entering displayed trepidation and unease, as if they were unsure whether it was part of the public museum or an office.

Once inside, few immediately grasped the significance or objective of the display or knew which way to follow it. The lighting was dim and the setting could be described as dreary and unwelcoming. Those that chose to stay skimmed over those parts that were not of particular interest to them, quickly moving on to other sections. These sections were most commonly those that incorporated a variety of objects, photographs and newspaper accounts, to displays dealing with earlier landowners and engineers whose lives were illustrated by paintings and a much thinner array of objects. A further detracting factor was the lack of continuity or 'theme' at such displays. This discontinuity only perpetrated disinterest. There was little to 'connect' the strands of these artefacts to illuminate the history of the period, and as such, milestones and events remained fragmented and unsupported by stimulating methods of presentation.

Nevertheless, to actually complete the circuit demanded excessive concentration. This was rare. Visitors started by exploring the opening demonstration and quickly built up momentum moving on to those that held greater appeal. Such displays included the later editions and accounts of social and economic conditions (late nineteenth century in particular). Here interpretation included photographs of, for example, back-to-back houses, alleyways and trams. Other artefacts consisted of extracts from documents detailing policies on education, newspaper clippings about crime and punishment, and medical reports which debated conditions such as rickets and head lice.

It was noted that there were differences in attitudes toward the paintings and the photographs. The photographs were perceived as 'real', the people had actually lived through and endured these conditions. These stimulated the greatest amount of discussion and prolonged interest. The older visitors discussed the settings, spoke about the nit nurse, laughed together and reminisced. The paintings on the other hand were perceived as cold and distant, there was little to relate to and they were largely ignored or given only cursory attention.

This exhibition illustrates a number of the issues that researchers have been debating with regard to the nature of the experience. It is, however, only one exhibition and a particular form of interpretation. Nonetheless, there are some fundamental points that appear to transcend museums as behaviour settings. These include the need to feel comfortable and orientated, the need to engage with the resource, which may take many different forms, ranging from imagination, to conversations with demonstrators, to piecing the jigsaw of the past together in a problem-solving manner. Consequently, interpretation needs context and continuity of theme if it is to make sense. The issue of cultural significance is a further area that warrants greater attention in future research, along with a much broader view of historical contributions to the construction and maintenance of society: in effect, continued research into the nature of the consumer experience utilizing methodologies that place the visitor at the heart of their study.

CONCLUSION

Stevens (1989) argues that interpretation should be close to its customer. Nevertheless, all too often the customer is ignored or given superficial treatment by researchers, despite exclamations of customer orientation. In order to widen appeal, interpreters need to be willing to take up the challenges facing them, which include consideration of methods to stimulate, engage and involve the visitor. Variation of stimulus is important for involvement and engagement, as is the provision of problem-solving exercises. Such approaches serve to enhance the experience and help create mindful activity, which can be either constructed through social interaction or on an individual basis. In essence, effective visitor and interpretation management involves the combination of research, proactive involvement and accessibility to a wide consumer base through the provision of stimulating and meaningful interpretation.

However, there are pitfalls to beware of. On the subject of interpretation, Lowenthal (1985) and Carr (1991) argue that often problems stem from the urge to 'over' interpret, to leave nothing to the imagination. Waterson (1989) suggests that far from enhancing the experience, over-interpretation may be an impairing factor to the visitor's enjoyment. A further challenge for interpreters it would appear, is knowing when to leave well alone and not interpret. Vergo (1989) adheres to these principles suggesting that the over-contextualized display, musty with documentation and earnest didacticism coupled with the audio-visual programme can drown out any occasion for private meditation and thought. There are more ways of transmitting information other than just verbal or written presentations. Printed family trees, photographs, newspaper accounts and evocative artefacts all serve to convey a sense of realism (Vergo 1989).

REFERENCES

Bennett, T. (1988) 'Museums and the people', in Lumley, R. (ed.) *The Museum Time Machine*, London: Routledge.

Bertens, H. (1995) *The Idea of the Postmodern: A History*, London: Routledge.

Bitgood, S. (1988) 'Visitor studies: coming of age', *Visitor Behaviour*, 3, 3.

Blud, L. M. (1990) 'Social interaction and learning among family groups visiting a museum', *Museum Management and Curatorship*, 9, 43–51.

Boisvert, D. and Slez, D. (1995) 'The relationship between exhibit characteristics and learning associated behaviours in a science museum', *Science Education*, 79, 5, 503–18.

Carr, J. (1991) 'Whose heritage is it anyway?', in Uzzell, D. (ed.) *Interpretation Newsletter: The Society for the Interpretation of Britain's Heritage*, March.

Chabot, J. (1990) 'A man called Lucy: self reflection in a museum display', in Baker, F. and Thomas, J. (eds) *Writing the Past in the Present*, Lampeter: University College.

Cossons, N. (1993) 'Rambling reflections of a museum man', in Boylan, P. (ed.) *Museums 2000*, London: Routledge.

Davis, F. (1979) *A Yearning For Yesterday: A Sociology of Nostalgia*, London: Collyer MacMillan.

Delaney, J. (1992) 'Ritual space in the Canadian Museum of Civilization', in Shields, R. (ed.) *Lifestyle Shopping*, London: Routledge.

Eason, L. P. and Linn, M. C. (1976) *Evaluation of the Effectiveness of Participatory Exhibits' Curator*, 19, 45–62.

Falk, J. H., Koran, J. J., Dierking, L. D. and Dreblow, L. (1985) 'Predicting visitor behaviour', *Curator*, 28, 249–257.

Fodness, D. (1994) 'Measuring tourist motivation', *Annals of Tourism Research*, 21, 3, 555–568.

Fowler, P. (1992) *The Past in Contemporary Society: Then and Now*, London: Routledge.

Garrison, L. (1990) 'The black industrial past in Britain', in Shore, P. and MacKenzie, R., *The Excluded Past: Archaeology in Education*, London: Unwin Hyman.

Gilmore, A. (1996) 'Services marketing research: the use of qualitative methods', paper presented at the Marketing Education Group Conference, Strathclyde University.

Goulding, C. (1997a) *A Grounded Theory Investigation of Contemporary Consumer Behaviour in Relation to Museum/Heritage Consumption: A Motivational and Experiential Analysis*, unpublished PhD Thesis: University of Wolverhampton.

Goulding, C. (1997b) 'Nostalgia and the concept of self: the case of themed living heritage and the elderly consumer', proceedings of the Academy of Marketing Conference, Manchester University, Manchester, July.

Haskell, F. (1993) *History and its Images*, New Haven: Yale University Press.

Hasted, R .(1990) 'Museums, racism and censorship', in Baker, F. and Thomas, J. (eds) *Writing the Past in the Present*, Lampeter: University College.

Hewison, R. (1987) *The Heritage Industry: Britain in a Climate of Decline*, London: Methuen.

Hooper-Greenhill, E. (1992) *Museums and the Shaping of Knowledge*, London: Routledge.

Hodder, I. (1982) *The Present Past*, London: Batsford.

Horne, D. (1992) 'Reading museums', in Boylan, P. (ed.) *Museums 2000*, London: Routledge.

Jenkins, K. (1991) *Re-Thinking History*, London: Routledge.

Jenkinson, P. (1989) 'Material culture, people's history and populism: where do we go from here?', in Pearce, S. (ed.) *Museum Studies in Material Culture*, London: Leicester University Press.

Katriel, T. (1993) 'Our future is where our past is: studying heritage museums as ideological and performing arenas', *Communications Monograph*, 16, March, 69–75.

Kelly, R. (1985) 'Museums as status symbols 2: obtaining a state of having been there', in Belk, R. (ed.) *Advances in Non Profit Marketing*, Greenwich CT: JAI Press.

Langer, E. and Newman, H. (1987) 'The prevention of mindlessness', *Journal of Personality & Social Psychology Bulletin*, 5, 295–299.

Lowenthal, D. (1985) *The Past is a Foreign Country*, Cambridge: Cambridge University Press.

Masberg, B. and Silverman, L. (1996) 'Visitor experiences at heritage sites: a phenomenological approach', *Journal of Travel Research*, 34, 4, 20–25.

McManus, P. (1989) 'What people say and how they think in a science museum', in Uzzell, D. (ed.) *Heritage Interpretation Volume 2*, London: Belhaven Press.

Merriman, N. (1989) 'The social basis of museum and heritage visiting', in Pearce, S. (ed.) *Museum Studies in Material Culture*, London: Leicester University Press.

Merriman, N. (1991) *Beyond the Glass Case: the Past, the Heritage and the Public in Britain*, London: Leicester University Press.

Merriman, N. (1995) 'Hidden history: the peopling of London project', *Museum International*, 47, 3, 12–16.

Moscardo, G. (1996) 'Mindful visitors: heritage and tourism', *Annals of Tourism Research*, 23, 2, 376–397.

Myerson, J. (1994) 'Talking shop', *Times Higher*, 3rd June.

Pearce, S. (ed.) (1989) *Museum Studies in Material Culture*, London: Leicester University Press.

Proesler, M. (1990) 'Museum masks and cultural change', in Baker, F. and Thomas, J. (eds) *Writing the Past in the Present*, Lampeter: University College.

Russell, J. (1993) 'Debating heritage: from artefacts to critical perception', *Australian Geographer*, 24, 1.

Squire, S. (1994) 'The cultural values of literary tourism', *Annals of Tourism Research*, 21, 103–120.

Smith, C. (1989) *Museums Artefacts and Meanings: The New Museology*, London: Reaktion Books.

Stapp, C. B. (1990) 'The "public" museum: a review of the literature', *Journal of Museum Education*, 11, Fall, 4–10.

Stevens, T. (1989) 'The visitor: who cares', in Uzzell, D. (ed.) *Heritage Interpretation Volume 2*, London: Belhaven Press.

Tilden, F. (1977) *Interpreting Our Heritage*, Chapel Hill: University of North Carolina Press.

Uzzell, D. (ed.) (1989) *Heritage Interpretation Volume 1*, London: Belhaven Press.

Uzzell, D. (ed.) (1989) *Heritage Interpretation Volume 2*, London: Belhaven Press.

Vergo, P. (ed.) (1989) *The New Museology*, London: Reaktion Books.

Vergo, P. (1989) 'The reticent object', in Vergo, P. (ed.) *The New Museology*, London: Reaktion Books.

Waterson, M. (1989) 'Opening doors on the past', in Uzzell, D. (ed.) *Heritage Interpretation Volume 1*, London: Belhaven Press.

West, A. (1990) 'Critical archaeology and black history', in Baker, F. and Thomas, J. (eds) *Writing the Past in the Present*, Lampeter: University College.

West, B. (1988) 'The making of the English working past: a critical view of the Ironbridge Gorge Museum', in Lumley, R. (ed.) *The Museum Time Machine*, London: Routledge.

MODEL QUESTIONS

1. While regular surveys are needed in order to identify demographic trends and the spending patterns of visitors:
   Consider the limitations of such approaches to understanding the nature of the experience gained from various types of interpretation, and
   Suggest other more appropriate approaches which may provide greater insights.

2. Surveys indicate that although the market for orthodox museums is becoming more diverse, the greatest number of visitors are still drawn from the middle-aged, middle-class, highly educated group.
   Keeping within the realm of feasibility, discuss ways of attracting and communicating the message to some of the under-represented groups in heritage visiting statistics. These may include:
   • The 16–24 age group.
   • Socio-economic groups E to C2.
   • The various ethnic groups that comprise British society.

3. Discuss the advantages and disadvantages of the more contemporary living, recreated heritage attractions such as open air museums, in terms of public appeal.

CHAPTER 5

Visitor Management

Myra Shackley

INTRODUCTION

Heritage visitor attractions are service operations and, as such, the management of visitors may be viewed as an integral part of their operational network of service task, service standards and service delivery system. However, there are many ways in which the service purchased by the visitor differs from that of, for example, a competing leisure attraction such as a garden centre, hotel or catering outlet. Visitors (customers) to heritage attractions are buying an experience, difficult to inventory and varying from person to person. Moreover, the attraction will probably be operating with severe capacity constraints which may be historical, architectural, financial or philosophical but will inevitably mean that it is impossible to deliver a service to visitors with optimal efficiency. In visitor management terms this is generally reflected by the need to control visitor demand and relate it to the attraction's fixed visitor capacity, often by employing methods which shift demand from peak to off-peak times (generally by pricing structures) or to offer ancillary services.

The scheduling of the delivery of the service to visitors (manipulated by adjustment of opening hours and the management of visitors to avoid long waits, queues and overcrowding) is as important a factor as the standards of exhibits or level of interpretation in the resulting visitor experience. It is therefore necessary to examine visitor management in the context of how the organization has defined its service task, what service standards are being set and how effectively that service is being delivered to the visitor. Schmenner (1995) highlighted those aspects of service delivery which make the management of service operations more challenging than the management of production or manufacturing businesses. He defined the nature of the service encounter through its critical components of service task, service standards and service delivery – an order followed within this chapter. The ultimate aim for the manager of a heritage visitor attraction is to ensure an effective service delivery, which creates a high quality visitor experience, encourages repeat business and builds customer satisfaction. However, this is particularly difficult to achieve within the limitations of an historic property.

SERVICE PRODUCTION

Describing the visitor as a customer is uncomfortable for many heritage visitor attraction managers, who may frequently see the quality of the visitor experience as secondary to preservation of the property or the display of particularly important collections. However, with the advent of a National Code of Practice for Visitor Attractions such managers must agree to provide, among many other things, high standards of customer care, courtesy, adequate maintenance to ensure visitor safety, adequate visitor facilities, access for disabled and special needs, and prompt response to enquiries. These are all features of good service delivery, and indicate that the customer/visitor should receive the same kind of service as that received in other parts of the leisure sector. The product offered to such visitors is not judged just on the basis of the experience during the visit, but on the pre-visit as well, which may include the adequacy of directional signs, availability of parking, access and welcome. Judgements during the visit involve both interpretation (how well the history and main features of the property or collections is presented) and the logistics of the visit (whether the attraction was crowded, how easy it was to find one's way around, the availability of facilities such as shops, refreshments and toilets). Comparatively few heritage attractions are purpose-built, with the exception of some museums and visitor centres, and many have been in existence for hundreds of years and are only now having to cope with considering themselves as deliverers of a product to an increasingly large, diverse and critical customer base. Many organizations with large numbers of heritage attractions, such as the National Trust, have gradually evolved procedures for coping with growing visitor numbers while maintaining physical fabric and sense of place. They have developed expertise in such matters as the repair and maintenance of footpaths, landscape screening of car parks, environmental interpretation, guided walks and other aspects of visitor management.

England alone has over 500,000 listed historic buildings and scheduled monuments, mostly in private ownership. Within the public sector there may be differences between the aims of organizations like English Heritage and the Historic Royal Palaces, and those of the National Trust – but all face the common difficulty that they cannot be purely commercial operations. Heritage visitor attractions are frequently properties of exceptional value and in order to open them to visitors a difficult balance must be drawn between the conflicting objectives of protecting and managing the heritage, maintaining integrity and aesthetic appeal, encouraging visitors and making profits (National Audit Office 1992). Unrestrained growth in visitors can present unacceptable threats to the integrity of the heritage property. An additional difficulty is presented by the sheer size of many attractions; the British Museum, for example, has 2.5 miles of corridors and several million items on show under a seven-acre roof, welcoming four million visitors per year. There is evidence to suggest that the size of the attraction directly affects visitor behaviour; visitors to smaller museums spend more time looking at exhibitions than visitors to larger ones (Falk and Dierking 1992).

Visitors are increasingly critical of facilities and value for money, with well-developed ideas of attractions which offer good and bad service quality. Brighton Pavilion, for example, generally receives excellent reviews for its free leaflet, information boards and video, with Buckingham Palace being considered overpriced and overcrowded. Aspects of visitor behaviour control the level of satisfaction with the product being bought; visitors hate paying out for a guidebook straight after entry, for example, so that attractions handing out a free map and guide which is supplemented by good on-site interpretation and no queuing are always highly regarded. Many museums and heritage attractions still demonstrate legacies from the time when visitors were not their core business: opening hours suiting the convenience of staff rather than visitors, for example, or the assumption that all visitors have access to a car (Ambrose and Paine 1993). A quality product has to be delivered to all visitors, necessitating the provision of facilities for visitors with disabilities, or specific facilities for children or the elderly.

The admissions policy of a heritage visitor attraction may not be specifically geared to maximize profits. Kew Gardens, for example, has an admissions policy dominated by the need to provide access for visitors from across the social spectrum which is just as important as long-term revenue generation, but has resulted in a complex ticketing system with thirteen different types of tickets at admissions prices below levels charged by competing attractions. Kew includes one historic attraction (the Pagoda) which cannot be opened to visitors at all since it is ten stories high with a single spiral stair.

VISITOR MANAGEMENT

Before the visit

Orientating the visitor and informing him/her about the nature of the product being offered begins with the pre-visit message. Critical issues here include the nature of the visitor's prior experiences and expectations, ease of obtaining directions to the attraction, and ease of following those directions. Visitor expectations about the proposed experience are diverse (Hayward and Brydon-Millar 1984) and complicated by the fact that the public has many stereotyped beliefs about what a heritage attraction should be all about. Despite the increasing amount of information about visitor expectations derived from academic studies of visitors, there is also a need to study the non-visitors (Hood 1983, 1986) since finding out about why people choose *not* to visit a heritage attraction is an important stage in planning the delivery of the product for those who do. Lack of parking, for example, is often an important reason for not visiting, and entrance orientation procedures are a significant element in visitor satisfaction (Loomis 1987). Parking may be severely limited (or non-existent) at many heritage attractions, particularly those in urban contexts. Solutions include the use of transit (shuttle) buses for large attractions as well as encouraging the use of public transport. The National Trust is trying to curb the use of cars by visitors to its properties, 90 per cent of whom currently arrive by car. A recent experiment took place at the new National Trust landscape garden which opened at Priory Close near Bath in 1996, without parking provision. The Trust argued that the valley, with a spectacular mid-eighteenth-century wooded landscape, was too narrow to accommodate parking and that alternative transport was to be encouraged. This policy was opposed by local residents who thought that visitors would ignore Trust advice to take the frequent bus service from the railway station one mile away and turn their village into a car park. Their fears proved unfounded. A visitor management policy including inducements to take the bus (£1 off a cream tea in Bath or £1 voucher at Bath National Trust shop) proved to be effective, with customers utilizing either the Trust's shuttle bus or council park-and-ride. The policy was relatively easy to implement since Priory Close had not been previously opened so that the visitor management strategy could compensate for the lack of parking and incorporate it into the information and marketing strategies. During the first season (1966) 50 per cent of arrivals used local buses and the rest took taxis, walked or cycled the one mile (uphill) from Bath city centre.

Major historic cities such as Bath frequently experience difficulties with visitors arriving at individual properties. Coach parties are a special problem, although they could be seen as an opportunity since more coaches theoretically means fewer cars. Stratford upon Avon addressed the coach-parking problem in 1993–6 by employing students on visitor information patrols who boarded coaches to explain the best routes and best places to park.

Once they have arrived at the attraction visitors require orientation towards its main features and facilities. This may be done by having a specific orientation centre separate from the main building or exhibition area, or (more commonly) by utilizing a small area near the entrance to the facility. Visitors require information about the shape, layout and displays within the attraction as well as directions towards support facilities such as shops, restaurants or toilets. They need to know the times of events or displays and any suggested routes. There is much evidence to suggest that visitors prefer a suggested path (such as themed route linking rooms or displays of interest) and knowledge of visitor preferences can aid in selecting a suggested route as well as planning the location of exhibits and facilities (Shettel-Neuber and O'Reilly 1981). Such routes can be the major features of an attraction. At Hampton Court Palace, for example, six specially-created visitor routes recreate the distinct atmosphere of different historic periods. A substantial body of literature exists on the planning of self-guided trails and routes through museums, outdoor and indoor visitor attractions (e.g.

Veverka 1994). Visitors prefer short trails starting near the point of arrival but actual route of trail determined by desired stops, potential problems, maintenance needs, location of particular displays. External routes (through heritage gardens and landscapes, for example) are predominantly half to three quarters of a mile in length which translates into a 45–60-minute trail walk on basically level ground. A good external trail includes 7–10 stops (too many are tiring) and should be a loop so that visitors can end up near where they started.

During the visit

The most common method utilized by the visitor to navigate his/her way round an attraction is still hand-held maps, although some people find these difficult to use and they must be supplemented by wall boards and direction signs for wayfaring and decision-making. The route chosen (Bitgood 1994) depends on the interaction of visitor characteristics (natural tendency to turn right, fatigue, boredom), architectural characteristics (sequence of rooms, placement of exits) and exhibit characteristics (size, movement). Classic studies of visitor characteristics by Robinson (1928) and Melton (1935) showed that, in the absence of more powerful factors vicitors showed a strong tendency to turn right. Some visitors just browse (Loomis 1987) without a clear pattern towards any specific destination.

The specific direction a visitor takes through the attraction depends both on the configuration of the attraction and the interests of visitor. Some have a specific goal in mind, this initial focus aided by good maps, but interest and energy flag after about an hour and most visitors have a time agenda . Most heritage visitor attractions have outmoded behaviour norms which are still adhered to by the majority of visitors and seem to have been tacitly adopted as appropriate for places of great antiquity, or where significant objects are kept. These norms are reverential, emphasise looking but not touching, keep voices low, wear appropriate clothes and show respect for the building or collection. The inappropriateness of many of these norms for children explains the popularity of science centres and interactive museums. Visitor behaviour is also stereotyped in other ways. Different flow patterns are typical of first-time, frequent and organized group visitors to museums and similar attractions. A first-time or occasional visit has four components: an orientation phase (4–10 minutes), intensive looking (15–40 minutes), exhibit cruising (20–45 minutes) and leave-taking (3–10 minutes) (Falk and Dierking 1992). Visitors leave an attraction because of hunger, fatigue or a feeling of having completed their visit (or a combination of all three) and during the leave-taking phase will ignore even the most enticing exhibits in favour of an exit sign. The frequent visitor, on the other hand, needs no orientation and has a simpler pattern with just intensive looking and leave-taking but seems to spend around the same amount of time. The behaviour of organized groups is different, as they may often be led by volunteers or staff members who may or may not be sensitive to the needs of the group. The usual pattern is a long period of guided intensive looking followed by a briefer period of cruising.

MANAGING WAITING

Visiting most historic attractions includes some form of waiting , and the process of managing waiting and queuing is part of the process of service provision. Mathematical models of queuing theory emphasise that in any system where the service capacity is exceeded by demand, waiting is the inevitable outcome (Dawes and Rowley 1996). Such models have been used to identify optimum levels of service and focus on minimizing the time that customers need to wait, within the resources available for the provision of the service. In heritage attraction terms such critical resources are generally dominated by space (room area available per specific number of visitors) and staff (numbers of guides, security staff, attendants or interpreters deemed necessary for that number of visitors). As with all service operations, the aim of a heritage visitor attraction is to provide customer satisfaction, informing existing customer intentions and future customer behaviour. Where the expectations of the customer are met or exceeded, visitor satisfaction is the result. Waiting for admission is central to this whole service quality experience because it is the first encounter which the customer has with the service provider, and because it is identifiable and memorable since the customer probably has little else to occupy them during that time (Dawes and Rowley 1996).

As in most service operations the customer's prior experience with waiting affects their tolerance level. For example, a customer who has never waited to visit a stately home or museum will be exceptionally irritated if they have to do so. Customers are more tolerant of longer waits when the operation is very busy (with some famously crowded properties like Beatrix Potter's Cottage or Shakespeare's birthplace a wait is anticipated) and may also be more tolerant if time is not important to them (since a long time has been allowed for their visit). Other distractions such as the proximity of a teashop or giftshop in conjunction with a timed ticket guaranteeing entry after a fixed period of waiting, minimize the problem. Such strategies can also restrict visitor numbers. The popularity of Chartwell in Kent (Sir Winston Churchill's home) resulted in the introduction of restricted tickets specifying the time of admission nearly twenty years ago, when considerable visitor damage had already been done to the gardens. Many National Trust managers take the view that the increased popularity of National Trust properties may mean that visitors will need to get used to theatre-style advance bookings for most popular properties. Overcrowding is a particular problem with gardens and does not just cause physical damage but changes in mood and atmosphere. 3,000 people turned up at Sissinghurst Garden on Good Friday 1991 although the National Trust had already raised ticket prices as a deterrent. A system of timed tickets has been introduced limiting the number of people in the garden at any one time to 400, effective for preservation but turning the garden into theatre with a subtle shift in the audience expectation of the performer (Pavord 1995).

Queues

Queuing at visitor attractions is commonplace, though more frequent at theme parks than heritage sites. Any attraction which regularly has a queue has to make a fundamental choice, whether to shorten the length of the queue or alter the way the customer perceives the waiting time. Good queue management reduces uncertainty, for example by posting notices along queues indicating likely waiting time, as at the Jorvik Viking Centre. Such signs do not stop visitors from entering the queue, which almost inevitably moves faster than the times indicated. Other possibilities include making the queue wider or hiding the queue by snaking it around barriers or corners and providing distractions for the waiting visitors. These can include tantalizing glimpses of the goal (perhaps seen through windows or over a hedge), a series of anterooms which make the visitor feel as though he has already arrived, or in-queue entertainment. Some attractions such as the London Hard Rock Cafe promote their desirability by ensuring a lengthy and highly visible queue; but most would prefer to prevent a queue by taking a more strategic approach to the planning of visitor arrivals. This involves estimating the most likely arrivals pattern (before lunchtime, late afternoon, between 3 p.m. and 4 p.m. etc.) and then increasing or decreasing arrivals management capacity to impact on waiting time. This is generally done either by adjusting the number of tills/arrival points open by going from a single to double or multiple channel system, or by increasing the speed of service. Professional exhibit designers use simulation models, but a private enterprise opening a new house to the public would be more likely to use guesswork and observation based on the first few months of operation of the experience of comparable attractions.

Queue members waiting for admission to an attraction may be entertained by buskers, informed by wallboards and provided (if necessary) with shade, shelter or seats. If regular queues are anticipated they can be incorporated into the design of an exhibition and accompanied by small display and information panels orientating visitors towards the attraction to come. Pierce (1991) recommends multiple line queues with single service personnel at large attractions for less intense use periods. In larger settings the take-a-ticket numbering system can free people from the queuing process which further frees up an entrance space to become a room or exhibit area. Even with models which aim to eliminate queues through a pricing mechanism, such as the social cost-benefit analysis of Wanhill (1980), queues are almost inevitable, either to enter an attraction, view a specific exhibit or room within the attraction, or obtain food, drink, merchandising or access to toilets.

Attempts can also be made to regulate visitor flow in advance by ticket sales. Tickets sold in advance motivate visitors, a fact yet to be come to terms with by many museums and galleries (Cramer 1995). Some museums, even when charging for temporary exhibitions, are reluctant to use the charge to ration the entry to congested facilities, taking the view that it is more egalitarian to allow crowding and control access only by the queue. The result is that many major 'blockbuster' exhibitions are so crowded that it is impossible to see the exhibits. Rationing by price rather than ordeal would make more sense, higher charges raise revenue but a queue does not. Only low-income groups could conceivably gain from the congested-but-free policy, and this difficulty can be overcome by a charging structure. It is also possible to dilute crowds by manipulating concessionary visiting, such as by making full charge days at weekends (which are more crowded but often utilized by visitors who are in employment and willing to pay to avoid congestion). Fine-tuning of pricing structures to eliminate queues can include diurnal variations such as adjusting for late entries or lunchtime visits.

The US White House operates self-guided walk-through tours on a free, timed ticket basis with visitors able to see videos and exhibits in the Visitor Centre while waiting their turn. Although the visit is not time limited it usually lasts just 20–35 minutes but tickets are only issued on the same day on a first-come, first-served basis. Admissions charges have just been instituted for Westminster Abbey, not (primarily) to raise revenue but to act as a break on visitor numbers which can reach 16,000 a day, with up to 40 groups at a time. This causes nightmarish congestion. Similar changes are likely to be started at the Sistine Chapel in the Vatican which receives up to three million visitors each year and where queues often reach half a mile in length. The introduction of advance bookings for routing visits to these attractions and to regular museum collections is becoming more widely accepted. 50 per cent of visitors to the Uffizi in Florence, for example, can now buy a ticket in advance for a pre-arranged time with no extra charge. They receive a special badge, utilize a special entrance and miss the queue. The Cezanne Exhibition at the Tate Gallery in 1996 drew 5,000 visitors per day who were willing to queue for up to two hours to see 90 paintings and only 70 watercolours/drawings (Kelly 1996). The organizers had taken the curious decision to limit the numbers of pictures being shown in order to control crowding, and to charge a high admissions price of £8.50 which was probably insufficient to deter visitors. A better scheme is to implement an advance booking system such as that utilized by the equally popular 1996 Vermeer Exhibition in The Hague, which had 350,000 reservable tickets and only 200 per day for walk-in visitors. Queuing was thus eliminated but the museum also assisted by extending opening hours until midnight for 23 nights, re-planning the visit and spreading the paintings over five rooms instead of the original four. Extra visitor facilities were installed, including a creche and dog kennel, all for 22 small paintings.

Bottlenecks

A bottleneck always causes the visitor to wait. Some are easily shifted (as by opening another till in response to peak time demand) while others are more subtle and unpredictable (such as a particularly attractive display that causes people to take longer than estimated to view, causing tailbacks). Coping with bottlenecks is a crucial aspect of visitor management but, unlike other service businesses, a heritage visitor attraction cannot store excess capacity; however, it can learn how to plan. Most admissions strategies allow the concept of peak visitation days ('design days') which are usually based on likely attendance patterns for August Bank Holiday weekends. Scaled-down models for off-peak operations can then be devised.

Chronic bottlenecks within the visitor flow generally arise from poor layout or inflexible processes, both of which can be solved by adjusting visitor circulation patterns. A poor display layout, inadequate capacity (in restaurant, toilets or shops) will inevitably create a bottleneck and queue. This can be prevented at the design stage by examining visitor flow and area space needs, utilizing (if necessary) computer models designed for this purpose (Schmenner 1995). It is not necessarily the case that visitors circulate the way that the designers intended. A strong body of theoretical literature exists about circulation, e.g. the classic studies of Melton (1935, 1936) which demonstrate that visitors have a strong tendency to turn right when they enter a gallery and that exits compete with exhibits. Levine (1982) looked at you-are-here maps for design of orientation and circulation system and Griggs (1983) and Hayward and Brydon-Millar (1984) looked at orientation and circulation in museums.

One of the most famous bottlenecks at any heritage attraction used to occur at the Jewel House at the Tower of London where a new visitor management system now enables some 20,000 people a day (2,700 per hour) to get within a few inches of the Imperial State Crown. During the summer visitors peak at 12–15,000 per day, with the Tower reaching gridlock at 18,000 visitors, estimated to be its maximum operating capacity. A wait of one to two hours was common for the Jewel House. Many visitors go to the Tower just for the Jewel House, although around half follow a tour and half just wander around. Despite signs at the ticket kiosk indicating the length of wait, few are dissuaded from visiting.

The old Jewel House (Murphy 1981) could only accommodate 5,000 people per day, sometimes less than 30 per cent of those who wished to visit. Improving the layout and circulation was hampered by the fact that the Jewel House is a subterranean vault designed to provide both security for the jewels and access for the visitor, the latter being subordinate to the former. The old model was a dual circulation system of slow foot passage and observation platforms. The new scheme, which cost £10 million to install, utilizes travelators (only switched on at the busiest time of the year) past the display cases after the visitor has queued slowly through various introductory rooms. The constantly moving queue spends exactly three minutes on each section of the display on the moving pavements, with viewing platforms located behind for those who wish to stay longer. Despite the fact that a notorious bottleneck has been avoided, the new exhibition has not excited the critics, who consider that it hardly justifies the Tower of London high admissions fee

(£8.20) which could probably be doubled before it would deter admissions. The new Jewel House lacks pace and story and is just an exercise in crowd management, beautifully lit and presented but literally mechanistic.

DELIVER A QUALITY SERVICE

Quality can only be delivered by an organization taking a long-term view of the way it is delivering its product, with success measured not solely by financial criteria but by visitor/customer satisfaction. Training and leadership are critical, and measures must be taken to permit pride in workmanship. In this context 'workmanship' can mean anything from the installation of visitor facilities to the skills with which a guide delivers a tour. At the Tower of London, for example, tours given by Yeoman Warders (Beefeaters) are not only popular visitor attractions in their own right but also perform a vital crowd management function, disseminating a large number of visitors into small, widely-spaced groups. The tours used to be repetitive and formulaic until new regulations were agreed which allowed each Beefeater considerable licence to devise and deliver their own script. Certain basic facts must be included but the guide is free to embellish these in his personal style. The resulting personalized tour is popular with visitors and with the guide, resulting in a quality product and enhanced visitor experience quality.

Maintaining quality standards in historic properties also involves protecting the property from its visitors by combination of education and enforcement (Butcher-Younghans 1993). Unfortunately, efforts to reduce visitor damage (blinds for light filtering, humidity control etc.) are never entirely effective and most vulnerable of all is that sense of intimacy so highly valued, if poorly defined, by all visitors to historic houses (Waterson 1994). These may be exemplified by the need to use physical barriers in some cases to block valuable areas with barriers varying from a simple rope to full-size sheet of Plexiglas, electric eye or alarm device. The barrier type affects visitor impression and visitor satisfaction; it being impossible, for example to appreciate a period room through a glass door. House museums are especially susceptible to visitor abuse as visitors feel comfortable enough with the experience to touch furnishings and objects on display.

Maintaining quality also means maintaining security, eliminating theft, training guards as well as guides. Staff are the most important element in quality control since visitors often draw their impressions of a collection or property from its staff. Security also means visitors being protected from themselves – maintaining a good state of repair and eliminating uneven stair treads or other safety hazards. The methods used to restore and protect houses can themselves be a visitor attraction as at the Royal Pavilion at Brighton, whose restoration took eleven years and £10 million pounds to restore it to the original Regency opulence. The Pavilion offered a popular ' behind the scenes' week after the restoration finished, showing the public the skills and techniques used with a programme of free lectures, displays and demonstrations. At Brighton, as in other historic properties, a major visitor management problem is caused by visitors' apparent need to touch everything, especially those things (like textiles) which should not be touched.

Public enjoyment of an historic site depends in important ways on how smoothly the site is managed. That, in turn, depends on the organization's rules and procedures which should enable visitors to view the site comfortably while protecting the collection and property and ensuring safety of staff and visitors. The effectiveness of such visitor regulations (which may be viewed as quality control mechanisms exerted on the visitor experience) varies with their enforcement, generally carried out by guides, interpreters or gallery attendants. These include rules for visitors (perhaps banning smoking or eating in a gallery), procedures for opening the site (recommended group sizes, where interpreters should stand, ideal traffic patterns and the sequence of which rooms or areas to be shown).

CONCLUSIONS

The management of visitors at heritage visitor attractions is complicated by a number of aspects of service delivery. There is frequently the need to maintain a delicate balance between the preservation of an historic property, archaeological site or monument and the desire to provide a quality service for its visitors. In the past many organizations have solved this problem by concentrating on the needs of the property rather than the visitor, but this is now changing, partly as a result of financial pressures. The managers of many heritage attractions are reluctant to view their activities as a product which must be sold to customers, yet this is the only attitude which will ensure that visitors receive adequate experience quality. A further problem for many attractions is the unpredictable nature of visitor demand. Demand for all types of heritage attractions is growing but it is difficult to predict the precise level of demand which may exist for a new attraction, or a special exhibit mounted within an existing attraction. Moreover, the customer base is always changing, making it necessary to continually adapt visitor management policies to cope, for example, with different foreign languages or changing patterns of visitor arrivals (Richards 1992).

Systematic research on the management of visitors at heritage attractions is a relatively new and frequently inexact science, although some museums have been researching their customer base systematically over a period of years. Since 1984 English Heritage and the Historic Royal Palaces, for example, have done market research on visitor enjoyment and perceived value for money as well as measuring how well their properties are presented. Surveys are commissioned at sample properties every two years to assist in forward planning. They generally show high levels of satisfaction with the visit but also highlight problems with service delivery, particularly identifying gaps in visitor facilities such as inadequate shops or catering as well as inadequacies in the provision of interpretative material. The most recently opened heritage attractions and facilities (such as the Tudor Kitchens at Hampton Court Palace or the re-vamped Brighton Pavilion) tend to score the highest in any visitor survey, for the simple reason that their designers have been able to build upon previous mistakes and utilize the body of visitor information and preferences that has accumulated over the last twenty years. It is much more difficult for an existing attraction which may have been open for some considerable time in a property with spatial constraints to alter visitor routes or add new facilities. Visitor research aids in identifying visitor requirements, planning the necessary level of service delivery and identifying pointers to potential trouble spots. It can aid in the management both of demand and supply. The methods by which this data is accumulated include both self-report by visitors (questionnaires, interviews, surveys) and direction observation (tracking). Measuring visitor behaviour is a complex business and results are not always either reliable or compatible; visitors do not always remember the routes they took, for example, tend to overestimate the time spent at an attraction and are only 60 per cent accurate in retracing their steps (Bitgood and Richardson 1986). Direct observation of visitors is labour intensive. It may also be misleading since the very act of being observed alters visitor behaviour. There is a need for a systematic study of visitor orientation and circulation rather than the existing small site-specific studies which are difficult to integrate into any working guidelines for the design of an effective orientation and circulation systems (Bitgood 1994).

The visitor to a heritage attraction is, like all tourists, becoming steadily better informed and more conscious of the power of his/her position as a consumer of a service product. Although there is a steady increase in the number of visits made to heritage visitor attractions, there is also a rise in the number of such attractions, making the provision of a high-quality visitor experience based on careful consideration of visitor needs an important element in competition between destinations. The customer no longer sees a visit to an historic house, for example, as a privilege, but rather a right bought within a framework of free choice of discretionary spend. Long queues, poor interpretation, lack of parking, difficult access, poor value for money will send the visitor elsewhere, removing both any current financial revenue for the attraction as well as future revenue from repeat business or word-of-mouth advertising. The proper management of visitors has thus become just as significant in heritage attraction management as the nature of the attraction itself and could, in some cases, be itself a determinant of demand to be ignored at a manager's peril.

SUMMARY

This chapter considers the management of a visit to a heritage attraction as a service operations problem, looking at the nature of the service task, ways in which service standards may be maintained and the manner in which the service is delivered. Visitors to historic properties are buying an experience, and the management of such properties may be complicated by historical, architectural or financial complexities, making it difficult to deliver optimum service. Particular problems are the need to control visitor demand and relate such demand to the attraction's fixed capacity. Service delivery includes pre-visit issues (parking, access, welcome) as well as interpretation, and strategies for managing the arrivals process may include queuing or special ticketing. There is often a need to maintain a delicate balance between conservation of a facility and the provision of high service quality, and this is complicated by fluctuating demand levels, a dynamic customer base and a lack of systematic research.

REFERENCES

Ambrose, T. and Paine, C. (1993) *Museum Basic*, London: Routledge.

Bitgood, S. (1994) 'Problems in visitor orientation and circulation', in Hooper-Greenhill, E. (ed.) *The Education Role of the Museum*, London: Routledge.

Bitgood, S. and Richardson, K. (1986) 'Wayfind at the Birmingham Zoo', *Visitor Behaviour*, 1, 4, 9–14.

Butcher-Younghans, S. (1993) *Historic House Museums: A Practical Handbook for their Care, Preservation and Management*, Oxford: Oxford University Press.

Cramer, J. (1995) 'Just the ticket', *Leisure Management*, 15, 10, 39–40.

Dawes, J. and Rowley, J. (1996) 'The waiting experience: towards service quality in the leisure industry', *International Journal of Contemporary Hospitality Management*, 8, 1, 16–21.

Falk, J. H. and Dierking, L. D. (1992) *The Museum Experience*, Washington DC: Whaleseback Books.

Griggs, S. (1983) 'Orientating visitors within a thematic display', *International Journal of Museum Management and Curatorship*, 2, 119–34.

Hayward, G. and Brydon-Miller, M. (1984) 'Spatial and conceptual aspects of orientation: visitor experiences at an outdoor museum', *Journal of Environmental Systems*, 13, 4, 317–32.

Hood, M. (1983) 'Staying away', *Museum News*, 61, 4, 50–7.

Hood, M. (1986) 'Beware of catch-22', *Visitor Behaviour*, 1, 2, 10.

Kelly, J. (1996) 'Status queue', *Museums Journal*, 5, 21–23.

Levine, M. (1982) 'You-are-here maps: psychological considerations', *Environment and Behaviour*, 14, 2, 221–37.

Loomis, R. (1987) *Museum Visitor Evaluation: New Tool for Management*, Nashville, TN: American Association for State and Local History.

Melton, A. W. (1935) *Problems of Installation in Museums of Art*, Washington DC: American Association of Museums New Series, 14.

Melton, A. W. (1936) 'Distribution of attention in galleries in a museum of science and industry', *Museum News*, 14, 3, 6–8.

Murphy, C. (1981) *Tourism*, London: Pitman.

National Audit Office (1992) *Protecting and Managing England's Heritage Properties*, London: HMSO.

Pavord, A. (1995) 'Gardens', in Newby, H. (ed.) *The National Trust: The Next Hundred Years*, London: The National Trust.

Pierce, P. (1991) 'Towards the better management of tourist queues', in Medlik, S. (ed.) *Managing Tourism*, Oxford: Butterworth-Heinemann.

Richards, B. (1992) *How to Market Tourist Attractions, Festivals and Special Events: A Practical Guide to Maximizing Visitor Attendance*, Essex: Longman Group.

Robinson, E. (1928) *The Behaviour of the Museum Visitor*, Washington DC: American Association of Museums, New Series 5.

Schmenner, R. W. (1995) *Service Operations Management*, Englewood Cliffs, NJ: Prentice-Hall.

Shettel-Neuber and O'Reilly (1981) 'Now where? A study of visitor orientation and circulation in the Arizona-Sonora Desert Museum', Technical Report No. 87-25, Jacksonville AL: Psychology Institute, Jacksonville State University.

Verveka, J. A.(1994) *Interpretive Master Planning*, Helena (Montana): Falcon Press Publishing.

Wanhill, S. R. C. (1980) 'Charging for congestion at tourist attractions', *International Journal of Tourism Management*, 1, 168–174.

Waterson, M. (1994) *The National Trust: The First Hundred Years*, London: BBC Books and National Trust Enterprises.

MODEL QUESTIONS

1. Why is it easier to deliver a higher quality of service to the visitor in a purpose-built attraction (such as a new visitor centre) than in an historic property?

2. You are planning to open a small country house to the public for first time. What steps would you take to prevent your visitors needing to queue?

3. The manager of a famous heritage garden has decided to develop a walking trail linking features of particular interest. What information would assist him/her in planning such a trail?

CHAPTER 6

The Role of Technology

Marion M. Bennett

INTRODUCTION

At first glance heritage and technology may seem an incongruous and arguably uncomfortable fit. One is concerned with the past, the other the embodiment of the present and all that the future has to offer. Yet increasingly examples of the marriage of these two opposites abound. Some of the most popular and traditional of HVAs make active use of technology, such as the National Gallery in London. In addition, conferences have focused on heritage and technology including 'The Future for Europe's Past' in 1995 which focused entirely on the application of technology, and the Museums and Heritage Show which in 1997 devoted a seminar to the subject of 'virtual interpretation'. All of this suggests that technology is becoming as much a fixture in HVAs as the heritage it purports to support. The aim of this chapter is to review the role played by technology within HVAs and to explore some of the issues emerging from the application of technology.

HERITAGE

To understand the role of technology within heritage visitor attractions, it is important to understand the term heritage and in particular HVAs. Heritage itself is a highly broad term which envelopes a panoply of forms including castles, museums, cathedrals, industrial sites, the built environment as well as natural heritage such as landscapes (Coulson and Herbert 1995). Notably Prentice (1993) developed a typology of heritage attractions comprising 23 subject types. This itself demonstrates the eclecticism of heritage, although a unifying thread is the historical or cultural significance associated with a place. Significant too is the use of the term 'attractions' by Prentice. Commonly, the noun used to describe heritage varies and includes institutions, sites, places and attractions. As a term, 'attractions' has quite definite connotations with tourism and in this sense heritage is a recognized part of the tourism industry. This chapter and indeed this book are concerned with heritage as attractions; therefore it follows that the issues raised are intrinsically related to the tourism industry.

FACTORS ENCOURAGING THE ADOPTION OF TECHNOLOGY

There are numerous incentives for HVAs to invest in and adopt technology, some of which pertain exclusively to heritage, others being generic in nature.

1. Interpretation

A principal role of a HVA is to tell a story and in this respect there are a panoply of tools available. However, the important point is that the tools should be used to convey the story as effectively as possible. According to Herbert (1989), the stages of interpretation are:

- relate to experience (educate);
- seek to reveal (inform);
- view as an art (enhance);
- seek to stimulate (entertain);
- aim for wholeness (manage).

While traditional audio-visual tools have performed the job up until recently, developments in information technology are such that new methods are increasingly becoming available to undertake this role. It is entirely debatable whether these new technological tools are more effective than traditional tools since the actual message remains the same. Nevertheless, it is a brave HVA which chooses not even to investigate the potential uses of new technology.

2. Enhancing the visitor experience

A contentious debate within heritage is the extent to which interpretation should exist to entertain or educate. Traditionally, heritage interpretation existed to educate primarily with a view to imparting an understanding of the need to conserve and preserve (Tilden 1957). While this premise remains fundamental, it is recognized that the role of heritage today has a much broader remit. Certainly, there is a need to make the visitor experience as interesting and pleasurable as possible, and one means of doing this is by adopting a range of tools to entertain the visitor. The very novelty of technology ensures a degree of entertainment. It can, of course, be argued that education and entertainment are interlinked and mutually compatible in that a visitor is more likely to absorb information if it is conveyed in an entertaining and interesting manner.

3. Competition

HVAs, like virtually all forms of heritage, are under increasing pressure to generate their own income. This is being felt in particular by traditional attractions such as museums which have previously relied upon a good measure of public sector funding to sustain them. Indeed, such is the squeeze that it has led to the MGC director to comment upon the 'revenue impoverishment' common among so many museums and galleries (MGC 1996). While, on the one hand, this renders it more difficult for HVAs to invest in 'expensive' IT solutions, on the other, it places a greater responsibility on HVAs to generate their own income. Consequently many HVAs may turn to IT to attract visitors by using it as a marketing tool in competition with other HVAs.

4. Cost savings

The sheer cost of IT is such that expenditure is inevitable before savings can be made. However, IT has to be viewed as a long-term strategic investment and in this respect there are undoubtedly gains to be made. For example, IT can be used to make the attraction more interesting and entertaining, therefore attracting more visitors over time; equally, IT can be employed for 'unseen' functions, such as archive documentation, compiling customer databases and electronic ticketing, which in the longer term provide valuable management information which can assist in optimizing operational efficiency. It is important too to remember that the costs of IT tend to spiral downwards – rendering IT, which is prohibitively expensive today, more affordable tomorrow.

5. Authenticity

The quest for authenticity is not a new one, but IT – in particular, virtual reality – is being employed to enable HVAs to bring to life the story being told. Virtual reality has a particular application to ruined sites as well as enabling the non-visitor to view inside a HVA. There are problems associated with this technology, the most important one being the inability to replicate history in an authentic manner.

6. Management efficiency

This has already been discussed under 'Cost savings' but it is worthy of separate mention, not least because it is a principal generic reason for the introduction of IT in any organization. If IT can be employed to render more efficient an entire operation then the organization's chances of long-term success and survival are considerably improved. In addition, IT can be used to improve the service offered to the visitor through a better understanding of the visitor's needs, their level of satisfaction, and through the use of IT to convey the message contained within the HVA.

ADOPTION OF TECHNOLOGY

There are a number of ways in which technology is being used by HVAs and on this basis it is possible to categorize the various applications. On a first level, there are two main categories: non-interaction with the visitor, and interaction with the visitor. At a second level, interaction with the visitor can be sub-divided into interaction on-site and interaction off-site. For the purposes of this chapter and consistency of argument, the focus is on interaction with the visitor as it is here where some of the most interesting developments are occurring particularly in relation to the issue of distribution and access. Nevertheless, it is important to briefly mention non-interaction as this is a facet of HVA management and operation.

Non-interaction

Non-interaction technology is largely concerned with the management of information at HVAs for the purposes of marketing and operational efficiency. In this respect, databases and electronic ticketing play a vital role in the collection and collation of information on the visitor. Such information can then be used to determine peaks and troughs in visitor numbers, pricing and marketing strategies, thereby forming a tool which enables the performance of an HVA to be measured on a cyclical basis. Of equal significance in museums is the use of information technology for the efficient documentation of collections (MGC 1996).

Interaction on-site

Interaction with the visitor on-site is one of the more obvious ways in which technology is having an impact. Multi-media is increasingly being adopted to convey information in an aesthetic and effective manner. The Micro Gallery in the Sainsbury Wing of the National Gallery provides visitors with an interactive database of image and text of over 2,000 paintings, 1,000 illustrations, and animation. It enables visitors to query a variety of art approaches by subject matter, period and geography. In addition, the system enables users to select paintings for their personal tour which can then be printed out in the form of a floor plan to show the locations of paintings.

Virtual Reality (VR), the simulation of reality, is also being used at many HVAs. In particular, it is providing the opportunity to recreate history, such as at the Natural History Museum, London which is using VR to simulate Captain Cook's ship *Endeavour*; the *Virtual Endeavour* is the outcome. Other opportunities include recreating ruined sites, such as Pompeii or the Colosseum in Rome, and then allowing the visitor to navigate their way through it. In this respect, VR can be viewed as an enhancing tool, helping the visitor to develop a greater understanding of the past.

These are just some examples of many, all of which demonstrate increasing interactivity within HVAs. The technology exists and is in use to provide the visitor with considerable flexibility in the manner in which information is conveyed and accessed. It also enables the actual attractions to tap into a new form of media to deliver their message.

Interaction off-site

Interaction off-site constitutes any form of technology used to enable non-visitors to access information about HVAs. Currently, there are three principal methods by which access is being extended. Firstly, information held on interactive multi-media systems is being packaged in CD-roms thereby facilitating broader distribution and consumption in the home. The Micro Gallery is one such example of how information is being made available on CD-rom. This particular CD-rom has sold over 50,000 copies worldwide (Bennett 1997).

Secondly, the Internet is facilitating on-line access to computer databases within HVAs. The Holocaust Memorial Museum in Washington DC, USA which has adopted an interactive multi-media system on-site is an example of an HVA which has made its system accessible through the Internet. Consequently, non-visitors are able to learn about what is contained within the museum by querying archive data which gives them access to documents and photographs. While there are limits to the amount of information that can be featured on the Web, it nevertheless identifies the range of information available within the museum. Hence, it becomes a useful tool for potential visitors as well as a means of obtaining information (including contact details) for those unable to make an actual visit.

Thirdly and finally is the concept of Virtual Reality (VR) and its application to HVAs. Taken to the logical conclusion, VR could enable consumers to visit a HVA 'virtually' from their homes or other convenient places resulting in a form of distance consumption. Potentially, this form of technology could enable HVAs to extend their audience reach well beyond their current numbers.

EMERGING ISSUES

The preceding discussion has highlighted the increasing use of technology within and by HVAs. Technology, in particular interactive multi-media technology, has proved to be highly applicable to HVAs. Certainly, there are benefits to be gained, but there are also a number of important issues to be grappled with before a value judgement can be made.

1. The media becomes the message

A frequent criticism of technology is that it has the potential to assume greater significance than the message it is there to convey. Given the importance of interpretation to heritage and given too that media, that is communication techniques, are the representatives of interpretation, the issue evolves into an even more important one. Stevens (1989) states:

> Interpretation is, today, in greater danger of being hijacked by the designers and media technocrats than ever before. The media is becoming the message.
>
> Technological wizardry, media consultants, audio-animatronics, innovative presentations – these are the buzz words to switch on the lights in tourist board offices around the world. Are we, however, being true to the spirit of interpretation?

Stevens goes on to argue that interpretation, instead of being consumer-led, is becoming 'designer-led' in order to make heritage more 'palatable and easier to digest'. This resurrects the issue of whether heritage, and by association, interpretation, exists to educate or entertain (Swarbrooke 1994). Referring to Herbert's (1989) schema of interpretation, both are mutually acceptable and, arguably, desired. Yet clearly there is a balance to be struck when employing modern communication methods such that the actual technology does not become the focal attraction.

2. High-tech requires high-touch

Tilden as far back as 1957 made this comment on gadgetry:

> There will never be a device of telecommunication as satisfactory as the direct contact not merely with the voice, but with the hand, the eye, the casual and meaningful ad lib, and with that something which flows out of the very constitution of the individual in his physical self.

In the 1980s Naisbitt (1982) referred to this as high-touch, in other words the need to balance technology with human contact. Technology, in itself, can be sterile and impersonal. Arguably, visitors interacting with technology generate sufficient high-touch to counterbalance the non-human aspects. As previously observed, current multi-media systems provide the visitor with a considerable degree of control over the mechanism for accessing information. In this respect technology must be viewed as being more consumer-orientated than it was in the 1980s.

3. The need for evaluation

Interpretation has traditionally been viewed as an art and in this respect an assessment of its effectiveness has been, at best, limited (Tilden 1957; Aldridge 1989; Prentice and Light 1994). As Prentice and Light (1994) observe, 'good practice has tended to be assumed, often on the basis of little evidence'. Given that technology serves an important interpretive role in many HVAs and that it is a relatively 'new' form of media, the case for undertaking a formal assessment and evaluation of interpretive technology is a strong one. Prentice and Light (1994) argue that evaluation of the impact of interpretative media is necessary for two key reasons: first, there is a need to determine whether intepretation fulfils its intended role; and second, interpretation should be evaluated to demonstrate accountability and cost-effectiveness. The latter is particularly pertinent given the tremendous cost of new technology such as Virtual Reality. It is incumbent on HVAs to undertake this type of evaluative research to justify the introduction of technology in terms of both cost and role.

4. Visitors do not learn

Arguably, a key role of interpretation at HVAs is to educate and inform (Herbert 1989). If technology is designed to help tell a story then it follows that as the medium for interpretation it should assist in an educational role. Significantly, however, studies show that visitors do not appear to learn very much (Miles 1986; Shettel 1968; Borun 1977; Screven 1975; Uzzell 1989). This suggests that a gap may exist between the objectives of the HVA and the motivations of visitors, which in turn demands that more research is needed. Without further research into this aspect of consumer behaviour it may be a misjudgement to claim that HVAs are failing in their educational and informative aims. By association then, it may be unfair to criticize the use of technology which in turn brings the discussion back to the issue of evaluation and the need to assess the role played by technology in HVAs.

5. Heritage: a value-added product of the tourism industry

As a constituent part of the tourism industry, heritage is highly valued. According to *English Heritage Monitor* (1995), visits to historic properties, for example, have risen by 15 per cent since 1975 and by 23 per cent since 1982. Consequently it is fair to argue that heritage has become an important income generator (Uzzell 1989). Hence the term 'heritage visitor attraction'. The question must be raised whether the aims of a tourist attraction are in conflict with those of heritage. An example of this is the issue of authenticity. Swarbrooke (1994) states:

> It has been argued that as interest in heritage has grown, the tourism industry has sacrificed authenticity in its desire to 'milk' this lucrative 'cash cow' by providing non-authentic heritage experiences to meet the desires and fantasies of the tourists.

Herbert (1995) corroborates this by referring to heritage in the context of visitor attractions. He states, 'Dangers arise because it is relatively easy to invert history and to turn heritage into a marketable product without proper regard for rigour, honesty and factual accuracy in the presentation of heritage.' The thrust of his argument is that the heritage is 'distorted' in the process of attracting visitors.

Clearly the issue of authenticity is a contentious one and it is being further stirred by technology. For example, virtual reality enables previously ruined sites to be recreated but doubts must be raised whether it is possible to accurately represent a structure which no longer exists. In such cases technology may be viewed as enhancing the appeal of the attraction while forsaking the authenticity of the heritage attraction.

6. Distribution and access

CD-roms and the Internet are providing HVAs with the opportunity to extend their reach beyond their actual sites (Bennett 1995a). Technology then is performing an important marketing tool in enabling consumers to learn about HVAs from a wider range of sources which may then encourage them to make a visit.

While the virtues of extending distribution beyond the physical site cannot be disputed, the question of access is one which requires some discussion. To benefit from electronic distribution requires that you have access to the technology. Arguably, technology is broadening access to people otherwise unable to make a visit in person. As Bottomley (1996) states:

> These developments (internet, multi-media systems) provide new access to the arts. They bring their own sense of wonder, and we are working to encourage the pace of change so that multi-media can enable as many people as possible to experience areas of the arts and heritage that may have been denied them in the past.

Equally, however, it could be argued that technology is re-defining access by differentiating between the 'haves' and the 'have nots'. If the ideal of heritage is access for all, then technology is only serving to destroy the ideal by enabling access for some, the techno-rich, and denying access for others, the techno-poor, resulting in a sort of technological apartheid (Bennett 1995b). This is a strategic and political issue which is not going to be resolved in the foreseeable future. It does, however, raise an important question: is it fair to discourage HVAs from adopting technology on the basis that not everyone would have equal access?

A second issue related to access concerns the problems museums have in displaying their collections. For many museums constraints on space and the need to conserve result in only a limited proportion of collections being publicly available at any one time. Technology now enables museums to provide access for the virtual visitor to reserve collections. In this respect, technology ought to be viewed in a positive light in enhancing access and in helping museums to overcome a growing problem.

7. Virtual Reality: substituting the experience

The emergence of VR as a major form of technology has generated a debate about the potential for VR to act as a surrogate form of tourism. Why visit a HVA, if you can do so virtually? There are a plethora of reasons why a visit is preferable to a technological simulation. These are perhaps best exemplified in a quotation from a discussion on the issue on the Internet:

> Putting on your virtual helmet and doing a virtual tour of the Acropolis is a totally different experience from climbing up to the hill in the intense heat, sweating, drinking, smelling the tavernas, flowers and gutters, hearing the multi-lingual background noise and car horns, etc. And what is central: by leaving home and travelling across space and time, transgressing some boundaries, the tourist who is climbing up the hill is in a different state of mind compared to the person in virtual reality.
>
> (Selanniemi 1997)

VR, by definition, is not real, and therefore sights, sounds and smells can never be accurately replicated. Regardless of how technologically advanced this technology may become, it is folly to believe that it will ever surmount such social limitations (Seaton and Bennett 1996). Rather then than being the killer application, on the contrary VR is more likely to stimulate interest in the 'real thing' (Bottomley 1996).

SUMMARY

What this discursive has attempted to show is that the introduction of technology into HVAs is immersed in a range of issues which extend well beyond the practical issues of type of application and cost. If technology is to be appropriately applied then it must address such issues as:

* What role is technology there to serve?
* What are the implications of its introduction?
* How can the objectives of introducing technology be measured and evaluated?
* Does technology enhance the visitor experience?
* Is technology consumer-orientated?

Crucial to the proper introduction of technology into HVAs is the basic need to ensure that the technology does not assume a greater significance than the message.

Obvious as this may sound, the risk of this happening is great, particularly with 'new' technology. It must always be remembered that technology is the servant, not the master. If this basic premise is adhered to then the potential benefits to be yielded by technology are great.

As far as presentation and interpretation are concerned, it is vital to recognize the importance of the consumer. If technology can enhance the service provided and convey the 'story' more effectively than other tools available, then there is merit in its application and introduction. All too often, however, excitement over the actual technology eclipses the more important role it is there to serve. In such cases the long term outcome is potentially disastrous.

CONCLUSION

This chapter has demonstrated the varied applications of technology within HVAs from non-interaction to interaction with the visitor both on- and off-site. It has also sought to explain some of the strategic reasons underlying the introduction of technology, including increasing competition among HVAs, the role of media in interpretation and the recognition of the increasing importance of technology to the tourism industry, of which heritage is a part. The issues raised by technology are far-reaching and highlight the need for careful consideration of the advantages to be gained before adopting technology. Clearly there are benefits, including extended distribution and marketing, but equally there are many potential pitfalls – not least the tendency for the medium to 'hijack' the message. The future will bring with it further advancements in technology. If such technology is able to fulfil clearly defined objectives then its worthiness will be assured.

REFERENCES

Aldridge, D. (1975) *Guide to Countryside Interpretation, Part One: Principles of Countryside Interpretation and Interpretive Planning*, Edinburgh: HMSO.

Bennett, M. M. (1995a) 'The consumer marketing revolution: the impact of IT on tourism', *Journal of Vacation Marketing*, 1, 4, 376–382.

Bennett, M. M. (1995b) 'New technologies and their role in cultural tourism marketing', *The Globalized Europe: A Cultural Bid*, European meeting on culture, leisure and tourism, 2nd–4th November, Guadalupe, Spain: Ministry of Culture.

Bennett, M. M. (1997) 'Heritage marketing: the role of information technology', *Journal of Vacation Marketing*, 3, 3, 272–280.

Borun, M. (1977) *Measuring the Immeasurable: A Pilot Study of Museum Effectiveness*, Washington DC: Association of Science-Technology Centres.

Bottomley, V. (1996) *Our Heritage, Our Future*, Lecture given to the Royal Society of Arts, Department of National Heritage, 14th October.

Coulson, M. C. and Herbert, D. T. (1995) 'Geographic information systems and heritage places', *The Future for Europe's Past*, Proceedings of COMETT workshops, ed. Stevens, T. and James, V., Swansea: Swansea Institute of Higher Education.

English Tourist Board (1995) *English Heritage Monitor*, London: BTA/ETB research services.

Herbert, D. T. (1989) 'Does interpretation help?', in Herbert, D. T., Prentice, R. C. and Thomas, C. J. (eds) *Heritage Sites: Strategies for Marketing and Development*, Aldershot: Avebury (Gower).

Lumley, R. (1988), 'Introduction', in Lumley, R. (ed.) *The Museum Time Machine: Putting Cultures on Display*, London: Routledge.

Miles, R. (1986) 'Museum audiences', *Museum Management and Curatorship*, 5, 73–80.

Museums and Galleries Commision (1996) *Annual Report*, London: MGC.

Naisbitt, J. (1982) *Megatrends: Ten New Directions Transforming Our Lives*, New York: Warner Brothers inc.

Prentice, R. and Light, D. (1994) 'Current issues in interpretative provision at heritage sites', in Seaton, A. V. *et al.* (eds), *Tourism: The State of the Art*, Chichester: John Wiley & Sons.

Prentice, R. (1993) *Tourism and Heritage Places*, London: Routledge.

Screven, C. G. (1975) *The Measurement and Facilitation of Learning in the Museum Environment: An Experimental Analysis*, Washington DC: Smithsonian Institution Press.

Seaton, A. V. and Bennett, M. M. (1996) *Marketing Tourism Products: Concepts, Issues, Cases*, London: International Thomson Business Press.

Selanniemi, T. (1997) 'TRINET discussion on "real/Virtual" world on internet', TRINET-L@hawaii.edu.

Shettel, H. H. *et al.* (1968). *Strategies for Determining Exhibit Effectiveness*, Pittsburgh, PA: American Institute for Research.

Stevens, T. (1989) 'The visitor – who cares? Interpretation and consumer relations', in Uzzell, D. L. (ed.) *Heritage Interpretation Volume 2*, London: Belhaven Press.

Swarbrooke, J. (1994) 'The future of the past: heritage tourism into the 21st century', in Seaton, A. V. *et al.* (eds) *Tourism: The State of the Art*, Chichester: John Wiley & Sons.

Tilden, F. (1957) *Interpreting our Heritage*, Chapel Hill: The University of North Carolina Press.

Uzzell, D. L. (1989) 'Introduction: the visitor experience', *Heritage Interpretation Volume 2*, London: Belhaven Press.

Walsh, K. (1992) *The Representation of the Past: Museums and Heritage in the Post-modern World*, London: Routledge.

MODEL QUESTIONS

1. Identify the different ways in which technology can be employed by HVAs.

2. Explain three pitfalls associated with introducing technology into HVAs.

3. To what extent is technology blurring the boundary between education and entertainment in HVAs?

CHAPTER 7

Job Design and Work Organization

Margaret Graham, Malcolm Foley, Bill Hughes and David Litteljohn

INTRODUCTION

Heritage is increasingly being recognized as a significant part of the leisure and tourism economy. Heritage visitor attractions (HVAs) have a central role to play in cultural tourism on a local, national and international level. The spatial dimensions of HVAs vary considerably from complete urban-built environments like Glasgow, as one of the best preserved Victorian cities, down to the many small community museums that interpret objects of local history. Indeed, museums, regardless of their scale and structure, are operating in an environment of change and as a result they are becoming involved in challenging new roles. Attitudes and values have become entrenched in the past and in many ways have hindered progress (Graham and Foley 1998). This chapter concentrates on the changing relationships between paid staff and volunteers in the context of museums in Glasgow. Primary research has involved predominantly a qualitative study undertaken in one independent, two university and six local authority museum sites in Glasgow. Research methods have included a series of sixteen elite interviews with professionals, and academics with an interest in museums and/or volunteers, along with a study of volunteers themselves utilizing a questionnaire survey involving 60 volunteers and a variety of ethnographic field research studies as participant observer. In many ways this chapter challenges traditional assumptions that have become attached to volunteers and their unpaid work.

MUSEUM TRANSFORMATION

From the outset, museums have reached a fairly crucial stage in their development. Maximizing the *efficient* and *effective* utility of resources at a time when the sector is having to cope with chronic financial difficulties has never before been so crucial. In the first instance museums must follow directions that ultimately aim to fulfil their primary organizational objectives. This was a problem being faced by one curator of a small independent museum, while preparing a job description for a vacant curatorial assistant:

... it has to be taken for granted that the care ... of the collection plays a primary role, but in a society where communication with the public plays such an essential part ... which skills then are to be of primary importance? How do we keep ourselves alive to the needs of the market place and still liaise with other museums ... and tourist attractions?

(Harvey 1993)

Harvey not only prioritizes the collection and keeping up with rival leisure activities, but also considers the obligations the museum has towards its visitors, tourism and other heritage organizations. As more skill is expected from museum professionals, their numbers are diminishing, either as an outcome of museum cost-cutting policy or through personal disillusionment (Conybeare 1995, 1996; Mason 1997; Sone 1997b). In order to provide the high degree of *skills flexibility* needed to cope with transformation and change, museums are being encouraged to maximize their utility of alternative employment opportunities to support the work of established staff (Carrington 1996; Sone 1997a; Hall 1995; Cordrey 1995; Reynolds 1997). In terms of financial worth and the number of museum tasks completed, voluntary work in many ways is a vastly underestimated or indeed hidden category of human capital.

MUSEUMS AS A PROCESS OF CHANGE

Most heritage organizations do not operate under the profit incentive, and changes in fund-raising procedures demand management styles that are not in widespread use in the sector. Applying techniques from the commercial sector began robustly with the introduction of the museum registration scheme in 1989, when the Museums and Galleries Commission in conjunction with the Museums Association and the Museums Training Institute set out minimum standards of management good practice. An association with charity no longer protects museums from poor organization and the utilization of basic administrative routines. Similarly, volunteers traditionally cannot be treated in the same way as paid employees. Their association with charity tends to protect them from being controlled in the same way because motivation is not tied to financial inducement. However, the issue of managing volunteers is currently being addressed more urgently by heritage agencies such as the Museums Association to encourage host museums to become more accountable and managerially effective by promoting good practice policy to raise standards of performance. Achieving a much broader core goal agenda that considers heritage as an internationally competitive cultural commodity alongside obligations towards the achievement of volunteer goal aspirations, touches on challenging new ground for museum managers. Inexperience and understaffing have hindered museums from developing and implementing effective volunteer management policy.

Concerning human resources, the utilization of Schmenner's (1994) model of operations management provides a useful starting point to consider job design and work organization in a changing museum setting. In terms of traditional museum service delivery, work would essentially be supply-led and include tasks associated with conservation, interpretation and education. However, as the *museum experience* broadens to accommodate a wider audience, task priorities fragment, placing more emphasis on the needs of existing and potential museum consumers.

Good museums, particularly those in the public sector, serve and involve their local community to their best ability, by maintaining their traditional role alongside their more innovative role as part of the local leisure and tourism economy. This involves a more flexible approach to work organization as new skills are being pulled in to meet a much broader core goal agenda at a time when financial constraints are intense. A more formal approach to managing personnel, therefore, becomes more pressing. However, as Schmenner argues, particular distinctive characteristics set apart one productive organization from another, which call for an element of customization. Museum collections and service provision varies from organization to organization and as a result the range of human capital specialisms can be considerably diverse.

Furthermore, employment status is structured from the high level of skill and expertise of established museum experts, through to the increasing pool of *flexible* workers such as staff on short-term contract, volunteers and other non-remunerated museum workers like university placements. The latter human capital category, that of unpaid staff, will provide the main focus for this chapter and will provide a framework to show the relationship between volunteers and paid employees within the context of *affordability, accountability* and *flexibility*. The intention is not to provide a prescriptive solution to managing museum volunteers, but merely to provide an insight into the potential opportunities volunteers have to offer museums. In line with Schmenner's approach to personnel, the intention is to provide a clearer understanding about museum volunteers and their increasing involvement in the delivery of the contemporary 'museum experience', with a special emphasis on museum volunteer policy, particularly supervisory issues. Like contemporary society, it would be a futile exercise to claim that museums and their relationship with their volunteers can be treated collectively. Like the individuals they serve and employ, museums are highly variable and diverse in their structure, context and purpose.

VOLUNTARISM AND VOLUNTEERISM DEFINED

Generally, voluntarism has been burdened by the myth that volunteers are unskilled, middle-class, middle-aged female individuals who channel their energy into good causes (Sheard 1995). Furthermore, in terms of motivation, it is assumed that voluntary work is carried out primarily as an act of selfless charity and not for any personal gain or benefit. It is this image that has become attached to museum voluntarism and has prevented volunteers from becoming completely assimilated with paid members of staff (Graham and Foley 1998). As a result of this, immense management implications have become associated with volunteer support, such as issues of control and discipline, levels of volunteer exploitation, commitment and reliability and employee relations between paid and unpaid staff.

It is relevant to consider at this point that as the government reduces its commitment to welfare provision, increasingly more is expected from the voluntary sector (Sheard 1995). Indeed, a new social consciousness and attitude towards voluntary work has been advanced, particularly since the late 1980s, by major political figures, not least Margaret Thatcher, when 'active citizenship' became a political catchphrase. This policy has been advanced more recently under Labour's New Deal with the development of Welfare to Work employment initiatives. In some cases Welfare to Work involves unemployed people in unpaid work. Apart from the addition of a modest expenses payment, unemployment benefit becomes replaced by a back-to-work allowance. In context, this has had a knock-on effect on most heritage sites. As public sector financial support becomes increasingly more difficult to secure, established and dormant volunteers and their potential are being scrutinized more formally as human capital resources. At the other end of the volunteering hierarchy, volunteers are becoming involved more in core activities, some innovative, alongside the periphery, routine tasks associated as traditional volunteer work roles. This shift can be viewed as a move away from the amateur label of volunteering towards a more professional one, thus elevating its former poor image. This new perspective of voluntary work is more appropriately defined by Tedrick et al.'s (1984) theory of *volunteerism*, which identifies a continuing upsurge in volunteering opportunities in leisure being accompanied by the development of a more cosmopolitan, professional and powerful label being attached to the image of volunteers.

Voluntary work is being viewed more positively, for example, as a means to transfer and/or develop personal skill as a prerequisite to paid work or as a leisure pursuit. Indeed, during the ethnographic study the proliferation of a highly professional assortment of instrumental volunteering types was identified that challenge the authenticity of the traditional stereotype and suggests a growing demand for a variety of museum experiences at all levels. Furthermore, as the pool of museum volunteers expands, expectation levels rise on both sides – the museum's of volunteers and the volunteers' of museums. Understandably, therefore, managing volunteers efficiently and effectively has become a major current issue instigating the impetus for research. In the process a whole raft of new roles and opportunities emerge for volunteers, not least in the area of skills development and the recent introduction of accredited courses in museum work. Indeed, more scrutiny is being placed on the work of volunteers, utilizing performance indicators. More importantly, there are signs that volunteer ability is becoming more visible in the museum job marketplace than the academic credentials of graduates lacking the same level of '*hands*-on' experience (Reynolds 1997). This in itself has implications for future volunteer aspirations and relationships between volunteers and existing paid staff.

The results from the study in Glasgow are intended to help provide a clearer understanding of the diversity of museum volunteering in one urban setting, while providing an insight into the current dilemma of managing volunteers and the relationships that exist between them and paid staff.

CONTEMPORARY MUSEUM VOLUNTEERISM IN GLASGOW

Generally, definitions of volunteering tend to be vague and inappropriate. Sheard (1995) and Burns (1996) argue that volunteering is not 'compulsory or coerced' but is 'freely given' through choice. In terms of contemporary non-remunerative, voluntary work carried out in museums in Glasgow, this definition would eliminate not only student unpaid placements but individuals on the Welfare to Work work experience/training initiatives mentioned earlier. For the purpose of this work, therefore, a general definition of museum volunteering identifies volunteers as people who do unpaid work for the mutual benefit of the museum and themselves. Unpaid means that no payment will be given for their voluntary work, with the exception of expenses like travelling costs. More specifically it was decided to create a customized volunteer typology, which would accommodate the variability of motivational characteristics identified in the field. This more formalized, precision-led approach was seen as a means to help rid volunteering of its poor stereotypical image that existing, typically vague, definitions tended to unintentionally propagate and allow to persist. Indeed volunteers in Glasgow have high expectations from their host museum, who collectively provide a supply of varied, some innovative, museum experiences. Gender and class have become less of an issue, although female volunteers still predominate.

Combining the whole range of ethnographic methods used in the study, including interview, observational and questionnaire techniques, five types of volunteer have been identified.

- *Type 1:* This category of volunteer is the 'Instrumental Hobbyist' who volunteers for leisure and recreational purposes. In this instance museum voluntary work is carried out on an irregular basis and tends to be one of many other leisure pursuits enjoyed by the volunteer. The results of the questionnaire survey involving 60 volunteers demonstrated that more than half of respondents primarily volunteered for leisure purposes, such as to further their interest in the subject matter of the museum, to meet people with similar interests or as a hobby.

- *Type 2:* This category of volunteer has been termed the 'Community Activist'. Burns (1996) identified a similar type but gave little information about their main characteristics. Glasgow Museums have a small elite group of volunteers, all are members of an independent association, the Glasgow Art Gallery and Museum Association (GAGMA) and are mainly retired professional people. The curator who manages them said that this group could be trusted, and confidences are regularly exchanged. Participant observation revealed this type of volunteer to be strongly opinionated regarding the future of Glasgow Museums and they demonstrated a willingness to lobby to resist any policy change they felt unacceptable. However, their commitment extends beyond this, and during observations at a meeting with them and a member of professional staff, they expressed concern about the conservation standards of a valuable work of art they felt was not kept under adequate environmental conditions. Similar responses were expressed in the questionnaire survey by several museum volunteers.

- *Type 3:* This category of volunteer is the 'Active Citizen' and is the nearest category to the 'Traditional Volunteer'. They tend to be older Glasgow citizens but there is evidence that a growing number of young people are participating. Primarily this group are female but there is a significant number of men emerging. Although most active citizen volunteers are retired there is a minority who are still in paid employment. All of this group in the public sector are registered with GAGMA. Active Citizen volunteers are driven predominantly by altruistic and/or social reasons. However, Bales (1996) casts doubt on the presence of solely altruistic motives being attached to volunteering. This was confirmed by the results of the questionnaire survey of volunteers. Only 1.7 per cent stated that they volunteered primarily for charitable reasons. However, some respondents who stated they were not motivated by charitable reasons, felt their voluntary work did benefit the community. One respondent felt compelled to comment 'I love Glasgow and its people', while another felt 'very happy to be involved in helping others appreciate Glasgow's bounty of art for the people'.

One volunteer organizer stated that the financial costs of volunteering in some cases were significant. More than 50 per cent of volunteer questionnaire respondents made a round trip of more than six miles, incurring significant travel costs. Organizers had increased costs such as telephone calls. Most of the volunteers did not receive expenses for their voluntary work. A GAGMA volunteer organizer agreed that, although volunteers did make sacrifices in order to volunteer, she believed there were personal gains to be made by them.

A new category of active citizen volunteer is one major growth area in voluntary work and involves the government-led employment initiatives mentioned earlier. Benefit becomes a back-to-work allowance and involves more job-seekers in voluntary work. The compulsory element of this category of unpaid museum work and its purpose as a pre-requisite to paid work introduces new ideas about active citizenship. This category of volunteer fits more comfortably under the following Type 4 definition.

- *Types 4 and 5:* A dominant category of volunteer is the 'Instrumental Economic Volunteer' and the 'Student Volunteer'. This group volunteer primarily to improve their paid employment prospects in some way. The former category, Type 4, includes volunteers involved in work experience initiatives for the unemployed and other types of voluntary work carried out as a pre-requisite to paid work. The former initiative has expanded since early 1998 under Labour's New Deal Welfare to Work Policy that channels the leisure time of various categories of able-bodied benefit-dependent individuals towards training for paid work. Participating in voluntary work is only one of several work experience options. The latter, Type 5 (Student Volunteer) covers student placements, student work experience and other student voluntary work carried out to enhance academic, educational and work experience credentials on a curriculum vitae (CV). Type 4 form a vital and in many ways innovative category of unpaid work. Type 5 provide a major supportive role to the museum function and have replaced paid postgraduate trainees. 25.4 per cent of volunteers involved in the questionnaire survey responded that they volunteered primarily to help gain work experience and/or to improve their career prospects. An additional 50 public sector Type 4 volunteers not participating in the questionnaire study were predominantly drawn from two inner-city job centres and included volunteers between the ages of 20 to 50. Most were involved in training in interview and audio-visual techniques to help compile an archive of 'life experiences' of Glasgow citizens. Interviews with a museum professional who supervised them and participant observation at a training session revealed that this group primarily volunteered to help in their search for paid work. Confidence-building and the development of interpersonal communication skills were particularly important personal objectives for this group of structurally unemployed individuals.

However, not every volunteer fits neatly under one category in the above typology. Most volunteers volunteer for more than one reason. The following model accommodates more flexibility and has been designed to plot volunteers more realistically according to their variable motivational and commitment priorities.

Although Figure 7.1 shows how volunteers can be plotted according to their motivational priorities, contemporary societal behaviour is fickle and susceptible to change, hence this model can act as a guideline only to help provide a clearer understanding about volunteers.

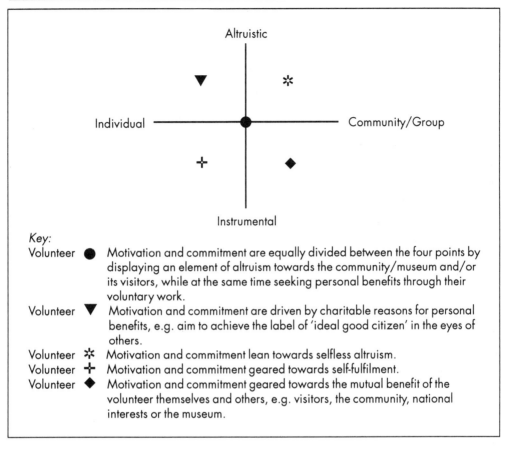

Figure 7.1: Motivation/commitment model.

VOLUNTEER POLICY ISSUES

Research confirmed that the term 'voluntarism' continues to attract negative gender-specific connotations, amateur occupational labels and poor image concepts like 'amateurism', 'exploitation' and 'unreliability', although the popular image of volunteers as older middle-class women with little skill is weakening. This appeared to restrict the maximum utility of volunteers in most museums. Drawing from Schmenner's ideas concerning personnel policy, training, recruitment, supervision and reward were key criteria in the *efficient scheduling* of people involved in operations.

Brian Martin, Director of Murray House Arts Institute in Edinburgh, stated the importance of staff development in raising standards:

The problem with this issue of volunteering is that it is seen by and large, certainly at Director and curatorial level, as a human resource management issue rather than perhaps a human resource development issue. The status of volunteering has to be raised and this can be achieved if more consideration was given to skills development.

Evidence of a variety of volunteer training examples have already been covered elsewhere in this chapter, although most museums tend to draw existing skills from their volunteers and offer hands-on museum experience rather than introduce them to new skills.

Although several museums had policy concerning their volunteers, there was little evidence that any was implemented to a great extent. Most volunteer supervisors were not trained in personnel management and did not feel confident about implementing policy, and all agreed that there was simply not enough time to provide this level of support. All volunteer organizers agreed that an effective management policy for volunteers would be very welcome. However, one influential Scottish museum head and management board member of various heritage associations said volunteering was 'unacceptable, blatant exploitation'. He argued that management policy would not provide the same sort of control and discipline one could expect from paid employees. He equated the right to work with the right to earn. This argument was backed up by an Employment Rights Officer at Glasgow's Low Pay Unit (LPU). He suggested the term 'volunteering' suggests an informal relationship, and preferred to refer to volunteers as 'unpaid' support. However, he also argued that, providing that technical and managerial training was provided for those managing volunteers, volunteering like this or in any other non-profit-making organization would be a positive experience and would have the support of the LPU.

There was a general consensus among most museum professionals that a standard management policy for volunteers would be a positive step forward. However, managing volunteers is unconventional and fairly unique in the service sector. For example, at the 1996 inaugural meeting and conference of the Scottish Association of Volunteers Managers, some delegates doubted whether formal management policy was in keeping with the spirit and values of some host organizations and volunteering itself. Management terminology was criticized as being inappropriate for organizing volunteers. However, there was a general consensus from the speakers and the audience that the current informal relationship was problematical, not only as far as the host organization is concerned, but for the volunteers themselves. The majority of delegates were involved in community welfare and were struggling to fill the gap left by the chronic decline in public sector provision. A more active approach, involving maximizing the utility and commitment of existing volunteers and pulling in new recruits, was viewed as a primary objective. Drawing ideas from business was seen as the inevitable solution to help relieve current management and supervision problems, thus developing a more formal relationship between volunteers and host organizations.

In context and in line with Schmenner's ideas, volunteers can be viewed as part of the service delivery system having a supportive role in delivering the 'museum experience' to visitors. This would tend to support the need for management guidelines to influence the work of volunteers.

However, the attitudes of volunteers themselves towards being managed tend to lean towards a more casual relationship with their host museum. From questionnaire results, 34 per cent of volunteers stated that they would welcome a contract with the museum, provided they could contribute to its contents and that it met their needs as well as the museum's. Of the remaining 66 per cent, 7 per cent did not respond while 59 per cent stated that a contract was either in conflict with the whole ethos of voluntary work or that a contract would make their voluntary work too much of a commitment.

Some volunteers commented that they felt they were not integrated into the organization to the same extent as paid employees, while museum professionals who managed volunteers felt that they had only limited control over volunteers when compared to paid employees. One museum professional stated that some volunteers are reliable, while others are not. Some need more supervision than others, an issue to be covered later in the chapter. A GAGMA organizer stated that an increasing number of volunteers want to use their voluntary work to help enhance their curriculum vitae. Indeed, as volunteers change their characteristics towards a more prevalent instrumental/professional profile where their supply exceeds demand, managing them becomes a more realistic and legitimate issue.

From the results so far, Figure 7.2 has been created and places various categories of volunteer on a sliding scale according to the amount of influence that may reasonably be applied to them.

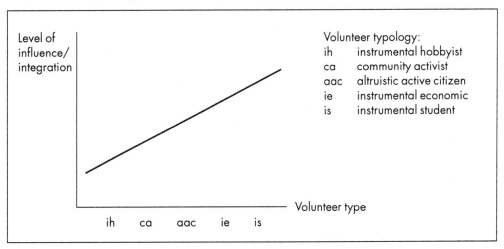

Figure 7.2: Boundary relationship diagram.

The term *boundary relationships* is used to measure the limits by which organizations can expect to legitimately exert influence over their volunteers. Conversely, 'boundary relationships' also refers to the limits by which volunteers may expect to be integrated into their host organization. Referring to Schmenner's Model, in terms of reward and recruitment, to replace payment incentives, contemporary volunteering has to be mutually beneficial. Therefore from a more prescriptive perspective, communication between the organization and the volunteer would be imperative at the recruitment stage so that volunteers can be placed in the correct category on the sliding scale. For example (refer to Figure 7.2), the 'instrumental hobbyist' volunteer may feel more comfortable having as informal a relationship as possible with the organization and may resist being controlled by the museum. However, the 'active citizen' volunteer may feel a stronger sense of belonging if his/her relationship with the organization was more formal. At the other end of the spectrum the student volunteer would be involved initially in a three-dimensional discussion between themselves, the host organizer, the instigator (for example, the university module or programme leader) to set minimum standards of commitment. The interview survey identified placements and casual student volunteers as the most problematical, particularly in terms of commitment, motivation and the use of false information on curriculum vitaes to further employment chances.

SUPERVISION

Supervision is essential in terms of *accountability*, in the drive to utilize volunteers to meet organizational aims while satisfying the needs of volunteers themselves. However, all museum specialists who manage volunteers agree that the most pressing dilemma involving volunteers is a lack of adequate supervision. There is more than enough work for volunteers to do but museums are restricted in the number of volunteers they can recruit because there are not enough paid staff to manage them. A former keeper of history, anthology and archaeology in Glasgow's public sector agreed with this:

> The more volunteers the more supervision provision the museum needs to provide. Glasgow Museums more than five years ago had a much smaller pool of volunteers to draw from. We had to take what we could get and there were immense problems involved with them. There is now a big market out there and museums can afford to be selective and the problems have been reduced.

Lack of supervision for volunteers threatens conservation standards. A local authority curator put forward his own experience:

Although our main direction is definitely the volunteer guide service, in the past we used volunteers in the workshop. They had skills that related to outdated mechanical maintenance work. Skills that even our specialists do not have. Recent restructuring has reduced the numbers that do this. Our specialist in conservation works with a small number of volunteers – between two and ten. Conservation is a bit up in the air at the moment. Conservation staff is eroding and this has meant volunteers having insufficient supervision with the result that most have had to be dismissed. Conservation generally is a big issue that appears to be falling in priority.

There is also a relationship between inadequate supervision and levels of job satisfaction for volunteers. This could pose a threat to volunteer standards as other opportunities emerge in other organizations, creaming off potentially good volunteers. A local authority spokesperson backed up this argument and stated that although more volunteers are working closely with specialist staff than ever before, because of other priorities volunteers are not getting the attention and gratitude they deserve. Some volunteers cope with a minimum of supervision and are, as one public sector curator suggests, 'worth their weight in gold while others need much more attention'.

Interviews also reveal that a lack of supervision and communication have had a negative effect on discipline. There was a general consensus that many volunteers do not understand the museum function. One curator managing student volunteers suggested that there needed to be more liaison between educational establishments sending placements when she commented:

We have had our placements from hell, even from universities dedicated to museum courses. School placements shadow one of the management staff and we have had some good pupils. However, some universities, colleges and schools do not prepare their students adequately enough and generally placements need to be more firmly controlled in many ways.

A specialist from the university museum agreed that placements from universities and schools proved to be most problematical when she stated:

Very few have displayed any genuine interest in the museum and some failed to be as reliable as I would have expected. This meant that I can only take on very few at a time.

Respondents were asked how they cope with the problems caused by deficient supervision. A conservationist from the public sector stated:

some volunteers, particularly older women, I have worked with in the past would rather talk than work. On the other hand others are hard working. You get to know who you can rely on.

A university museum commentator said:

We are under pressure to continue taking as many placements as we can cope with. However, we had to deal with the traditional type of volunteer. They were our main problem and are no longer front of house as they tended to give the wrong message. There are not so many of this type now. We simply cannot provide them with the supervision they require.

A GAGMA organizer said that volunteers themselves play a supervisory role to compensate:

In some local authority museum departments incompatible volunteers do not seem to fit in so much anymore and they do not tend to stay.

It was evident that there is a hierarchy of managerial control over the work of volunteers in Glasgow's Museums which accommodates considerable functional and numeric *flexibility*. In all categories of museum, a museum specialist is in overall control of volunteers and placements. It is this professional who decides who and how many volunteers will be recruited. In the case of Glasgow's local authority museums which physically span thirteen spatially spread buildings peppered across the city, with approximately 500 members of paid staff prior to recent cost-cutting redundancies, conservation and curatorial staff submitted requests for volunteers to their volunteer liaison officer, a museum curator. As far as student placements are concerned she stated:

I know by the end of October what projects there are available in which sections, and who the people are who want to manage the students and how many students they want. Generally all student volunteers tend to be involved in specific tasks or projects such as cataloguing and conservation and many are involved in general administrative work.

She added that with adequate supervision paid staff working with volunteers can identify volunteers with specific skills that may otherwise go unnoticed. She gave an example of this when she said that some placements volunteer beyond what their course expects:

We had an 18-year-old who volunteered over the summer on her own account. You cannot usually allow volunteers to handle priceless porcelains and other fragile pieces. But this young girl packed Pollok house porcelain – she had a natural gift. She has since gone on to do some paid short-contract work.

Supervision is also carried out in some museums by specially trained volunteers. This has an important role to play in making volunteer supervision more flexible, particularly in Glasgow's local authority museums. Older volunteers in the public sector, all members of GAGMA, are controlled by volunteer organizers – all of whom are retired professional people. Each of these organizers lead and administer all the volunteers who are assigned to their particular museum. They liaise between museum specialists on matters such as identifying volunteers who have special skills or interests that specialist staff could utilize. In many instances museum volunteers other than placements are supervised in specific projects by a museum specialist. The work they carry out leaves paid staff free to carry out other tasks. They also manage routine voluntary work and social events for volunteers. Their most important task is co-ordinator and trainer of the voluntary guide service.

Several volunteers have expertise beyond that of the museum experts. In this way museum professionals learn from their volunteers. However, this can have an adverse effect on the relationship between volunteers and paid staff. Graham and Foley (1998) look at the issue of patriarchy, where an elderly male volunteer marginalizes the authority of a female museum professional. Similarly, the more active museum volunteers become in core functions, the more they threaten paid functions. For example, graduate and student volunteering can be viewed as threatening to established museum staff. Consultants and freelances on contract have already been identified as a new generation of museum professionals. As establish staff erode, opportunities arise where a graduate volunteer may compete with redundant museum professionals to secure short- or long-term museum contract work. Following a stream of redundancies in Glasgow Museums during the period of the survey, three museum professionals from the public sector stated that there was a vast reduction in the number of volunteers taken on. Another museum professional stated that as establish staff disappear, museums can host fewer volunteers. With the exception of the volunteer guide service which is organized by the volunteers themselves, lack of supervision has been viewed as a serious problem for all categories of museum due to professional supervisory under-staffing. There is more than enough work for volunteers to do, but fewer museum experts are available to supervise their work.

CONCLUSION

No longer can the stereotypical image of volunteers be applied to contemporary museum volunteerism. The relationship between paid and unpaid staff has developed considerably, not least in the area of supervision and skills development. In the first instance, it is important to consider the profile of contemporary museum volunteers, in the context of motivation and professionalism. Increasingly, there is a cross-over between the work of paid employees and the volunteers who support them. Perhaps the most problematical issue concerns the threat posed by volunteers on paid staff, be it imagined or real. In terms of value, it is also worth considering the financial value of museum volunteerism in terms of museum tasks completed and alternatively the skills and other personal benefits gained by the volunteers themselves. The opportunities in management that have been touched on in this chapter by drawing on Schmenner's approach to personnel management pave the way for more research into this area of innovation.

REFERENCES

Bales, K. (1996) 'Measuring propensity to volunteer', in *Social Policy and Administration*, 30, 3, September, 206–226.

Burns, L. (1996) 'The context: the future of volunteering', in *AIM Focus*, 3, April, 2.

Carrington, L. (1996) 'Solo so good and here today, gone . . .', in *Museums Journal*, August, 21–25.

Conybeare (1995) 'Curator loses job in regiment museum reorganization', in *Museums Journal*, November.

Conybeare (1996) 'Bristol faces cash squeeze', in *Museums Journal*, March, 11.

Cordrey, T. (1995) 'What are friends for?', in *Museums Journal*, October, 19–20.

Graham, M. and Foley, M. (1998) 'Volunteering in an urban museums service', in *Tourism and Visitor Attractions*, ed. Ravenscroft, N. *et al.*, Eastbourne: Leisure Studies Association Publications.

Hall, L. (1995) 'All for the love', in *Museums Journal*, October, 25–28.

Harvey, R. (1993) 'Professionals wanted', in *Scottish Museum News*, 9, 2, Summer, Edinburgh: Scottish Museums Council.

Mason, R. (1997) 'Steel but not brass', in *Museums Journal*, January, 25–29.

Reynolds, P. (1997) 'Museum skills way forward for unemployed volunteers', in *Museums Journal*, March, 9.

Schmenner, R. (1994) *Plant and Service Tours in Operations Management*, 4th edition, New York: MacMillan Publishing Ltd.

Sheard, J. (1995) 'From Lady Bountiful to active citizen', in Smith, J. *et al.* (eds) *An Introduction to the Voluntary Sector*, London: Routledge.

Sone, K. (1997a) 'Here today, gone tomorrow', in *Museums Journal*, March, 22–23.

Sone, K. (1997b) 'MoD indecision prolongs the agony over cutbacks', in *Museums Journal*, May, 19.

Tedrick, T. *et al.* (1984) 'The effective management of a volunteer corps', in *Department of Parks and Recreation*, Arlington, USA, 19, 2, 55–59, 70 (unpublished source).

MODEL QUESTIONS

1. Why has the management of volunteers become such an important contemporary issue in the museum sector?

2. What are the main negative characteristics that have burdened museum volunteering with its poor image, and why have they been allowed to persist?

3. Identify four reasons why museum volunteering is losing its poor image.

CHAPTER 8

Design of the Process and Product Interface

Paul Reynolds

Millar (1989) and Simons (1996) suggest that the development of cultural and heritage tourism should ideally proceed within a management framework which gives priority to the conservation and preservation of unique heritage resources. This framework has to balance the often conflicting needs of both conservation and tourism. It is in the natural heritage areas that this problem has become most acute.

This chapter will discuss operational management aspects of visitor management, product and process design and managing customer expectations, using boat trips in a World Heritage listed site (Kakadu National Park) as a case study. The case will illustrate some of the problems that are faced by product designers in natural heritage areas and fitting a tourist product into theoretical frameworks.

NATURAL HERITAGE MANAGEMENT

The word 'heritage' in its broader meaning is generally associated with the words 'inheritance' and 'ancestry': something transferred from one generation to another.

In the natural arena, heritage has been used to describe gardens, landscapes, national parks, wilderness, rivers, islands and components thereof, such as flora and fauna (Herbert 1989; Zeppel and Hall 1992). In many countries certain areas have significant heritage value and cultural importance. Governments have decided to designate particular areas as National Parks and put boundaries around them to 'preserve and protect' them. Questions arise as to what precisely is being preserved, and what are these areas being protected from. Similarly, decisions have to be made as to whether National Parks are more valuable as cultural artefacts than as commodity resources.

The idea of natural areas having heritage value has taken credence since the adoption in 1972 of the *Convention Concerning the Protection of World Natural and Cultural Heritage*. Since that time some 450 sites throughout the world have been formally designated as World Heritage Sites. The general objectives of the convention were to enhance worldwide understanding and appreciation of heritage conservation and to recognize and preserve natural and cultural properties throughout the world. One of the primary goals of the setting up of the World Heritage list was to attract visitors to different areas in the world and thereby encourage greater understanding and sharing of experiences and culture amongst people. It is therefore important to embrace the concept of natural heritage when methods of heritage management are being discussed.

OPERATIONAL MANAGEMENT AND THE SERVICE INDUSTRIES

Increasingly in business operations which involve serving customers, companies are moving their general focus from just looking at their core product to trying to understand what the customer requires and utilizes from the total package or bundle that is on offer. Tourism is no different from other service industries in the move towards understanding more about the nature of customer satisfaction and how total quality is perceived in customer relationships.

There have been several attempts to classify services to gain a richer understanding of their complexity, notably Rathmell (1966) and Shostack (1977). A common theme running through these authors' work is the classification of services into tangible and intangible components in order to help choose an effective marketing strategy. Eiglier and Langeard (1977) went further than this. They added the effect of the organization and client interface and user participation on the customer's perception of the product.

Approaches that address subjective aspects of service to a greater extent are given by Sasser, Olsen and Wyckoff (1978), who defined the three components of a service package as follows:

- Physical items or facilitating goods.
- Sensual benefits or explicit services.
- Psychological benefits or implicit services.

They suggested that the key to an effective design of a service is to recognize and properly define all the items that make up the service package. The mix of facilitating goods, explicit services and implicit services must be appropriate for the customer base and the resources available. Further, each part of these components must be specified as part of the service and not left to chance.

Chase (1981) arranged various kinds of service along a continuum from high to low 'contact'. The 'contact' refers to the duration of the customer in the service system, but not what happens to the customer while they are in the system. Lovelock (1983) focused on specific categories of services and proposed five schemes for classifying them in ways that transcended narrow industry boundaries. Other writers discussing operational management design for services suggest other methods of categorization. Slack *et al.* (1995), for instance, have developed a meaningful 'volume-variety continuum' which helps a business focus on its performance objectives.

While all the categorizations above are useful in their various ways in understanding the nature of services, it is sometimes difficult to see how the categories aid managerial decision-making, especially for tourism destination managers. Schmenner (1995) comes closest to providing assistance here by outlining challenges to managers for several categories of service organization. However, the tourism product is not often a comfortable fit into the classification chosen.

Notwithstanding the above, it is a mistake to assume that most tourists are anything more than consumers, whose primary goal is the consumption of the tourism experience. Even eco-tourists or visitors to heritage sites, who may have strong ethical, environmental or historical motives for travel, are still consumers when they participate in tourism activities. As deKadt (1977) stated, 'the normal tourist is not to be compared with the anthropologist or any other researcher. Tourists are pleasure-seekers, temporarily unemployed, and above all consumers.'

To expect most tourists to act in any other way is naive, although widespread. While a limited number of people will be prepared to modify their actions according to the environment they enter, the vast majority of tourists appear to be uninterested in doing so. It must be remembered that tourists are seeking escape from their everyday existence. While on vacation, they do not want to be burdened with the concerns of their normal world.

Tourism should be seen as entertainment, striving to satisfy tourist needs, wants and demands. To be successful, and therefore commercially viable, the tourism product must be manipulated and packaged in such a way that can be easily consumed by the public. Clearly learning opportunities can and should be created from the tourism experiences provided. But even in this the primary role of tourist attractions should be to entertain. Even large museums and art galleries that are ostensibly developed to provide educational and cultural experiences have recognized that they are in the entertainment business and have arranged their displays accordingly.

AUTHENTICITY

It has been argued by commentators such as MacCannell (1973) and Pearce (1982, 1984) that the notion of authenticity provides us with one of the most important insights into the behaviour of tourists. Tysoe (1985) has written of the widespread belief that tourists are basically shallow and foolish individuals, typically satisfied with superficial, staged, unauthentic glimpses into the life of the country or region they are visiting. In contrast with this are the views of MacCannell (1973, 1976) who claims that many tourists and travellers are seeking authentic and genuine contact with the people and places they visit, and that few visitors seek superficial or contrived experiences.

CASE STUDY

Yellow Water Billabong in Kakadu National Park

Kakadu National Park (KNP) is the largest terrestrial National Park in Australia. In 1992 the whole was added to the World Heritage List after partial listings in 1981 and 1987.

The Park covers approximately 20,000 square kilometres and is a place of spectacular landscapes with a remarkable abundance and variety of plants and animals. All the major habitats of the Top End are found within the Park. Some of the plants and animals are rare or do not occur elsewhere and so it provides a sanctuary for their continued existence.

Traditional ownership

Kakadu is a living landscape. It is a place where the Aboriginal custodians maintain personal and spiritual links with their traditional lands. People have inhabited the area for possibly 60,000 years. It is a place of immense cultural importance with a wealth of archaeological and rock art sites, which provide insights into Aboriginal culture and environmental changes through the ages.

Aboriginal culture, like any other, continues to develop as it adapts to changing circumstances, particularly the changes caused by the dominant (European) culture. There are far fewer Aboriginal people (*bining*) than there were before European (*balanda*) colonization, perhaps as few as a tenth. However, the culture is strong and has survived and adapted.

Kakadu is unusual in the extent to which its culture is intact. There remains a wealth of traditional knowledge. Not only do the more senior *bining* residents recognize the importance of passing their knowledge on to younger generations but they realize too the value of sharing some of this knowledge with *balanda*.

From the beginning there was an expressed desire to involve Aboriginal people in the management of the Park. This primarily stemmed from the philosophy under which the Park was established, that of Aboriginal ownership and joint management (Hill and Press 1994). Now, approximately 35 per cent of the permanent Australian Nature Conservation Agency (ANCA) staff and about 40 per cent of people on temporary contracts are Aboriginal. Most of them are Park residents with strong traditional links with the land. Such Aboriginal people have brought much experience and cultural outlook to their jobs. Moreover, as they work alongside *balanda*, there is considerable transfer of traditional knowledge.

Studies of tourists in the Park have indicated that there is a need for more visible Aboriginal involvement in tourism activities (Knapman 1990; Braithwaite and Reynolds 1996).

Tourism

The landscape values of the region, the opportunity to learn about Australian Aboriginal culture and the expectation of a wilderness experience are the main reasons people visit the Top End of Australia, and particularly Kakadu. Over 200,000 people visit Kakadu each year. The most significant characteristic of tourism is the marked seasonality, with the majority of visitors arriving between May and October. Approximately half of visitors to the Park are on commercial tours.

The boat tours at Yellow Waters are superb for giving people a great opportunity to see and photograph animals. Thus they are of great importance in fulfilling people's expectations at the Park. They are a wonderful way of effortlessly experiencing some of the spirit of Kakadu in a short time. As a wildlife experience available to a relatively large number of people, it is without comparison in Australia.

Yellow Water

Knapman (1990) rightly calls Yellow Water 'that recognized jewel in the Kakadu crown'. Around 55 per cent of visitors to Kakadu went on the Yellow Waters cruise in 1995 (Braithwaite and Reynolds 1996). Of the various activities available in the Park, wildlife viewing (essentially boat tours) rated for satisfaction ahead of all other activities (bushwalking, camping, fishing, boating, scenic driving/tours, visiting rock art sites) for both domestic and international visitors (Knapman, 1990). Water cruises accounted for 13 per cent of domestic and 11 per cent of international expenditure in Kakadu National Park.

The current fleet of boats consists of three 66-seaters bought in 1988 (upgraded with quieter four-stroke engines in 1994), plus two 22-seater vessels from circa 1985. The price of a trip is $22.50 a head. Australian Kakadu Tours operate another 22-seater under an arrangement with Gagudju. Currently there are proposals to acquire a new 60-seater and a new 30-seater and dispose of the two older small boats.

The numbers of people wishing to visit Yellow Water have been steadily increasing along with the numbers of people visiting Kakadu. This may be putting an increasing strain on the facilities and the environment.

The facilities are constantly being improved, with new quieter and more efficient engines fitted to the boats, new walkways and landing areas being recent additions.

Wildlife and humans

Humans now seek wildlife not for food, clothing and other such basic commodities as they have for millions of years, but for the satisfaction of intellectual and spiritual needs, through that peculiar psychological succour called entertainment or tourism.

Success at creating intimate encounters with wildlife increases the demand for that tourism product. Therein lies its vulnerability. If the impact of that intimacy is too great, the animals will cease breeding, cease feeding and ultimately stop using the area. In other words, the quality of the tourist experience will decline, the reputation will be lost, the people will go elsewhere and, by past experience around the world, be unlikely to return.

The relationship between the visitor and the fauna is largely determined by the guide. Therefore ultimately the behaviour of the guides on the boats will determine what happens to the fauna, and thus the long-term sustainability of the boat tour operation.

In studying the case above from a management perspective, it is important to consider the following trade-offs and compromise options that present themselves.

SERVICE AND THE TOURISM PRODUCT

The provision of a service is a complicated phenomenon. The word has many meanings, ranging from personal service to service as a product.

One of the better definitions of a service is provided by Gronroos (1990):

A service is an activity or series of activities of more or less intangible nature that normally take place in interactions between the customer and service employees and/or physical resources or goods and/or systems of the service provider, which are provided as solutions to customer problems.

Within this definition lie four basic characteristics that relate to a tourist experience such as the Yellow Water boat trips. By understanding more of the nature of the experience, we can then attempt to understand what might lead to satisfaction or dissatisfaction of the experience.

1. The experience is intangible.
2. The experience consists of activities rather than things.
3. The experience is produced and consumed simultaneously.
4. The customer (tourist) has to be present and participate in the production process.

This approach can be useful for pinpointing characteristics of tourism products. In these respects, tourism is in fact no different from other services in general. However, Faulkner (1994) argues that there other features that are generally not emphasised, such as the notion that tourism is an amalgam of complementary services that are destination-specific. Any service delivery system can be looked at as a series of experience points for the customer. These points can be seen as a chain, one experience affecting the next. Each experience point may be classified for 'high', 'medium' or 'low' effect on the customer's experience, or how the customer perceives the experience. It is the customer who perceives value in a product or a service and, through that perception, bestows value on it. As such, the industry must be aware of how customers perceive the value of each of the links in the value chain, and that customers have a pre-phase and post-phase perception of the values they receive (Braithwaite 1992).

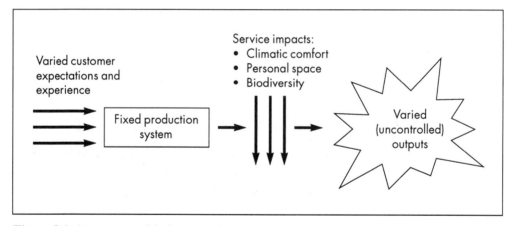

Figure 8.1: A process model of a nature-based attraction.

Customer satisfaction is based on all the products and services a customer has bought *or perceives they have bought*. It is therefore important the product is understood. The *core* product at Yellow Water is:

- a wildlife experience;
- a birdwatching trip;
- a scenic boat trip.

The marketing of any core product needs to be focused and accurate and not lead to false expectations. If people have an expectation of seeing crocodiles, for example, and this is not realized, it may lead to low satisfaction.

The peripheral areas impact greatly on the final satisfaction rating. At Yellow Water, these include other passengers, other boats, the commentary and the boat design. It therefore becomes clear that analysis needs to be done to ascertain what tourists think or perceive they are buying, before real management of the experience can begin.

A tourist experience such as wildlife viewing is normally perceived in a subjective manner. The perception will be coloured by values already held by the visitor, previous similar experiences and information received. This information may have been self-sought, or supplied by another party such as a tour operator. Each visitor, although receiving the same stimulus, interprets it in a different way. It is therefore difficult to quantify satisfaction of the intangible parts of the experience. Satisfaction of the tangible segments is easier to gauge, for instance: boat comfort, visibility and quality of hardware.

At Yellow Water the delivery system is fixed. Visitors sit on a boat and are moved through the 'exhibits'. The customer is passive during this stage, although they are given information by the guide. The operation would fit into the 'service factory' area in Schmenner's (1986) service process matrix. However, it is expected in a service factory that the outcomes are controlled and unvaried. This cannot be the case here. Flora, fauna and climate are constantly changing with the time of day and certainly the time of year.

Successful tourism services require a sense of uniqueness. A tourist experience should be a personal one (even though the visitor may be in a group), and if the visitor came a minute, an hour or a day later the experience would be different. The guide commentary or written word can add to this, by heightening awareness of the rarity, or uniqueness of an experience.

To a large extent, wildlife experiences cannot be planned. However, the more that is known about an animal's natural behaviour, daily movements, breeding and feeding patterns and other regular changes, the greater chance there is of managing a successful tourist experience concerning that species.

This heterogeneity creates one of the major problems in managing an operation such as Yellow Water, that is, how to maintain an evenly perceived quality of the trip.

MEASUREMENT AND STRATEGIES

A goal of the Yellow Water operation should be to deliver the highest value of total experiences to customers throughout the value chain. Given the notion that 'value given equals value received' then the pursuit of this goal is likely to be the surest road to long-term profit maximization.

Attaining this goal means designing and implementing appropriate strategies. Ideally a sound value-delivery system would be based on a value-measurement system. A fine-tuned measurement system will help to quantify the nature of high, moderate and low experience.

In the absence of a measurement system, both quantity-based and quality-based service strategies are possible within a value-chain framework. A quantity-based strategy suggests delivering many high-value experiences, a modest number of moderate ones and only those low-value ones that are needed to keep the chain connected. The quality-based strategy recommends intensifying the customer's exposure to high-value experiences, limiting those of moderate value and minimizing the low-value ones.

One of the terms in vogue amongst the travel industry is 'giving value for money'. Yet, decision-makers in the industry find considerable problems when it comes to measuring value given or value received. The value-chain framework provides a basis for measuring value of services delivered and experiences received by relating value to the attribute of time. Tourism seems sometimes to be seen by operators as an unconnected series of experiences. It clearly is not.

ECONOMIC AND ENVIRONMENTAL FACTORS

Tourism is an activity that is likely to generate environmental impacts. This is especially true when it is the natural environment or areas of heritage value that is the attraction for tourists. It should also be recognized that not all externalities generated by tourism are negative. It can generate positive effects. For example, the opportunity for people to learn more about the importance of the Yellow Water system and Aboriginal culture in the area has not been fully explored. In the long run, successful tourism at Yellow Water will depend on the environmental preservation.

There are two types of environmental cost (Clarke, Dwyer and Forsyth 1995). One is the direct cost of degradation of the environment, where tourism has adverse consequences for the flora or fauna in the area, or leads to pollution of the site. The second is the monetary cost of preventing or limiting the impact: constructing paths, putting new motors in boats and lessening pollution in general. This latter area is more readily evaluated than the former, although it is part of the purpose of this study to add to methods of measurement of the former, although not to put an economic value on it.

It is also important to distinguish between immediate and long-term effects. Some impacts may be adverse, but they may not have long-term or widespread consequences. An example of the latter would be when a species no longer visits an area due to disturbance by tourists.

Instruments

There is a wide variety of instruments that can be termed 'economic' and which can be used to control environmental impacts (for review see Tisdell 1993; and for the Australian experience, James 1993).

1. Price-based instruments

This is often referred to as 'user pays'. It can be interpreted as making a charge to use a fragile environment. The fees may or may not be related to costs, and these costs may be the costs of environmental damage, or the monetary costs incurred in preventing such damage. In most cases, user charges are made for an activity that generates a probability of pollution or other impact, rather than the cost of the impact itself.

Price can be used to regulate demand and supply. By making a product a high price, customers may be deterred in making the purchase. A high price may open the organization to allegations of profiteering. Also, customers who do make the purchase will expect an equal benefit. Fittings, fixtures and levels of service must be at a high level as well as the event itself.

2. Quantitative limits

The use of many environmentally sensitive areas is controlled by the imposition of quantity limits. The number of cars, boats, visitors or permits may be set in advance. An advantage of quantitative limits is that they can result in precise environmental impacts. However, they will, if effective, give rise to excess demand.

Limits may also be placed on complementary services, such as accommodation, or car parking near a site so that use is rationed or at least spread throughout a sensitive area.

3. Other instruments

There are several other instruments that can be used to control impacts, but two that are worth mentioning are education and codes of conduct. Users and operators of fragile environments can be educated into ways of lessening impacts. Codes of conduct apply more to operators than visitors as such. Both of these methods may be as an added economic cost to the consumer, or the operator.

ENVIRONMENTAL AND SATISFACTION FACTORS

Many of the determinants of satisfaction at Yellow Water are biological. These are basically 'givens' which must be worked around. Once these patterns are genuinely recognized, it is possible to tailor the cruises in a manner that is appropriate to those biological patterns. In other words, it is accepted that there are times of year and of day when there are more crocodiles around, and boats are therefore scheduled to concentrate around those times (if crocodile viewing is accepted as a major attraction of the tour).

The other approach is to manage the wildlife populations of interest. This can involve habitat manipulation involving either natural processes such as fire, restoring pre-European conditions such as by culling introduced mammals, or by artificial means of enhancing numbers and behaviour, such as by providing supplementary food. This latter approach might compromise the authenticity of the experience, thereby diminishing the experience for some segments of the market.

One particularly difficult satisfaction issue is that of managing customer expectations. Most people coming to Yellow Water will have seen a nature documentary of television, or spectacular still photography of animals in action – a crocodile leaping into the water, a sea eagle launching itself into the air or a large flock of Magpie Geese flying off. They are all spectacular sights. Pressure is brought to bear on the tour guide to manage such experiences, and severely disturbing wildlife often increases customer satisfaction greatly. It is, in fact, a sign of acute disturbance. It is energetically costly for the birds to do this, and if it happens too often the birds will avoid the area. It is a form of environmental degradation. However, it is not recognized in this way by most people.

SATISFACTION AND ECONOMIC FACTORS

A major component of satisfaction is comfort. If people are comfortable they are less likely to be irritated. Conversely, if people are well entertained, they are more tolerant of discomfort. It is a matter of minimizing the opportunities for synergism of a number of negative factors, some of which will be beyond the control of the operator. There are a number of trade-offs involved. Filling boats to capacity minimizes overhead costs per customer but leads to lower satisfaction. The cost of a sustainable operation includes the difference between the loading level of maximum satisfaction and maximum boat capacity.

In order to maximize customer satisfaction the operator should therefore supply the customer with a comfortable environment (both physical and climatic), and ensure that there is much available to entertain the visitor. From the available data these factors would appear to come together for the early morning and the evening cruises, especially in the dry season. Temperature and humidity are at their lowest (early dry), the water levels are low, leading to a concentration of wildlife, especially crocodiles (late dry).

Authenticity and enthralment

While the categorizations referred to place a service in a continuum with other services, it is necessary to understand where tourist attractions are placed in the visitor's consciousness.

Two measures that are useful in regard to heritage attractions are the degree of authenticity, and the degree of enthralment.

1. Authenticity

In the case of Yellow Water the degree of natural behaviour exhibited by the fauna would be examined, together with the environment in which it is viewed. The authenticity is perceived to be high if it is not obviously contrived. Subtle unnaturalness such as habituation of fauna probably does not count.

2. Enthralment

The degree to which the experience captivates, fascinates and thrills the visitor. This, in turn, is to do with several factors:

1. The sense of uniqueness that the visitor is made to feel.
2. The degree of involvement with the environment and the closeness of the animals (a good example of this is the difference between viewing in an aquarium and snorkelling).
3. The degree of information given to the visitor and the way it is given.

An experience that rates highly in this regard would make the guest feel that their visit was unique – a distinctive, special and individual encounter that they are privileged to be part of. This can be managed in several ways. Firstly, the visitor must be close to the environment, with as few impediments or barriers to the seeing, feeling and generally experiencing the environment as possible. Secondly, the degree of exclusivity and privilege of the experience needs to be impressed, by the guide, and with the pre- and post-experience information.

An experience that rates high on both authenticity and enthralment, while still having a high regard for service, passenger safety and care of the natural environment in which it operates, would be an exemplar.

A museum would score low on both counts. It is high on visitor-based control, in that the exhibits are always on view (they are dead), and the visitor can spend as much or as little time viewing as they so please, and there is much information on offer. However, it does not set out to be a 'natural experience', and the degree of enthralment, captivation and risk are low in spite of great advances in visitor management.

The zoo is set as much as possible in a natural habitat with fauna in specific

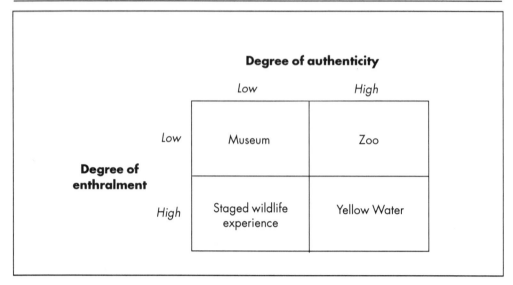

Figure 8.2: A model of attractiveness of nature-based attractions in relation to degree of authenticity and degree of enthralment.

enclosures, so that visitors can view them. However, often the enclosures are large and the animals are not always visible, especially in the middle of the day when they are resting. It therefore rates fairly high in authenticity. The visitor does have control over management of their experience, in what and how long they wish to see an exhibit. Most zoos have regular displays of specific fauna, but there will not be a high degree of uniqueness or distinctiveness about the experience provided.

A staged 'natural' experience where animals are encouraged to interact with or for humans would fall into another quadrant. The Jumping Crocodile Cruise on the Adelaide River in Australia is a good example. Passengers are taken along the river, and crocodiles are enticed to jump out of the water for food that is suspended several metres above the water. Although the cruise takes place in a natural setting, and crocodiles do jump out of the water for prey on low branches, this is a performance, staged specifically for tourists, and has little authenticity to endorse it. The cruise is undoubtedly high on the thrill-and-fascination factor.

A nature based boat trip such as the Yellow Water cruise has the potential to be high on both counts. It takes place in a natural setting, with fauna exhibiting natural behaviour (the habituation will not be obvious to most passengers). The authenticity of the experience should be greatest when the disturbance is lowest. Each cruise is also unique. The passengers see and experience different things, although it is, to a large part, up to the guide to make the passengers feel as if this trip is unique and exciting. The guide must make seeing fauna a fascinating incident, as if this was the first time that the species had been seen – and, for many passengers on the trip, this will be the case.

COMPENSATING SATISFACTION FACTORS

A final stage in design of a visitor attraction should be an examination of the elements that go towards satisfying the visitor, or might affect adversely the visitor experience.

Albrecht and Zemke (1985) suggest that managers should try to find out what problems the customer wants solved. Similarly, a tourism manager should examine the range of things that might satisfy or dissatisfy a visitor. All too often service organizations concentrate only on the core part of the product and neglect the peripherals even though these have profound impacts on satisfaction levels.

The core product marketed at Yellow Water is birds and animals (fauna), yet if biodiversity is measured (Figure 8.3) it can be clearly seen that there is a great variation in the amount of species to be seen throughout the year. Yet the general level of satisfaction throughout the year appears to be high, indicating that other factors affect satisfaction levels such as climatic influences and the number of other passengers. These ecological and social impacts affect visitor satisfaction at different levels at different times of the year. Some have a more marked effect on overall satisfaction than others. For instance, in September/October the number of birds and crocodiles visible is at its highest, giving great satisfaction. However, a negative impact, Relative Stress Index (RSI) (temperature and humidity) is also very high.

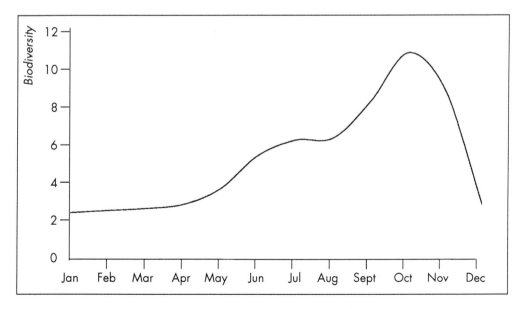

Figure 8.3: Biodiversity at Yellow Water billabong, 1995 (measured by number and importance rating of species able to be seen). *Source:* Braithwaite and Reynolds 1996.

Four major factors that influence satisfaction at Yellow Water are:

- Biodiversity (measured by the number and importance rating of species able to be seen).
- Climatic comfort (measured by the inverse of Relative Stress Index [RSI]); RSI is a measure of human discomfort based on temperature and humidity; Desplace and Drosdowsky 1981).
- Vastness – the sense of enormity and spaciousness derived from being with a few people in a large open wilderness area. This is especially prevalent during the wet season when the area is in flood.
- Personal space. Defined by number of other people on the boat (loading factor) and the number of other boats.

All of these factors have an effect on satisfaction and should be seen as a continuum of positive and negative influences on the customer, each strong one replacing the other rather than cancelling the other out (Figure 8.4). However, there is likely to be synergism operating also, so management should aim to maximize the positives and minimize the unavoidable negatives. Satisfaction ratings are likely to be highest when the actual experience matches or exceeds the expectation raised by the marketing information supplied. However this is tempered by the fact that visitors may have few comparable experiences on which to base expectations.

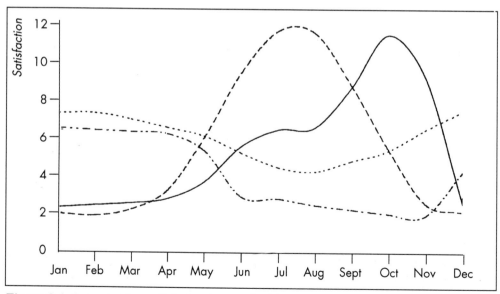

Figure 8.4: Compensating satisfaction factors thought to be affecting customer perceptions at Yellow Water. *Source:* Braithwaite and Reynolds 1996.

CONCLUSIONS

Nature-based tourism is becoming integrated into the popular tourism market, and the preservation of the environment should be seen as part of protecting our culture and heritage. Without effective management, the pressures of mass tourism can lead to the exploitation and degradation of irreplaceable heritage resources. The protection and conservation of these assets must be balanced with appropriate and suitable levels of tourist use, along with appropriate development projects. A better understanding of the operational issues and the determinants of customer motivations for visiting these sites must be a prerequisite for any manager who has a connection to tourism and environmental welfare.

REFERENCES

Albrecht, K. and Zemke, R. (1985) *Service America*, New York: Warner Books.

Braithwaite, R. W. and Reynolds, P. C. (1996) *Wildlife Tourism at Yellow Waters*. CSIRO Australia.

Braithwaite, R. (1992) 'Value-chain assessment of the travel experience', *Cornell HRA Quarterly*, October, 41–49.

Chase, R. B. (1981) *Operations Research*, Operations Research Society of America, 29, 4, 698–706.

Clarke, H., Dwyer, L. and Forsythe, P. (1995) 'Economic instruments and the control of tourism's environmental impacts', Australian National Tourism and Hospitality Research Conference, ed. Shaw, R. N., Melbourne: CAUTHE, 159–176.

de Kadt, E. (1977) *Tourism: Passport to Development?*, New York: Oxford University Press.

Desplace, P. and Drosdowsky, W. (1981) 'Meteorological influences on comfort in the Northern Territory', *Translations of the Menzies Foundation*, 2, Melbourne: The Menzies Foundation, 31–50.

Eiglier, P. and Langeard, E. (1977) 'A new approach to service marketing', in *Marketing Consumer Services: New Insights*, Report 77–115, Boston: Marketing Science Institute.

Faulkner, H. W. (1994) 'Towards a strategic approach to tourism development: the Australian experience', in Theobald, W. F. (ed.) *Global Tourism: the Next Decade*, Oxford: Butterworth-Heinemann, 231–44.

Gronroos, C. (1990) *Service Management and Marketing*. USA: Lexington Books.

Herbert, D. (1989) 'Leisure trends and the heritage market', in Herbert, D. T., Prentice, R. L., Thomas, C. J. and Brookfield, V. T. (eds) *Heritage Sites: Strategies for Marketing and Development*, Avebury Press, 1–14.

Hill, M. A. and Press, A. J. (1994) 'Kakadu National Park – a history', *Biodiversity – Broadening the Debate*, Canberra: Australian Nature Conservation Agency, 2, 4–23.

James, D. (1993) Using Economic Instruments for Meeting Environmental Objectives: Australia's Experience, Environmental Economics Research Paper No 1. Canberra: Department of the Environment State and Territories.

Knapman, B. (1990) *Tourists in Kakadu National Park: Some Results from a 1990 Visitor Survey*, Darwin: North Australia Research Unit, Australian National University.

Lovelock, C. H. (1983) 'Classifying services to gain strategic marketing insights', *Journal of Marketing*, 47, 9–20.

MacCannell, D. (1973) 'Staged authenticity: arrangements of social space in tourist settings', *American Journal of Sociology*, 79, 589–603.

MacCannell, D. (1976) *The Tourist*, New York: Schocken.

Millar, S. (1989) 'Heritage management for heritage tourism', *Tourism Management*, 10, 3, 9–14.

Pearce, P. L. (1982) *The Social Psychology of Tourist Behaviour*, Oxford: Pergamon.

Pearce, P. L. (1984) 'Tourist guide interaction', *Annals of Tourism Research*, 11, 129–146.

Rathmell, J .M. (1966) 'What is meant by services?', *Journal of Marketing*, 30, 32–36.

Sasser, W. E., Olsen, R. P. and Wyckoff, D. D. (1978) *Management of Service Operations*, Boston: Allyn & Bacon.

Schmenner, R. W. (1986) 'How can service businesses survive and prosper?', *Sloan Management Review*, Spring 1986, 21–32.

Schmenner, R. W. (1995) *Service Operations Management*, Englewood Cliffs, NJ: Prentice-Hall.

Shostack, G. L. (1977) 'Breaking free from product marketing', *Journal of Marketing*, 41, 73–80.

Simons, M. (1996) 'The protection of heritage sites and special places', in Prosser, G. (ed.) (1996) *Tourism and Hospitality Research: Australian and International Perspectives*, Proceedings on annual conference of CAUTHE, Council of Australian University Tourism and Hospitality Educators, Canberra: Bureau of Tourism Research.

Slack, N., Chambers, S., Harland, C. and Johnson, R. (1995) *Operations Management*, London: Pitman.

Tisdell, C. (1993) *Environmental Economics: Policies for Environmental Management and Sustainable Development*, Aldershot: Edward Elgar.

Tysoe, M. (1985) 'Tourism is good for you', *New Society*, 16th August, 226–230.

World Heritage Convention, General Conference of the United Nations Education, Scientific and Cultural Organisation (UNESCO), November 1972, Paris.

Zeppel, H. and Hall, M. C. (1992) 'Arts and special interest tourism', in Weiler, B. and Hall M.C. (eds) *Special Interest Tourism*, London: Bellhaven, 47–69.

MODEL QUESTIONS

1. Create lists of tangible and intangible impacts on the visitors.
   Divide the lists into variable (unmanageable) and unvariable (manageable) impacts.
   a) What would it take to move an item from variable to unvariable?
   b) What implications does this have for management, especially in managing visitors' satisfaction levels?

2. Given that the Yellow Water boat tour operation is a major revenue generator for the Gagudju people, how can revenue be increased, while preserving (or not degrading further) cultural and environmental standards?

3. How can you categorize/segment the visitors to Yellow Water? How can you create a good level of satisfaction within each segment?

CHAPTER 9

Quality

Nick Johns

INTRODUCTION

Heritage attractions must continually upgrade and improve quality in order to cope with changes in the marketplace. A quality attraction attracts and satisfies more visitors, who in turn are prepared to pay a higher price for the extra value that has been added. The quality of services (such as heritage attractions) has attracted a great deal of attention from practitioners and scholars, and a considerable body of literature has been produced, covering conceptual models of how quality is perceived by service customers (e.g. attraction visitors), how it may be measured, and how measurements may be integrated into effective management. This chapter presents an overview of service quality literature and discusses how they may be applied to practical heritage management situations.

As has been seen in Chapter 8, there is already something of a consensus about the nature of attraction quality, but the heritage attractions industry is new to the concept of service quality. Some of the quality management concepts which underpin developments in other services, such as banks and retail operations, are relevant to heritage attractions, but are hardly ever employed there. The heritage industry also has its own specific service-related problems, which have been discussed by comparatively few authors (e.g. Boniface 1995).

Authors in some service industries treat 'service' as more or less independent from other components of the visitor/customer experience. For example Martin (1986) breaks down restaurant service into a series of actions and activities of service staff. This is helpful in terms of the management of waiting staff, but does not express the overall quality of the customer's experience, which features the food and the environment in which it is eaten, at least as much as the service. Heritage attractions likewise depend for their 'service quality' upon exhibits, interpretation devices, shopping and eating opportunities. The actions of service staff are certainly important, but must be considered in the context of the whole visitor experience.

This chapter discusses service quality in heritage attractions along three lines. It examines some of the attempts authors have made to define quality, and particularly service quality. It presents various approaches to quality assessment and measurement and it discusses issues of managing attraction quality.

DEFINITIONS OF QUALITY

The concept of quality originated in manufacturing industry, and was originally considered simply to mean 'excellence'. For instance, artefacts of the Victorian era – railway engines, the stations which housed them, and even the benches and sanitary ware in the stations – were all 'built to last', reflecting a value system where permanence was a virtue in its own right and quality equated with excellence. Later, quality took on a more relative connotation of 'fitness for purpose'. At much the same time, the concept of quality control arose, which relied on testing products and intermediates regularly, in order to ensure that their designed-in characteristics (i.e. their 'quality') stayed within narrow, measurable limits. This engendered a new view of quality as 'conformance to specifications'. Another way to regard quality is as an absence of defects, which brings a subtle shift in emphasis. 'Fitness for purpose' and 'conformance to specifications' assume that quality is completely describable (i.e. by the product's purpose or specifications) and that the description is realizable. Thus once a product is fit for its purpose, or meets its specifications, it is counterproductive to try to improve on its quality. However, the zero defects approach introduces a position where new defects can always be identified and eliminated, as manufacturing processes or measuring techniques are refined, or consumer demand evolves. By starting from a negative position, the zero defects approach helps manufacturers to be consistently critical about their work. Manufacturing approaches assume that quality can be measured and specified, that defects are objective and identifiable, that quality may be achieved through standardization, and that any kind of product variability must be avoided. Few, if any, of these precepts apply to the quality of services.

Services such as heritage attractions are differentiated from manufactured products by three basic characteristics: time-dependence, person-dependence and customization. These have been elaborated by a number of authors, but can be summarized as follows:

Time dependence
- Services are 'instant'. An attraction opens in 'real time' and it is impossible to 'stockpile' its services for future use.
- Use is linked directly to demand. An attraction only provides its service while its visitors are there.
- Services are absolutely perishable. A heritage exhibit which fails to attract the Bank Holiday crowd cannot do so on another day. Attractions generally deteriorate with time and use. This applies not only to exhibits, paintings or

buildings, but also to landscapes and beauty spots, which may become disfigured through erosion and pollution.

Person-dependence

- Services often contain a considerable amount of person-to-person interaction. Attraction quality may depend upon the personality and behaviour of the 'front line staff' who actually deal with the visitor.
- These include the people who provide interpretation, e.g. actors who portray life in historic times. Such individuals may need to fulfil several roles, such as providing information and policing exhibits.
- Service effectiveness and quality are partly dependent upon the personality and behaviour of the visitor, or of other visitor groups.
- A specific problem may be presented by volunteers, who often need to feel a sense of ownership, for example by interpreting sites on their own terms. A visitor's enjoyment of a heritage attraction may also centre around personal involvement, through gaining new knowledge, or through a feeling of participation in historic or cultural re-enactments.

Customization

- In principle, services offer considerable scope for individual adaptation to each customer's need. In practice the style and content of a visit is highly variable depending upon the visitor's reaction to it or participation in it.
- Thus in heritage attractions there is scope for tailoring the content to visitor needs, both through interpersonal interaction and through technology.
- For example, live interpretation may be conducted in different languages, and information may be provided through interactive computer programs.

It is generally believed that quality of a service such as an attraction visit is subjective and intangible, existing only in the visitor's perception. As Parasuraman *et al.* (1986) put it, service quality is: 'an inference about the superiority of a product or service based on rational assessment of characteristics or attributes, or an affective judgement, an emotional response similar to an attitude'. Thus cultural heritage often means many different things to different individuals, and quality depends heavily upon interpretation, participation and customization. However, the practicalities of getting to the attraction, getting round it, eating, buying souvenirs and getting away again also influence the overall quality of the visitor's experience. Thus the visit may be considered a journey, which takes a fairly clear path to, and through, the attraction (Johns and Clark 1993).

According to expectancy-disconfirmation theory (Oliver 1980; Bolton and Drew 1991) visitors' expectations are another important ingredient of an attraction's quality. This theory proposes that satisfaction and dissatisfaction are determined by the disconfirmation of visitors' expectations when they actually experience the attraction. Positive disconfirmation occurs when the visit exceeds expectations, and negative disconfirmation when the opposite is the case. Positive or zero disconfirmation is thought to indicate satisfaction, while negative disconfirmation indicates dissatisfaction. However, the nature of expectations is unclear. They can be regarded as a kind of 'memory' of past service encounters, but individuals also build expectations of services they have not yet experienced from hearsay and from past experiences. Johns and Tyas (1997) suggest that expectations and perceptions are built up from three components:

- *Mythologies*: commonly held perceptions of a particular service, not necessarily grounded in experience. (These may be particularly important in cultural heritage situations, where the 'buzz' of visiting an attraction often comes from an individual's fascination with some particular, personal aspect of history or travel.)
- *Critical incidents*: important events during a visit or a previous visit, which enhance or spoil the visitor's experience. (For example a particularly informative guide, or the unexpected and annoying closure of an exhibition.)
- *Gestalt perceptions*: overall images built up from mythologies, upon which the visitor overlays experienced incidents. (The final impression that the visitor takes away with them from the attraction.)

Bitner and Hubbert (1994) consider *satisfaction* to be the outcome of a specific service experience and service quality as the visitor's overall perception of a particular brand or type of service experience. Intuitively it would seem that visitor satisfaction is a *consequence* of good or adequate attraction quality, but for Bitner and Hubbert visitors' satisfaction is a *precursor* of the 'quality image' they form about the attraction. Thus a number of service incidents go to make a single customer-satisfying visit, while several such visits build up an impression of attraction quality. Repeat visits are less relevant to heritage attractions than to other services, because many people only visit a site once, but 'overall satisfaction' perceived by visitors as their memory of the visit matures, may play a significant part in word-of-mouth recommendation and the development of expectations.

Assessment of attraction quality is ultimately to aid attraction managers, and to do this must be expressed in managers' terms. However, the quality of a cultural visit exists only in the visitor's mind, so the most effective way to access it is in the visitor's terms, and putting this into management terms may be difficult. *Provided* quality consists of distinct, separately managed elements: exhibits, interpretation, behaviour of front-line service staff and various facilities, and it is unlikely that these correspond precisely with visitors' *experienced* quality. For example, a faithfully reproduced historical experience may in fact be lost upon the majority of visitors, if it is not interpreted adequately. The full effect of an improvement initiative can only be understood if evidence is gathered by a variety of quality assessment techniques.

MEASUREMENT OF QUALITY

Quality *provided* is ultimately the subjective perception of planners, managers and front-line staff. Quality *experienced* is a matter of visitors' own subjective perceptions. Both 'qualities' must be assessed in order to monitor and manage the development of a satisfactory heritage 'product', but neither has an independent, objective existence.

Measuring the quality provided

Provider-oriented assessment often assumes that quality can be defined and specified, and that defects in the attraction 'service' are identifiable and finite in number. Two main approaches are used to measure 'quality provided': critical incident analysis and various types of audit.

Critical incident analysis identifies the aspects of a service which particularly satisfy or dissatisfy the visitor. In principle this implies a visitor-focused approach, but in many cases, staff are asked to identify the incidents. The technique can also be a very effective way of focusing staff awareness, by asking front-line staff to read and discuss visitors' comments.

Critical incidents are arranged in order of importance or urgency of corrective action. They can also be identified as satisfiers and dissatisfiers. The former correspond to Herzberg's 'motivating factors', i.e. the more they are present, the more they contribute to visitor satisfaction. Dissatisfiers are equivalent to 'hygiene factors', producing dissatisfaction if they are present, but not increasing satisfaction by their absence. Lockwood (1994) recommends that critical incidents be analysed on the basis of the grid shown in Figure 9.1. Managers can thus identify and classify the most important satisfiers and dissatisfiers for appropriate action.

A service quality audit involves drawing up a checklist covering all aspects of the service. For example, a list might specify the way staff greet visitors – as 'polite' or 'friendly', the minimum time a visitor should wait, or the maximum number of times the telephone should ring before it is answered. Consultants then grade each aspect of the service. Assessors are often specialists in a particular type of attraction, and may therefore view service quality through a manager's eyes. In order to achieve a more visitor-oriented view, some operators view the visitor's passage through the heritage attraction as consisting of distinct stages, as shown in Figure 9.2. A checklist of the stages of this 'visitor journey' (Johns and Clark 1993) ensures that all aspects of the attraction are included, and are audited in the same sequence as they would be by visitors. Despite this, service journey audits still tend to present a 'service provider's view' to some extent.

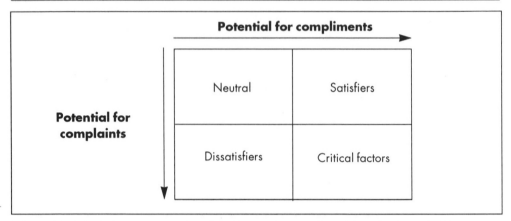

Figure 9.1: Matrix for analysing critical incidents. *Source:* adapted from Lockwood (1994).

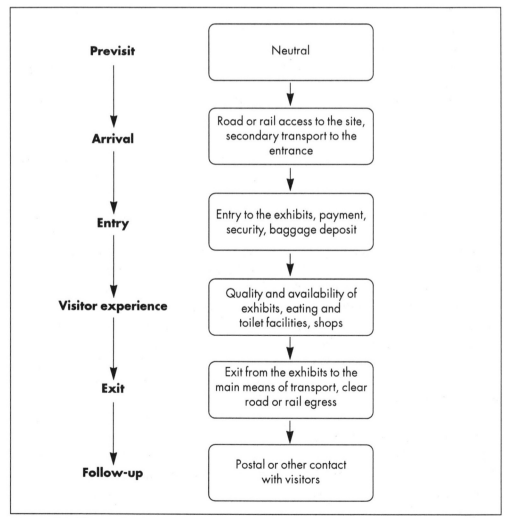

Figure 9.2: The service journey in a visitor attraction. *Source:* adapted from Johns and Clark (1993), p. 362.

Barsky (1992) suggests that they can be made less clumsy with a comparative style of wording such as: 'Better than/worse than expected', replacing the duplicated SERVQUAL questions. This approach is useful for heritage attraction situations, where visitors are often unwilling to complete long questionnaires, and a comparison between experience and expectations eliminates the need for duplicate series of questions. However, it has not yet received enough validation to be generally accepted, and respondents may have difficulty making such comparisons without other reference points (Johns and Tyas 1997).

An alternative way to assess the visitor experience is to use the profile accumulation technique (PAT) developed by Johns and Lee-Ross (1996) and others. In this free-response approach customers are asked to write down the best and worst aspects of their experience, together with the reasons for their selection. The data are coded using key words, and quantified to build up a profile showing what visitors like and dislike, and why. Like critical incident technique, profile accumulation can identify which aspects of the visit are satisfiers and which dissatisfiers. PAT accesses the responses of visitors directly, with questions so open that they do not lead respondents or bias the data. In contrast to the tick-boxes and numerical data of conventional questionnaires, PAT's free responses are easily read and understood by busy managers and staff. Thus the technique provides a new perspective on the quality experienced by attraction visitors, and complements the results from other questionnaire approaches.

Practicalities of measurement

In order to assess the quality of service provided and also to get as close to the visitor's experience as possible, a variety of quality assessment techniques needs to be integrated into a coherent operational strategy. There is also a need to distinguish between service quality and visitor satisfaction. Questionnaire approaches are generally used during or immediately after the visit and therefore according to Bitner and Hubbert actually measure satisfaction. Visitors may not form an overall view of quality until some time after the visit.

Quality *provided* may be measured through critical incident analysis if the objective is to concentrate upon the interaction of visitors with staff, or upon suspected but as yet unidentified problems. However, service quality audits are more effective for assessing the quality of the physical facilities and systems. Audit results should be saved on a database, because they can be used to map the effects of constant small improvements made from year to year. Data from both critical incidents and audits can provide valuable training materials for management and staff.

Quality *experienced* can be assessed with strategically placed comment cards which visitors can fill in. Results can be accumulated in a database, but in practice response rates may not be high, and it may be better to conduct more coherent, one-off surveys with questionnaires or interviewers. Such surveys should be held regularly, and as far as possible should use the same questionnaire or interview schedule for several years, making the results comparable over time. Results should be stored on a database, and in fact such surveys offer a good opportunity to collect marketing information about visitors' demographic characteristics, their activities within the attraction, and their preferences. A database also makes it possible to benchmark quality at a particular point in time and to monitor progress from quarter to quarter or year to year. Measurements of experienced service quality are of interest to staff and should be shared with them, at team briefing meetings and training sessions. It may be worthwhile surveying people at some time after their visit. In any case it is often useful to collect and database as many names and addresses of local visitors as far as possible, to whom brochures and information (e.g. about special promotions, sale items, courses etc.) may be sent.

Internal service quality

'Internal service quality' refers to the quality of interactions between staff within the organization. The total quality management (TQM) philosophy regards each interaction between employees as a separate 'service encounter', in which one individual takes the role of 'service provider' and the other that of 'service consumer'. Internal service quality reflects the cultural 'climate' of an organization, which affects both employees and visitors, and it is particularly important in organizations such as attractions. The measurement of internal service quality is in its infancy, particularly in heritage attractions, but some researchers have attempted to measure it using questionnaires of the comparative 'Better/worse than expected' type (Javier and Moores 1995). Critical incident approaches based upon the reports of service staff may also indirectly uncover some problems of internal service quality.

MANAGEMENT OF QUALITY

Formal approaches

As mentioned above, expectancy-disconfirmation theory regards service quality as a 'gap' between visitors' expectations and their perceptions of actual attraction quality. Various authors have attempted to extend this 'gap' concept to include the management of services, and Brogowicz et al. (1990) have summarized their work in the form of a two-cycle model, a greatly simplified version of which is shown in Figure 9.3. According to this model, management can assure quality by closing the first four 'gaps', shown in Table 9.2 (page 138).

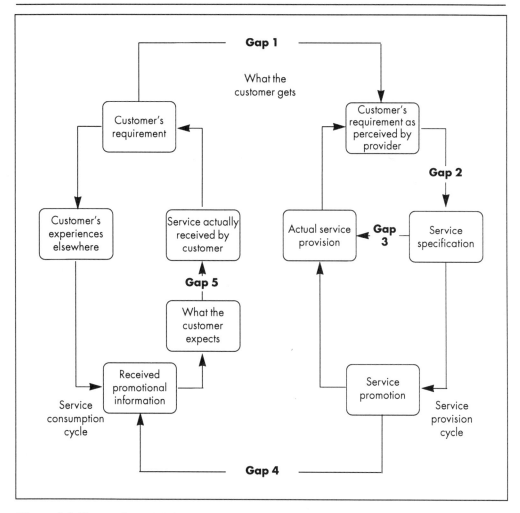

Figure 9.3: Two-cycle model. *Source:* Brogowicz *et al.* (1990).

Gap no. 5, the perception gap, is the one predicted by expectation-disconfirmation theory, and the others represent target areas for management action. Possible actions that can be taken are discussed below.

The positioning gap

This gap may be bridged or narrowed by improving feedback from visitors, the goal being to minimize divergence between quality provided and quality experienced.

Heritage attractions often face the problem that conservation attitudes prevail among curators and senior staff, which may not reflect what customers want from the attraction. One way to deal with this is by providing extensive interpretation of exhibits, through staff or technology.

Table 9.2: Description of the five gaps in the two-cycle model.

Conceptual gap	Description
1. The positioning gap	The gap between management's view of what the visitor expects and what the visitor actually expects.
2. The specification gap	The gap between management's view of what the visitor expects and the actual attraction quality that is specified.
3. The delivery gap	The gap between what is specified and what is actually delivered (i.e. the actual technical quality of the attraction).
4. The communication gap	The gap between what is delivered by the attraction and what is advertised to visitors (i.e. the information they receive to shape their expectations).
5. The perception gap	The gap between the quality that visitors feel they receive and the quality they expect (i.e. the gap discussed earlier in this chapter).

The specification gap

This gap may be bridged or narrowed by making the technical attraction quality as similar as possible to that indicated by visitor feedback. Critical incident analysis and quality audits may provide valuable tools for assessing this gap.

There is often a need to continually update and adjust quality, and this may present a problem for heritage attractions, which must simultaneously conserve cultural quality and maintain the credibility of all customer segments.

The delivery gap

This gap may be bridged or narrowed by improving communication between those who deliver the service and those who design it. Training of front-line staff is also important, and should include the results of service quality assessment, particularly that from qualitative techniques such as critical incident analysis or profile accumulation.

Heritage attractions generally face a delivery conflict. Exhibits must be conserved, but there is also a need to interpret them for the public. Visitors may also need to touch or walk over parts of the attraction in order to experience 'participation'.

Heritage attractions may also have a specific problem of managing volunteers or temporary staff. Often these individuals are committed to the attraction itself, but may need to be motivated and trained to cope with visitors , whom volunteers may even see as 'outsiders'.

These different needs may produce conflicting attitudes among attraction staff, which need to be managed by carefully controlling the organizational culture.

The communication gap

This gap may be bridged or narrowed by relating advertising to survey data about visitor satisfaction and perceived quality.

It is particularly important to ensure that visitors see the specific things that they have been promised. For instance, Reynolds (1996) notes that visitors to a Northern Australian National Park were dissatisfied if they did not see a crocodile, because this had been promised in the holiday brochures. Satisfaction was particularly low during the rainy season, which scattered the animals. The Park achieved much higher satisfaction ratings when it decided to advertise aboriginal tribal culture as 'the thing to see' during the wet season.

The perception gap

This gap can be bridged or narrowed only by closing the other four gaps in the model.

The gap model of quality provision is a convenient way of understanding the role of quality assurance in heritage attractions. Quality is a matter of 'getting it right first time' and it is not possible to put errors right after they have occurred. However, the gap model does not take into account the distinction discussed above between service quality and visitor satisfaction, and it fails to consider what action should be taken in respect of informal shapers of visitor expectations, such as word-of-mouth or mythology. By concentrating upon a few easily identifiable gaps, it also neglects many less obvious places where service provision may go wrong. Thus the gap model should be regarded as a helpful source of insight, rather than a comprehensive checklist of quality defects or remedial actions.

Total quality approaches

Quality management originated from the need to control output in manufacturing industry, and at first was mainly concerned with monitoring products to ensure that they matched design specifications. The scope of monitoring was widened to include intermediates, but it was eventually realized that it is more effective to control the *process* during manufacture (and so stop problems occurring) than to control products or intermediates to find out *post hoc* if anything has gone wrong with them. This process-control approach, known as *quality assurance*, is particularly appropriate for services. Quality assurance has undergone many developments over the years, of which the most effective have been amalgamated under names such as total quality management (TQM) or continuous quality improvement (CQI).

In its generalized form, the total quality concept considers a service process as a chain of events in which there is a flow of work from one employee to another. The individuals who pass on or receive the work in each transaction are considered internal 'suppliers' and 'customers' respectively. In theory, if there is a good working relationship between each supplier/customer team, the process should be working at its most efficient, and quality should be optimized. TQM programmes try to make employees aware of their internal customers and suppliers, ensuring that they obtain and give feedback about the quality of their work and the work that is passed on to them. In service organizations employees are usually also given training in customer care (i.e. in interpersonal skills and the way they treat customers). They may also be given 'empowerment training', i.e. trained to use their own initiative in order to identify what guests need and to provide it. TQM and empowerment are typical components of quality assurance programmes in hospitality and tourism organizations (see for example Stewart and Johns 1996).

Continuous quality improvement (CQI) attempts to actually improve the quality of service processes by continuously removing defects from operational processes to make them more and more efficient. Most examples of CQI are found in manufacturing industry, where defects are comparatively easy to identify. CQI has scope in heritage attractions, for example to gain improvements in layout and in the balance between visitor needs and those of conservation. Like TQM programmes, CQI initiatives involve training to sensitize employees to internal supplier/customer relationships, but employees are also trained to identify defects and to report them. CQI implementation usually involves two type of 'quality team'. Some trouble-shoot defects as they are identified, while others look for ways in which processes can be proactively improved.

TQM and CQI are interpreted differently in different organizations, and overlap to a considerable extent. Organizations vary enormously in their cultures and activities and it is always necessary to design a specific programme for a given situation. However, there are certain ingredients which should always be considered. These are:

- Clear commitment to the programme from top management.
- Training, preferably by a cascade process starting with top management, so that it includes everybody in the organization, including volunteers and part-time workers.
- An organizational culture emphasising sensitivity to visitor needs and a commitment to quality.
- A comprehensive system of quality measurement, including both the quality supplied and the quality experienced.
- Efficient communication between employees and management.
- A team structure for correcting defects, identifying possible improvements and monitoring the whole process.
- Systems of recognition and reward, to maintain the corporate culture and let everyone know how they are doing.

Thus TQM/CQI programmes in heritage attractions need to consider all of the aspects of quality measurement discussed in this chapter, including provided service quality, experienced service quality and internal service quality. They also need to standardize and benchmark quality from season to season and year to year. It is important that the results of such studies are shared with staff on an ongoing basis. It may be appropriate to do this within departmental briefing sessions, during appraisals, during training, through the medium of newsletters or noticeboards, or *ad hoc* as part of a system of recognition or reward.

TQM and CQI represent helpful models for the management of quality in service industries generally. However, heritage attractions may present specific problems which may make their application difficult. For instance, the concept of 'top management' may apply to a historic building or museum. It may be much less relevant to a National Park or a working island, which happens to be designated as a heritage site. In such circumstances it may be necessary to adopt a political approach, ensuring that all stakeholders are adequately consulted, but providing enough leadership to make sure that quality management decisions are made at a high level.

The concept of 'front-line staff' may be equally inappropriate in many heritage attractions. It has already been pointed out that such staff may have various, and possibly conflicting roles, including:

- an interpretive role of providing information about exhibits and features;
- a conservation role of reflecting culture or history as accurately as possible;
- a guiding role of ensuring that visitors keep to paths, avoid damaging exhibits and generally behave appropriately.

These roles are often associated with particular values, attitudes and strong perceptions of history or culture which may conflict with a need to be 'customer-friendly'. Heritage attractions often rely upon volunteers, or employ many part-time staff, and this can further strain these roles.

In principle, staff-related problems may be resolved by adequate training, but this is a problem with volunteers, part-time or short-term contracts. However, volunteers in historical enactment can be motivated by maintaining strict historical accuracy (e.g. by 'outlawing' wristwatches, trainers, jeans and modern money). Closed communities such as islanders or villagers may also be motivated to provide 'visitor care' through a common purpose such as the future of their community.

Action research approaches

Action research has been used extensively in educational and social research, but comparatively little in service industries. It involves identifying 'research teams' consisting of members of the organization (e.g. Argyris and Putnam 1985; Sanger 1996) who meet regularly, gather and analyse data. Action research is a very flexible approach which can cope with wide differences between organizations, and with the inherent subjectivity of service quality. Team members become highly involved and committed to assessing and improving quality, and the action research process can be tailored to specific organizational needs. Perhaps such approaches represent the future of service quality, assessment and management in heritage attractions.

FURTHER READING

Boniface, P. (1995) *Managing Quality Cultural Tourism*, London: Routledge.
Johns, N. (1995) 'Managing Quality', in Jones, P. L. and Merricks, P. (eds) *The Management of Foodservice Operations*, London: Cassell, 245–261.
Olsen, M., Gummesson, E. and Teare, R. (1995) *Quality Management in the Hospitality Industry*, London: Cassell.
Teare, R., Atkinson, C. and Westwood, C. (eds) (1994) *Achieving Quality Performance: Lessons from British Industry*, ed. R. Teare, London: Cassell.

REFERENCES

Barsky, J. D. (1992) 'Visitor satisfaction in the hotel industry: meaning and measurement', *Hospitality Research Journal*, 16, 1, 51–73.
Bitner, M. J. and Hubbert, A. R. (1994) 'Encounter satisfaction versus service quality: the consumer's voice', in Rust, R. T. and Oliver, R. L. (eds) *Service Quality: New Directions in Theory and Practice*, Thousand Oaks, California: Sage Publications.
Bolton, R. N. and Drew, J. H. (1991) 'A multistage model of visitors' assessment of service quality and value', *Journal of Consumer Research*, 17, 375–384.
Brogowicz, A. A., Delene, L. M. and Lyth, D. M. (1990) 'A synthesized service quality model with managerial implications', *International Journal of Service Industry Management*, 1, 1, 27–46.
Farouk, S. and Ryan, C. (1991) 'Analysing service quality in the hospitality industry using the SERVQUAL model', *Service Industries' Journal*, 11, 3, 324–343.
Javier, R. and Moores, B. (1995) 'Towards the measurement of internal service quality', *International Journal of Service Industry Management*, 6, 3, 64–83.
Johns, N. and Clark, S. L. (1993) 'The quality audit: a means of monitoring the service provided by museums and galleries', *Journal of Museum Managership and Curatorship*, 12, 1994, 360–366.
Johns, N. and Lee-Ross, D. (1996) 'Profile accumulation: a quality assessment technique for hospitality SMEs', in Teare, R. and Armistead, C. (eds), *Services Management: New Directions and Perspectives*, London: Cassell.
Johns, N. and Tyas, P. (1996) 'Use of service quality gap theory to differentiate between foodservice outlets', *Service Industries Journal*, 16, 3, 321–346.
Johns, N. and Tyas, P. (1997) 'Customer perceptions of service operations: *gestalt*, incident or mythology?', *Service Industries Journal*, 17, 3, 474–488.
Knutson, B., Stevens, P., Wullaert, C., Patton, M. and Yokoyama, F. (1991) 'LODGSERV: a service quality index for the lodging industry', *Hospitality Research Journal*, 14, 3, 277–284.
Lewis, R. C. and Pizam, A. (1982) 'The measurement of guest satisfaction', in Pizam, A., Lewis, R. C.

and Manning, P. (eds), *The Practice of Hospitality Management*, New York: AVI Publishing, 189–201.

Lockwood, A. (1994) 'Using service incidents to identify quality improvement points', *International Journal of Contemporary Hospitality Management*, 6, 1/2, 75–80.

Martin, W. B. (1986) 'Defining what quality service is for you', *Cornell Hotel and Restaurant Administration Quarterly*, February, 32–38.

Oberoi, U. and Hales, C. (1990) 'Assessing the quality of the conference hotel service product: Towards an empirically based model', *Service Industries Journal*, 10, 4, 700–721.

Oliver, R. L. (1980) 'A cognitive model of the antecedents and consequences of satisfaction decisions', *Journal of Marketing Research*, 17, 460–469.

Parasuraman, A., Zeithaml, V. A. and Berry, L. L. (1985) 'A conceptual model of service quality and its implications for future research', *Journal of Marketing*, 49, 41–50.

Parasuraman, A., Zeithaml, V. A. and Berry, L. L. (1986) 'SERVQUAL: a multiple-item scale for measuring visitor perceptions of service quality', *Marketing Science Institute*, Working Paper Report No 86–108, August.

Reynolds, P. (1996) 'Whose yield is it anyway? Compromise options for sustainable boat tour ventures', in *Proceedings of the First Annual International Yield Management Conference*, Birmingham College of Food/Napier University, Walton Hall, Stratford-upon-Avon.

Stevens, P., Knutson, B. and Patton, M. (1995) 'DINESERVE: A tool for measuring service quality in restaurants', *Cornell Hotel and Restaurant Administration Quarterly*, 36, 2, 56–60.

Stewart, S. and Johns, N. (1996) 'Total quality: an approach to managing productivity in the hotel industry', in *Managing Productivity in Hospitality and Tourism* (1995) (edited volume from IAHMS Conference), London: Cassell.

Teas, R. K. (1993) 'Consumer expectations and the measurement of perceived service quality', *Journal of Professional Services Marketing*, 8, 2, 33–54.

MODEL QUESTIONS

1. Discuss the advantages and disadvantages of the expectancy disconfirmation paradigm as a means of understanding service quality in heritage attractions.

2. What practical issues are involved in measuring service quality in heritage attractions, using a customer questionnaire?

3. Having measured service quality in a heritage attraction, what steps can a manager take to improve and develop performance?

CHAPTER 10

Productivity

John Heap

Productivity is important because it is a key determinant of value and a useful measure of organizational well-being. It is particularly useful because it offers an alternative assessment of well-being – alternative to profitability. Although profitability, perhaps the most commonly used measure, offers valuable insight into company health, its benefit lies mainly as a short-term indicator: although highly desirable, profitability is influenced too readily by external factors and short-term actions. Productivity allows an assessment of the future profitability of an organization and is a better reflection of the robustness and quality of the underlying policies and management practices.

Although the basic concept of productivity is simple, it is not an easy word to define. However, it can be relatively easily, and variably, explained. Even in one industry, it can be interpreted in many ways, all of which reflect the basic underlying concept (Sasse and Harwood-Richardson 1996). Thus, it is easily understood.

The concept of productivity was established in the eighteenth century: expressed in its most simple form it is the ratio of output to input. In manufacturing industry, this ratio is easily converted into measures of output (goods produced) and measures of input (resources consumed), and measured and analysed as a means of ensuring operational efficiency.

However, the concept of productivity can be used at a number of levels. The term is used with reference to the performance of an industry, of a region, of a nation – such 'global' measures are used as the basis of performance and competitiveness benchmarks. The productivity of service industries, here, is of growing importance as they contribute an increasingly large percentage of national gross domestic product.

Because of its nature, productivity is not an absolute. Productivity is only 'good' or 'high' when compared to competitors or when compared to the productivity of the organization in a preceding period. Thus productivity measurement and improvement needs to take place over reasonably long periods and in a consistent manner if real success (or failure) is to be identified. This is, of course, an advantage: organizations should be considering the productivity of their operations on a continual basis.

The study of productivity and the use of productivity improvement techniques has largely, and perhaps not surprisingly, followed the major trends in organization and management theory. Thus, scientific management in the early part of this century resulted in the systematic analysis of work in order to identify its basic components: work can then be rationalized and its ineffective components removed. This analytical approach to productivity improvement was extended in the post-World War II era to the organizational level, when structures were deemed to be important factors in determining efficiency. Detailed work measurement became popular, largely as the basis of payment-by-results schemes, but also as an aid to evaluating alternative methods of working and as the basis for accurate job estimating and costing.

The 1960s and 1970s saw the development of industrial behavioural science – and with it came the realization that human beings were more complex than mechanical equipment, their effectiveness being determined by such vague notions as their working inter-relationships and levels of satisfaction and motivation. Thus, attention on the productive use of resources moved from the task carried out to the individual (and groups of individuals) carrying out the task.

The 1980s and 1990s have brought the productivity movement up-to-date: firstly, by almost denying the concept of productivity and insisting that quality is the major determinant of organizational well-being – and then, on reflection, by realizing that quality is perhaps simply a component of productivity, a complex concept with no quick and easy answers. Thus, all of the above approaches have merit. It is necessary to analyse the work undertaken – to break it down into components that can themselves be analysed to see if they can be eliminated, modified or assisted. But it is also important to look at 'non-work'; in many systems there is considerable wastage of time and effort through delay, system faults, unco-ordinated working, poor communication, poorly trained staff, quality defects and so on. These also need to be addressed. Quality working systems produce quality products (and services) and are highly productive.

The resources dealt with are essentially:

- materials;
- physical plant and equipment;
- energy;
- direct labour;
- indirect labour;
- general overheads.

However, for most service industries, the primary resource input is labour, and productivity is seen most often as a measure of labour utilization. In such industries, attempts have been made to use the productivity ratio in the same way as in manufacturing – using simple output/input measures such as meals per hour in fast-food establishments. However, in many service industries it is difficult to express the output component of the productivity ratio in terms of simple measures – and a 'meta-measure' of value-added, of revenue generated is often used to represent output. This raises interesting questions, addressed below, about the way in which value is measured. Value is more than simple utility: it encompasses 'quality' measures. A 'good meal' does more than simply nourish.

Productivity in the service sector has long been regarded as lower than that in manufacturing, although it is possible to argue that productivity gains in certain service industries such as banking have been quite dramatic in the last decade. However, within the service sector productivity in the tourism sector is still generally regarded as being low. As a rule, the net value added per employee in a high-class urban hotel is three to four times less than in the case of a bank employee (OECD 1995).

Of course within banking, labour productivity has increased markedly because there have been massive strides in rationalization of service and because capital (in the form of technology) has been substituted for labour in many areas. In tourism, there are some areas which are relatively open to such rationalization and substitution – yield management, portion control, reservation systems, etc. – but others remain doggedly (and often quite properly) bespoke and labour intensive. Ironically, it can be argued that the hospitality and tourism sector (including the heritage sub-sector) generally employs lowly-qualified staff carrying out relatively unskilled work – just the kinds of labour that were first mechanized out of manufacturing and then financial services. Of course, in those industries, the numbers involved (and especially the numbers involved in any one location by any one organization) were sufficiently large to justify the level of investment required: this is almost never so in the heritage industry. This does not mean that the potential benefits of technology should be ignored: indeed, there is evidence that the heritage industry is starting to recognize a role for technology in both productivity improvement and enhancing visitor satisfaction. The Heritage Lottery Fund in the UK, for example, is undertaking a research study in 1997/98.

> ... to assist in developing a policy framework and funding guidelines to support the Heritage Lottery Fund's wider powers under new legislation to fund projects involving:
> • compilation and dissemination of information about the heritage;
> • the encouragement of study, understanding and enjoyment of the heritage.

As part of the brief for the research study, it is explained that these new purposes, taken with the HLF's established role in funding conservation of the heritage, imply that information technology will play a much greater part in future HLF grant activity. The study will examine, amongst other issues, the possible future use of image datasets, and the use of interactive on-site and on-line systems.

Schmenner (1995) outlines some of the different challenges to managers arising from the differing nature of service industries, and in particular from the degree of labour intensity. In, for example, highly labour-intensive operations, there is a paramount importance attached to the management of staff – hiring, firing, training, developing, deploying, scheduling etc. However, he points out that labour-intensive operations have an inherent flexibility that cannot be matched by capital-intensive operations. This degree of flexibility can also be difficult to maintain when technology is substituted for manual labour.

It is important to learn lessons from other related (and not-so-related) industries. HVAs, for example, have much in common with the retail industry – and many HVAs have particular synergy with the more modern manifestations of retailing – the hypermarket and retail park, with their out-of-town location, and insatiable demand for car parking. Indeed, many HVAs rely on retailing for a major secondary income stream. It is worth examining how the local supermarket attracts its customers, organizes its displays, targets its special offers, rewards regular customers, etc.

Treating the concept of (added) 'value' as the numerator of the productivity ratio allows attention to be focused on the outputs of a process. Accepting that much of the activity within tourism is labour intensive and there is limited (but still important) ability to control labour costs, it is necessary to consider addressing productivity improvement on the basis of adding additional value. Customers do not buy 'quantity' and thus, even in those industries where output can be easily measured in quantitative terms, it should not be regarded as the exclusive component of the productivity numerator. Organizations selling goods and services most often operate in some form of competitive marketplace (even if, as with some visitor attractions, they are competing for their customers' money against alternative leisure pursuits) in which the customer selects the goods or services on the basis of some vague, even unknown, criteria which are aggregated into the concept of 'value'. In terms of productivity, the components of value are the 'top-line factors' affecting the productivity ratio (Heap 1992).

Another methodology for addressing the concept of added value is that of importance-performance (IP). This is a popular analytical tool in areas such as financial services, health care and education (Vaske et al. 1996). IP analyses are concerned with the importance individuals attach to a given set of attributes and how well the organization performs with respect to those attributes. For example, in education a study of student satisfaction with various facilities and services should be informed not only by the level of satisfaction (measured by the 'scores' attributed to the performance of each of these facilities and services), but also to the degree of importance attached to each by the students. High marks on unimportant issues obviously carry less weight; low marks on important issues need to be addressed. For a HVA, the attributes (facilities and services) will include the 'added value' facilities such as information displays, toilets, catering, helpfulness of staff, etc. Surveys to establish IP ratings can help management identify those areas (considered important by visitors) that need attention. This approach works best where visitors have a similar motivation for visiting (this is often so in a HVA). However, even where this is not so, there are approaches to IP analysis that attempt to accommodate non-homogeneous visitors. One problem with establishing the views of visitors from surveys is that it is difficult to get the views of visitors about parts of the attraction that are not yet in place. Thus, if investment in additional facilities or services is being contemplated – and there are different possible targets for that investment – visitors may find difficulty in making comparative judgements about proposed enhancements. The 'focus group' approach, in which a small number of visitors (real or potential) is provided with a venue (and hospitality) for a meeting in which issues and proposals can be explored in more depth, is more likely to yield useful comment.

Customer satisfaction is not a straightforward, mechanical issue. Teare suggests that satisfaction is derived from two sources: firstly, the sum of positive assessments of the various components of the product or service; and secondly from the psychological impact of the overall service. Did, for example, the consumer feel rested and refreshed after consuming the service? (Teare 1991). In the case of a HVA, there may be a need to define the nature of the overall impact that the attraction is aimed at creating (relaxation? education?) before assessing how each component contributes to it – recognizing, of course, that the aim may be to create different impacts on different types of customers (children and their parents, for example).

Whenever productivity is discussed, two other 'measures' normally follow: those of effectiveness and efficiency. These are often commonly expressed as 'doing the right things' (effectiveness) and 'doing things right' (efficiency). In the absence of simple output measures in the HVA arena, an alternative view of productivity – which helps to give a fully-rounded understanding – is the ratio of effectiveness (the ability to satisfy client needs) to efficiency (the ability to cover costs and make a profit) (Wood *et al.* 1993).

Of course, recognizing that productivity – in any of its manifestations – is a ratio provides two means of attacking productivity improvement:

1. The bottom-line, productivity (efficiency) enhancement model, using the manufacturing approach of technology transfer and process improvement.
2. The top-line, service quality (effectiveness) model – improving the likelihood of client satisfaction and adding value (thus justifying higher charges).

It may be that one of these is more appropriate in any given situation or environment – but it should be selected because it is more appropriate, not on the basis of default.

This means that, although recognizing that service industries may be different from manufacturing industries in a number of ways, and that the operation of heritage attractions may be different from the operation of other service industries, it is still possible to learn lessons from the productivity movement within manufacturing (where it first started and is probably most mature). Indeed, Schmenner (1995) draws direct analogies between 'traditional' manufacturing processes and methodologies (the concepts of factory, shop and mass production) and service industries, citing specific similarities between quoted service industries and these manufacturing processes.

'Heritage' can be, and often is, subjected to a form of 'production process' by which raw material such as land or a building undergoes a transformation to add value (Johnson and Thomas 1995). This transformation can include the addition of secondary factors such as visitor centres, shops, tea rooms, dramatic reconstructions, etc. although there is a limit to the value enhancement of such additions. For example, there is evidence that many visitors do not use high-tech presentation aids (such as tape players, computer workstations and CD-roms), much preferring 'live' displays (Prentice 1993).

If a heritage attraction is to be considered (at least temporarily) as the raw material of such a production process, it is useful to apply some of the same techniques and methodologies that would be applied in other manufacturing industries. For example, many of the key decisions in manufacturing are built around a robust and reliable sales forecast: this enables us to determine how many of the product should be made, and to what time schedules. Forecasting demand in the leisure market is equally as important, if not more so. Perhaps unfortunately, and certainly unlike in some manufacturing industries, there will not be a regular and consistent demand. Most visitor attractions are seasonal to some degree and many are at the mercy of the elements, strongly affected by weather conditions. This means that the value being created by the attraction varies – and therefore so must the resource inputs, especially the staffing levels. So the first purpose of forecasting visitor numbers is as the basis of (e.g.) temporary/peak staffing (Johnson and Sullivan 1993).

The simple aim of forecasting is to predict the most probable level of demand in the light of known circumstances (Archer 1994). Of course this assumes that there is sufficient understanding of the situation to be able to identify and quantify these 'circumstances'. Seasonal variations are possible to predict on the basis of past records. Predicting the weather is, however, slightly more problematic!

In addition to forecasting demand (usually based on past demand), forecasting (and modelling) can also be used to predict the effects of different policies and actions. Whenever a change is made to the way a visitor attraction is operated, presumably it is made in the expectation that it will 'improve' the situation – by attracting more visitors, retaining visitors for longer, extracting more from them while they are visiting, making them more likely to return, etc. Ideally, it should be possible to predict the quantitative effects of the change before any investment is made. This allows a cost/benefit analysis to be carried out. If it is not possible to estimate, however crudely, the effects on 'demand', such investment decisions become simply an 'act of faith' – never the best (but sometimes the only) basis for investment.

The comparison with manufacturing can also relate to a consideration of the potential for technology application. Placing a particular HVA operation into the appropriate category of Schmenner's comparative analysis of service industries – into Service factory, Service shop, Mass service and Professional service – (Schmenner 1995) allows the drawing of parallels with the way that technology is used within the relevant manufacturing operation. Mass services, for example, with high throughput, low customization, low flexibility delivery may be highly suitable for certain types of technology – such as that to control access and throughput.

The 'market' – in terms of the visitors attracted – is unlikely to be homogeneous. The nature of the attraction, and its location, may determine the profile of the visitors attracted – in terms of age, sex, social class, etc. The more is known of the visitors (that are most likely to be) attracted, the more secondary attractions can be targeted to them or, depending on the strategy, the more changes can be made to attract other sections of the potential market.

Typically historic and heritage site visitors are older visitors (Taylor, Fletcher and Clabaugh 1993). If an attraction wants to extend its appeal to younger visitors, it must meet their particular expectations – of enjoyment and of value. However, in attempting to increase the customer base by adding attractions for a younger market, it is important not to alienate the 'natural' market.

If additional visitors are to be attracted, it is necessary to know something about the visitors that are not attracted. Little research has been carried out into 'non-visitors', and what there is is hard to interpret since it is difficult to tell how accurately people respond to questions about what they do not do (Davies and Prentice 1995). Such information would obviously be of use in assessing latent demand.

Of course, in some circumstances it may be necessary to limit visitors: to protect the attraction itself (protection may be, for example, seasonal allowing a time for the site to recover) or to preserve the quality of the visitor experience. (Of course, price can be used to ration visitor numbers.) A well-managed site with visitors educated to 'behave properly' can sustain a higher throughput of visitors without affecting the local eco-system or the quality of the visitor experience (Mark and Moncur 1995). Remember also, that a satisfied visitor is much more likely to recommend the attraction to others.

Of course, if labour is the greatest resource (both in terms of its importance – excluding the attraction itself, of course! – and its cost) it makes sense to pay particular attention to controlling labour costs.

The general inability to 'automate out' the intensive use of labour (as has happened in manufacturing) means that there is an in-built tendency to 'cost drift'.

To counter this and control costs, organizations often resort to paying low wages and providing poor terms and conditions of employment – whilst expecting employees to provide quality service! This cannot be a recipe for long-term success built on repeat and recommended business.

Ironically, however, some HVAs make almost a virtue out of their financial non-viability and resort to the use of voluntary labour for guiding and information-giving. Although this obviously reduces labour costs, it does need careful management if it is to reduce overall costs. There is the danger of such volunteer labour (which is often part-time on a 'fragmented' attendance pattern) costing excessive amounts in ancillary costs of training, insurance, supervision, etc. The use of volunteer labour should be regarded as an alternative labour strategy rather than as a 'cheap' labour option. It can have significant advantages – for example if volunteers are on duty for relatively short time periods – in terms of providing a continually refreshed 'face' to the public.

An alternative strategy is to outsource some of the required services. Although there is an argument that a specialized service provider can take advantage of economies of scale and the flexibility inherent in size, this is often just a mechanism for passing the responsibility for wage reduction onto a third party! Concentrating simply on reduction of labour costs is a symptom that an organization is focusing on bottom-line attempts at productivity improvement, rather than on a fuller examination of both top- and bottom-line contributors to value and productivity. Poorly paid, under-valued (and often inadequately-trained) staff are unlikely to make the extra effort to add value, to communicate positively with visitors and to stimulate visitor satisfaction, repeat visits and word-of-mouth recommendations. This is, obviously, particularly important for front-line, front-of-house staff.

If reducing wage levels is not an appropriate way of addressing labour costs, there is a need to examine all the other components of 'labour' that determine the cost. The number of staff employed is the obvious parameter to control – and it must be controlled – but it is important to remember that if staff numbers are cut in reaction to (what could be) a temporary problem, those existing staff have skills and experience that may be difficult to replace when the temporary problem has been overcome. It is more effective to consider staff as a valuable asset, but nevertheless an asset that requires careful and systematic management. Thus, there is a need to examine:

- roles and structures (what people do and how they interrelate);
- training (linked to how well they do what they do, and thus a determinant of quality);
- work patterns (when and how often they do what they do);
- motivation (the degree to which they do what they do).

The aim should be to examine each of the above in order to make changes that increase the flexibility of the workforce. In order to make employees flexible, it is important to ensure that they have an appropriate range of skills (and are confident in their ability to demonstrate those skills) and feel adequately rewarded for demonstrating the full range of such skills. Thus, it may cost more – in terms of training costs, and in terms of slightly higher unit wage costs. However, the flexibility gained (in addition to any 'quality' benefits accruing from a better trained workforce) allows them to be used in different ways at different times, to have an ability to cover for absent employees, and to cover emergency situations.

Atkinson (1985) identified a number of forms of flexibility:

- functional flexibility – the versatility of individuals to handle different jobs/tasks;
- numerical flexibility – the extent to which the system allows the number of workers to be adjusted to demand/throughput levels;
- pay flexibility – the degree to which functional flexibility and/or performance are rewarded;
- distancing flexibility – the extent to which operations can be contracted out.

Any productivity review should address all these forms and should address all the components of the attraction. It has been suggested (Medlik 1980) that the attractiveness of a hotel is determined by:

- location;
- facilities;
- service;
- image;
- price.

An HVA has all the above except that location is normally a 'given'. However, 'location' of a fixed attraction can be affected by increasing accessibility, itself influenced by such issues as changing road networks, improved access routes, better local signage, etc. Thus, all of these components must be addressed in any systematic review.

An approach to productivity improvement might therefore be:

1. Understand the nature of the problem: this is important. It is necessary to understand the context of a need to improve productivity – and the broad intention of so doing. For newcomers to work analysis and productivity improvement, it may be beneficial to get outside help. The most obvious way is to employ a specialist consultant (who, if 'targeted' well enough, will have specific experience and expertise in addressing the productivity of HVAs). However, consultants can be expensive (they might claim that it can be very

expensive not to employ consultants) and so cheaper forms of help should be investigated first. These can include anything from simply reading the generic and specialist literature, to approaching industry bodies, to finding out what is on offer from your local university in the way of student projects.

2. Focus on a limited set of issues: from an understanding of the particular problem, it is necessary to decide on whether the prime need is to prioritize value, visitor numbers, visitor throughput rates, repeat visits, cost reduction or some other elements of the productivity ratio. Once this decision is taken, it is much easier to direct effort to the generation of as many ideas, involving all the HVA components identified above, as possible in this focused direction. For example, consider improving 'attractability' by:
    *   adding wet weather facilities;
    *   adding attractions;
    *   varying (seasonal) pricing;
    *   linking with other nearby (complementary) attractions (to form a heritage trail?);
    *   adding education services/facilities (this may help in obtaining grant aid!).
    Consider improving throughput by:
    *   improving accessibility;
    *   extending opening hours;
    *   increasing throughput speed (by pacing, by minimizing congestion, by routing/signing);
    *   using parallel versions – models, reproductions, simulations, VR, etc.
    Consider improving the rate of repeat visits by:
    *   multi-visit/season tickets;
    *   special events.

3. Involve employees: employees have a vested interest in the success of the enterprise; they also often have valuable ideas about how (some part of) the enterprise can be improved. They will invariably value being asked to contribute, assuming they are asked with a real view to treating their input with respect. More ideas come more easily from more people.

4. Set realistic goals: goals are important in terms of motivating action, and in terms of measuring progress.

5. Plan and then control implementation: as ever, 'the devil is in the detail'. Changes must be well planned, and then the actual changeover to the new situation must be well-organized and effectively handled.

6. Evaluate: when a particular project has been completed, it is important to reflect on both the process and the results. This reflective process should be used as a learning experience so that the next project will be more effective.

MODEL QUESTIONS

1. Service industries generally, and the heritage visitor attraction sector more specifically, are labour intensive. Discuss the degree to which it is therefore appropriate to concentrate on measuring and improving labour productivity.

2. What steps can be taken by an organization which is considered to exhibit 'poor service' to gain a reputation for 'good service'? Can this transformation be achieved whilst improving productivity?

3. Comment on the statement that in a well-managed organization, there should be no need to address productivity improvement – it happens anyway.

CHAPTER 11

Managing Supply and Demand

Gerald Barlow

Schmenner (1995), in his book *Service Operations Management*, addresses the problem of capacity management in two chapters: the first looking at approaches suitable for the management of supply and demand issues, and the second dealing with issues caused by capacity change. The purpose of this chapter is to explain the dimension and principles discussed by Schmenner that are applicable and unique to heritage visitor attractions.

STRATEGIES FOR MANAGING DEMAND

Many heritage organizations seem to accept excessive fluctuations in their demand, although this does not need to be regarded as inevitable. Service systems and techniques are available to help smooth demand patterns. Through smoothing techniques, organizations are able to reduce the cyclical variations, whilst the arrivals will still occur at random intervals.

LONG-TERM CAPACITY PLANNING

One normal approach to dealing with capacity problems is to increase the level of capacity. Most services can deal with substantial long-term capacity shortages only by increasing capacity. This type of increase will require as a minimum redesigning of layout, expansion of existing or additional facilities. This option is not, however, always available and, when it is, the cost can be considerable. For example, the current proposed plans for Stonehenge are estimated at £35–40 million. Prior to any planning process, it is essential to undertake future forecasts of existing demand, plus additional demand predictions from the new plans. It is equally necessary, when considering new capacity, that the plans take into consideration all the potential effects, such as parking and road congestion. For example, the proposed development of Stonehenge will also include the re-routing of main and access roads.

Long-term capacity planning decisions are generally strategic and will inevitably involve investments in buildings and equipment.

A significant decision for an organization is how it might provide extra capacity. One option may be major new extensions, design and layouts, dedicated to expected visitors, which may be undertaken in one clean move or in a series of incremental steps. Alternatively, it may be small-scale adjustments, to help create better facilities or improve the flows and add value to the visitor experience. It may, however, be that no real alteration is deemed appropriate or possible. Under these circumstances an organization needs to consider if it can deal with the existing high levels of demand or future predicted levels. If so, the possible alternatives may be in short- to medium-term demand management techniques, or possibly using alternative entertainment facilities appropriate to the site and environment. Examples such as balloon events in the gardens, steam engine meetings and falconry exhibitions are aimed at creating alternative attractions and diversions during peak demand periods.

However, many managers within the heritage industry will seldom if ever have the opportunity or problems of considering long-term capacity planning. The facilities, size and design is in itself fixed and the reason for its existence within the sector, and its demand, is related to this fact.

SHORT- TO MEDIUM-TERM CAPACITY PLANNING

This area of an organization relates to the methods used in attempting to match supply sources and demand. There are two main options available outlined in Figure 11.1:

1.   To try to adjust the organization's resources to meet demand.
2.   To try to manage demand, in order to avoid the need for any changes in resources.

The methods of managing demand can vary from simple approaches to very sophisticated techniques. The period that medium-term capacity management relates to, varies from weeks to many months.

Managing demand is often seen as the best solution for service operations in areas where inventory cannot be stored, whereas permitting the management of capacity to follow demand is seen as the preferred method by successful organizations who can store inventory.

Partitioning demand

Also available to demand management. Demand for the services in heritage operations or sites does not come from a single homogeneous source. In fact it is gathered from a range of different groups and types, with a range of random and pre-determined arrival patterns. For example, arrivals at Warwick Castle will range from

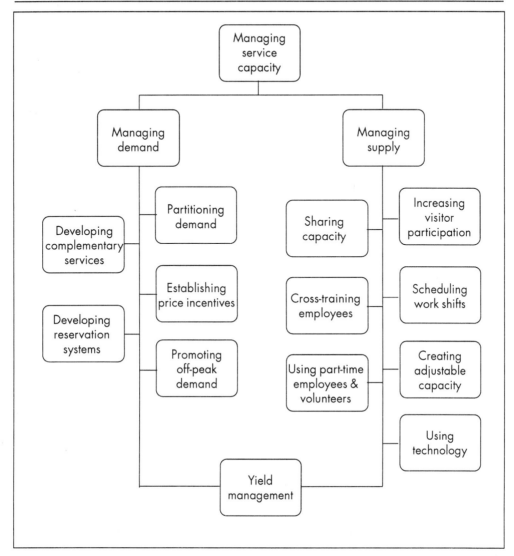

Figure 11.1: Strategies for matching supply of and demand for services. *Source:* adapted from J. A. and M. A. Fitzsimmons (1984), *Service Management for Competitive Advantage.*

the individual arriving in Warwick for another reason, a day at the races with time to spare, to the family who have planned a day out; from the group who made the spur-of-the-moment decision because it was a nice day, and seemed a good idea, to the pre-booked and planned coach group. It can also expect the random arrival of visitors with season tickets.

The daily smoothing of demand can be improved by scheduling the booking and arrival times for groups, or even the entry times for season tickets. This form of management can offer the following benefits:

1. The flow of visitors can be better planned.
2. More and varied entry points helps plan the flow of visitors.
3. Booking bulk arrivals permits better staff planning, particularly in ancillary services, entertainment, catering etc.
4. It speeds up the waiting time for the non-group visitors at the entry point, and reduces the risk of reneging.

Establishing price incentives

There are many examples of price incentives to help smooth demand:

1. Special discounts for out-of-season visits, to increase demand.
2. Special prices for early arrivals and late entry, to spread demand.
3. Limited number of group prices at peak times, and dates, to ensure satisfied visitors, and a good spread and mix of visitors.
4. Peak loaded prices for special days, to stop overcrowding and spread demand (although this is often considered a risky policy, and the preferred one is reducing prices on other days).
5. The use of mid-week price structures.
6. Special process for groups at off-peak times.

Many organizations appear reluctant to use the pricing mechanism for fear of losing visitors, but fail to identify the fact that overcrowding is likely to cause complaints and loss of future business, through word of mouth and loss of reputation. Whereas, if the heritage site is truly unique, then the clients will undoubtedly still visit on an alternative date.

Promoting off-peak demand

In addition to pricing, creative use of off-peak capacity results from investigating different sources of demand. For example encouraging group visits, or special events for quiet periods. Special prices for groups as introductory services, or to encourage future visitors, for example school parties, which may well encourage future visits with families.

Developing complementary services

As a complementary service, it is possible to offer additional services to encourage better off-peak demand, services such as exhibitions, displays, and sporting or similar events. Although popular at all times, it would be inappropriate to offer these at peak times, if capacity is already exceeded at these times. However, these services can increase demand at quiet times, or offer alternative extra opening periods, for example the open-air theatre performances or music concerts in many heritage sites during normally closed hours.

Developing reservation systems

Although widely used in many sectors of the service industries, this is an area often ignored, or felt inappropriate by many in the heritage sector. True it is difficult or all but impossible to apply to the large volumes of individual families or small groups of visitors. However, it is still a method that needs serious consideration for adoption by medium- and large-sized parties, as does the possibility of having separate points of admission and entry for such groups.

STRATEGIES FOR MANAGING SUPPLY

For many heritage organizations, demand cannot be smoothed very effectively. Therefore, control must come from adjusting service supply to match demand. Several strategies can be used to achieve this goal.

Increasing visitor participation

This is an area where many service industry organizations have achieved great benefits. For example, entry systems do not need to be fully manned; the type of ticket system used in London's underground could be adopted, as the pricing would be quite simple, with a single service area for visitors needing attention or assistance. Self-service food counters in catering outlets permit the customer to feel involved and not simply part of a waiting process, and reduce staffing levels. Similarly, visitor participation can be seen in the increasing use of techniques like touch-screen and interactive displays at heritage centres, thus saving the need for attendants in these areas.

Effective workshift schedules

By accurately scheduling the pattern of working shifts throughout the day, the profile of service supply can be made to match or shadow the appropriate demand. This will inevitably mean having a successful pattern of past demand, by using good forecasting techniques. Working patterns and schedules are vital areas of management in many service organizations. Where staff scheduling is being effectively managed, areas such as hospitals, telephone companies, banks and fast-food restaurants have resulted in a changing pattern of working hours, and provide lessons for the heritage sector. The successful service operator needs to match the working hours to the demand patterns, and so maximize the use of the workforce; it should also be remembered that a busy workforce is normally a happy and satisfied workforce. Finally, the use and value of volunteers in the heritage sector cannot be ignored. Their scheduling and planning needs careful consideration and must be linked and integrated into the entire manpower planning. A volunteer workforce can provide the appropriate levels of additional staff to cover periods of extra demand, whilst in some cases ensuring the financial viability of an operation.

Providing an adjustable capacity and alternative service location

Through effective design, a portion of capacity can be variable, with better use of space, opening of area not normally used or the use of outside facilities during peak periods, for example. This strategy requires some cross-training of staff and the use of additional part-time employees to ensure effective use of additional facilities and the knowledge of the additional facilities by all relevant employees to ensure visitor satisfaction.

Using technology

This technique ties in with many of the techniques mentioned earlier, for example the use of an effective admissions system to record numbers and time of arrivals, thus enabling better forecasting.

Other methods already discussed are the use of interactive videos and computer systems to advise and inform visitors. Simpler techniques like information boards to entertain and inform queues are simple but appropriate methods. The more advanced techniques like computer-based or electronic display systems can be used to help manage demand by increasing the speed of the programme, or slowing the programme so permitting a faster through flow. For example, a timed film display or computerized display outlining information on a section of an exhibit can be speeded up without affecting the watcher's interest, thus enabling a higher number of potential viewers.

Using part-time workers

Part-time workers have been used in the heritage sector for many years and this is a common technique of supplementing regular workers during known peak periods. However, one problem is that if it is not managed well this may create unskilled and untrained staff, who can create as many problems as solutions. The successful organization using part-time staff trains these employees to the same level and extent as the full-time employees and offers similar conditions and benefits.

Staff training

If the organization is to manage its capacity well, it is essential that the employees are fully trained, not simply in their specific job but in service standards and visitor satisfaction, in many ways to enable empowerment. That is, empower the staff to handle the visitor in all aspects of their specific job, including problem situations and problem-solving, which will result in a more satisfied visitor and employee.

Cross-training employees

Many of the heritage industry jobs are made up of a range of operations. On occasions when one operation is busy, another is idle. Cross-training employees to perform tasks in several areas creates a flexible capacity to meet localized peaks in demand.

Sharing capacity

A service delivery system often requires a large investment in equipment and facilities. During periods of under-utilization it may be possible to find other uses for this capacity. It may also be possible to arrive at a reciprocal agreement with operators within the same area, to help share the high investment costs.

Preparing for peak demand

One additional way of preparing for peak demand, as suggested by Schmenner (1995) is to decide ahead of time to create enough capacity to cover the expected demand. This may mean reducing or increasing the capacity, often by employing normally unused areas of capacity, or by better use of existing capacity by creative use of space and layout, the opening of areas not always open, or conversely, by reducing capacity at quiet times. Similarly the organization may create more available capacity by speeding up the flow of traffic throughout the site, or specific areas of bottlenecks, caused by slow through-flows. There are two main ways of justifying such actions:

1. *Margins earned at the peak.* The profits created may be so lucrative at the peak periods, or the costs of the increase capacity so low, that it pays for an organization to create this excess at appropriate times, or conversely reduce the capacity in periods of low demand, so giving a desired effect of higher usage. These policies can be easy to operate by simply opening areas not normally used, or by removing or closing less popular items, or areas to create more space for throughput or more space for additional services or exhibits. For example, an operation may have an area set aside for a specific display, running

163

alongside its traditional daily business; in this case it may be necessary to create more space for the increase in demand itself, as well as the extra exhibits (that is ,the increased space needed for the number of people). Examples of this were seen at the British Museum for the Tutankhamun exhibition in the 1970s, where little consideration was given to the crowds. Better use of space and queue management, and the improved handling of throughput of the visitors at a number of major exhibitions at the National Maritime Museum in the late 1980s and 1990s contrasts with this.

2. *Countercyclical services.* Some services and facilities have more than one use, additional and complementary. Proceeds from an off-peak or complementary service can be used to create the extra capacity needed for peak times. Additionally, they may cover the costs incurred, when the prices charged at such peak periods cannot be increased, and the extra revenue generated may not actually cover or adequately increase the profits to justify the effort and costs incurred. However, any loss in goodwill or reputation caused by poor services, or lack of services during such peaks in demand, would be very damaging. Examples of such countercyclical services may be seen in many heritage houses opening during normally closed hours for music and theatre shows, either indoors or more often in the gardens during summer evenings, or the use of heritage sites for such events as advertising campaigns and even parties and functions in the evenings.

Other major ways of preparing for increases in demand are by ensuring that the capacity chosen is being used to its maximum. This is where operational planning comes to the fore. These plans should exist to guarantee that the service operation does not fail to satisfy the visitors' desires. These plans should cover the following areas:

*   Dealing with the scheduling of labour (the number of people, the hours of work, the type of skills required).
*   Dealing with the use of equipment (which machines, and the location).
*   Dealing with the use of technology (the siting and most advantageous use).
*   Ensuring adequate and full use of inventory (including areas like shops, programmes, catering etc.).
*   Planning and dealing with maintenance (what is to be maintained and when).

Extending service hours

This has already been mentioned, but the best examples are the use of extended hours to provide complementary services, the use of the gardens for music evening, concerts or theatre events, the use of the indoor facilities for private evening functions, advertising campaigns, product launches etc. All provide an additional source of income, without affecting existing business; in fact they serve as an introduction to potential new visitors for normal business.

Forecasting demand daily

Demand needs to be forecast on a regular basis, not a weekly or even daily basis but perhaps an hourly one. With advances in electronic technology, it is possible for the terminal recording entry to do so on a timed basis, thus providing necessary basic data. Similarly this can be matched with known bookings if the organization is using a reservations system, and can result in accurate use of forecasting techniques, good staff scheduling and effective movement of a multi-skilled workforce to the correct site at the appropriate time. Similarly, shift schedules need to ensure the right staff, with the correct numbers available on the right days, thus scheduling the working days to match needed or expected peaks. This in some cases also involves matching short-term shift work (often part-time staffing) with specific forecasting like weather forecasts: where a period of hot or wet weather will result in an increase or decrease in business, this can be coupled with medium-term meteorological forecasts.

FIXED SUPPLY

In many cases, the capacity of service per time period in a heritage site is limited because of the fixed nature of the business, the fixed number of staff supplying a service, the rate of entry, the capital equipment used, or the nature of the facilities and building. The two major ways of dealing with the visitors in such cases are by the use of appointments or use of queues.

APPOINTMENTS AND RESERVATIONS

This has already been discussed, but one of the problems with appointments and reservation systems is that some visitors do not show up, and small groups and individuals (the bulk of the business) are unlikely to book in advance.

Any successful reservation system will need careful planning to decide the segments needing to make reservations, how to deal with late or early arrivals, and how to deal with 'no shows' – that is, visitors who fail to keep their reservation.

QUEUING

The result of the imbalance within supply and demand in the heritage sector is likely to lead to queuing; it is therefore important for operations managers to understand queuing, its causes and effects, and any possible ways of managing the queues.

Queuing theory suggests that, in the long run, the capacity to serve must exceed the demand for service. Failure will result in at least one of the following adjustments occurring:

1. Excessive waiting by visitors, which will result in reneging and thus a loss in demand.
2. Excessive waiting, if known or observed by potential visitors, will cause them to reconsider the need for the service and thus a decease in demand.
3. Under the pressures created by long queues, staff will attempt to speed up, thus spend less time with the visitor to increase service capacity. This may result in poor quality of service and less-satisfied visitors and poorer staff moral.
4. Sustained pressure from increased queues may result in increased pressure on the staff and visitors to hurry, which can result in the elimination of time-consuming features, a reduction in performance to a minimum, thus a reduction in overall levels of service, to attempt to increase service capacity. But, at what cost – lost or unhappy, unsatisfied visitors, and less happy staff?

The body of knowledge regarding queuing theory is a very valuable tool for an operations manager. Systems are measured and classified to permit the use of mathematical models to allow the forecasting and managing of queues. This is well covered in many texts: Cox and Smith (1968) extensively cover the mathematical methodology, whilst Murdick, Render and Russell (1990), and Fitzsimmons and Fitzsimmons (1994) apply these to the service sector. Additionally, these models are now easily available in queuing simulation models, which permit computerized simulation of complex tasks. They generate random numbers, simulate thousands of time periods in a matter of seconds or minutes, and provide management with reports that make decision-making easier. The computer model can also simulate the queuing process pictorially and permit the 'What if?' scenarios.

Psychology of queuing

Queuing psychology reflects the potential psychological effects of queues and of the management of queues. Queuing has many causes and reasons, but the ideal queue is still one which forms just as the last visitor(s) is/are about to depart, leaving the service available to the next visitor. Therefore just as the visitor is about to leave having paid his entry fee, the next visitor(s) arrives and the process repeats itself.

However, this is the ideal and at certain locations like a tourist or heritage attraction this is highly unlikely. Most attraction centres are not of the single-server, single-queue nature, nor of a multi-server, single queue, as found at the supermarket or post office. Although they may be at the entry point, the actual process may have a variety of areas which result in queues.

The psychology of queuing is summarized by Maister (1985) as:

1. *Visitor expectation versus visitor perception:* If a visitor receives better service than he/she expects, then they will depart a happy, satisfied visitor – they will convey this satisfaction on to their friends.
2. *It's 'Hard to play catch-up':* First impressions can influence the rest of the service experience, therefore, if your visitors have to wait (queue), make it a pleasant experience – or alternatively tolerable – and at the best, pleasant and productive.

To attempt to satisfy the customer and make the wait at least tolerable, the management must consider the following psychological types found in the queuing process:

1. That old empty feeling.
2. The foot in the door.
3. The light at the end of the tunnel.
4. Excuse me, but I was next!
5. They also serve who only stand and wait.

How can managers minimize complaints?

So how do heritage managers best manage this process and ensure they get the demand they need, whilst best satisfying visitor requirements and minimizing or removing the risk of complaints?

*   Treat visitors as you would like to be treated yourself.
*   Snake the queues – straight lines move slower (or appear to) mainly because of the gaps created in the snakes of the queues; but if a queue is moving, it seems to be quicker.
*   Entertain the queues.
*   Use literature, information boards.
*   Use technology, video systems, touchscreen systems etc.
*   Involve the waiting public.
*   Treat everyone the same.
*   Use the queue to mutual benefit:
    – sell to them products such as drinks, ice creams etc.;
    – conduct surveys, or hand out survey forms; you will get a guaranteed return.
*   Communicate with the queues.
*   Deal openly and honestly with the queues, particularly in advising anticipated waiting times.
*   Deal quickly and openly with any problems and complaints, but wherever possible away from the actual queue.

FORECASTING

Forecasting is a logical starting-point for most planning. Forecasting permits management to translate much of the data and information available into strategies that can give a service a competitive edge or advantage. One of the more interesting decisions is which method to engage, but in many cases before this can even be considered it is necessary to take other issues into consideration. Murdick, Render and Russell (1990) suggest that service operations need to consider the following areas alongside the cost-benefit perspective. The factors to be considered are:

1. Time:
    a: Span of the forecast.
    b: Urgency with which the forecast is needed.
    c: Frequency that the updates must be made.

2. Resource requirements:
    a: Mathematical sophistication available to the company.
    b: Computer resources.
    c: Financial resources.

3. Input characteristics:
    a: Antecedent data available.
    b: Variability or fluctuation range and frequency.
    c: External stability.

4. Output characteristics required:
    a: Detail or degree of desegregation.
    b: Accuracy.

CHOOSING A FORECASTING METHOD

Table 11.1 outlines a brief listing of the well-known forecasting methods, which can be broken down into four categories:

1. Judgement.
2. Counting.
3. Time series.
4. Associated or causal.

Table 11.2 explains these forecasting methods in greater detail.

Table 11.1: Brief description of methods. *Source:* D. M. Georgoff and R. G. Murdick, from 'Managers' Guide to Forecasting' (*Harvard Business Review*, Vol. 64, No.1, January/February 1986, pp. 110–120).

Judgement methods	Counting methods
Naive extrapolation: the application of a simple assumption about the economic outcome of the next time period, or a simple, if subjective, extension of the results of current events. *Sales-force composite:* a compilation of estimates by salespeople (or dealers) of expected sales in their territories, adjusted for presumed biases and expected changes. *Jury of execution opinion:* the consensus of a group of 'experts', often from a variety of functional areas within a company. *Delphi technique:* a successive series of estimates independently developed by a group of 'experts', each of whom, at each step in the process, uses a summary of the group's previous results to make new estimates.	*Market testing:* representative buyers' responses to new offerings, tested and extrapolated to estimate the products' future prospects. *Consumer market survey:* attitudinal and purchase intentions data gathered from representative buyers. *Industrial market survey:* data similar to consumer surveys but fewer, more knowledgeable subjects sampled, resulting in more informed evaluations.

Time series methods	Associated or causal methods
Moving averages: recent values of the forecast variables averaged to predict future outcomes. *Exponential smoothing:* an estimate for the coming period based on a constantly weighted combination of the forecast estimate for the previous period and the most recent outcome. *Time series extrapolation:* a prediction of outcomes derived from the future extension of a least squared function fitted to a data series that uses time as an independent variable. *Time series decomposition:* a prediction of expected outcomes from trend, seasonal, cyclical and random components, which are isolated from a data series. *Box-Jenkins:* a complex, computer-based iterative procedure that produces an autoregressive, integrated moving average model, adjusts for seasonal and trend factors, estimates appropriate weighting parameters, tests the model, and repeats the cycle as appropriate.	*Correlation methods:* predictions of values based on historic patterns of co-variation between variables. *Regression models:* estimates produced from a predictive equation derived by minimizing the residual variance of one or more predictor (independent) variables. *Econometric models:* outcomes forecast from an integrated system of simultaneous equations that represent relationships among elements of the national economy derived from combining history and economic theory.

Table 11.2: Overview of 15 forecasting techniques.

Dimensions/ Questions	JUDGEMENT METHODS			
	Naive extrapolation	Sales-force composite	Jury of execution opinion	Delphi technique
Time: Span: is the forecast period a present need or a short-, medium- or long-term projection?	Present need to medium need.	Short or medium.	Short or medium.	Medium or long.
Urgency: is the forecast needed immediately?	Rapid results are a string advantage of this technqiue.	Forecast can be assembled, combined and adjusted relatively quickly.	In-house group forecasts are quicker than outside experts.	Urgency seriously compromises quality.
Frequency: are frequent forecast updates needed?	Dev. short. Ex. short. Can easily accommodate frequent updates.	Dev. short. Ex. moderate. Forecasts can be quickly compiled, but data collection restricts rapidity.	Dev. short. Ex. short to moderate. Can accomplish quickly.	Dev. moderate. Ex. moderate or long. Usually used for one-time forecasts, but they can revised as new information becomes available.
Resource requirements: Mathematical sophistication: are quantititave skills limited?	Minimal: quantitative capabilities are required.			
Computers: are computer capabilities limited?	Computer capabilities are not essential.	Normal processing does not need a computer.		
Financial: are only limited financial resources available?	Very inexpensive to implement and maintain.	Inexpensive to implement and maintain.	Financial require-ments are normally for executive groups; they may be higher for outside experts.	Expense depends on make-up and affiliation of participants.
Input: Antecedant: are only limited past data available?	Some past data is required, but extended history is not essential.	Past data is helpful but not always essential.		
Variability: does the primary series fluctuate substantially?	Has difficulty adequately handling wide fluctuations.		Does not handle fluctuation well but can accommodate them if the panel meets frequently.	
External stability: are significant shifts expected among variable relationships?	Often insensitive to shifts, can reflect changes but quality can vary.		Usually aware of shifts and can reflect them in the forecast.	
Output: Detail: are component forecasts required?	Focus can be readily restricted.	Can often provide useful breakdowns.	Can reflect component forecasts, but is gen-erally concerned with aggregate forecast.	
Accuracy: is a high level of accuracy critical?	Often provides a limited practical level of accuracy.	Can be very accurate or subject to substantial bias.	May be most accurate under dynamic conditions.	

| Market testing | COUNTING METHODS | |
| | Market survey: | |
	Consumer market survey	Industrial market survey
Time: Medium.	Medium.	Medium or long.
Substantial lag is involved.	Method of gathering data may cause a substantial time lag.	
Dev. moderate. Ex. long to extended. Extended, basically used for one-time forecasts.	Dev. moderate. Ex. long to extended. Depending on methodology, frequent updates are possible, updates are provided at extended intervals.	
Resource requirements: Technical competences are generally needed.		
A computer is generally needed for analysis. Generally very expensive.	Generally expensive for good controls.	Moderately expensive, depending on conditions.
Input: Past data is useful but not essential.		Past data very helpful but not essential.
Substantial fluctuations, limit the accuracy of projections.	Handles fluctuations poorly, but tracking improves performance.	Wide fluctuations are frequently a significant concern.
Seriously weak in accommodating shifts.	Seldom reflects significant shifts.	If carefully controlled, can handle shifts well.
Output: Handles details but scope can be limited.		
Provides highest accuracy in new product and limited data conditions.	Has limited predictability with durables, somewhat better with non-durables.	Can be most accurate approach in special cases.

171

TIME SERIES METHODS

Dimensions/ Questions	Moving averages	Exponential smoothing	Time series extrapolation	Time series decomposition
Time:				
Span: is the forecast period a present need or a short-, medium- or long-term projection?	Short, medium or long.	Present need to short or medium.	Short, medium or long.	Short or medium.
Urgency: is the forecast needed immediately?	Rapid results are a string advantage of this technqiue. Dev. short. Ex. short.		Computation is quick if data is available; data-gathering can cause delays. Dev. short to mod. Ex. short.	Programme set-up and data-gathering may cause delays but once programme med. computations is quick. Dev. moderate. Ex. short.
Frequency: are frequent forecasts updates needed?				
Resource requirements:				
Mathematical sophistication: are quantititave skills limited?	Minimal: quantitative capabilities are required.			
Computers: are computer capabilities limited?	A computer is helpful for repetitive updating.		A computer is helpful for repetitive updating.	
Financial: are only limited financial esources available?	If data are readily available, out-of-pocket costs are minimal.		If data are readily available, out-of-pocket costs are minimal.	Moderately expensive to acquire, develop and modify.
Input:				
Antecedant: are only limited past data available?	Past history is essential.	Only recent forecasts and current data are required once alpha is determined.		Past history is essential with some detail required.
Variability: does the primary series fluctuate substantially?	Can accommodate fluctuations with appropriate averaging period.	Can accommodate fluctuations with suitable alpha.	Wide fluctuations result in decreased confidence in projected outcomes.	Can isolate and determine the level of component effects.
External stability: are significant shifts expected among variable relationships?	Cannot validly reflect shifts.	Cannot moderately reflect shifts with prior trend.	Cannot validly reflect shifts.	Can only moderately reflect shifts with prior trends.
Output:				
Detail: are component forecasts required?	Focus can be readily restricted.			
Accuracy: is a high level of accuracy critical?	Accurate under stable conditions.	Generally rates high in accuracy for short-term forecasts.	Normally accurate for trends and stationary series.	Effectively isolates identifiable components.

Box-Jenkins	ASSOCIATED OR CAUSAL METHODS		
	Correlation methods	Regression models	Econometric models
Time: Short, medium or long.	Short, medium or long.	Short, medium or long.	Short, medium or long.
Operationalizing programme can take time, but forecasts can be produced quickly.	Data evaluation may cause delays, but forecasts computation is quick.	Model formation takes time, but forecast computation is quick.	Model-building is lengthy, but producing forecasts is quick.
Dev. long. Ex. moderate.	Dev. moderate. Ex. short or moderate.	Dev. moderate to long. Ex. shor t to moderate.	Dev. long to extended. Ex. short to moderate. Forecast can be updated quickly if data are available.
Resource requirements: A high level of understanding is required.	A fundamental competency level is required.		A high level of understanding is required.
A computer is essential.	A computer is desirable.	A computer is essential for most cases.	A computer is essential for all cases.
Acquisition and modification costs are expensive.	If data are on hand, development costs are moderate.		Development costs are substantial; operating costs are moderate.
Input: Past history is essential with detail required. Handles variability effectively.	Technique is good if covariation is high; otherwise it is poor. Predictive accuracy is weakened if shifts occur.	May handle large fluctuations well with appropriate independent variables.	
Output: Frequently the most accurate for short to medium range forecasts.	Predicitve accuracy can vary widely.	A restricted focus might substantially comprise technique's predictive accuracy. Accurate if variable relationships are stable & proportion of explained variance is high.	Generally confined to aggregate forecasts. Gives spotty performance in dynamic environments.

173

SUMMARY

The inherent variability of demand coupled with the inability to store spare capacity creates a challenge for managers in the heritage sector attempting to achieve the best use of their available service capacity.

One approach can be to attempt to smooth visitor demand, to enable the best use of the fixed capacity. There is a variety of other potential alternatives available, such as partitioning demand, the use of price incentives, promoting off-peak demand, the development of complementary services and the potential for the use of reservation systems.

A second strategy to consider is the problems that fluctuation of demand create from the supply side. There have been a number of alternatives suggested: the development of better work-shift schedules, the potential for better use of part-time employee and volunteers, as well as cross-training and multi-skilling of the staff. Increased participation of the visitor in the service process and the use of technology to the process will reduce some of the problems created at peak times. Finally it is possible to create extra capacity by opening extra facilities for peak periods.

Despite the best plans of management and staff, situations will still occur when demand exceeds the available capacity and queues will result, here the options to help create a better experience for the waiting visitor have been discussed.

REFERENCES

Cox, D. R. and Smith, W. L. (1968) *Queues*, London: Chapman and Hall.

Fitzsimmons, J. A. and Fitzsimmons, M. A. (1984) *Service Management for Competitive Advantage*, London: McGraw-Hill.

Georgoff, D. M. and Murdick, R. G. (1986) 'From managers guide to forecasting', *Harvard Business Review*, 64, 1, January–February, 110–120.

Maister, D. H. (1985) 'The psychology of waiting lines,' in Czepiel, J. A., Soloman, M. R. and Surprenant, C. F. (eds) *The Service Encounters*, Lexington, Mass.: Lexington Press, 113–123.

Murdick, R. G., Render, B. and Russell, R. S. (1990) *Service Operations Management*, Needham Heights, Mass.: Allyn & Bacon.

Schmenner, R. W. (1995) *Service Operations Management*, Englewood Cliffs, NJ: Prentice-Hall.

MODEL QUESTIONS

1. Identify three different service environments within a heritage site, and describe the planning processes in each case. Outline how the characteristics of service contribute to the complexity of these processes.

2. What are the organizational problems that can arise from the use of part-time or volunteer employees, in trying to manage capacity planning within a heritage organization?

3. What are the possible dangers associated with developing complementary services?

CHAPTER 12

Yield Management

Ian Yeoman and Anna Leask

INTRODUCTION

The heritage visitor attraction sector plays a significant role in the structure of Scotland's tourism industry. While visitor statistics are published annually in a variety of sources, much of this data is of variable standard, based on differing definitions and general in nature.

Heritage visitor attractions range from small, unmanned individual sites to clearly defined small-scale geographical areas that people visit for a limited period of time. The attractions offer 'an experience', an intangible product that visitors participate in to varying degrees and add their own values to. It is the perishable nature of the product, in common with many aspects of the service industries, that creates some of the revenue-generating issues and necessitates a more commercial and formal manner of operation. In addition, the current operating environment and possible reduction of public funding support in the future, also necessitates further commercial awareness. Whilst approximately 6,000 visitor attractions are currently operating in the UK (BTA 1997), only 38 per cent of these attract over 10,000 visits per annum. Many heritage visitor attractions do not operate as viable commercial businesses, with many having wider community and educational aims. As a result, they often rely upon financial or voluntary assistance from local authorities or Trusts or within organizations where a small number of sites raise the money for a larger number of less revenue-generating-orientated sites. High-profile ventures can attract large amounts of funding, particularly from Lottery sources, and may raise industry standards, while few offer long-term financial viability and return on investment, resulting in little opportunity for reinvestment.

Visits to heritage visitor attractions in Scotland in 1996 have varied when compared to those in 1995. While historic houses recorded a decrease of 1 per cent, with only 16 per cent of these occurring in the shoulder months of October to March, castles recorded an increase of 8 per cent, with only 6 per cent of visits between October and March (STB 1997). It is this highly seasonal nature of business that necessitates a stronger, revenue management approach, to maximize the revenue generated during busy periods, whilst encouraging appropriate use during quiet ones.

YIELD MANAGEMENT

The Association of Scottish Visitor Attractions (ASVA) has been working closely with Scottish Tourist Board (STB) and operators to develop a number of ways to improve and support visitor attractions, particularly during the planning stages and in areas such as retailing and catering, prime revenue-generating opportunities. One such approach is yield management. Kimes (1997) defines yield management as a method which 'helps the firm sell the right inventory unit to the right type of customer at the right time, and for the right price'.

Yield management assists the operations manager to allocate undifferentiated units of capacity to available demand in such a way as to maximize profit or revenue. Yield management originated with the deregulation of the US airline industry in the late 1970s. One airline, People's Express, offered its customers low-priced tickets with minimal service. Other airlines, i.e. American, decided to compete head-on with People's Express by offering a limited number of seats at even lower fares, therefore maintaining higher fares on the remainder of their seats. By adopting this strategy, many airlines were able to squeeze People's Express business, resulting in People's Express eventually being declared bankrupt.

Yield management is a useful method for organizations that are constrained by capacity. Such unsold capacity cannot be inventoried. The HVA experience, the inventory, is a moment in time; it cannot be used again and therefore represents a missed opportunity when left unsold. The perishable nature of the HVA experience adds to the difficulty experienced in managing capacity in the sector. In addition, it should be noted that many HVAs may not wish to attract visitors and sell to maximum capacity all year round. Management conflicts between the objectives of revenue and conservation objectives, for example, may arise, with the wider aims of the organizations taking precedence. Many properties rely on the quiet, shoulder periods to undertake necessary preservation work or simply allow the building to rest.

YIELD MANAGEMENT FACTORS

Kimes' (1997) presentation of the necessary conditions and necessary ingredients were elaborated by Goulding and Leask (1997), as providing a framework for analysing the application of yield management to HVAs. Goulding and Leask concluded that visitor attractions in their widest sense do display some of the economic, operational and market characteristics that pertain to the airline and hotel business. However, the diversity of visitor attractions, in terms of both supply and demand characteristics, highlights the difficulties of applying the principles of yield management. This point was also mentioned by Middleton (1988) and Wanhill (1993) who stated that visitor attractions' cost structures typically contain a significant high element of fixed costs in relation to variable or operating costs. Furthermore, capital building costs for new attractions tend to be high in relation to annual revenue potential for many attractions (Robinson 1994). Wanhill goes on to suggest that market-orientated pricing policies are appropriate for attraction operators who have to meet the costs of servicing the investment in their attractions and the fixed costs of operation. Therefore, it is the function of pricing to optimize yield through a variety of segmentation and promotional pricing techniques in much the same way as airline and hotel operators do. Goulding and Leask (1997), in their final analysis of the application of yield management, state the application comes down to two fundamental issues. Firstly, the sector is at the mercy of a set of demand variables over which it has little influence and even less control, and secondly, there is the difficulty in solving the relationship between how visitor attractions define their capacity in sale volume terms and how they measure their unit of production.

Yeoman and Ingold (1997) discuss yield management as a process of decision support, to enable an operations manager to take decisions about the relationships of price to capacity, and vice versa. By providing the operations manager with a rational framework, a focus on the journey to optimal revenue is achieved. Therefore, by defining yield management as:

> the ability to sell the right experience to the right visitor at the right time,
> for the right price in order to maximize revenue or yield,

this enables the operations manager to be placed into the mainstream of the HVAs' decision-making activity with the emphasis on focusing decisions about the yield management equation, in order to develop HVAs' decision-making capability.

Therefore, the factors of yield management are enhanced in the next sections.

NECESSARY CONDITIONS FOR YIELD MANAGEMENT

For yield management to be adopted as an appropriate operations strategy, necessary conditions are required. These conditions include fixed capacity, high fixed costs, low variable cost, time-varied demand and units of inventory (Kimes 1997).

Fixed capacity

Yield management is designed for capacity-constrained service firms, which an HVA experience is. HVAs have a fixed capacity, which cannot be varied to deal with fluctuations in demand.

High fixed costs

Attached to fixed capacity is the additional cost of adding incremental capacity. There is high marginal cost of extending capacity beyond full production cost according to Goulding and Leask (1997). This cost is extremely expensive and cannot be rapidly adjusted to meet demand.

Low variable cost

As most of the costs are high, the additional cost of an additional visitor in unused capacity is very low. Low variable costs per visitor will vary according to the size of attraction, level of admission charge, promotional spend and market base. The sector is unique in business in having low staff costs through using volunteers as part of the visitor experience. Therefore, HVAs must understand the concept of adding extra visitors as contribution towards fixed costs.

Time-varied demand

An HVA cannot alter its capacity to match changing demand patterns. When demand varies, HVAs can concentrate on price when demand is high. When demand is low, HVAs can concentrate on volume. Independent visitors' decision to visit an attraction is usually discretionary within the destination choice and not normally time specified. This must be also seen in connection with HVAs' high reliance on the leisure market causing unpredictability in demand patterns. The success of managing time-varied demand is based upon good information management systems, in order to make decisions about yield. More emphasis needs to placed upon time utilization given the generalized nature of demand for HVAs.

Units of inventory

The unit of inventory is a perishable service or an experience caught up in the elements of physical structures of attractions. This physical permanency is the core product, but non-core amenities, such as catering and retail, provide opportunities for additional revenue. Special attractions also generate revenue in certain visitor attractions, i.e. Santa Trains (Graham *et al.* 1998). Alternatively, the unit of inventory could be defined as:

The visitor experience per visitor profile in a specific time period.

Therefore the operations management must be able to sort and place different tariff rates onto this unit of inventory.

NECESSARY INGREDIENTS FOR A YIELD MANAGEMENT SYSTEM

In order to operate a yield management system, HVAs must have market segmentation information, demand management strategies, pricing knowledge, information technology and a conservation policy.

Market segmentation

HVAs must be able to segment their market by willingness to pay. This information provides the operations manager with valuable knowledge in determining strategies in preparing for the peak and extending peaking period into off-season. It allows the operations manager to decide which visitors are time-sensitive and price-sensitive. For example, HVAs may experiment with discounts for pre-booking. At present the HVAs gear themselves towards market segmentation for the leisure and discretionary demand, with little emphasis placed on the business and corporate opportunities (Goulding and Leask 1997).

Historical demand, advanced sales and booking patterns

HVAs need to be able to anticipate low and high demand periods. Therefore detailed sales and booking data are essential. HVAs must be able to gather information on booking patterns and track future visitor purchases. At present, according to Goulding and Leask (1997), there is little evidence of operations managing capacity and advanced purchase in harmony. HVAs tend to use promotional methods to stimulate advance purchase of admission, i.e. discount vouchers and passport schemes, though they constitute a small proportion of sales. Most of advanced purchases are through intermediary sales channels. The success of any yield management system also depends on the visitor perception of the tourism area, as the success of an HVA depends on the performance of the tourism area. Demand is also influenced by the leisure day-trip patterns and activity (Goulding and Leask 1997).

Without this information it is impossible to develop a pricing policy that determines the level of discounts, specific exclusions, family tickets, multi-site tickets and membership benefits.

Pricing knowledge

In the airline industry people believe (Kimes 1997) yield management is a method by which firms change their price several times a day. But in reality, airlines rely on a rate control methods and dynamic pricing systems (Curry 1995). Yield management is a process of decision-making, enabling the operations manager to concentrate activity in determining the most appropriate price for the HVA inventory. When demand is low, discounted prices become available and when demand is high, discounted rates are unavailable. Instead of using discounts, operations managers may consider additional charges for certain aspects of the HVA experience. During the period of high demand, the focus is on price to optimize revenue. The operations manager must operate a pricing policy based upon periodicity of demand (time of day, day of the week) to maximize yield. Therefore by operating a range of tariffs, the operations manager can match demand and supply.

Information technology

In order for yield management to work, the data that assists the operations manager in making decisions about yield must be managed, accessible, accurate and useful. In order to achieve this, an appropriate information system is required. The lack of an information system is one of the largest reasons why yield management is not implemented. Therefore this is a must, as decisions taken by operations managers depend on the appropriateness of the knowledge provided.

Conservation policy

The unique nature of HVAs involves conserving the nature of the attraction, as too many visitors will erode the heritage aspects of the site and spoil the experience for present and future visitors. The operations manager has to judge a range of options in the terms of revenue generation and conservation. This is very much a process of cost-benefit analysis.

YIELD MANAGEMENT: A MODEL OF IMPLEMENTATION

A yield management approach will make a contribution towards improved revenue management within HVAs. For yield management to be effective, operations managers must adopt a proactive approach to managing of capacity. Therefore the organization must gear itself up towards a clearly defined process of yield management to enable the operations manager to concentrate and make the best decisions in the yield management process of 'selling the right experience to the right visitor at the right time, for the right price in order to maximize revenue or yield'.

Donaghy *et al.* (1997) and Lewin (1951) provide an overview of the implementation of yield management comprising three stages:

1. Unfreezing is the process whereby need for change is emphasized. This is applied within the context, for example in the promotion of a yield management

strategy as a means to increase revenue when state funding is being reduced. Managers, employees and volunteers are shown the importance of yield management and how their roles will benefit from such a strategy. Staff should be motivated to highlight the benefits of such a system and the disadvantages of historical procedures.

2. Change is the second stage. This is the transition from old to new systems. The HVA must adopt new procedures for restructuring, designing and implementing a yield management system.

3. The final stage involves refreezing in the process of new systems and procedures adopted. This ensures a continuous evaluation of yield management systems, ensuring the new systems minimize resistance to change.

Donaghy *et al.* (1997) found that developing an understanding for a yield management approach depended significantly on the training provided. Operations managers believed that clarification of the concepts, methods and aims of yield management were of primary importance. Yeoman and Watson (1997) found that organizations needed to adopt a systemic approach to yield management, placing a strategic and operational emphasis on the concepts for success to be delivered. This point is reinforced by Donaghy *et al.* (1997) and Huyton and Peters (1997), who state that yield management must be integrated into the daily management procedures for managing inventory. The yield management system adopted must be unambiguous and simple, in order to allow transferability of the concepts throughout the organization. By adopting this approach, yield management reinforces the ability of managers to improve their decision-making capability (Yeoman and Ingold 1997).

For the successful implementation of a yield management strategy, a co-ordinator needs to be appointed. The fundamental role of the co-ordinator is to ensure that yield management systems and procedures work within the HVA. They will be involved with all lines of management, employees and volunteers. They will develop functional specialists within HVAs, who will become core people in the development and implementation of yield management.

The transition from old systems to new systems is the process where resistance to change surfaces. Operations managers must be aware of reasons given by staff 'for yield management not to work'.

The main reasons identified by Yeoman and Ingold (1997) of 'why things fail' are in two forms: errors and violations. Errors are mistakes in judgements, where with hindsight a person should have done something different and the outcome is a deviation from the normal operation. Violations are acts which obstruct procedure. It can be difficult to distinguish between errors and violations in decision-making. Yeoman and Ingold (1997) also concluded that yield management systems failed because of the following reasons:

- *Organizational culture.* Many HVAs are not geared to a team approach in management decision-making. Many organizations have a clear hierarchy of decision-making authority, and a team approach is inconsistent with this.
- *Quality of decisions.* Many operations managers follow the satisficing heuristic in decision-making, i.e. they follow a course of action that yields an outcome that is good enough rather than the best possible option. Most yield decisions are influenced by social and political factors which are underpinned by the weight given to qualitative rather than quantitative information. The biggest influence is seen to be time pressure, with insufficient time available to make quality decisions.
- *Overconfidence.* Operations managers do not have the foresight to see how events might unfold. Decisions are taken based on one particular anchoring when operations managers search for the information to support a favoured course of action.
- *Flexibility of decision-makers.* Many HVAs managers involved in revenue management decisions adopt systems and procedures that are appropriate in one circumstance but not in another.

Therefore commitment to the concepts of yield management is of fundamental importance. A fundamental role of the co-ordinator must be the need for communication between the parties involved in the programme.

Yeoman and Watson (1997) highlight a systemic and holistic approach to the implementation of yield management. It can be seen from Figure 12.1 that yield management is based on three interactive subsystems: people, forecasting and strategy.

1. *Forecasting.* This is the ability to forecast accurately. Factors such as demand for tourism in the area, weather, competition and historical booking patterns influence the decision-maker's ability to forecast yield. These factors are combined with visitor information and profiles. The forecasting subsystem is an ongoing process, as information is constantly entering and leaving the subsystem.
2. *People.* The process of managing yield is basically a human activity. This requires the organization to make a commitment in terms of resources and authority to the principles of yield management. An organization should have a yield management-designated team to manage the process.
3. *Strategy.* Clear guidelines of policy are required in determining the strategies for low demand and high demand situations. Options and tactics that are sensitive to the environment of decisions are necessary. Clear guidelines are required to understand the relationship between revenue generation and conservation of the HVA.

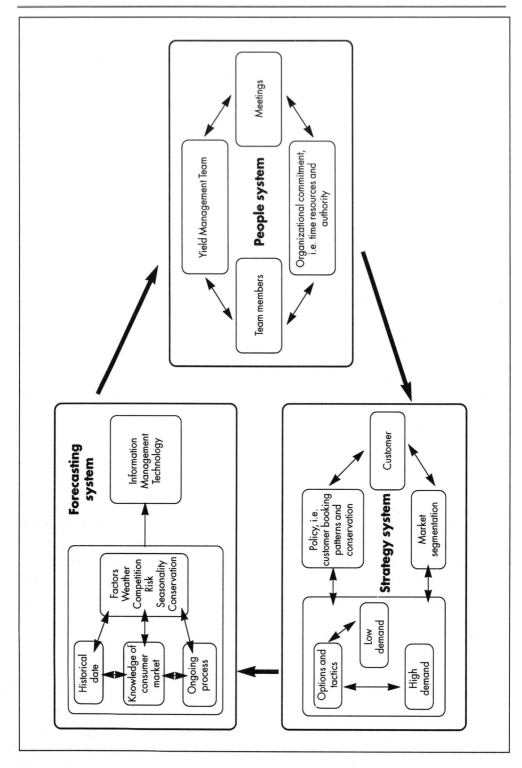

Figure 12.1: Yield management: a systems model.

By adopting the model in Figure 12.1, the operations manager is provided with a rational framework to examine the decision-making process of yield management. An holistic and systemic approach is suggested because of the inter-relationships of the sub-systems involved. The subsystems have mutual interflows, for example where outflows form the inflows of others. One subsystems residue becomes another's subsystems energy source. Therefore the success of yield management implementation depends on the mutual success of each of the subsystems. No one subsystem can operate in isolation.

The adoption of certain principles of yield management is highlighted through two case studies, namely Historic Scotland and National Trust for Scotland.

HISTORIC SCOTLAND

Historic Scotland (HS) is responsible for the care of 330 properties that are within the guardianship of the Secretary of State for Scotland. The basis of the operation is 'not for profit' and all proceeds generated at any of the 60 admission-charging properties goes towards the 'conservation and presentation' of the other sites within care. The properties range from Scotland's most popular paid entry attraction at Edinburgh Castle, to much smaller, unmanned sites such as the Ring of Brodgar in Orkney. In income-generating terms, Edinburgh Castle is the most successful property, generating £6.25 million in 1996, with £4.5 million from admissions and £1.75 million in retail. These figures represent an on-going increase in visitor activity, partly as a result of the expansion of retail and catering facilities in recent years. In terms of visitor numbers, Edinburgh Castle recorded a total of 1.2 million in 1996, followed by Stirling Castle at approximately 400,000 and Urquhart Castle on 250,000. Six further properties attract approximately 50,000 visitors per annum, with the remaining 50 income-generating properties recording approximately 10,000 visitors per annum. A representative figure relating to the spend-per-visitor split would be two-thirds on admission, plus one-third on retail/catering (Leask and Goulding 1996).

The agency was reviewed in 1994, resulting in the setting of 'key performance targets', relating to visitor numbers, income and the primary area of the protection and preservation of Scotland's built heritage. The commercial revenue objectives are pursued via three main means:

- marketing initiatives with travel trade;
- development of on-site retailing and catering;
- the implementation of a central information system which monitors costs, revenues and budgets on individual property, regional and state basis.

Visitor numbers and revenue targets are still set centrally, though with involvement of the individual property managers, with a business plan now being produced for each property. Visitor spend is monitored monthly and has recently shown dramatic increases in retail spend, without substantial increases in admission. Prices are usually increased bi-annually, with the aim of increasing revenue, whilst continuing to offer value for money.

In 1997 the pricing strategy included:

- Price banding monuments into five main adult price bands covering 56 of the 60 properties. Edinburgh Castle, Stirling Castle, Urquhart Castle and Whithorn Priory each have higher price levels due to their national significance.
- Streamlined market pricing with three standard admission charge levels per property: adult, reduced (which included disabled and student categories for the first time in 1998), and child.
- Joint ticketing for properties in close proximity, for example Stirling Castle and Argyll's Lodgings.
- Scottish Explorer Tickets covering admission to all HS properties over a 14-day period.
- Group discounts.
- Voucher incentive schemes offered to accredited tour operators.
- Membership rates for Friends of HS, memberships standing at approximately 40,000, the highest level to date.
- Free entry for pre-booked educational parties.
- Participation in the Great British Heritage Pass scheme, for overseas visitors.
- Participation in STB promotions such as Autumn Gold and Spring into Summer.

Another area where this is seen is in the pricing policy, which is standardly limited to set groups. The only flexibility apparent is that the 'reduced' group requirements are being expanded in 1998. HS is the largest operator of heritage visitor attractions in Scotland and is fully aware of the increasingly competitive environment. Market research indicates a 97 per cent satisfaction rate from visitors, though there is no room for complacency. The continued improvement of the quality of the product, visitor experience and staff awareness are all issues currently being considered, with constant market research activity being carried out. The introduction of 'mystery visits' to properties is only one of the range of methods employed. Whilst it is acknowledged that a more commercial approach to management may be appropriate, with areas such as events suitable for development, these need to be viewed in light of the aims of the agency – to 'preserve and protect' the properties – with decisions not always based on a return on investment basis. This could manifest itself through further analysis of pricing policy, facility layout and labour use to develop the properties in a suitable manner – ensuring an improvement in the customer experience plus realization of the revenue targets.

NATIONAL TRUST FOR SCOTLAND

The National Trust for Scotland (NTS) is a voluntary organization with charity status, established by an Act of Parliament in 1931. Its remit includes the care and conservation of landscapes, historic buildings and their contents, and the promotion of these attractions. The NTS had 230,000 members in 1997 and has a mutual free entry policy for members of the National Trust in England and Wales. The NTS is responsible for 120 properties in total, with 44 of those having a retail presence, of which 22 also have catering facilities. Only 20 properties have a significant level of trade, with investment dictated by the anticipated return and the need to maintain visitor experience.

They are actively involved in the process of operating their properties to allow access to the public, generate revenue plus conservation and preservation. This means that some properties may not be operated purely to generate revenue, if conservation is given priority, shown through the general policy to close many properties in the winter to allow conservation work and allow the buildings/sites to rest. One main service operations feature adopted by NTS is to charge a higher price for access to properties at risk – for example Craigievar Castle, where higher prices and timed ticketing have been introduced to reduce the visitor numbers in the building. This is an example conserving the limiting demand to conserve the experience, in that demand can be influenced by increasing the price, to still ensure revenue generation, whilst reducing the pressure on the service product itself. NTS agrees individual management plans for each property via consultation with the Managing Director for Trading, the management group and individual property managers. At a few sites, where visitor numbers have an adverse effect on conservation or enjoyment of the visitor experience, carrying capacities are set to limit visitor numbers. It is at these sites that yield management strategies could be employed to achieve the most appropriate use of the resources, whilst still achieving required revenue targets. The most popular methods currently adopted by the NTS include variable pricing, timed ticketing and restricted entry to a maximum number at any one time.

The NTS is actively involved in Autumn Gold and Spring into Summer – Scottish Tourist Board (STB) initiatives – and has developed a pricing structure based on property bandings and pricing sectors. For example, the family ticket is calculated on the basis of two adults plus one child, although the visitors may take up to six children per two adults. Again, this is partly an indication of the wider educational and community aims of the NTS. The membership scheme also admits visitors on reduced prices, with 230,000 members recorded in 1997. The membership subscription system is becoming increasingly important in the push to generate income to support the conservation work. It can be clearly seen that although increasing commercialization may affect the operation of NTS properties, through development of yield management, retailing and catering outlets, the key priority for the organization is conservation.

CONCLUSIONS

Yield management offers HVAs an opportunity for a focused methodology for improving revenue that integrates the characteristics of the HVA experience. The HVAs sector is both distinct and diverse in the style of attractions offered to the visitor. The benefits of yield management are drawn from the hotel and airline industries, but tailored to suit the characteristics of HVAs. Many visitor attractions serve broader objectives, other than business, but the financial pressures are focusing the operations manager to come up with imaginative and new ways of managing sites. A yield management approach allows decisions to be taken in an holistic and systemic manner. Before a yield management system can be implemented both necessary conditions and ingredients need to be in place. For successful implementation of a yield management strategy, a systems model approach is suggested based upon strategy, information and people for successful implementation.

REFERENCES

British Tourist Authority (1997) *Sightseeing in the UK 1996*, London: BTA.

Curry, R. E. (1995) 'A market level pricing model for airlines', *Scorecard Technical Brief Second Quarter*, Atlanta: Aeronomics.

Donaghy, K., McMahon-Beattie and McDowell, D. (1997) 'Implementing yield management: Lessons for the hotel sector', *International Journal of Contemporary Hospitality Management*, 9, 2, 50–54.

Huyton, J. and Peters, S. (1997) 'Application of yield management to the hotel industry', in Yeoman, I. and Ingold, A. (eds) *Yield Management: Strategies for the Service Industries*, London: Cassell.

Goulding, P. and Leask, A. (1997) 'Scottish visitor attractions: Revenue verse capacity', in Yeoman, I. and Ingold, A. (eds) *Yield Management: Strategies for the Service Industries*, London: Cassell.

Graham, J., Morrison, D., Yeoman, I. and Leask, A. (1998) 'Santa trains', in Leask, A. and Yeoman, I. (eds) *Heritage Visitor Attractions: An Operations Management Perspective*, London: Cassell.

Kimes, S. (1997) 'The principles of yield management: An overview', in Yeoman, I. and Ingold, A. (eds) *Yield Management: Strategies for the Service Industries*, London: Cassell.

Leask, A. and Goulding, P. (1996) 'What price our heritage?', in Robinson, M., Evans, N. and Callaghan, P. (eds) *Managing Cultural Resources for the Tourist*, Sunderland: Centre for Travel & Tourism.

Lewin, K. (1951) *Field Theory in Social Sciences*, New York: Harper & Row.

Middleton, V. (1988) *Marketing in Travel and Tourism*, Oxford: Heinemann.

Robinson, K. (1994) 'Future for tourism attractions', *Insights*, March, D29-40, London: English Tourist Board.

Scottish Tourist Board (1997) *Visitor Attraction Survey 1996*, Edinburgh: STB.

Wanhill, S. (1993) 'Attractions', in Cooper, C., Fletcher, J., Gilbert, D. and Wanhill, S. (eds) *Tourism Principles and Practice*, London: Pitman.

Yeoman, I. and Ingold, A. (1997) 'Decision-making', in Yeoman, I. and Ingold, A. (eds) *Yield Management: Strategies for the Service Industries*, London: Cassell.

Yeoman, I. and Watson, S. (1997) 'Yield management: A human activity system', *International Journal of Contemporary Hospitality Management*, 9, 2, 80–83.

MODEL QUESTIONS

1. Evaluate either Historic Scotland's or National Trust for Scotland's approach to yield management using Yeoman and Watson's (1997) model.

2. How would you measure the success of the implementation of a yield management system for an HVA?

3. Identify the issues both for and against the applicability of yield management in HVAs.

CHAPTER 13

Risk and Environment

Neil McGregor

INTRODUCTION

The operations function of the heritage visitor attraction involves the management of resources devoted to the customer experience. Harris (1989) characterizes the major resource inputs to any operational system as skills, physical assets, information, materials and finance. He further defines physical assets to include machinery, vehicles, computers and other office equipment. In the current chapter it is argued that such resource definitions are inappropriate to the operation of HVAs as they fail to take account of the critical role that the heritage assets themselves play in the service delivery system and, ultimately, the quality of the customer experience.

In situations where the heritage resource itself is not managed effectively, the likely outcomes will be either financial and economic benefits foregone, damage to, or destruction of, the heritage resource, or both (Tunbridge and Ashworth 1996). The current chapter therefore attempts to identify how the heritage resource issue can be integrated into the service delivery system via the operations management function. Based on the principles of risk management, this chapter identifies the critical balance required between organizational (financial and economic) and environmental (heritage resource) risks in order to promote the sustainable management of the service delivery process in HVAs.

The purpose of this chapter is to consider how, at the operations level, HVA managers can achieve organizational objectives in terms of economic performance while preserving the quality of the heritage resources involved. The specific objectives of the chapter are:

- to identify the nature of risks associated with the operation of HVAs;
- to develop a framework by which such risks can be assessed; and
- to outline a range of options designed to promote the effective management of those risks at the operations level.

SERVICE PROCESS DECISIONS

Schmenner (1995) defines service processes according to the degree of labour intensity and the degree of interaction and customization involved. HVAs, being a heterogeneous group of service organizations, do not fall neatly into any one of the four categories identified by Schmenner.[1] Potentially, therefore, HVAs may face a diverse range of management challenges. A critical consideration in the choice of service process lies in the productivity and capacity of the heritage assets which form the basic element of the HVA service product and, derived from that, visitor expectations relating to the type of service available.

Consider, for example, a heritage attraction such as an historic building. If at the strategic level preference is given to a *service factory* approach, that would imply no guided tours and little staff-visitor contact. This would suggest that operations managers would face the challenges associated with low labour intensity such as making investment decisions (those relating to interpretive provision and security, for example) and managing fluctuations in demand. Challenges associated with low interaction/customization would be likely to involve activities to promote visitor satisfaction and attention to the physical environment, such as problems with litter, vandalism, theft, and wear and tear.

A *professional service* approach, however, would involve small-group guided tours of the building. The hazards of the service factory approach would be replaced by challenges associated with high labour intensity such as hiring, training and scheduling of the workforce. In addition, high interaction/customization would result in challenges such as controlling staff costs while maintaining quality of experience and minimizing employee turnover.

The potential to operate on a service factory basis is likely to be severely limited in the case of HVAs utilizing resources which are highly fragile and susceptible to visitor impacts – as the risks of resource damage are likely to become unacceptable. At the same time the ability to operate certain HVAs on a professional service basis would be equally inappropriate due, for example, to the magnitude of the site, the number of entry and exit points and the sheer volume of visitors. It is likely that such an approach would lead to financial risks associated with the high costs involved. In both situations it is unlikely that customer satisfaction would be maximized.

It is clear that both strategic and operating decisions in HVAs must take account of the heritage assets upon which the service product is based. If managers are to maximize the long-term benefits derived from the heritage resource, then operations must be both economically and environmentally sustainable.

SUSTAINABILITY AND
HERITAGE VISITOR ATTRACTIONS

The concept of sustainability requires 'that the conditions necessary for equal access to the resource base be met for each generation' (Pearce *et al.* 1991). The concept of sustainability is now widely recognized as a societal goal potentially consistent with the objectives of commercial enterprises, economic development agencies, conservation bodies and local communities;

> Most successful tourism destinations today depend upon clean physical surroundings, protected environment and often the distinctive cultural patterns of local communities. Destinations that do not offer these attributes are suffering a decline in quality and tourist use.
>
> (McIntyre *et al.* 1993)

At the organizational level, however, managers have found it difficult to relate the broad concept of sustainability to their own activities. The management challenge, of attempting to balance commercial and resource management objectives, represents a microcosm of the far wider issue of sustainability. Cohen (1978) highlights the needs of HVAs to generate income from visitors and to conserve the heritage product which those visitors come to experience.

The process of commodification of environments[2] into marketable heritage products introduces the potential for conflict in the management of heritage visitor attractions. If managers get the balance wrong then either income levels will be too low to sustain the organization commercially, or visitor pressures will be so great that the heritage resource becomes damaged in some way (Berry 1994).

RISK AND HERITAGE VISITOR ATTRACTIONS

Risk can be defined as a concept involving the possibility of an adverse outcome *and* uncertainty surrounding the likelihood, timing or magnitude of that adverse outcome.[3] The UK Department of the Environment (1995) defines risk as 'a combination of the probability, or frequency, of occurrence of a defined hazard and the magnitude of the consequences of the occurrence'.

The terms 'hazard', 'consequences' and 'probability' may also be defined as follows:

*   *Hazard* – a situation that could lead to harm.
*   *Consequences* – the adverse effects as a result of a realized hazard.
*   *Probability* – the likelihood of a particular event taking place.

In the context of HVAs, two distinct forms of risk can be identified, organizational risk and environmental risk. To promote the sustainable and efficient management of HVA resources it is critical that these risks are both recognized and managed effectively.

Organizational risk

Organizational risk issues can be defined as a situation whereby visitor numbers, and revenues, are at such a level that the organization fails to meet its financial, or wider economic, performance objectives. In the framework of heritage *production* (Figure 13.1), adapted from Tunbridge and Ashworth (1996), commodification of heritage resources involves the investment of human, financial and physical capital. Most investment decisions are characterized by commitment of financial resources in the uncertain expectation of obtaining higher financial returns in future periods.

Ownership, whether public, private, voluntary/charitable or some combination of these, is likely to influence strategic organizational objectives, and hence activities, of HVA operations managers. It is likely, however, that the attraction be required to generate some level of income to contribute towards costs (such as preservation costs), cover all costs or generate profit. Declining funding and the removal of other support from government means that revenue generation is increasingly important in publicly-owned HVAs. The risk to investors will be the possibility that the resources invested in the HVA will not yield a suitable rate of return, with consequent repercussions for the HVA management team.

In order to calculate the rate of return and assess commercial viability it is usual to perform an appraisal based on techniques such as *discounted pay-back* and *net*

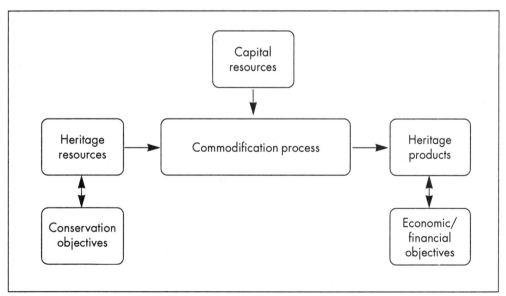

Figure 13.1: The commodification process. *Source:* adapted from Tunbridge and Ashworth (1996).

present value. These techniques emphasize the importance of short-term financial returns in investment decision-making and provide far lower weight to cashflows arising in the longer term. This leads to a preference for rapid resource development relative to a resource conservation approach.[4]

Environmental risk

The concept of environmental risk, in the context of HVAs, relates to the situations whereby the heritage resources upon which the heritage product is based are damaged in some way. The realization of environmental hazards in HVAs is, unfortunately, all too common:

- In the Galapagos Islands, with its unique eco-system, over one hundred non-native species of flora and fauna have been introduced (Woodley 1993).
- White-water rafting has been linked to declines in the Harlequin Duck population in the Banff/ Bow Valley National Park in Canada (Woodley 1993).
- Damage to coral reef eco-systems such as those in Australia (Davis and Tisdell 1995), French Polynesia (Gabrie *et al.* 1994), and the Red Sea (Prior *et al.* 1995), are well documented.
- Damage to the Stonehenge site in England has been widely reported.
- Deterioration in the prehistoric cave art at Lascaux in France (Delluc and Delluc 1984).
- The problems associated with visitor pressures in historic towns and cities such as Venice in Italy and Canterbury in England (Murphy 1997).

The risk trade-off

While the operational situation may not be as clear-cut in practice, it is useful to assume that as organizational risk increases, environmental risk falls, and vice-versa. This trade-off situation is illustrated in Table 13.1. In this scenario it is clear that the ideal *visitors per hectare* figure would lie in the range 201–300: anything below that level would represent an unacceptable risk in terms of the achievement of organizational (financial and economic) objectives, whereas a figure greater than 300 would represent an unacceptable environmental (resource) risk on site.

CAPACITY AND DESTINATION LIFE-CYCLES

Haywood (1991) suggests that the concept of the destination life-cycle is widely accepted as an illustration of the typical pattern of growth for a wide variety of tourist destinations. Butler (1980) states that this pattern indicates the need for long-term planning in order to extend the tourism product/ destination life over a longer period,

Table 13.1: Organizational and environmental risk trade-off.

Visitor numbers per hectare	Organizational risk level	Environmental risk level
0–100	Unacceptable/ Intolerable	Negligible
101–200		Acceptable/ Tolerable
201–300	Acceptable/ Tolerable	
301–400		
401–500	Negligible	Unacceptable/ Intolerable
500+		

Tourist attractions are not infinite and timeless but should be viewed and treated as finite and possibly non-renewable resources. They could then be more carefully protected and preserved. The development of the tourist area could be kept within predetermined capacity limits, and its potential competitiveness maintained over a longer period.

The life-cycle concept relating to heritage visitor attractions goes beyond the basic product life-cycle applicable to typical goods and services.[5]

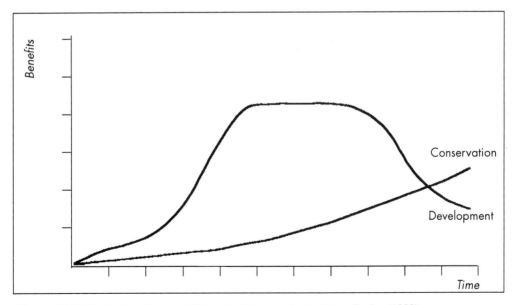

Figure 13.2: The destination area life-cycle. *Source:* adapted from Butler (1980).

The development scenario exhibits an initial *introduction stage* leading on to rapid *growth, consolidation, stagnation* and ultimately *decline,* or *rejuvenation* if there is action taken to improve the heritage product. While stagnation and decline may be a natural process associated with the appeal of substitute products, the decline may well be exacerbated by the social, cultural and environmental problems associated with the rapid, uncontrolled growth in visitor numbers (Martin and Uysal 1990). In other words, resource carrying capacity levels will have been exceeded, leading to the eventual demise of the attraction itself in the longer term. The conservation option will not create the short-term cashflows associated with development, although in the longer term the sustainable net benefits are potentially far greater.

These alternative scenarios imply that the optimal strategic approach is one of conservation. If environmental risk is reduced then the long-term prospects for the HVA as an income-generating venture are enhanced and long-term organizational risk is reduced. The problem, however, arises in the short term. At the strategic level, for the reasons outlined previously, there will be pressure for enhanced economic performance, with a consequent short-term reduction in organizational risk. Increasing visitor numbers, however, create additional pressure on the heritage resource and hence an increased risk that the resource will be damaged.

THE RISK MANAGEMENT PROCESS

Beck (1992) suggests that, in order to determine current actions, risks should be recognized, their implications identified and preventative action taken to both reduce the probability of hazards being realized and manage any adverse consequences arising from them.

Risk assessment

The UK strategy for sustainable development, HM Government Cm 2426 (1994) suggests that, where potential resource damage is uncertain and significant, the precautionary principle should be adopted. Risk assessment is designed to assist in the application of the precautionary principle by identifying the potential hazards, and their consequences, associated with an intention or action. In the context of environmental protection the UK Department of the Environment (1995) provides a framework for the analysis and management of risks adapted in Figure 13.3.

The model indicates that risk assessment will involve a series of key stages.

1. Define proposed actions

In the context of HVAs the *actions* may include such activities as opening a cave decorated with prehistoric art to the public or implementing a marketing campaign designed to increase visitors in off-peak periods. This stage in the risk management

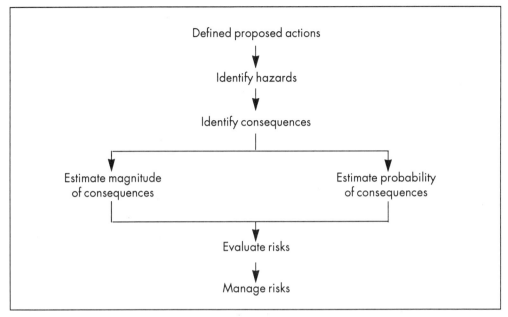

Figure 13.3: The risk management process. *Source:* adapted from Department of the Environment (1995).

process involves determining the changes in environmental conditions on site specifically resulting from implementation of the proposed actions. This requires knowledge of the baseline situation, the key aspects of the proposed actions and the predicted environmental conditions post-implementation.

2. Identify hazards
Hazard identification involves determining which of the properties of the intended action could lead to adverse effects on the heritage resource *and/or* the heritage product. Where, and to what extent, might an action or its individual elements cause harm to the heritage resource and/or heritage product?

3. Identify consequences
The key issue for the HVA manager is in determining the consequences for the heritage resource, in terms of damage to the environment, and the consequences for the heritage product, in terms of product quality and future income-generating potential.

4. Determine the consequences
In some cases it will be possible to quantify the magnitude of such effects in terms of, say, revenues and costs, visitor numbers and species population changes. Techniques have also been developed which can be used to assign a monetary value to heritage resources (Hanley and Spash 1993). Certain effects, however, do not lend

themselves to quantification, and semi-quantitative and qualitative approaches may be required.

The probability that a hazard will be realized may be expressed quantitatively (e.g. a 75 per cent chance of serious path erosion) or qualitatively (e.g. the chances of serious path erosion are high). A range of possibilities may also be expressed for each potential hazard. Judgements as to the probability of particular events occurring can be made through a wide range of methods such as comparisons with similar sites/situations, Delphi panels and a range of modelling techniques.

The HVA management system

In order to both assess and manage risks effectively, the HVA operations manager must initiate a system which provides the necessary information on variables relating to:

- visitor, and other on-site activities;
- the heritage resources available on-site; and
- their utilization relative to carrying capacity estimates or agreed limits of acceptable change.

For this purpose a basic HVA management model, such as that illustrated in Figure 13.4, could be used and adapted to specific HVAs. If operated effectively such a system would provide the information required to conduct a risk assessment and the management tools capable of dealing with those risks through a combination of supply and demand management techniques.

Baseline evaluation: visitor activity assessment and resource inventory analysis
The visitor activity assessment will involve collection, storage and analysis of information relating to the range of activities associated with the attraction of visitors to the site such as:

- Mode of transport to, and on, site.
- Services utilized on site such as accommodation and infrastructure provision.
- Visitor information including totals, profiles and spend.
- Environmental information such as waste generation per visitor day.
- Development information such as existing land-use patterns.

Visitor and visitor services information could be collected via one, or a combination of methods such as admission records, visitor surveys, visual observation and electronic/infra-red counters.

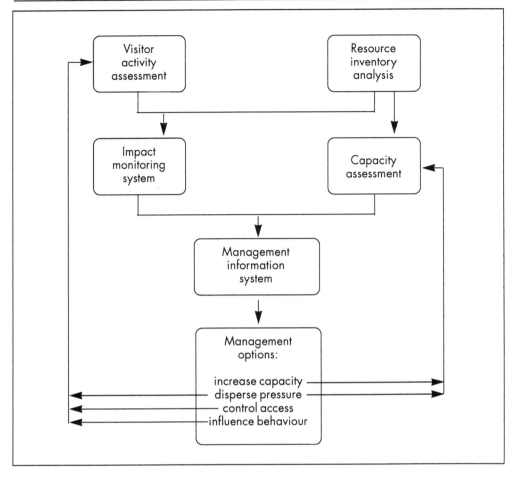

Figure 13.4: The attraction management process.

A resource inventory in the context of the management model used could include both a natural resource inventory and an inventory of man-made and socio-cultural resources. Natural resource assessments could, for example, be undertaken according to a *resource suitability classification* or a *resource depletability analysis*. In the case of a resource suitability classification, for example, each major resource in the attraction area is considered in light of current and potential future uses according to a four-stage assessment process, as shown below. A resource suitability report can then be produced for each main area on site, ⟨   ⟩site report covering the entire attraction.

- *Basic suitability:* is the resource suitable or not for current/
- *Order of suitability:* if suitable, is it highly suitable, mode
  unsuitable is this currently not suitable or permanently no⟨

- *Limitations of suitability:* what are the basic reasons for the order of suitability? e.g. erosion, pollution, health risk, fragile eco-system competing higher use.
- *Improvement opportunities:* what measures, if any, might raise the order of suitability? e.g. coastal protection, boardwalks, visitor education.

The interaction between resources and visitor activities is critical to the management system. These elements in the model should, therefore, be undertaken in tandem. Service blueprinting is one approach which could provide the basis of an assessment of the HVA service delivery system which emphasises the relationship between organizational resources (including heritage resources) and the customer. Developed by Shostack (1984), service blueprinting helps to analyse how changes in resource use affect the service process. In addition, the technique can highlight potential hazards in the system and, in particular, where quality may be adversely affected (Gronroos 1990).

Carrying capacity/ limits of acceptable change assessment
The interaction between resources and visitors is expressed in the concept of capacity. The ability of a heritage attraction to absorb visitor pressures is a critical element in the HVA's potential to survive in the long term. Archer and Cooper (1994) suggest that: 'Any consideration of tourism's impact must recognize the pivotal role which carrying capacity plays by intervening in the relationship between visitor and resource.'

There is a diverse range of variables which are likely to limit the ability of an HVA to absorb infinite numbers of visitors (Inskeep 1991). The relative importance of each of these elements will depend on a range of factors such as the nature of the site, the characteristics of visitors and the stage in the attraction life-cycle. The management problem is in determining what are the critical indicators to adopt, and what are the threshold stress levels for these?

In the case of some HVAs the answers to these questions may be relatively straightforward. A critical issue in the management of visitors to limestone cave systems, for example, is in the concentration of carbon dioxide (CO_2) levels. The critical thresholds for CO_2 concentrations are estimated to be 2,400 parts per million (ppm) with regard to damage to limestone formations (as water becomes corrosive through the absorption of CO_2 in concentrations above 2,400ppm) and concentrations in excess of 5,000ppm causing visitor discomfort. Levels of CO_2 are, not surprisingly, strongly correlated with increased visitor numbers. A carrying capacity limit in terms of CO_2 concentrations can be translated into visitors per day and this could act as an indication of maximum visitation levels for site managers ˜agovich and Grose 1990).

The carrying capacity approach, which implies a particular maximum number of visitors at any given time, is often seen as inappropriate in the context of particular heritage attractions (Wallace 1993). An alternative approach relates to *limits of acceptable* change which establishes a set of target conditions for the site within which managers need to operate, or work towards (Stankey *et al.* 1985).

Impact monitoring system

The impact monitoring system should be designed to address the key indicators relevant to both organizational risk and environmental risk. The system is a way of combining and continually updating the base-line information collected via the visitor activity and resource inventory assessments. The monitoring system should be developed with the primary objective being to provide information relating to the potential realization of serious hazards or threats and the identification of significant opportunities. Key issues in establishing the monitoring programme will include the selection of key indicators and the use of appropriate collection and sampling methods.

Management information system (MIS)

The MIS provides a mechanism for the storage, retrieval and analysis of the information collected via the base-line assessments and monitoring system. A key element in this activity will be the ability to reference indicator levels against the threshold values established via carrying capacity estimation and/or agreed limits of acceptable change. The MIS therefore provides managers with the ability to assess risk levels and indicate whether intervention is required to manage those risks.

Risk management practices

The risk of financial distress or environmental stress can be managed by the operations manager through a range of practices. These practices are reviewed here, although a number are examined in considerably more detail in other chapters of the book.

Increasing resource capacity

Traditional discussion of capacity issues in the context of service operations management, such as by Schmenner (1995), generally refer to capacity as a factor entirely controlled by the organization and largely dictated by levels of demand. This approach fails to recognize the problem in HVAs that available supply may dictate sales (visitor numbers), and not demand, even in the long run. Archer and Cooper (1994) suggest that:

> The issue of management is closely related to the notion of carrying capacity as a destination can be 'managed' to take any number of visitors.

Simply by 'hardening' the environment and managing the visitor, large volumes can be accommodated without an unacceptable decline in the environment or the experience.'

While it may be possible to expand HVA site capacity it is unlikely that the number of visitors which can be absorbed without significant organizational and/or environmental consequences, is infinite. Capacity could be increased through, for example: staff training, improvement to/expansion of infrastructure (e.g. transport, waste management and utilities provision), design and layout changes, and physical protection of the resource (such as the use of specialized wood treatment and preservation techniques in historic attractions and the construction of raised boardwalks to avoid trampling of rare plant species).

Controlling access to the resource
Access management can involve two main alternatives:

1. Limiting access to the heritage attraction site.
2. Limiting access to areas within the site.

Limiting access to the attraction itself may be a valid management response, particularly during peak periods of demand. In HVAs a maximum number of visitors may be imposed externally via health/safety/fire regulations, or internally, in recognition of capacity limitations. Approaches to limiting site access may involve direct entry prevention measures or indirect measures such as parking restrictions, traffic routing and limits to accommodation supply. Sanson (1994) provides an example of access limitation policy in New Zealand's Sub-Antarctic Islands where the tourism management plan for the area includes policies which state:

- Islands in pristine or near-pristine condition remain strictly closed to all entry.
- Ship capacity is limited to 180 passengers.
- Only one ship may visit a site per day.
- A maximum of 600 visitors per site per cruise season.

In regard to access management, the HVA operations manager would be concerned with identifying the appropriate cut-off point for access through monitoring visitor numbers and/or indicators of acceptable change, determining the process by which access may be controlled, and dealing with customers (particularly those not permitted entry).

Limiting access to areas on site will involve some form of zoning policy which, either permanently or temporarily, precludes visitor access to specified areas within the overall site. An alternative to this is to zone the overall site according to permissible visitor activities, as is common in National Parks with competing recreational and other uses, such as keeping separate white-water rafting and fishing, or mountain-biking and walking activities. Wallace (1993), for example, suggests a zoning system for the Galapagos National Park based on factors such as intensity of use, location relative to communities and environmental sensitivity. The management of access to zones on site will involve issues such as information provision (sign-posting, guides, maps and leaflets), visitor monitoring, dispute resolution and security procedures for occasions when zoning regulations are infringed.

Environmental management and audit programmes

The introduction of an effective environmental management and audit programme, such as the British Standard on environmental management systems (BS7750 1992) or the international environmental standard (ISO14001), can help to reduce both organizational risk and environmental risk. Environmental management can have a direct impact on the bottom-line through the achievement of operational cost savings in areas such as water and energy conservation – often for minimal capital outlay. In addition, revenues may be enhanced through *green product* marketing advantages. Less tangible, but still important benefits can also arise in terms of community and employee relations. At the same time effective environmental management will help to conserve the heritage asset upon which the organization depends by maintaining or improving service quality leading to long-run performance enhancement and preventing problems of obsolescence resulting from deterioration of the heritage asset.

Influencing levels of demand

In situations where managers of heritage attractions are constrained as to the level by which the physical capacity of a site may be expanded, demand management policies may be appropriate, via promotion or de-marketing activities. The introduction or revision of pricing policies, for example, can be seen as not only a method of generating income but also as a means of rationing the consumption of limited resources in pursuit of a conservation objective.

In the majority of attractions there are likely to be peak and off-peak periods of demand. Demand management policies can help to reduce demand in peak periods and increase demand in off-peak periods. If at peak periods of demand some element of site-carrying capacity is exceeded then operations managers should attempt to reduce demand in those periods. This could simply involve increasing prices in periods of peak demand, reducing levels of demand at that time and, potentially, overall revenues.[6] Alternatives to price variations would involve other forms of 'de-marketing' in peak periods and increased marketing efforts in shoulder and off-peak periods. If demand management policies can be planned and implemented effectively then overall revenues may be increased while reducing the risk of damage in the demand peaks. A management tool which can be adopted to achieve this is *yield management*. The objective of a yield management policy is to maximize revenues (and profits) by generating sufficient demand to reach, but not exceed, capacity by varying prices. Kimes (1989) lists the key conditions under which a yield management strategy is likely to be effective such as: where there is relatively fixed capacity; the product cannot be stored; sales can be made in advance of consumption; demand fluctuates and marginal costs are low. Each of these conditions will be applicable to the majority of heritage visitor attractions. Warnick *et al.* (1994) suggest that the implementation of a yield management strategy will require a strategic approach including effective analysis of temporal demand patterns and market segmentation.

Developing Revenue-generating opportunities
Additional on-site products can be integrated with the primary heritage product to generate additional revenues without creating additional environmental risk. In other words, the operations of the attraction can be modified to maximize spend per visitor through the introduction of products designed not to attract additional visitors but to increase their spending on site through discretionary purchasing. Typical examples would involve provision of catering services, merchandizing and car-park charges.

Influencing visitor behaviour
Tilden (1975) developed the concept of interpretation designed to enhance visitor experiences on recreational visits and in doing so recognized that greater awareness and understanding of a recreational resource would lead to a greater desire to care for and preserve that resource. The use of interpretation in heritage attractions involves communicating the significance of a place or object to visitors. Interpretation can be seen as a management tool to aid resource conservation by changing visitor behaviour patterns and as such can assist in the promotion of sustainable heritage resource use. In addition, by raising visitor awareness, interpretation can enhance product quality and therefore have a significant impact on organizational risk.

Interpretative methods can be adopted to promote a number of organizational objectives. Greater respect for the heritage assets among visitors means that visitor numbers can be increased without fear of wholesale destruction of the environment, whether natural, built or social. In addition, effective interpretative design can help to disperse pressure away from 'honey-pot' areas and alleviate bottlenecks throughout an attraction.

Techniques for communicating information to visitors can range from the relatively simple, such as informal contact with attraction staff, to highly sophisticated multi-media presentations. Information on the effectiveness of interpretative provision is generally anecdotal, although Roggenbuck (1992) conducts a review of evidence on the effectiveness of persuasive messages in recreation settings, concluding that:

- Persuasive messages often prompt a reduction of depreciative behaviours such as littering.
- Verbal appeals can be effective in encouraging litter pick-up although, in more developed attraction areas, incentives are required.
- Combined verbal and written requests to reduce litter and resource damage are often more effective than a written message alone.

While the potential for interpretation to promote sustainable heritage resource use is widely accepted, Bramwell and Lane (1993) identify a number of potential pitfalls in its use. These include:

- The neglect of less-favoured heritage assets and the compromise of themes developed for interpretation.
- Over-interpretation which may reduce levels of visitor satisfaction and have a negative impact on local communities.
- Elitism.
- The construction of false histories.
- The creation of 'quaint' tourist landscapes.

Influencing the location of visitor use
Congestion and the concentration of large numbers of visitors on particular routes or in particular areas may cause such problems as noise pollution, erosion, deterioration in heritage assets and wildlife disturbance, thus representing a source of environmental risk. At the same time such congestion, often associated with queuing, will be detrimental to the visitor experience and thus impact on the popularity of the HVA representing a source of organizational risk. The flow of visitors within an HVA will, coupled with visitor numbers, be largely determined by the layout and design of the site itself. The spatial relationship between main points of interest on site will determine the desired routes for visitors. The provision, design and construction of routes on site will also be critical in the movement and flow of visitors. Where possible, poor site layout should be adapted to enhance visitor flow and prevent bottlenecks. The appropriate siting of facilities such as camp sites, catering/picnic areas, car parks, and a range of other site services can help to alleviate pressure on areas subject to intense use, or confine visitor activities to areas resilient to intensive use.

Management of visitor movement on site is also strongly linked to the interpretative provision available. Signposting, maps and trail-markers can direct visitors on self-guided tours of the site. Guided tours can be used to maintain visitor flow on site and avoid congestion and bottlenecks. Roggenbuck (1992) suggests, for example, that:

- Persuasive messages are effective in altering the places visited, particularly within the site.
- Provision of information to visitors early on trip/visit increases the effectiveness of persuasion.
- Visitors with low knowledge and experience of the attraction are most likely to be influenced by information relating to route selection and where to visit.

Interpretative techniques can also be used to contain visitors within particular areas, such as those which are more resistant to intense visitor use, as may be appropriate in the case of coral reef eco-systems (Marion and Rogers 1994). In such cases the management decision involves determining whether to enforce access limits to particular areas, to persuade visitors to confine their activities away from sensitive areas or to induce the desired outcome indirectly. Approaches could involve access management, interpretation and limiting the provision of facilities to specific areas. The provision of transport routes, parking facilities and other services in particular areas, and their absence in others, is seen as a highly effective approach to the concentration/dispersal of visitor use.

SUMMARY

The operations function, in any context, will involve the reconciliation of customer satisfaction and resource productivity objectives. Effective operations management in heritage attractions requires that the heritage assets themselves be considered as resource inputs to the service delivery system. This characteristic, which differentiates HVA operations management from more general approaches to service operations, has considerable implications for the role and activities of the HVA operations manager.

This chapter has illustrated that the role of the operations manager involves attempting to balance the organizational and environmental risks associated with HVA activities. This will involve both an assessment of the risks and the design and implementation of appropriate management responses to those risks. Effective risk assessment and management requires utilization of a management system which involves certain critical elements:

- Analysis of the base-line conditions on site.
- Assessment of the interaction between visitor activities and site resources in terms of capacity levels.

- The systematic monitoring of key indicators and a managerial capacity to retrieve and analyse the information.
- A range of management options to be implemented in response to potential hazards.

If the risks to heritage assets themselves are not integrated into the design of service tasks and the service delivery system, then operations managers will lose control over a vital aspect of product and service quality in their organization. The implications of this are both potential reductions in both customer satisfaction (organizational risk) and reductions in resource productivity and longevity (environmental risk).

In order to achieve this balance at the operations level, however, strategic organizational objectives must be framed in such a way as to encourage the efficient and sustainable use of resources.

NOTES

1. Schmenner (1995) defines the four service process categories as service factory (low labour intensity-low interaction), service shop (low labour intensity-high interaction), mass service (high labour intensity-low interaction) and professional service (high labour intensity-high interaction). It is conceivable that an HVA could fall into any one or more of these categories, dependant on the nature and range of visitor services provided.
2. The term 'environments' throughout this chapter, encompasses the idea of natural, built and socio-cultural resources. Tunbridge and Ashworth (1996) discuss the similarities in both the natural and built environments, as well as the integration of cultural issues, in the context of sustainable heritage resource management.
3. The focus of this chapter is on the negative or *downside* aspect of risk. The issue of *upside* risk and the identification and exploitation of opportunities represents an important derivative of effective risk management (Chapman and Ward 1997). The HVA Management Model presented later in the chapter is designed to allow operations managers to identify and react to both threats and opportunities.
4. For a discussion of investment appraisal techniques see, for example, Lumby, S. (1994) *Investment Appraisal and Financial Decisions*, London: Chapman & Hall.
5. See, for example, Kotler (1994).
6. The impact of price changes on total revenues will depend on the price elasticity of demand for the heritage product.

REFERENCES

Archer, B. and Cooper, C. (1994) 'The positive and negative impacts of tourism', in Theobald, W. F. *Global Tourism: The Next Decade*, Oxford: Butterworth-Heinemann.
Beck, U. (1992) *Risk Society: Towards a New Modernity*, London: Sage.
Berry, S. (1994) 'Conservation, capacity and cashflows – tourism and historic building management', in Seaton, A. V. *et al.*, *Tourism: The State of the Art*, Chichester: John Wiley & Sons.

Bramwell, B. and Lane, D. (1993) 'Interpretation and sustainable tourism: the potential and the pitfalls', *Journal of Sustainable Tourism*, 1, 2, 71–80.

BSI (1992) British Standard 7750: Environmental Management Systems, Milton Keynes: BSI.

Butler, R. W. (1980) 'The concept of a tourist area cycle of evolution: Implications for management of resources', *Canadian Geographer*, 24, 5–12.

Chapman, C. and Ward, S. (1997) *Project Risk Management: Processes, Techniques and Insights*, Chichester: John Wiley & Sons.

Cohen, E. (1978) 'The impact of tourism on the physical environment', *Annals of Tourism Research*, 5, 2, 215–37.

Davis, D. and Tisdell, C. (1995) 'Recreational scuba-diving and carrying capacity in marine protected areas', *Ocean and Coastal Management*, 26, 1, 19–40.

Delluc, B. and Delluc, G. (1984) 'Lascaux II: a faithful copy', *Antiquity*, 58, 194–196.

Department of the Environment, UK (1995) *Guide to Risk Assessment and Risk Management for Environmental Protection*, London: HMSO.

Dragovich, D. and Grose, J. (1990) 'Impact of tourists on carbon dioxide levels at Jenolan Caves, Australia: an examination of microclimatic constraints on tourist cave management', *Geoforum*, 21, 1, 111–120.

Gabrie, C. *et al.* (1994) 'Study of the coral reefs of Bora-Bora (Society Archipelago, French Polynesia) for the development of a conservation and management plan', *Ocean and Coastal Management*, 25, 189–216.

Gronroos, C. (1990) *Service Management and Marketing: Managing the Moment of Truth in Service Competition*, Mass./Toronto: Lexington.

Hanley, N. and Spash C. L. (1993) *Cost-Benefit Analysis and the Environment*, Cheltenham: Edward Elgar.

Harris, N. D. (1989) *Service Operations Management*, London: Cassell.

Haywood, K. M. (1991) 'Can the tourist-area life-cycle be made operational?', in Medlik, S. *Managing Tourism*, Oxford: Butterworth-Heinemann.

HM Government Cm 2426 (1994) *Sustainable Development: The UK Strategy*, London: HMSO.

Inskeep (1991) *Tourism Planning: An Integrated and Sustainable Development Approach*, New York: Van Nostrand Reinhold.

Kimes, S. E. (1989) 'The basics of yield management', *Cornell H.R.A. Quarterly*, 29, 4, 14–19.

Kotler, P. (1994) *Principles of Marketing*, Englewood Cliffs: Prentice-Hall.

Marion and Rogers (1994) 'The applicability of terrestrial visitor impact management strategies to the protection of coral reefs', *Ocean and Coastal Management*, 22, 153–163.

Martin, B. S. and Uysal, M. (1990) 'An examination of the relationship between carrying capacity and the tourism lifecycle: management and policy implications', *Journal of Environmental Management*, 31, 327–333.

McIntyre *et al.* (1993) *Sustainable Tourism Development: A Guide for Local Planners*, Madrid: World Tourism Organization.

Murphy, P. E. (1997) *Quality Management in Urban Tourism*, New York/Toronto: John Wiley & Sons.

Pearce, D.W., Markandya, A. and Barbier, E. B. (1991) *Blueprint for a Green Economy*, London: Earthscan.

Prior, M. *et al.* (1995) 'The impact on natural resources of activity tourism: a case study of diving in Egypt', *International Journal of Environmental Studies*, 48, 201–209.

Roggenbuck, J. W. (1992) 'Use of persuasion to reduce resource impacts and visitor conflicts' in Manfredo, M. J. (ed.) *Influencing Human Behaviour: Theory and Applications in Recreation, Tourism and Natural Resources Management*, Champagne: Sagamore.

Sanson, L. V. (1994) 'An ecotourism case study in sub-antarctic islands', *Annals of Tourism Research*, 21, 2, 344–354.

Shostack, G. L. (1984) 'Designing services that deliver', *Harvard Business Review*, January–February.

Schmenner, R. W. (1995) *Service Operations Management*, Englewood Cliffs, NJ: Prentice-Hall.

Stankey, G. H., Cole, D. N., Lucas, R. C., Peterson, M. E. and Frissell, S. S. (1985) 'The Limits of Acceptable Change (LAC) system of wilderness planning', Forest Service General Technical Report INT-176, Washington DC: US Department of Agriculture.

Tilden, F. (1975) *Interpreting Our Heritage*, Chapel Hill: University of North Carolina Press.

Tunbridge, J. E. and Ashworth, G. J. (1996) *Dissonant Heritage: The Management of the Past as a Resource in Conflict*, Chichester: John Wiley & Sons.

Wallace (1993) 'Visitor management: lessons from Galapagos National Park', in Lindberg, K. and Hawkins, D. E. (eds) *Ecotourism: A Guide for Planners and Managers*, North Bennington: Ecotourism Society.

Warnick *et al.* (1994) 'Yield management in recreation resources management', *Journal of Parks and Recreation Administration*, 12, 3, 71–90.

Woodley, S. (1993) 'Tourism and sustainable development in parks and protected areas', in Nelson *et al.* (eds) *Tourism and Sustainable Development: Monitoring, Planning, Managing*, Department of Geography Publication Series Number 37, University of Waterloo: University of Waterloo.

MODEL QUESTIONS

1. In what respect do fluctuations in demand represent a source of risk to HVAs, and how can such risks be addressed at the operations level?

2. Explain why HVAs may opt for the development scenario at the strategic level, and discuss the potential consequences of this for operations managers.

3. Explain the importance of the interaction between visitor activity and heritage resources and suggest how operations managers can intervene in this relationship in order to address risk levels. (This could also be examined in the context of a specific HVA such as an historic town, historic building, wildlife area, cave system, coral reef, museum or art gallery.)

CHAPTER 14

Decision-making

Phyllis Laybourn

INTRODUCTION

Operations managers in service organizations, e.g. heritage visitor attractions, are responsible for providing the supply of services in an efficient and effective manner. They handle the transformation process, converting inputs to service outputs (Schroeder 1993). They strive to nurture the 'moments of truth' of a service encounter so that they equate to a high quality experience (Albrecht and Zemke 1985). The role of operations functions is to support strategy, translate strategy into reality, and drive strategy. Quality must be maintained and improved, problems solved and opportunities seized. Making decisions, taking responsibility for decisions and implementing decisions are the central and most crucial of these management functions (Mintzberg 1973).

The pursuit of excellence requires a constant critical review of decisions made, a process made possible through the development and use of knowledge of the decision-making process. This type of reflective practice is now seen to be fundamental to the successful, learning organization of today (Schon 1983). An understanding of decision-making is therefore of central concern to the operations manager.

Current forecasts suggest that the potential growth in demand for heritage tourism will continue throughout the 1990s (Middleton 1994). However, times of plenty, when demand outstrips supply, do not necessarily sharpen the appetite for management efficiency and effectiveness. But circumstances change and only those organizations that have been proactive in developing effective management procedures will be well placed to survive and succeed. There are lessons to be learned from the manufacturing industry. In the absence of negative external pressures many companies in the USA fell behind in terms of the efficiency of their operations systems and thus lost the competitive edge to Japan (Hall 1989).

According to Riddle (1994) 'Management by lip service was a very common phenomenon in heritage organizations in the 1980s.' Have heritage organizations facing the third millennium moved away from this position? Is there a greater acceptance of Middleton's (1994) view that no matter how small, the heritage organization must operate as a business?

Access to informed discussion of decision-making for operations management in heritage organizations is not straightforward. In operations management textbooks the focus tends to be on specific operational concerns, e.g. the service encounter as service task, service standards and service delivery (Schmenner 1995); or types of decision-making responsibilities – quality, process, capacity, inventory, workforce (Schroeder 1993). Few examples can be found of the decision-making process *per se* being discussed (Harris 1989). Furthermore, in the past, heritage visitor attractions were given very little attention in mainstream tourist texts (Millar 1991).

Looking beyond the disciplines of tourism and operations management to decision-making literature, even a superficial appraisal reveals the awesome breadth and complexity of the area. Economics, statistics, management sciences, organizational theory, philosophy of science and psychology (Jungermann and De Zeeuw 1977) have all contributed to the analysis, and each discipline tends to have preserved its own terminology, methods and domain of interest: a somewhat indigestible feast for the uninitiated reader.

In this chapter, emphasis will be placed on providing a framework to assist understanding of the decision-making process. It will highlight key aspects of selected models of decision-making, giving an indication of the fundamental issues and the scope of current thinking. It will explore factors which may undermine the quality of decisions made (see also Abelson and Levi 1985; Slovic, Lichtenstein and Fischoff 1988; Stevenson, Busmeyer and Naylor 1990; Harrison 1987). It will do so in the context of selected central issues in heritage visitor management which have profound implications for decision-making.

AN INDUSTRY IN DEMAND

In recent years travel and tourism has become the world's largest industry (Price 1996). There is evidence of a growing dissatisfaction with the mass tourist experience, towards encounters which provide links to authenticity, identity and communication with the past (Nuryanti 1996). Thus, heritage visitor attractions relating to the natural, cultural or built environment have become a burgeoning sector of the industry (see Swarbrooke 1995 for a typology of visitor attractions).

Critiques of the 'heritage industry' by people such as Hewison (1987) and Eco (1986) provide a refreshing analysis of the underlying origins of demand and the resulting services provided. Eco (1986) draws attention to America's obsession with reconstructions of the heritage and culture: 'The frantic desire for the Almost Real . . . the Absolute Fake is offspring of the unhappy awareness of a present without depth' (Eco 1986). Hewison (1987) questions the authenticity of heritage centres and museums, describing them as providing carefully constructed versions of history and culture.

Ecotourism has seen particularly rapid growth in the last decade (Boyd and Butler 1996). Variously defined, ecotourism is usually associated with concerns about conservation. (Whether this is real or merely a marketing ploy is a matter of current debate (Wight 1993).) Urban, technological living appears to make areas of isolation even more attractive (Price 1996).

BALANCING SUSTAINABILITY AND CUSTOMER NEEDS

Central to the role of operations management is the 'marketing concept', that is, every operation is designed and directed to meet the customer's requirements (Schroeder 1993). Today's discerning customer has relatively high expectations about the quality of service delivery (Middleton 1994). Heritage visitor attractions are highly dependent on the preservation of the quality of the resource base (be that historic building, museum or natural landscape). Thus they are 'in the centre of the struggle between the potentially conflicting aspirations of conservation and tourism' (Millar 1991). There are instances of American National Parks (Yellowstone, Grand Canyon, Yosemite) in which tourist demand has reached catastrophic levels. Price (1996) aptly describes the situation: 'Little patches of real estate so sought after for their "natural beauty" that four million persons per year try to squeeze into each of them and park rangers are trained in riot control.'

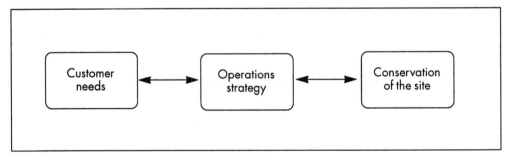

Figure 14.1: Customer needs and conservation.

Achieving sustainable tourism is rightly a major focus of concern today. Riddle (1994) said that conservation should be placed as the first premise out of which planning and operations strategy develop. For the manager of the day-to-day running of the operation, fulfilling the often conflicting demands of sustainability and customer needs is a difficult task.

HERITAGE VISITOR ATTRACTIONS: SERVICE TYPE AND OPERATIONAL DECISIONS

Schmenner (1995) highlights the customer in his analysis of the three attributes of service management that relate to the service encounter. Understanding the service encounter is the bedrock of operations strategy in service organizations. Service task is the essence of what the service provides for the customer: it is the voice of the customer. It provides a goal, a creed or slogan for the management and the workforce. Service task informs the design of the service delivery system and also translates into service standards which benchmark the quality of the service. He further classifies service organizations into type according to capital to labour ratio, amount of service contact and degree of customization. Heritage attractions have a high capital to labour ratio which presents the manager with decisions relating to resource utilization and demand management (rather than an emphasis on managing and controlling the workforce). High customer contact may introduce uncertainty into the system: their needs and demands may be varied, difficult to predict; their reactions difficult to assess (Chase and Tansik 1983). High customization requires better interpersonal skills in the workforce and the manager will be faced with concerns such as the prevention of employee turnover.

The level of customer contact varies widely across heritage visitor attractions. For many organizations e.g. museums and historic buildings, the service product involves a low level of face-to-face contact with staff by using careful sign-posting, unobtrusive security and freedom of interaction with the heritage resource. This may be supplemented by the provision of an optional higher contact service, e.g. a guided tour. Other heritage organizations provide a higher level of contact which also serves to limit the volume of customers, gives greater opportunities to monitor use of the resource and assists security checks, e.g. R.R.S. Discovery, Heritage Point, Dundee; Handa Island. The high contact type of service is more costly in both staff time and expertise and sets clear limits on the access and the potential revenue of a site.

OPERATIONAL AND STRATEGIC DECISIONS

A theme running through this chapter is the need to relate operations management and decision-making to strategic planning. Traditionally, operations has placed the emphasis on internal concerns and efficiency. Linking operations management to strategic issues is critical for the organization (Hayes 1985). Slack *et al.* (1995) identify three roles of operations functions in relation to business strategy: Operations as follower: supporting strategy by developing appropriate objectives and policies to guide operations management; operations as effector: making strategy happen by translating strategic decisions into reality; operations as leader: driving strategy, providing a means to achieve competitive advantage.

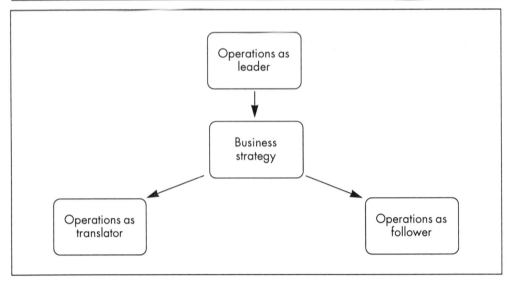

Figure 14.2: The three roles of operations management

The operational/strategic dimension is fundamental in descriptive classifications of decision type. Cooke and Slack (1991) use three descriptive dimensions: operational/strategic (how repetitive, novel; scope of impact; short or long-term concern); structured/unstructured (clarity of definition; degree of ambiguity; distinctiveness – relates to probabilities, uncertainty, risk); dependent /independent (scale of influence; links to past/future decisions; isolated or wide-ranging effects in other areas of the organization). Whilst these three dimensions could render an infinite range of decision types, in practice the strategic/operational dimension is the superordinate category. Strategic decisions tend to be unstructured and dependent whilst operational decisions are more often structured and independent. According to this typology, therefore, the decisions involving operations managers will tend to be more structured and independent.

The classification into operational and strategic decisions is not always easy to sustain. The operational decision taken by a Scottish skiing company to improve the skiing surface by the use of a snow-smoothing machine turned out to have far reaching negative consequences. The company suffered prosecution, a fine and the ignominy of the resulting bad publicity for failing to inform the Nature Conservancy Council and damaging a special nature conservation area (Millar 1991). The operations manager of the heritage visitor attraction must always consider the wider implications. This inevitably involves taking the concerns of stakeholders into account.

Schroeder (1993) describes the value of an operations strategy which develops out of and is informed by the corporate strategy. The operations strategy has a mission, distinctive competence definitions, objectives and policies. Its primary task is to define a set of operations policies to guide decision-making for each of five

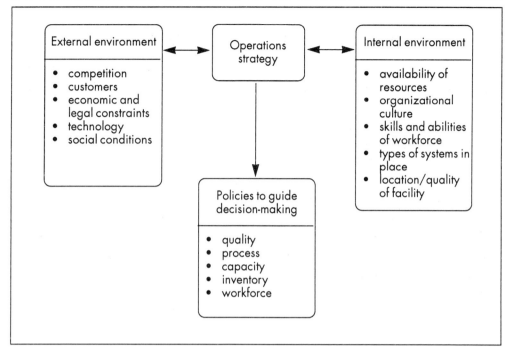

Figure 14.3: Operations strategy, defining policy, guiding decision-making.

decision categories which are the primary concerns of the operations manager: quality; process; capacity; inventory; workforce.

Examples of decisions under each of the five decision categories are given below.

- *Quality:* Decisions about matching the service to standards set. Involves measurement, informs staffing needs and resource requirements.
- *Process:* Decisions about the process and procedures used to provide the service. Concerns about layout design, purchase and maintenance of physical resources (often involving long-term, high capital investment).
- *Capacity:* Decisions relating to planning the level of access so that the appropriate number of visitors use the attraction at the suitable time.
- *Inventory:* Relates to the ordering of materials and products needed to run the operation e.g. food for the cafe; information leaflets.
- *Workforce:* relates to the selection, hiring, training, supervision, even dismissal of staff.

Maintaining clear, day-to-day links between operational and strategic levels is the key to a responsive, outward-looking organization. It allows it to operate efficiently but also provides a platform on which to respond to internal and external change.

WHAT INITIATES THE DECISION-MAKING PROCESS?

Decision-making arises out of effective environmental scanning, involving the assembling of up-to-date, meaningful information (Drummond 1991). This is the pre-decisional problem recognition stage. Heritage managers will be faced with opportunity decisions, where making a decision is optional, e.g. whether or not to landscape an area of ground at the entrance to a heritage site; and crisis decisions, e.g. how to prevent damage to the fabric of a building caused by visitor contact (Mintzberg 1973). Hogarth (1987) describes the decision-maker undertaking an intuitive cost-benefit analysis in deciding whether to enter the 'decision conflict'. Avoidance of decision-making is common. Entering 'decision conflict' can give rise to uncomfortable feelings of uncertainty, not only about preferences and values, but even about how best to describe or structure the problem. Many other factors lead to avoidance, e.g. memories of past mistakes, group pressures, role confusion, time pressure.

The next sections look more closely at the processes underlying decision-making. What is happening when a decision is being made?

ASPIRATIONS OF RATIONALITY – TRYING TO CAPTURE A RAINBOW?

Rational/normative theories of decision-making such as classical economic theory (von Neumann and Morgenstern 1944) rest on the assumption that decision-makers ought to follow a rational, systematic procedure for making decisions. This has much intuitive appeal for the manager (Cooke and Slack 1992). Rational theories are concerned with analysing and modelling the structure of decision-making. The decision is broken down into component parts and mathematical equations used to model the decision-making process. Decision-makers are assumed to have perfect knowledge of alternatives and their importance, know their preferences and have information on the probabilities of outcome. They are also expected to use perfect judgement, i.e. select the best possible outcome, requiring an exhaustive appraisal of alternatives. These theories were not originally intended to describe how people *do* behave but how the ideal hypothetical decision-maker *should* behave.

Models have been produced for riskless decision-making, e.g. Keeney and Raiffa 1976, and for risky decision-making e.g. Savage 1954; Edwards 1954. A riskless decision involves a choice between alternatives. The outcomes of the choice are known with certainty, e.g. choose between three job candidates.

A risky decision is one in which probabilities (the likelihood that something will occur) are involved. Risky decisions vary between situations in which the probabilities of outcome are objectively known, e.g. tossing a coin, to those in which objective probabilities of outcome are unknown and in practice are not easily estimated. In this sense risk relates to probability rather than danger. As has been said earlier one factor which raises the level of uncertainty in the situation is high customer contact. Decisions of risk under uncertainty are the most intractable, arising when dynamic, changeable and unknowable variables, events or states of the world influence the outcome e.g. global economy, the weather i.e. unstructured decisions (Cooke and Slack 1991). (See Wright 1984 for an introduction to Rational theories.)

DECISION MODELLING

The generic term decision modelling is used to describe techniques used to analyse and represent the decision. This can range from a very simple descriptive analysis by the decision-maker to the construction of a complex mathematical model of the decision situation, usually with the help of a specialist management science consultant. This modelling process is used for different purposes: to help represent or 'capture' the essence of the decision-maker's judgement policy; to make comparative judgements of the quality of decisions made; to 'bootstrap' or replace the decision-maker (Dawes and Corrigan 1974). The quantitative, specialist decision models come under the area of 'operations research' or 'management science' (Buffa and Dyer 1978). Leigh (1983) reports that one-third of the top 500 American firms use some form of decision analysis at board level.

What are the benefits of rational based decision modelling for the operations decision-maker? Firstly, it promotes a systematic approach to decision-making. For example, one of its legacies is the continued endorsement of frameworks which break the decision-making process into a sequence of more manageable phases. There are many alternative configurations; e.g. Simon (1957) describes three: searching the environment for conditions calling for a decision; inventing, developing and analysing possible courses of action; selecting a particular course of action from those available. Leigh (1983) favours a nine-phase framework:

1. Monitor the environment.
2. Define the decision problem or situation.
3. Specify the decision objectives.
4. Diagnose the problem or situation and analyse causes.
5. Develop alternative solutions.
6. Establish the methodology or criteria for appraising alternatives.
7. Appraise alternative solutions.
8. Choose the best alternative solution.
9. Implement the chosen solution.

This framework was reported to improve performance by a sample of several

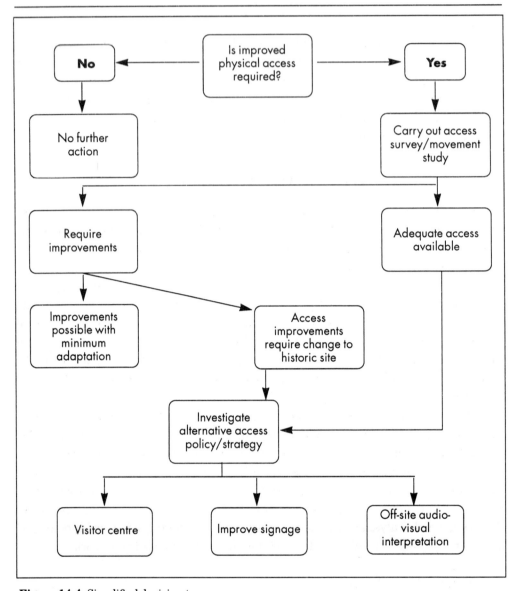

Figure 14.4: Simplified decision tree.

hundred managers (Leigh 1983). Frameworks attempt to simplify the decision-making process. They also make explicit the decision-maker's interpretation of the salient aspects of the decision. This may promote understanding and critical analysis (Cooke and Slack 1991).

Examples of the application of simplified versions of a decision tree are provided in the Historic Scotland guidance booklet providing advice on the provision of access for people with disabilities (Young and Urquhart 1996). Several decision trees illustrate the assessment and adaptation of a site to improve access. These decisions relate to the design and delivery of the service process. Ideas about decision alternatives to accommodate the Disability Discrimination Act (1995), which establishes that there is a duty on the part of the service provider to overcome access problems and legislation relating to listed buildings and scheduled monuments restricting the adaptation of recorded sites, are presented.

This example is purely descriptive modelling. It does not go to the extent of using techniques to assist in the evaluation of alternatives, which would normally be part of what is termed a decision tree. This simple approach also demonstrates a potential indirect benefit of decision modelling: improved communication and discussion of the decision. This could promote a more searching analysis and development of ideas beyond the individual decision-maker. A further benefit of systematic modelling is that it provides quantified and documented data which may prove useful in promoting and justifying a decision.

Harris (1989) discusses the value of decision models such as the decision tree to assist and optimize decision-making in relation to resource management. These involve estimating chance and risk, enabling comparisons to be made between outcomes associated with alternative decisions. They require the application of statistics. Given that the operations manager is rarely an expert in statistics, mathematics or computing, Harris (1989) suggests they should aim for a good understanding of the problem and the ability to interpret information provided by statistical software. Most importantly, they must be totally confident that the information being gathered and used is valid.

The cost of the expertise and resources for these more complex management support solutions is likely to be prohibitive in most heritage contexts. One way around this would be to form networks or consortia to share knowledge and skill to reduce the duplication of effort and share costs (Griffin 1994).

To sum up, the benefits of the rational approach are in the promotion of a more systematic, explicit approach to decision-making. It may be applied at a simple, descriptive level by the individual manager or be extended to the use of generic software to assist quantitative decision-making. This might involve the more costly option of using a specialist consultant to help develop bespoke systems.

RATIONAL MODELS – A CRITIQUE

There are criticisms of the rational approach. Many managers find these techniques time-consuming, cumbersome or difficult to understand. Beach and Lipshitz (1993) state that 'Even when they have been trained to use classical decision theory (and even when they have decision aids to help them apply it) managers rarely use it.' Isenberg (1984 1985) further adds that they seldom implement decisions prescribed by these procedures if they conflict with their own subjective intuitions.

Perhaps support for the more complex, rational models relates more to aspirations rather than actual full implementation? The reality of decision-making is somewhat more messy than the rational models would suggest. Phases of decision-making are inter-related, not easily distinguished, not always sequentially operated, may involve back-tracking and missing out of phases. Simplification may in some contexts be useful, but it can also be dangerous. It inevitably means excluding things – this could mean that critical information is ignored (Drummond 1991).

DECISION-MAKING – THE BROADER PERSPECTIVE

Key criticisms of 'rational' theories have centred around whether it is valid to accept the assumptions of 'perfect knowledge' and 'perfect judgement' in relation to the real-life decision-maker (Wright 1984). There is a large and ever-growing body of research which indicates that decision-makers are not naturally rational in their approach (Plous 1993). They apply short cuts and make-do strategies which curtail the process of selection. Full understanding of decision-making also involves extending the analysis far beyond the point of selection. The cognitive processes involved in appraisal and selection of alternatives are not cocooned from other influences. It is in the research areas of psychology, naturalistic decision-making and management that many of the answers to these broader questions are found.

Figure 14.5 models the range of individual and organizational factors affecting the decision process as a wheel moving along the uneven terrain of external factors or influences. All factors or elements are interdependent. Changes in one will affect the others. The decision-maker is at the centre of the process, the hub of the activity.

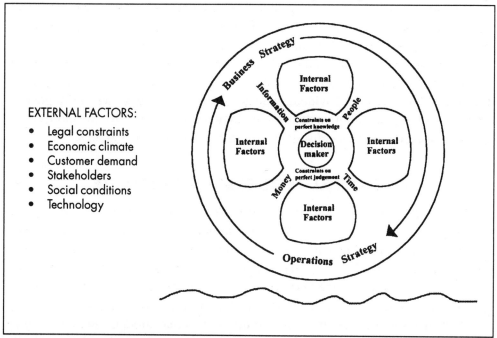

Figure 14.5: Decision-making: the broader context.

THE DECISION-MAKER

The cognitive processes leading to the point of appraisal and selection are subject to systematic biases. Decision-making is about recognizing problems and perceiving opportunities. The foundation of good decision-making is the effective gathering, interpretation and use of valid information sources (Drummond 1991). It requires measuring the service process outputs and matching these against standards set (Harrison 1996). The decision-maker must decide whether or not changes must be made (to standards set, inputs, or the service process). An example is given in Figure 14.6.

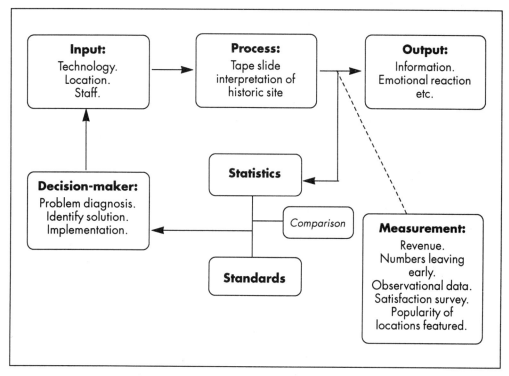

Figure 14.6: Effective use of information in decision-making.

In an ideal scenario, the decision-maker is interested, has time to devote to the process, has the ability to plan and interpret and comprehend information-gathering, is aware of the goals and has the experience and skills to implement a decision once made – rarely are these fully realized in real life (Drummond 1991). One particularly important influence on information-gathering and appraisal is the process of perception. Perception is an active, selective, interpretative process. It often involves adding in, missing out or amending data (Gregory 1974; Neisser 1967, 1976). It is influenced and guided by the personal characteristics of the perceiver, e.g. attitudes, motivation, past experience, personality, mood. Pennington and Hastie's (1986) Explanation Based Decision Model echoes these processes. Derived from naturalistic decision research, it describes how the interpretation of evidence involves the construction of a coherent story or explanation. A large part of the story structure is based not on direct evidence but inference. Information appraisal, therefore, is inevitably a very subjective process influencing problem diagnosis (Pfeffer 1978) and selection of alternatives (Plous 1993).

There are interesting references made to perceptual-like processes in decision-making amongst other naturalistic decision-making models, derived from research into real-life, complex situations. The Recognition-Primed Decision Model (Klein *et al.* 1993) emphasizes situation assessment. The decision-maker draws on experience to classify a situation as typical or novel. This is then matched in a serial way with viable options for action. It clearly shows the value of past experience on decision-making. The model was originally designed for application to time pressure decisions but has since been explored in service contexts (Gore 1995; Yeoman and Ingold 1997).

ANCHORING AND ADJUSTMENT

Cognitive processes involving the decision itself utilize simplifying shortcuts or heuristics which provide quicker routes to a decision by reducing the complexity – but in so doing introduce severe and systematic biases (Kahneman, Slovic and Tversky 1982). For example, judgements are strongly influenced by an initially observed value. This is termed anchoring and adjustment. The initial value seems to act as a reference point which influences the decision-maker's future estimates and judgements. 'Anchoring' has been demonstrated in a wide range of different decision scenarios, e.g. estate agents' estimates of property value being influenced by the seller's asking price (Northcraft and Neale 1987).

AVAILABILITY

Another heuristic or bias is termed 'availability'. This is whereby instances or examples which are readily brought to mind bias our estimation or judgement of the likelihood of an event. For example, people tend to overestimate the likelihood of a 'newsworthy' cause of death occurring, i.e. murder is overestimated. Outcomes which are easier to imagine (Sherman *et al.* 1985) and those which are more often mentally rehearsed (Gregory, Cialdini and Carpenter 1982) are more likely to be selected. Thus managers who dwell on the difficulties or drawbacks of a new venture or innovation may be less likely to embark on it. 'Availability' bias has been linked to errors in disaster forecasting and perception (Slovic, Fischoff and Lichtenstein 1977). In forecasting future disasters people are strongly conditioned by their immediate past. If someone has never experienced a flood they are unlikely to be able to conceptualize it, therefore they will play down the likelihood of its occurrence. In this context, another common decision bias further adds to erroneous forecasting.

There is a tendency to underestimate the likelihood of negative events (Plous 1993). It is tempting to suggest that this plus an 'availability' bias contributed to the decisions and actions observed on the island of Monserrat preceding the major eruption of the volcano in 1997. Prior to that event the economic strategy of the island had been to increase the emphasis on tourism, despite significant environmental warnings of an impending disaster.

VALUE OF GAINS AND LOSSES

Perhaps one of the most significant findings, contributing to our understanding of decision-making relates to our perception of 'value' or 'utility'. Kahneman and Tversky (1979) discovered that a given quantity of 'loss' was more keenly felt than the equivalent quantity of 'gain'. This situation was the foundation of what was termed 'Prospect theory'. When people stand to gain, they will avoid risky situations i.e. they will select the sure bet, avoid long odds. If they stand to lose they become risk-seeking, i.e. they will take more chances in an attempt to avoid a loss. Perceptual factors also enter into this decisional bias. If something is semantically framed as a 'loss', there is more likelihood that the decision will be daring; if framed as 'gain' there will likely be a more cautious decision. Likewise the reference point someone adopts, e.g. current, immediate losses, as opposed to cumulative losses over a period, will affect the bias. The latter leads to more devil-may care gambles in an effort to avoid further loss (Abelson and Levi 1985). Decisions are strongly influenced by previous decisions made. Previous financial investment, costs of withdrawal, fear of failure and losing face all contribute to a potentially disastrous sequence of entrapment leading to risky decisions in favour of a losing course of action (Drummond 1991; Staw and Ross 1987; Bazerman 1994).

LIMITS ON PERFECT JUDGEMENT

Constraints on 'perfect judgement' are also evident in decision-making processes. 'Perfect judgement', according to rational models, relates to an exhaustive appraisal of alternatives and selecting the alternative which generates the maximum utility or gain. Herbert Simon's (1956) Nobel prize-winning work suggests that reality is somewhat different. He showed that rather than optimizing, the decision-maker chooses an option which is 'good enough', i.e. which will 'satisfice'. Thus the decision-maker operates according to 'bounded rationality'. Simon's research stimulated the search for decision rules which might guide the selection process, e.g. elimination by aspects (Tversky 1972). The art of decision-making rests on selecting the appropriate rule to fit the requirements of the situation. Beach and Mitchell (1978) suggest that rules are selected so as to balance the benefits of making better choices against the costs of using more complex but better decision rules.

Image theory (Beach and Mitchell 1990), from naturalistic decision-making research, is interesting in that it explicitly raises the importance of principles, i.e. morals, ethics, values in the decision-making process. Principles are the ultimate rejection criteria used to guide the decision maker's choices (goals) and actions (plans). This theory has been applied in a wide range of contexts and may be particularly apt in heritage settings. The variance in ethics, values etc. of stakeholders may lead to conflict over the development and operation of a site.

Finally, decision-makers tend to be over-confident of the accuracy of their judgements, particularly in situations where subjective estimates are called for (Oskamp 1965; Lichtenstein and Fischoff 1977; Janis 1982). Furthermore, they fall into the trap of seeking out or selectively emphasising evidence which supports or endorses their own views or decisions (Plous 1993).

BUSINESS AND OPERATIONS STRATEGY

The importance of operations management developing from and influencing business strategy has already been discussed. Business strategy and the operations strategy which develop from it are the boundaries set for the operations manager. For maximum operational effectiveness of heritage attractions the decision-maker must be fully aware of the mission, goals and policy of the organization, and must also facilitate the translation of these into operational success. Inevitably, there will be a mixture of motives underlying decision-making, involving, amongst other things, the need for personal success, career advancement, the desire to be popular amongst employees. Lack of clarity in mission and goals, lack of definition in terms of action and measurement compound this problem, creating a vacuum into which personal interpretations and motives (which may conflict with organizational goals) can grow.

INTERNAL FACTORS

Figure 14.7 shows the complex interplay of personal and internal environment factors combining to limit perfect judgement and perfect knowledge.

Firstly, constraints of time and money set limits on decision-making. Information-gathering takes time and costs money, therefore a trade-off is necessary. Scarce resources must be selectively divided according to the importance of the decision.

An organization consists of a collection of people with their own needs, wants and interests. They are internal stakeholders in the heritage concern. The concept of a decision aiming to achieve the maximum gain is, therefore, a logical impossibility. Decisions will be good for some, not for others. Politics arising out of, among other things, unequal distribution of resources, leads to the further development of 'interests'. Individuals will attempt to influence decisions made for various reasons.

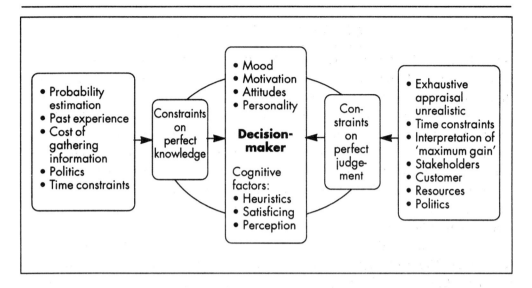

Figure 14.7: Constraints on the decision-maker.

There are numerous ways in which this will happen, some deliberate strategies, some unconscious expressions of personal goals. For example, information flow can be affected. People may conceal problems, implement information-gathering methods differently, provide selective interpretations of data, selectively release information, control the setting of agendas, constrain the diagnosis of a problem, hold back the implementation of a decision (Drummond 1991).

It has now been firmly established that the presence of other people has a profound influence on decision-making (Asch 1956; Stoner 1968). Furthermore, influence may still occur even when there is no direct physical presence of others (Kelman 1958). The majority of research in this area has been directed towards illuminating group decision-making. Janis (1982), for example, has demonstrated the development of 'groupthink'. This is particularly problematic since it involves an involuntary withholding of critical faculties and can result in superficial problem analysis, biased and selective search and appraisal of information, limited discussion of alternatives, and overconfidence and feelings of invulnerability.

The Delphi technique used to forecast change attempts to gather consensus judgement on an issue whilst circumventing the problems of group processes by engaging the services of an independent consultant to act as an intermediary. The consultant gathers views relating to an issue through individual interviews and questionnaires. The collective intelligence of an organization is gathered together by avoiding the use of meetings and group discussions which, it is argued, would be more susceptible to such things as political influence and group influence (Department of Trade and Industry 1973; Harris 1989).

EXTERNAL FACTORS

A whole range of external factors complete the broader context in which decision-making occurs. The organization wheel is designed to operate successfully within a given environment. Drastic changes in the broader environment will necessitate fundamental organizational change. These external, environmental factors are the most difficult to predict and control. One major problem associated with predicting change at this level relates to the difficulty of obtaining relevant information. In estimating probabilities, 'Research mostly looks down the hill and gives an idea where you are' (Griffin 1994) rather than where you would like to be. Organizational defences are constructed to cope with the preceding war rather than the next one (Drummond 1991; Toffler 1975; Heller 1989).

The local and national economy, the legislative position will have far-reaching influences. The economy affects demand, customer buying power and funding, amongst other things. Funding pressures increase the necessity of heritage sites to look for ways of becoming financially more self-reliant. Middleton (1994) describes how withdrawal of Manpower Services Commission and Training Agency funding left many heritage organizations foundering – they had failed to respond to funding changes.

Achieving greater financial self-reliance could involve the adoption of some of the standard techniques of tourism. However, as has been discussed, commercial tourism and conservation are frequently incompatible bedfellows. Implementing such techniques could lead to interpretation of the site which is 'demeaning falsehood... heritage then degenerates into little beyond an evocation of the taste of the present' (Lowenthal 1989). At worst it could result in irrevocable damage or destruction of the site.

Legislation controls the development and use of a site. For example, rights of access to the natural environment vary widely between countries and are subject to constant critical debate. At the moment, the unique Allemansratt (the right to freely use public and private land for leisure and recreation) which applies in Sweden is under scrutiny. There is mounting criticism from landowners and local communities directed towards 'tourists' as opposed to native users of the land (pollution, danger of fire, disturbance) (Mortazavi 1997). If this debate leads to legislative change, the effects on ecotourism and tourism in general could be marked, requiring complete redesign of the operational strategy. Ironically, the current climate of legislative change in the UK is in the opposite direction, towards greater freedom of access. Since February 1998 in England and Wales a voluntary code of practice is on trial to allow the public access to uncultivated and non-environmentally sensitive land.

In Scotland, proposals are currently being developed to create National Parks in a few large areas which 'are of national importance for their outstanding natural heritage and the opportunities they provide for enjoyment by the public' (Scottish

Natural Heritage 1998). If these plans come to fruition, they would probably include the Cairngorms. This would have a profound impact on the recent controversial plans to further develop the plateau for commercial tourism. This site provides an excellent example of the difficulties of achieving a management plan which is compatible with the views of various stakeholders, e.g. landowners, con- servationists, mountaineers and hill-walkers, skiing and other tourism developers, local community, members of the public. This highlights the difficulty of establishing legitimacy in site management (Lawrence and Wickens 1997). Appeasing the demands of varying vested interests at an operational level may be extremely difficult, and too often the cost of error is too high. Arctic tundra (relevant to the Cairngorm plateau) disturbed for construction averages a re-growth of only one inch in 50 years (Price 1996).

How can these issues be reconciled to assist and guide operational concerns? Clearly, where our fragile, precious heritage is at stake ethics must play a major part in decision-making. All parties using or associated with the resource should take ownership of ethical codes of practice (Wight 1993) which establish the importance of conservation. These should guide and inform the development and management of a site. Moreover, conservation relates not only to the physical environment; decisions must also take account of the impact of site development and day-to-day usage on the economic and socio-cultural welfare of the community (Uzzell 1994; Boyd and Butler 1996; Fennell 1996).

SUMMARY

1. Decision-making is the key function of operations management.
2. Decisions must balance the needs of the customer with the need to ensure conservation of the heritage site.
3. Defining the type of service organization helps predict the range of decisions facing the operations manager.
4. The forward-thinking, successful organization maintains clear links between business strategy and operations management.
5. The operations strategy defines operations policies which guide decision-making.
6. Rational theories describe how decisions ought to be made. They promote a systematic approach, use frameworks or models to break down and analyse decisions.
7. The rational premises of perfect knowledge and perfect judgement are rarely fully sustained in real life decision-making. Full understanding of decision-making requires exploration of the complex interplay of influences: within the decision-maker; the internal environment (including business and operational strategy); the external environment.

REFERENCES

Abelson, R. P. and Levi, A. (1985) 'Decision-making and decision theory', in Lindzey, G. and Aronson, E. (eds) *Handbook of Social Psychology* 1, New York: Random House.

Albrecht, K. and Zemke, R. (1985) *Service America*, Illinois: Dow Jones-Irwin.

Asch, S. E. (1956) 'Studies of independence and conformity: a minority of one against a unanimous majority', *Psychological Monographs*, 70, 6.

Bazerman, M. (1994) *Judgement in Managerial Decision-making*, 3rd edition, New York: John Wiley & Sons.

Beach, L. R. and Lipshitz, R. (1993) 'Why classical decision theory is an inappropriate standard for evaluating and aiding most human decision-making', in Klein *et al.*, *op cit*.

Beach, L. R. and Mitchell, T. R. (1978) 'A contingency model for the selection of decision strategies', *Academy of Management Review*, 3, 439–449.

Beach, L. R. and Mitchell, T. R. (1990) 'Image theory: a behavioural theory of decisions in organizations', in Staw, B. M. and Cummings, L. L. (eds) *Research in Organizational Behaviour vol 12*, Greenwich: JAI Press.

Boyd, S. and Butler, R. (1996) 'Managing ecotourism: an opportunity spectrum approach', *Tourism Management* 17, 8, 557–566.

Buffa, E. and Dyer, J. S. (1978) *Essentials of Management Science/Operations Research*, Santa Barbara: John Wiley & Sons.

Chase, R. B. and Tansik, D. A. (1983) 'The customer contact model for organization design', *Management Science*, 29, 9 1037–1050.

Cooke, S. and Slack, N. (1991) *Making Management Decisions*, 2nd edition, Hemel Hempstead: Prentice-Hall.

Dawes, R. M. and Corrigan, B. (1974) 'Linear models in decision-making', *Psychological Bulletin*, 81, 95–106.

Department of Trade and Industry (1973) 'Delphi forecasting', Technolink no. 1312.

Drummond, H. (1991) *Effective Decision-making*, London: Kogan Page.

Eco, U. (1986) *Travels in Hyper-Reality*, London: Picador.

Edwards, W. (1954) 'The theory of decision-making', *Psychological Bulletin*, 51, 380–417.

Fennell, D. (1996) 'A tourist space-time budget in the Shetland Islands', *Annals of Tourism Research*, 23, 4, 811–829.

Gore, J. (1995) 'Hotel manager's decision-making: can psychology help?', *International Journal of Contemporary Hospitality Management*, 7, 213 19–23.

Gregory, R. L. (1974) 'Perception as hypothesis', in Brown, S. C., *Philosophy of Psychology*, London: Macmillan.

Gregory, W. L., Cialdini, R. B. and Carpenter, K. B. (1982) 'Self reliant scenarios as mediators of liklihood and compliance: does imagining make it so?', *Journal of Personality and Social Psychology*, 43, 89–99.

Griffin, J. (1994) 'Strategic linkages and networks', in Harrison, R. (1994) *op cit*.

Hall, E. H. (1989) 'Just in time management: A critical assessment', *The Academy of Management Executive*, 3, 4, 315–318.

Harris, N. D. (1989) *Service Operations Management: Management Techniques for the Service Sector*, London: Cassell.

Harrison, E. F. (1987) *The Managerial Decision-making Process*, 3rd edition, Boston: Houghton Mifflin.

Harrison, M. (1996) *Principles of Operations Management*, London: Pitman.

Harrison, R. (ed.) (1994) *Manual of Heritage Management*, Oxford: Butterworth Heinemann.

Hayes, R. (1985) 'Strategic decision-making – forward in reverse?', *Harvard Business Review* 1, November–December 111–119.

Heller, H. (1989) *The Decision Makers*, London: Hodder and Stoughton.

Hewison, R. (1987) *The Heritage Industry*, London: Methuen.

Hogarth, R. M. (1987) *Judgement and Choice*, 2nd edition, New York: John Wiley & Sons.

Isenberg, D. J. (1984) 'How senior managers think', *Harvard Business Review*, November–December, 81–90.

Isenberg, D. J. (1985) 'Some hows and whats of managerial thinking: implications for future army leaders', in Hunt, J. G. and Blain, J. (eds), *Military Leadership in the Future Battlefield*, New York: Pergamon Press.

Janis, I. L. (1982) *Groupthink: Psychological Studies of Policy Decisions and Fiascoes*, 2nd edition, Boston: Houghton Mifflin.

Jungermann, H. and De Zeeuw, G. (1977) *Decision-making and Change in Human Affairs Proceedings of the Fifth Research Conference on Subjective Probability, Utility and decision-making* 1st–4th September 1975, Dordrecht, Holland: D. Reidel.

Kahneman, D. and Tversky, A. (1979) 'Prospect theory: An analysis of decision under risk', *Econometrica*, 47, 263–291.

Kahneman, D., Slovic, D. and Tversky, A. (1982) *Judgement Under Uncertainty*, Cambridge: Cambridge University Press.

Keeney, R. L. and Raiffa, H. (1976) *Decisions with Multiple Objectives and Value Trade-offs*, New York: John Wiley & Sons.

Kelman, H. C. (1958) 'Compliance, identification and internalization, three processes of attitude change', *Journal of Conflict Resolution* 11, 1, 51–60.

Klein, G. A., Orasanu, J., Calderwood, R. and Zsambok, C. E. (1993) *Decision-making in Action: Models and Methods*, Norwood, NJ: Ablex.

Lawrence, T. B. and Wickins, D. (1997) 'Managing legitimacy in ecotourism', *Tourism Management* 18, 5, 307–316.

Leigh, A. (1983) *Decisions, Decisions! A Practical Management Guide to Problem Solving and Decision-making*, London: IPM.

Lichtenstein, S. and Fischoff, B. (1988) 'Do those who know more also know more about how much they know?', *Organizational Behaviour and Human Performance*, 26 149–171.',

Lowenthal, D. (1989) 'Heritage revisited: a concluding address', in Uzzell, D. L. (1989) *op cit.*

Medlik, S. (1991) *Managing Tourism*, Oxford: Butterworth Heinemann.

Middleton, V. (1994) 'Vision, strategy and corporate planning: an overview', in Harrison, R. (1994) *op cit.*

Millar, S. (1991) 'Heritage management for heritage tourism', in Medlik, S. (1991) *op cit.*

Mintzberg, H. A. (1973) *The Nature of Managerial Work*, New York/London: Harper Row.

Mortazavi, R. (1997) 'The right of public access in Sweden', *Annals of Tourism Research*, 24, 3, July, 609–623.

Neisser, U. (1967) *Cognitive Psychology*, New York: Appleton-Century-Crofts.

Neisser, U. (1976) *Cognition and Reality*, San Francisco: W. H. Freeman.

Northcraft, G. B. and Neale, M. A. (1987) 'Experts, amateurs and real estate. An anchoring and adjustment perspective on property pricing decisions', *Organizational Behaviour and Human Decision Processes*, 39, 84–97.

Nuryanti, W. (1996) 'Heritage and postmodern tourism', *Annals of Tourism Research*, 23, 2, 249–260.

Oskamp, S. (1965) 'Overconfidence in case study judgements', *Journal of Consulting Psychology*, 29, 261–265.

Pennington, N. and Hastie, R. (1986) 'Evidence evaluation in complex decision-making', *Journal of Personality and Social Psychology*, 51, 242–258.

Pfeffer, J. (1978) *Organizational Design*, Illinois: AHM.

Plous, S. (1993) *The Psychology of Judgement and Decision-making*, New York: McGraw-Hill.

Price, M. F. (1996) *People and Tourism in Fragile Environments*, Chichester: John Wiley & Sons.

Riddle, G. (1994) 'Visitor and user services', in Harrison, R. (1994) *op cit.*

Savage, L. J. (1954) *The Foundations of Statistics*, New York: John Wiley & Sons.

Schmenner, R. W. (1995) *Service Operations Management*, Englewood Cliffs, NJ: Prentice-Hall.

Schon, D. A. (1983) *The Reflective Practitioner: How Professionals Think in Action*, USA: Basic Books.

Schroeder, R. G. (1993) *Operations Management: Decision-making in the Operations Function*, New York: McGraw-Hill.

Scottish Natural Heritage (1998) *Developing Proposals for National Parks in Scotland* (information leaflet), Scottish Natural Heritage.

Sherman, S. J., Cialdini, R. B., Schwartzman, D. F. and Reynolds, K. D. (1985) 'Imagining can heighten or lower perceived liklihood of contracting a disease: The mediating effect of imagery', *Personality and Social Psychology Bulletin* 11 118–127.

Simon, H. A. (1956) 'Rational choice and the structure of the environment', *Psychological Review*, 63 129–138.

Simon, H. A. (1957) *Models of Man*, New York: John Wiley & Sons.

Slack, N., Chambers, S., Harland, C., Harrison, A. and Johnston, R. (1995) *Operations Management*, London: Pitman.

Slovic, P. Fischoff, B. and Lichtenstein, S. (1977) 'Cognitive processes and societal risk taking', in Jungermann, H. and De Zeeuw, G. (eds) *Decision-making and Change in Human Affairs*, Dordrecht: D. Reidel.

Slovic, P., Lichtenstein, S. and Fischoff, B. (1988) 'Decision-making', in Atkinson, R. D., Herrnstein, R. J., Lindzey, G. and Luce, R. D. (eds) *Stevens Handbook of Experimental Psychology. Vol. 2, Learning and Cognition*, 673–738, New York: John Wiley & Sons.

Staw, B. M. and Ross, J. (1987) 'Behaviour in escalation situations: Antecedents, prototypes and solutions', *Research in Organizational Behaviour*, 9, 39–78.

Stevenson, M. K., Busemeyer, J. R. and Naylor, J. C. (1990) 'Judgement and decision-making theory', 283–374, in Dunnette, M. D., Hengen, H. M. (eds) *Handbook of Industrial and Organizational Psychology*, 2nd edition, Palo Alto: Consulting Psychologists Press.

Stoner, J. (1968) 'Risky and cautious shifts in group decision: the influence of widely held beliefs', *Journal of Experimental Social Psychology*, 4, 442–459.

Swarbrooke, J. (1995) *The Development and Management of Visitor Attractions*, Oxford: Butterworth Heinemann.

Toffler, A. (1975) *The Ecospasm Report*, New York: Bantam.

Tversky, A. (1972) 'Elimination by aspects', *Psychological Review*, 79, 281–299.

Uzzell, D. L. (1989) *Heritage Interpretation* 1 and 2, London, New York: Belhaven.

Uzzell, D. L. (1994) 'Heritage interpretation four decades after Tilden', in Harrison, R. (1994) *op cit*.

von Neumann, J. and Morgenstern, O. (1944) *Theory of Games and Economic Behaviour*, Princeton, NJ: Princeton University Press.

Wight, P. (1993) 'Ecotourism: Ethics or eco-sell?', *Journal of Travel Research*, 31, 3, 3–9.

Wright, G. (1984) *Behavioural Decision Theory*, Harmondsworth: Penguin.

Yeoman, I. and Ingold, T. (1997) *Yield Management: Strategies for the Service Industries*, London: Cassell.

Young, V. and Urquhart, D. (1996) *Access to Built Heritage: Advice on the Provision of Access for People with Disabilities to Historic Sites Open to the Public*, Edinburgh: Historic Scotland.

MODEL QUESTIONS

1. Use Schmenner's descriptive classification of service organizations and Schroeder's analysis of operations strategy to analyse decisions made in heritage organizations. In your answer you should:
   (a) Use examples from at least two heritage organizations to provide a comparative analysis.
   (b) Explore key differences in decision concerns which arise from differences in type of service organization.
   (c) Identify the relationship between operational decision-making and corporate or business strategy.

2. Critically assess applications of rational decision modelling in operations decision-making.

3. Explain why an understanding of decision-making must extend beyond the application of a rational model of the point of selection. Use examples from the heritage context to clarify your answer.

CHAPTER 15

Strategy and Policy

Ros Derrett

INTRODUCTION

The challenge of providing heritage services to visitors requires an understanding of several aspects of management culture. Contemporary heritage visitor attractions have appropriated relevant elements of the business world, in particular the service sector, to better deliver what has long been a piecemeal passion for sharing materials and ideas shrouded in the culture of conservative academia. The following outlines practical frameworks which deal with the contribution that the marketing concept, the human resources and particularly the operations concept can make to clearly representing the organization's mission.

The role of operations management is about implementation. Therefore the appropriate interface between operations and strategy is discussed. The chapter aims to provide a guide to theory and practice in key areas of heritage visitor attraction management and planning, with an emphasis on three functional concepts. These concepts need to be integrated to deliver effective and efficient tourism experiences. The marketing concept, the human resource concept and the operations concept all have the visitor or customer as their focus.

Heritage visitor attraction managers need to understand the service sector and require a framework to better deliver the services demanded by visitors. Policy needs to be in place which stimulates strategies to address the external environments in which the business operates; the internal factors which will influence the implementation of day-to-day operations, and the monitoring and measurement of performance. Policy will be influenced by the legislative context in which the enterprise operates. A statement needs to be developed by the organization firmly establishing the statutory responsibility it owes to appropriate levels of government.

Identification of external and internal factors which could become policy issues need to be monitored and prepared for by the organization. Adequate consideration needs to be given to relevant guiding principles, constraints and other significant issues affecting stakeholders before policies and strategies are agreed. The heritage visitor attraction's goals are supported by policies and need to be endorsed by relevant authorities with which the organization is obliged to have dealings. Policies need to be clearly articulated and communicated to all parties in a way which promotes understanding and support. Strategies provide an outline of an intended course of action. They relate directly to policies, are comprehensive and are designed to achieve specified outcomes.

Policies and strategies may deal with aspects of any of the heritage visitor attraction's functions. These could include: collection management; conservation and preservation; research and dissemination of information; public programmes and community access; commercial and marketing activities; culturally sensitive issues; employment and training practices.

> The management of heritage presents a paradox. How do we allow people to visit and experience heritage without heritage becoming so degraded that it loses its value and attraction? Or, to put it another way, how do we ensure that we don't love heritage to death?
>
> (Hall and McArthur 1993)

Hall and McArthur (1993) suggest that the traditional approach to heritage management ignored a fundamental element of the management process, the visitor experience. The quality of visitor experience highlights the need to not just focus on the supply side but to recognize the characteristics of satisfying visitor expectations, motivations and needs.

Heritage visitor attractions recognize the process nature of policy-making and strategic planning. It is not a one-off exercise, and the notion of monitoring and evaluating progress can be as important as creating a document. In planning for effective management of heritage visitor attractions, a range of options are discussed. Some examples commonly used include: direct management and conservation by a public authority; adaptation for management or commercial use; commercial lease for use and/or conservation; stabilization of structures as ruins; minimal necessary preservation of remote sites; visitor control (or exclusion); management involvement by special interest groups; abandonment to benign neglect; and active removal of all or part of the fabric of the place (Pearson and Sullivan 1995).

Management policy and thus planning options are based on factors such as the purpose of the dedication and use of the area involved; the appropriate level of conservation entailed, based on the assessment of the significance of the place and assessment of other constraints; the amount and kind of public use; the feasibility of leasing or other uses; and the costs of conservation. Basic planning elements such as the investigation of resources, assessment and statement of significance, definitions of management objectives and constraints, statements of conservation policy, interest in authenticity, legitimacy, sympathy and interpretation become central to policy and strategic development.

External factors such as globalization, information technology, changes in regulation and marketing practices and competition for tourism revenue all impact on the design and delivery of heritage services. The management decisions to be made by commercial, public and non-profit organizations involved with providing heritage services include concerns for declining human and financial resources and the need to take a businesslike approach to recruitment, training and marketing. Strategies need to be in place to deal with increasing the number and effectiveness of the profit centres within the organization like innovative merchandising, museum shops, educational service provision, restaurants and consultancies. Management needs to plan for results. Consistency is the key for identifying goals, objectives and priorities which are achievable within existing constraints and make for seamless operations.

Planning for appropriate heritage place management includes the recognition of the organization's conservation plan. Management must understand the nature of heritage value and its conservation. Conservation must be seen as a primary objective in the integrated policy, planning and practice. The International Council of Museums' definition of Conservation Policy (Australia ICOMOS 1992) states that 'The conservation policy should identify the most appropriate way of caring for the fabric and setting of the place arising out of the statement of significance and other constraints.'

The strategy devised outlines personnel, resources, management structure and technical requirements and details the timing and sequence of particular conservation actions. Staff need to be alert to the need to maintain, update and document the records of the resource it is attempting share with the public; mitigate against inappropriate visitor impacts and vandalism; be prepared to conserve work, protect the physical resources, control any impinging development or potentially conflicting management practices; control research; prepare effective visitor-use and interpretation practices; curate movable artefacts; arrange ongoing con-sultation with and/or involvement of particular relevant community groups; and maintain the amenity of the heritage visitor attraction in good condition (Pearson and Sullivan 1995). These are principles of implementation.

The organization's strategic objectives are informed by the environment in which the enterprise operates; resources available to allow effective management and where it wishes to position itself in the marketplace. Operational efficiency and customer satisfaction seem like conflicting goals. In the day-to-day activities of heritage attractions, the agendas of all participants in the delivery of a variety of services have their own agendas. It is the role of management to identify their needs and seek resolution for the compatible elements that each stakeholder wants.

Management processes include conceptualizing, carrying out the plan and obtaining results through people, seeking improvements and monitoring and appraising results, assisting subordinates, and inspiring and motivating them. A simple strategic plan will include the following elements: a mission statement; organizational aims; objectives which are SMART: S – Specific, M – Manageable, A – Achievable, R – Realistic, T – Timebound; priorities; performance indicators; monitoring and evaluation. Each element has actionable status to ensure all stakeholders appreciate their role and how their efforts contribute to the dedicated thrust of the organization's mission.

Those in leadership positions within the organization can create a vision and define a strategy to get there by offering direction, setting objectives and eliminating uncertainty; their drive provides motivation, inspires confidence and builds team cohesion; and their communication and representation to the outside world and from outside to the team is critical and delicate. Successful attraction managers satisfy almost universal criteria, sound leadership, objectivity; staff motivation; care of customers and operational excellence (Torkildsen 1993).

The manager is responsible supervising the marketing, operational and human resource issues influencing the effective development of a successful heritage enterprise. They will see their job as effectively maximizing the efforts of others and be familiar with all the disciplines represented among the staff. While there may be differences between the public, volunteer and commercial sectors, there are similarities in terms of management. Managing people across two main areas, the operational tasks and the relationships inside and outside the organization between individuals and groups, requires attention to detail.

Delivering quality services in a heritage tourism attraction is generally a labour intensive activity. The variety of professional services provided requires significant customer interaction, and more and more enterprises are recognizing visitor interest in tailored interpretive experiences. These additional services value add to the visitor experience, but generate high demand for specialist staff. To provide a full range of prompt, accurate, courteous services will demand high levels of customer interaction and the organization needs to be mindful of the costs associated with wages and on costs. The time taken to enhance the visitor experience will need to be monitored. A busload of visitors arriving at a venue may require 'mass service' involving a high degree of labour intensity but a low degree of interaction and customization.

Clear-thinking managers utilize the three functional perspectives involved in service management described by Lovelock (1992). Lovelock identifies a model for integrating three functional concepts for managing services. All have a customer focus and are inter-related. The marketing concept, the human resources concept and the operations concept can be readily applied to the effective management of heritage visitor attraction.

THE MARKETING CONCEPT

Marketing heritage visitor attractions provides managers with an opportunity to research the demand for their facilities, target visitors, monitor their interest, regulate and manage the flow of visitation, ensure the provision of quality presentation, interpretation, conservation and authenticity standards. The issues of sustainability are as connected to preservation, restoration and conservation as they are to good business practice in attracting the right levels of visitation, offering quality experiences and encouraging sound word-of-mouth promotion, for example, as outcomes. Heritage visitor attractions need to offer quality products, which are matched with appropriate markets through accurate and stimulating promotion.

Creating relationships with specific types of customers by delivering a carefully defined service package of consistent quality that meets their needs and is perceived as offering superior value to competitive alternatives are crucial elements of the marketing concept. Marketing of heritage is a conservation technique often overlooked by managers. The targeting of specific visitors to regulate volume and frequency can lead to desirable sustainable practices for a product which will be attractive.

Managers take advantage of information on societal and market trends. An understanding of consumer demand is reached through research and public consultation. Data is available through public collections, government and community agencies and initiatives of individuals. The management needs to be able to adequately predict the future behaviour of the organization's potential visitors, provide a guide to policy formulation, reduce the risk in decision-making and monitor the reaction of visitors to the facility.

Organizations which enlist the support of their visitors in what is termed *relationship marketing* accrue benefits outside the traditional framework on tourism and hospitality marketing. Philip Kotler (cited in Keily 1993) identifies five stages in the development of relationship marketing which readily translate to the experience of heritage attractions. Firstly, the *basic* stage where a salesperson makes a sale and waves the customer goodbye and usually never sees that person again; the *reactive* stage occurs when the salesperson might say 'Call me if you have any problems or you want more information'; thirdly, the *accountable* stage when the organization calls some time later to check if the customer has been satisfied with the product or service; the *proactive* stage when the organization calls the customer periodically with helpful, updated information of the services being provided and the customer gets a sense that the organization is still interested in them; and finally the *partnership* stage when the organization enlists the support of the customer as an adviser and advocate for the products and services on offer.

Organizations which have a membership constituency or a volunteer work-base or a substantial working relationship with a host community exploit the partnership stage of the marketing relationship. Visitors to sites, museums, heritage attractions can be solicited through successful experiences to become an advocate for the organization. Word-of-mouth promotion is readily understood as a valuable marketing tool. Personal referral is a powerful tool to be harnessed and is generally regarded as more influential than advertising and promotions. Now, it becomes an objective of the organization's marketing plan to ask customers to help in the design of products and services. Feedback from satisfied customers encourages the appropriate development of attractive amenities, projects or activities for visitors.

Customers can provide useful feedback on how to best reach specific markets; school students, community networks, special-interest groups. A simple survey asking existing regular visitors how they best like receiving news elicits a useful picture for the organization's future media promotions. It may suggest the development of a newsletter, a regular newspaper column etc. Visitors like to feel they are being delivered a thoughtful quality product and often the display of a guarantee, a manifestation of the organization's mission statement, is sufficient to satisfy expectations. Visitors are utilized on occasion to provide support for staff training sessions where they can share feedback on their experience.

This feedback can sometimes be translated into useful promotional copy. Endorsements from satisfied customers allows the visitor to become a copywriter for the organization. Informal exchanges between staff and visitors may elicit important information about best practice in competitor's establishments. The organization's *swipe file*, where they collect good ideas for preparation and presentation of activities and resources, can be enhanced by suggestions from visitors gleaned from their experiences in other places. This research is sufficiently valuable for organizations to invest in some incentives for people to share their experience, vouchers to be redeemed at the museum shop or snack bar. Sometimes visitors are so struck by their experience at the heritage attraction that they can be encouraged to invest in the organization's ongoing heritage programme. Memberships, benefactors, 'Friends' of the organization, frequent visitor pro-grammes, host community discounts are strategies which generate much-needed finance, but also provide opportunities to develop brand loyalty.

Successful marketing requires planning and careful implementation, as well as an understanding of marketing concepts and strategies. A marketing plan is a useful document. Managers recognize the collaborative process of creating a marketing plan by bringing staff together, stimulating input from all levels of the organization, and consolidating the corporate vision and engaging the strategic vision of the organization. It is not a stand-alone document.

It provides a framework for the activities of the enterprise for a given period of time; allows for articulation of marketing activities into the organization's strategic/business plan; encourages regular monitoring of all steps in the marketing process to ensure realistic and expected outcomes; assists in the budgeting process matching resources to objectives.

The essential elements are:

- *An executive summary* which outlines the year's objectives in qualitative terms; describing strategies to meet goals and objectives including target markets and the resources required to implement marketing activities effectively.
- *A marketing rationale* which identifies current situation of the organization; any relevant research, any competitive analysis, any segmentation decisions made based on target market selection, any positioning approaches suggested and the objectives identified for the period.
- *A detailed implementation plan* which is designed to identify the marketing mix to be utilized; the personnel responsible for effecting the actions; the timeframe and activity scheduling; the budgetary and contingency funding for the activities; the expected results; the measurements to be used; the progress reporting procedures; any performance indicators to be used to measure outcomes; and an evaluation timetable.
- *Integration with other plans* indicating the links required between marketing and other (often independent) policy-making and planning conducted within the organization. These could include communication policy, customer service policy, marketing research and pricing. The plan must reflect the mission statement, the corporate philosophy and goals of the organization.

The heritage attraction ensures that its networks and wider host community regularly receives promotional material. This material presents a positive, attractive image of the facility and its activities. Press briefings for special events, opportunities to interview relevant personnel or visitors need to be simple, accurate and directed so that the media, particularly, recognize a 'hook' on which to hang a story. Picture opportunities are provided for the electronic media. The sound documentation of the organization's regular activities serves as an archive to enhance any press release distributed.

Sponsorship opportunities are identified in the organization's marketing plan. A pitch to prospective participants in a sponsorship partnership is prepared and delivered by articulate advocates of the organization whether staff, board members or volunteers. Once an arrangement has been successfully negotiated, terms are agreed which satisfy all parties. The legal, financial, cultural, ethical requirements provide an acceptable style which satisfies the expected benefits for all parties. Organizations can offer naming rights for spaces or events, signage opportunities, free admissions for special guests and public acknowledgement of good corporate citizenship in exchange for financial or 'in-kind' support.

Heritage venues are identifying new opportunities for commercial activity to complement the more traditional approach to delivery heritage services.

Supplementary income is now attracted for services in the areas of food and beverage; retail through shops or mail order; presentation of formal entertainments; hiring out space; merchandising of items reflecting the ethos and the collections held at the attraction; sale of expertise of staff and archival services for research.

With the recognition of the growth of the leisure, recreation and arts sectors, expectations of visitors are rising. There are specific niche markets to be attracted. The age, income, and education profiles of visitors need to be taken into account, there is increased education, awareness, appreciation and respect for heritage, new technologies are being applied to attract visitors, facilities can be integrated into other community-based cultural facilities, participation is a significant ingredient, tradition and new fashions are to be dealt with.

THE HUMAN RESOURCES CONCEPT

The people who deliver the services of the heritage visitor attraction need to identify and communicate the essential work requirements to each other. These are determined by an assessment of the strengths and weaknesses of available personnel compared to organizational needs. Policy frameworks are required for other human resource management tasks like recruiting, training, motivating and retaining managers and other employees who can work well together for a realistic compensation package to balance the twin goals of customer satisfaction and operational effectiveness.

The work to be undertaken within the organization needs to be attended to in an atmosphere of trust, encouragement and effective communication. Management delegates responsibility to make best use of staff skills and experience. An appropriate degree of autonomy and supervision ensures staff feel secure and well compensated for their efforts. Management can introduce incentive programmes as a corporate tool to motivate staff. Creative conditions for staff to feel motivated in desirable ways which benefit to core business of the attraction need to be generated. Management recognizes what most people want from their jobs. Such variables include (in no particular order) recognition, genuine appreciation and encouragement, challenge, personal satisfaction, opportunity to grow, proper training, to be part of a winning team; an enjoyable environment, trust, acceptance and approval as an individual, opportunity for advancement, proper reward for effort, constructive and regular performance feedback. So, management needs to apply strategies which will harness the power of the individual worker.

Deal and Kennedy (1982) identified the features of an organization's corporate culture, how dominant views are transmitted, how expectations are explained and outcomes prescribed and these are being adopted by heritage attraction managers. Peters and Waterman (1982) documented their research into corporate cultures in *In Search of Excellence,* linking strong and distinctive organizational culture with the organization's success. These can be readily applied to small/large scale operations with volunteer, public or private business structures through which they deliver their service.

Selecting personnel for the organization requires attention to job and contract specifications. Recruiting policies need to be in accord with non-discriminatory practices and legislation. Candidates for positions need to be kept informed of progress and decisions need to be made and communicated with the minimum of delay. Opportunities for transfer and promotions need to be monitored and acted on when justified and all records need to be kept according to legal and organizational requirements. This will involve the performance appraisal mechanisms and any remedial grievance actions which may be required.

THE OPERATIONS CONCEPT

Specific operational techniques utilized by heritage visitor attractions need to be executed by personnel with the necessary skills and supported by appropriate facilities, equipment and information technology so that they can create and deliver the specified service package to target customers, while consistently meeting quality and productivity standards. Management needs to have in place systems and procedures which facilitate effective information management and documentation. This includes registering, accessioning, recording, numbering, locating, (un)packing, transporting and storing objects; purchasing or commissioning objects, equipment or services; co-ordinating security, safety and disaster planning; managing visitor traffic, group visits and site access. These tasks can be undertaken by in-house staff or outsourced to commercial or community experts.

Staff need to have specific work areas in which they can safely carry out their work in protected and well-equipped environments. Appropriate tools and supplies need to be readily available, stored, labelled properly and maintained in working order so that there can be efficient delivery of the required service, any problems or deficiencies in the workplace need to be quickly rectified and amenities offered to the public not jeopardized. Amenities to be included in the facility for staff and visitors may include toilets, showers, laundry, snack bars, restaurants, canteen, staffrooms and recreation facilities.

The choice of facilities, equipment, techniques and activities undertaken by the organization are influenced by the questions of historical authenticity and conservation and presentation issues. Environmental factors which impact on these include climate, temperature, light, humidity, pests, pollution, air quality, site location, e.g. proximity to hazards, likelihood of accidents, vandalism and theft. Management needs to provide protection for staff and amenities through either electronic, human or physical systems.

Legal duties for management to undertake include, duties owed to visitors as participants so that staff must not be negligent; i.e. eliminate any opportunities for danger through risk minimization for static displays, demonstrations, performances. Care must be taken of the property of visitors. Management needs to inform visitors of their commitment to care and responsibility. The organization has a duty to comply with any contracts made; the duty not to discriminate; duties to neighbours and community, i.e. not to be negligent or create a nuisance. There are duties owed to employees, through contracts of employment, payment of wages, discrimination, occupational health and safety, unfair dismissal and references and the duty to comply with the law in relation to building codes, sale of food and alcohol, organizing entertainment, occupational health and safety needs.

Visitors' attitudes to their experience to a heritage visitor attraction will be influenced by the level and type of attention they receive. Effective, friendly, informative directional signage introducing some pleasant and helpful direct contact with well-trained and well-motivated staff will satisfy most people's needs. A welcoming, well-maintained entrance, with well-maintained facilities and an accessible interpretive programme are important too.

Finance considerations provide a substantial influence on operations. Budgets for the whole organization and specific (small/large/individual) projects within the annual programme need to be negotiated and agreed upon. Proposals for expenditure need to be justified, with explanations of how funds will be sought and the concise, timely benefits identified. Following fund allocation comes monitoring and control mechanisms to be put in place. The need for accountability guidelines will assist in shoring up sound internal relationships as well as outside authorities like government, funding agencies, members and benefactors. Management needs to consider pricing regulation policy, limits to group size, limits placed on physical amenity, booking procedures, siting of facilities, zoning of areas within the site, control of access points to enhance the visitor experience.

General operational concerns in a heritage visitor attraction can focus on specific projects and their management. The activities connected with such projects are finite and have agreed components requiring monitoring and clear performance indicators. These can be exhibition planning, research projects, field studies, up-grading or modifying facilities, systems or procedures, visitor activities and events, interpretive programmes and conservation activities. Appropriate resources are directed to each project over specified periods of time. Project managers may be sought from among the staff to ensure consistency with overall organization aims or engaged for their expertise from outside.

The heritage visitor attraction needs to maintain effective links with the host community. It is important for there to be sound liaison and support for annual programmes. Opportunities exist to strengthen links with specific interest groups, community-based networks, the commercial sector, the general community. Benefits seen to emanate from close working relationships include increased visitation and 'ownership' by locals with increased advocacy resulting for this empowerment, increased financial support, better marketing opportunities with the VFR (visiting friends and relative) market, linking to community events, exhibitions and promotional and sponsorship activities, with educational and outreach programmes for youth, disadvantaged groups and maybe to generate wider national and international audiences for localized material.

The heritage attraction can be utilized as a venue for a variety of activities and events which sharpen the focus of the organization's work while providing opportunities to broaden audiences for current programmes. The event may be seen to be part of a long-term strategy to promote the scope of the work undertaken at the attraction. It is a way to target specific linkages within the cultural, community or special-interest areas, and resulting partnerships should be of mutual benefit. These special occasions may include performances in grounds, indoors, experiments, workshops, festivals, demonstrations, conferences and special ceremonies.

The learning programmes at a heritage attraction need to be educationally sound, providing adequate information for the needs, interests and priorities of the visitors. A variety of suitable delivery techniques are used by staff or consultants. Arrangements for booking the appropriate equipment, facilities and relevant support materials and the provision of simple access for potential audiences are recommended. Programmes need to be adapted, refined in response to feedback from participants and outside assessors. Some formats include formal lectures, guided tours, demonstrations, sessions where artefacts can be handled, practical activities where skills are developed by participants interacting with experts, technology may enhance understanding and generate a dynamic range of experiences. Attendances and user satisfaction of the interpretation services provided needs to be monitored and documented.

The development of print and graphic materials which underpin the learning programmes and substantiate the marketing strategies needs to be professional. Numerous options exist now with the various levels of technology available to heritage attractions. The material may be prepared and maintained in-house or outsourced using professional graphic designers, printers and researchers.

The books, cards, leaflets, promotional collateral, school kits, materials in other languages, signage and captions need to directly enhance the messages being delivered orally and through other media with which the visitor may have been targeted at other stages of the relationship between them and the attraction. Consistency of representation of logos and merchandising allows for the reinforcement of an image and identity for the attraction in the minds of past, present and potential visitors.

Specialist (short-/long-term) exhibitions are generated to satisfy the organization's mission. All internal stakeholders can contribute to the development of themed displays and exhibitions. The proposed development needs to be checked against the available research into suitable objects/artefacts, potential audiences, resources (human and material), ensuring that environmental controls are in place. Some of these exhibitions will be temporary, seasonal exhibitions; they may be on loan from outside establishments, or be travelling to other venues; and this will have implications for budget and timing.

An understanding of the importance of the three overlapping concepts outlined in this chapter will enable management to better satisfy all stakeholders. There exist frameworks which will allow for management, staff, visitors, government agencies and local communities to better access and appreciate the heritage at the core of the enterprise. Business practices need to reflect the needs of the internal and external environments in which the HVA operates. This will be articulated in the policy and strategic planning of the organization and implemented by management and staff.

FURTHER READING

Arts Training Australia (1994) *National Museums Competency Standards*, Commonwealth Canberra: Department of Employment, Education & Training.

Blackall, S. and Meek, J. (eds) (1992) *Marketing the Arts, Every Vital Aspect of Museum Management*, London: ICOM (International Council of Museums).

Brown, C. (1995) 'Making the most of family visits: some observations of parents with children in a museum science centre', *Museum Management and Curatorship*, 14, 1, 65–71.

Cameron, D. Ferguson (1995) 'The pilgrim and the shrine: The icon and the oracle – A perspective on museology for tomorrow', *Museum Management and Curatorship*, 14, 1, 47–55.

Kotler, P., Bowen, J. and Makens, J. (1996) *Marketing for Hospitality and Tourism*, NJ: Prentice-Hall.

Morrison, A. M. (1989) *Hospitality and Travel Marketing*, Albany, New York: Delmar Publishers Inc.

REFERENCES

Australia ICOMOS (1992) Marquis-Kyle, P. and Walker, M. (eds) *The Illustrated Burra Charter*, Sydney: Australia ICOMOS.

Deal, T. and Kennedy, A. (1982) *Corporate Cultures*, Harmondsworth: Penguin.

Hall, C. M. and McArthur, S. (eds) (1993) 'Heritage management in New Zealand and Australia', *Visitor Management, Interpretation and Marketing*, Auckland: OUP.

Kiely, M. (1993) 'Relationship marketing: the customer as God the creator', *Marketing*, October, 61–64.

Lovelock, C. H. (1992) (2nd edn) *Managing Services – Marketing, Operations and Human Resources*, Englewood Cliffs: Prentice-Hall.

Pearson, M. and Sullivan, S. (1995) *Looking After Heritage Places, The Basics of Heritage Planning for Managers, Landowners and Administrators*, Melbourne: Melbourne University Press.

Peters, T. and Waterman, R. (1982) *In Search of Excellence*, New York: Harper and Row.

Torkildsen, G. (1993) *Leisure and Recreation Management*, 3rd edition, London: E & FN Spon.

MODEL QUESTIONS

1. Heritage visitor attraction management can be divided into the three overlapping systems mentioned in this chapter. What are they? How can they assist the effective delivery of the organization's aims and objectives?

2. Write paragraph responses to the following marketing concept issues faced by heritage visitor attractions:
    a. The importance of internal marketing.
    b. Explain the benefits of service quality.
    c. Explain the role of public relations in the context of heritage attraction management.
    d. Recognize the ethical, authenticity and legitimacy considerations involved in marketing.

3. Discuss the challenges of sharing the significance of heritage places to visitors who may not be immediately familiar with attractions new to them.

CHAPTER 16

Ray's Farm: A Case Study

Anthony Ingold, Ian Yeoman and Anna Leask

INTRODUCTION

'Ray's Farm Country Matters' is a very unusual heritage tourism attraction. The farm is thought to originate in Saxon times and parts of the current farm are thought to date back to the fourteenth century. Until 25 years ago, the farm was of average size (350 acres) and comprised mainly beef, pigs and dairy. Parts of the land were sold piecemeal and when purchased by the current owners in 1982, the farm had only ten acres of land left attached to the farmhouse.

The farm as it remains today is in Shropshire, about ten miles west of Bridgnorth. It incorporates the final western spur of the Wyre Forest, it has a brook, Ray's Brook, and is at the start of Shropshire's longest footpath, the Jack Mytton Way. In addition to the woodland walk, along the banks of the brook, the farm is home to a number of rare breeds of animal, many of indigenous species, together with a large collection of owls.

This chapter will examine the operations management of this attraction in terms of the mission of the owners and in the context of Schmenner's (1995) service operations functions and processes. Schmenner outlines the well-known characteristics of services, e.g. intangibility, service product and consumption usually occur together both temporally and spatially, etc. However, he then goes on to produce a matrix that he calls the Service Process Mix (Schmenner, 1995) which defines four major groups. These are Service Factory, Service Shop, Mass Service and Professional Service.

They are characterized by Schmenner on the basis of their degree of interaction and customization on the one hand, then by the degree of labour intensity on the other.

BACKGROUND

The present owner of Ray's Farm, Frank Cartwright, has an engineering background. On retiring from his engineering business, Mr Cartwright decided to change his focus, and invested in the purchase of Ray's Farm. Following a variety of ventures which were only partially successful, Mr Cartwright and his wife decided upon setting up Ray's Farm as a heritage visitor attraction. The emphasis on the attraction has always been upon the quality of provision for the visitor rather than upon maximizing revenue generation. In fact, the Cartwrights are unusual for entrepreneurs in that they wish to keep visitor levels relatively low, in order that the attraction maintains its distinctive natural appeal. Their mission could be described as running a natural resource attraction in such a way as to minimize impact upon the plants and animals, both natural (e.g. kingfishers along Ray's Brook) and farmed (the rare breed species which are maintained in enclosures) whilst providing a memorable visitor experience. Visitors are welcomed at the farmhouse entrance and given a map showing the location of the footpaths around the farm, suggested routeways, and where and how to view the highlights of the attraction.

The collection of owls was started serendipitously by Mrs Cartwright, when she took in an injured owl for care and recuperation. Under her care, the owl was nursed back to good health and Mrs Cartwright began to find a small stream of injured or unwanted owls being bequeathed to her. Originally the intention of the Cartwrights was to care for the owls, then release them or return them to their owners. However, this soon became impossible in many cases, and so began the owl collection, with a considerable diversity of species, and now over fifty in number.

The Cartwrights are now well known for their good animal husbandry, developed from an initial base of interest and dedication. They now have an excellent collection of both wild and domestic animals, many of which are rare British breeds, including pigs and goats. The following sections will examine this heritage attraction from an operational perspective.

MANAGEMENT PERSPECTIVES

A review of Ray's Farm, even superficially as above, will demonstrate that it does not fit neatly into any of Schmenner's categories in the Service Process Mix. Reviewing the challenges for managers which are proposed by Schmenner, it can be proposed that the management of Rays Farm borrows attributes from each of the proposed areas.

Low labour intensity (Service Factory/Service Shop)

As will be shown later, Ray's Farm is a low labour intensity operation, not due to mechanization, but by the nature of the operation. Capital expenditure decisions that are made are relatively low key and rather than being based on expansion of the operation are based on quality of provision. However, the owners have obtained grants for capital improvement of the farm from the European Union. Because the operation is heritage based rather than profit driven, much of the work is carried out by traditional methods and little use is made of new technology for the farm operation. The farm also is seen very much to have an educational role, but again, the educational methods are traditional, developing students' interpretative and observational skills. Demand management is limited and promotion is carefully controlled to avoid mass market inflows of visitors. There is no promotion of off-peak visits, but the farm is open to visitors every day of the year, except Christmas Day and weekdays in January and February.

High interaction and customization (Service Shop/Professional Service)

At Ray's Farm, there is considerable scope for economies of scale. Mr Cartwright is Vice-chairman of the Marches Countryside Attractions Group, and the group are able to negotiate contracts which provide such economies. For example, Ray's Farm have 150,000 leaflets printed and distributed at a reduced cost because of this membership. Much of the cost control relies upon the family orientation of the operation, with family members providing most of the labour in both manpower and administrative functions. However, the administrative functions are kept to a minimum. With regard to maintaining quality, the main focus of the operation is continual quality improvement; this is the main thrust of any capital outlay. Reacting to consumer intervention in the service delivery process is quite low key in the Ray's Farm operation. There can be little immediate interaction on a daily basis, since the owners are involved in the farm operation and the visitors are allowed to wander along the pathways etc. at will. However, the owners do interact with visitors on an *ad hoc* basis, for example when the visitors are welcomed and when they leave. Thus the owners do gain better-quality visitor information than, for example, an hotel operation does of its customers. Additionally, the owners get feedback from visiting schoolteachers which provides information which can be used to improve the educational value of visits.

The management of the advancement of the people who deliver the service is an interesting area, and one in which Ray's Farm is involved. At present there is very little provision for development of managers or operatives who work in farm tourism/farm heritage operations. This shortfall of provision is currently being addressed (Alexander, Ingold and McKenna 1997) in a European Union project which is assessing the availability and requirement for education and training in four European countries. It is an issue to which the owners of Ray's Farm had given little consideration until the issue was raised by the researchers, but one which the Cartwrights now consider to be of importance. Management of hierarchies of managers and operatives is definitely not an issue at Ray's Farm, as the personnel consist of Mr Cartwright, his wife and his daughter plus two casual workers. Likewise, gaining employee loyalty is not an issue.

High labour intensity (Mass Service/Professional Service)

It is quite clear that Ray's Farm cannot be related to any of Schmenner's criteria – hiring, training, methods development and control, employee welfare, scheduling workforces, control of far-flung locations, startups, managing growth – except in the most limited and parochial of interpretations. Thus it can at least exclude these from being relevant to this operation.

Low interaction/low customization (Service Factory/Mass Service)

In this category there is a re-emergence of some important issues for Ray's Farm. Marketing is one area of importance. Although, as has been stated earlier, the operators of Ray's Farm wish to maintain a high quality product with restricted visitor numbers, they do undertake certain marketing functions. One of these could be said to derive from a modern engineering focus, that of competitive benchmarking for product improvement and quality enhancement. Instead of taking normal vacations to sunny climes, the owners spend their holidays visiting other tourism/heritage attractions to learn and to gather ideas for their own operation. It is during this period that family loyalty is sought, and their daughter looks after the operation while they are away. It could be proposed that there is only limited scope for giving a 'warmth' to the service (particularly in a typical British summer); however, the owners do greet and make visitors feel welcome without stifling any sense of adventure or experiment.

It could be stated that the one key issue for Ray's Farm is the ambience of the physical surroundings and their perception by the visitor. The owners understand this very well and all the management and planning decisions that are taken, are on the basis of providing the visitor with a stimulating yet relaxing environment, which is at the same time tranquil yet encourages a spirit of enquiry. The owners have carried out some limited but detailed market research. This has provided them with a profile of their visitor and their needs and wants. They are thus able to plan the operation to meet these expectations, whilst at the same time attracting the type of visitor that they wish to attract and exclude those visitors they do not wish to encourage.

Finally, whilst there is no hierarchy in the operation other than operates within any family, there is undoubtedly a need for standard operating systems on any farm-type activity. It is possibly in these areas that the previous industrial/engineering background of Mr Cartwright will have had most influence. One good example of this is the flow process which has been arranged for the visitor. This takes the visitor right around the farm, with good views of all of the attractions, whilst maintaining security for the visitors, reasonably respecting the environment for the animals, and protecting the natural environments.

CHALLENGES TO MANAGEMENT SUMMARIZED

It is perhaps interesting that Ray's Farm, an unusual heritage attraction and definitely a service operation, does not fit easily into any of Schmenner's management challenge categories. In addition, as can be seen from Table 16.1 below, Ray's Farm does not compare clearly with any of Schmenner's four groupings.

Table 16.1: Service characteristics of Ray's Farm. *Source:* after Schmenner 1995.

Ray's Farm	Schmenner typology	
Service features		
Mix of services	Limited	Service Factory/Mass Service
Basis of competition	Wide choice	Service Shop
Introduction of new services	Limited experimentation	Mass Service
Process features		
Capital intensity	Moderate	None
Pattern of process	Rigid	Service Factory/Mass Service
Ties to equipment	Integral	Service Factory
Importance of balance of tasks	Critical	Service Factory
Tolerance for excess capacity	Unwanted	Service Factory/Professional Service
Ease of scheduling	Not done	None
Economies of scale	Not possible	None
Notion of capacity	Unclear	Professional Service
Layout	Line flow	Service Factory
Additions to capacity	Limited and unwanted	None
Bottlenecks	Unlikely to occur	None
Nature of process change	Seldom occurs	Mass Service
Importance of material flow to provision	Incidental	Professional Service
Customer-orientated features		
Importance of attractive physical surrounding	Essential	Similar Mass Service
Customer-process interaction	Great and essential	Professional Service
Customization	Little	Service Factory/Mass Service
Ease of demand management	Not done	None
Process quality control	Informal	Mass Service/Professional Service
Labour-related features		
Pay	Not relevant	None
Skill levels	High	Service Shop
Job content	Very large and high variety	Professional Service
Advancement	Not relevant	None
Management features		
Staff-line needs	No line	None
Means of control	Variable	None

In terms of the challenges provided, Ray's Farm draws heavily upon two of the proposed groupings, but has little to draw from the other two. Schmenner provides a useful framework for analysing service operations, but his categorizations now perhaps require some readjustment since his framework is rather too rigid. It could be argued that this is particularly important for service operations in Europe, where farm tourism and similar service operations are becoming increasingly important.

REFERENCES

Alexander, N., Ingold, A. and McKenna, A. (1997) Unpublished data.
Schmenner, R.W. (1995) *Service Operations Management*, Englewood Cliffs, NJ: Prentice-Hall.

MODEL QUESTIONS

1. Discuss the advantages and disadvantages of using Schmenner's Service Process Mix to assist Frank Cartwright decide the style of appropriate service.

2. What changes would you recommend to Frank Cartwright for the visitor attraction to be classified as professional service?

3. What changes would you recommend to Frank Cartwright for the visitor attraction to be classified as mass service?

CHAPTER 17

Developing the Concept for the Thackray Medical Museum, Leeds

Graham Black

INTRODUCTION

The Thackray Medical Museum, which opened to the public on 25th March 1997, was built around a collection of historic medical equipment brought together by Paul Thackray, initially during his career as a director and shareholder of the private company, Chas F. Thackray Ltd, a supplier of surgical goods. A charitable trust was established to take responsibility for the collection in 1990. This trust provided seed core funding for the museum project. In 1995, the Heritage Lottery Fund granted £3 million towards the cost of the creation of the museum.

The museum is located in the former Leeds Poor Law Union Workhouse, opened in 1861, an impressive Grade II listed building which later became part of St James' Hospital. By 1992 the hospital authorities considered it to be no longer suitable for their use and it was leased to the Thackray Museum Trust. Work on the development of the concept for the museum displays began in March 1993.

FACTORS INFLUENCING THE CONCEPT

The Museum Mission Statement

The objectives of the museum were defined within its Mission Statement. The concept for the museum displays was developed to meet these objectives and other priorities defined by the trustees of the Museum Trust:

- To present a history of medicine from ancient times to the present day with particular emphasis on the social and political influences and, in particular, the commercial pressures which spurred technical developments.
- To describe and explain the effects that these developments had, at the time, on the quality of life of the population at all social levels.
- To give visitors an understanding of the impact of current and projected medical techniques upon daily life and long-term healthcare issues.

251

The collections

A central objective was that all the displays should be object-rich and should encourage people to explore the objects and gain additional insight into them.

While the museum held some material relating to the early history of medicine, the bulk of its collections were of post-1840 date and were related to surgery rather than other forms of medical care. There was a possibility of supplementing these holdings with material borrowed from other institutions. However, it was clear that the displays would be biased towards the strengths of the collections.

As most of the major advances in Western medicine took place after 1840, it was decided to use that date as a starting-point. Displays would begin with an exploration of the medical care available in 1840 and its limitations, moving on from there to outline developments over the last 150 years.

The building

Housing a museum in a building with a substantial history of its own was both an advantage and a disadvantage. Apart from limitations on what alterations were permissible in a listed building, there was the issue of how much of the history of the site should be incorporated in the final displays when the overall exhibition covered a much wider theme. In the end, the imposing entrance hall was retained as a feature of the museum and the route by which visitors would enter and leave the building. Relevant aspects of the site's history were referred to within the main displays but there was no separate interpretation of the building and its occupants.

The building was long and relatively narrow, with a substantial corridor running full length down the middle of each floor (see Figure 17.1). For exhibition purposes, only the ground floor and half of the first floor were available. It was clear that the exhibition layout must make the corridor 'disappear' by incorporating displays in it and by directing the visitor route across it. This was necessary both because of the square meterage represented by the corridor and because the continuing presence of the corridor would adversely affect the whole atmosphere created by the displays. In the event, 'removal' of the corridor was not fully achievable as much of the corridor had to act as a fire escape route.

The shape of the building also dictated the visitor route through it (see Figure 17.1) and divided the displays into three discrete areas. This had a major impact on the development of the concept, making it necessary to divide the storyline into three elements, each separated by a staircase.

Location

When concept work on the museum began, construction of the new Royal Armouries Museum, on Leeds waterfront, was already under way. Despite the £42 million

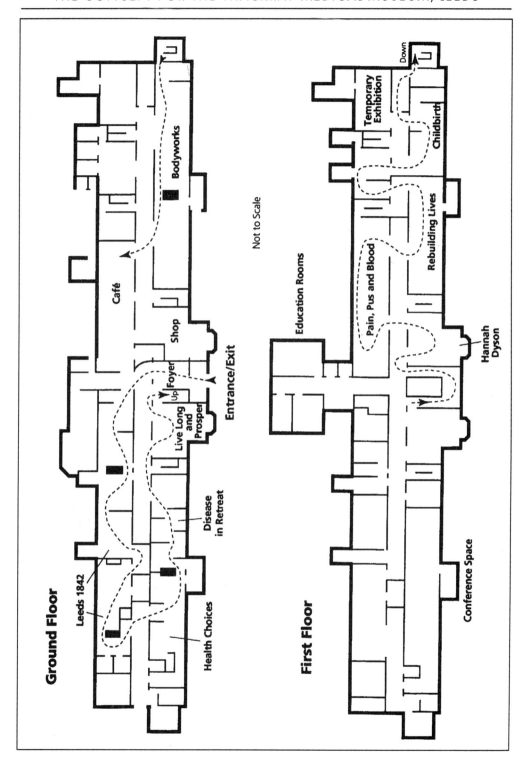

Figure 17.1: Thackray Medical Museum: layout and visitor route.

committed to this, and its target audience of 750,000 per year, the potential of Leeds as a tourist destination remained uncertain. The key audiences, it was believed, would be local people, schools, day-trippers, and visitors staying with friends and relatives.

The Leeds-Bradford conurbation and its environs contain a population of over five million people within one hour's drive of the Thackray Museum. However, it is not easy driving, more an urban and suburban crawl. An analysis of experience at sites in comparable locations suggested that those living within the half-hour drive range would form the most important audience and that only a small percentage of users would travel for more than one hour.

The Thackray Museum is located some 1.5 miles from Leeds city centre, in a not particularly salubrious area. Visitors to the museum would make a specific decision to come, would not have enjoyed their journey, would want a parking space and would be unlikely to combine their visit to the museum with another activity such as city-centre shopping. Location dictated, therefore, that the museum would have to act as a stand-alone, 'day-out' attraction, capable of holding visitors for an average of at least three hours. This had a major impact on the concept.

Interpretative principles

Underpinning the whole concept was a commitment to *engaging* the audience as fully as possible in the subject and the collections, based on principles of interpretation and reflecting both the rise of new technology and increasing visitor demand to participate actively in exhibitions.

For the Thackray Museum this meant initially the establishment of a thematic storyline which was 'people-led'. The theme was medical advance, but this was to be explored through its impact on people's lives rather than in terms of scientific achievement or technological innovation. It also meant that the exhibition should be 'paced' with regular changes in display approach, for example from 'experiential' to contemplative, to 'inter-active', in order to retain visitor concentration and involvement.

It was essential that the exhibition content and media used should match the needs of the museum's target audience, starting from an assumption of no real knowledge or understanding of the subject. However, the needs of those with background expertise could not be forgotten and, equally, it was important to allow all visitors to explore individual issues more deeply if they wished. This was done by 'layering' the information provided. Key messages were provided for all, with additional material available in a range of forms, from discovery boxes to flip-books and computer databases. The intention was to engender a sense of discovery, encouraging people to make connections for themselves rather than simply providing a didactic account.

Educational use

The museum also saw the development of substantial use of the site by structured educational groups as one of its central objectives.

St James' is a teaching hospital, with a potential student audience on site. However, this is limited in scale. The chief targets were primary and secondary schoolchildren. The most relevant primary level history study unit was the Victorians, at Key Stage II (7–11 years). There was also considerable potential to meet the needs of the science curriculum. At Key Stage IV (GCSE – 14–16 years), 'Medicine through Time' is a popular unit of study, with more than 60,000 pupils taking part each year, giving the museum a potentially strong appeal at secondary level also.

The museum was committed to building school project work into the initial concept, rather than attempting to graft it on afterwards. Museums have travelled a long way beyond the old 'death by worksheet' principle in which pupils made their way in Indian file through displays, failing to notice much beyond the information required for the next answer. The ambition now is to develop investigative project work which involves groups of pupils carrying out specific tasks within limited areas of an exhibition.

Teachers and teacher advisers were involved from the initial development of the concept and played an active role throughout the project. This resulted in a continuing input into the exhibition, the development of educational resource materials for use in pre-visit and follow-up work, and their running familiarization sessions for other teachers to encourage quality use of the museum.

Visitor needs

In this context, concept development and operational criteria overlap:

- Visitors will only be in the right 'frame of mind' for the exhibition if the journey has been well signposted, it has been easy to park and they have felt welcomed into the building.
- Toilets must be easily accessible, the temperature right, noise levels acceptable, plenty of seating available in appropriate places, and a good cafe and shop incorporated into the site.
- Every reasonable effort must be made to meet the needs of disabled visitors, not only those in wheelchairs but also the visually- and hearing-impaired and all those who simply have difficulty walking. This involves not only physical access, but also 'representation' within the displays.
- The Thackray Museum was also committed to encouraging use by ethnic minority groups, and this, too, is reflected in display content.
- From the beginning, staff were seen as an integral part of the concept, playing an enabling/demonstrator role within the displays rather than performing a purely security function.

Target: 80,000 paying visitors

To ensure that revenue income from visitors could meet a substantial proportion of its running costs, the museum commissioned a visitor potential appraisal from John Brown & Company. Based on the concept outline provided, this suggested a likely audience of between 70,000 to 120,000 per year. The museum business plan, central to its long-term survival and development, set a target of 80,000 visitors to be achieved within three years of opening and, thereafter, sustained.

In marketing terms, this target dictated a popular, highly participative exhibition approach, with key 'draws', a suitable balance between education and entertainment, a high satisfaction level to encourage word-of-mouth recommendation, and a capacity for substantial change to encourage return visits. It also meant that the needs of specific target audiences, particularly family groups and schools, must be catered for. These requirements linked readily to the interpretative principles on which the concept was based.

The real concern lay with the ability of the museum to attract return visitors. There is a serious risk that a charging museum in a non-tourist area will reach saturation point with its potential audience (i.e. all those who wish to see it have done so) within five years of opening, with a resulting decline in audience figures and revenue income.

The need to ensure a high percentage of return visitors dictated that the exhibition had to contain displays which many people would wish to re-discover and that changes could be introduced on a scale substantial enough to act as draws in their own right. As a result, it was decided that the final part of the exhibition, eventually named 'Bodyworks', would be highly interactive and capable both of expansion and redevelopment independently of the main thematic storyline in the remainder of the museum. As this is on the ground floor of the museum, it would also be possible for visitors to come to this section alone in the long term.

Visitor flow

Visitors to heritage attractions do not come at a steady rate throughout the year or even throughout the day. Experience nationally suggests audiences can vary from a total of less than 3 per cent of the annual target in December to more than 17.5 per cent in August.

It is impossible to cater fully for the two busiest days of the year, Easter Monday and August Bank Holiday, but it is essential that an exhibition can handle satisfactorily a normal daily audience in August. For the Thackray Museum, attracting 80,000 people a year, this meant 630 people in a day, with up to 240 of these arriving between 11.00 a.m. and 12.30 p.m. With an average length of stay of three hours, there could be up to 480 people in the building at one time.

It was important to be able to bring visitors into the exhibition rapidly, to prevent a problem with queues, and to ensure an even spread throughout the building, to prevent 'traffic jams' in particular areas. In devising the concept, attention was given to estimating the average time visitors would spend in each section of the exhibition and to ensuring that the content of each section warranted that amount of time. This is a difficult exercise because, except in the case of timed film presentations, the visitor has total control of how he or she explores the exhibits.

THE FINAL CONCEPT

The physical split of the public area of the museum into three separate sections forced a similar split in the development of the concept. It was decided to devote two of the areas to the main storyline (an artificial split into Infectious Diseases and Surgery), with the third being devoted to highly interactive exhibits targeted at children (Bodyworks).

The following is a brief description of gallery contents and intentions, as visitors follow the route through the museum:

A. Ground floor (left): Infectious Diseases

Gallery 1: Medical Puzzlers, a series of life-size exhibits with associated questions intended to engage the audience from the outset and to move them rapidly into the main body of the displays. (Also to act as a waiting area while group members visited the toilet.)

Gallery 2: Dr Baker, a two-minute filmed presentation based on a Leeds doctor who carried out an investigation of Leeds slums in 1842 for a national report on working-class living conditions – devised as a brief introduction to Gallery 3.

Gallery 3: Leeds 1842, a reconstruction of a section of a Leeds slum. Visitors walk through the slum to explore the lives and illnesses of its inhabitants. They select an individual character to identify with – devised as a powerful introduction to infectious diseases, as the basis for project work particularly for Key Stage II pupils and as one of the three major public marketing draws for the museum.

Gallery 4: Health Choices, where visitors use the same characters to explore the alternative medical treatments available to the citizens of Victorian England. What treatments will the characters select for their diseases? What influences their decisions? What are the results? Devised to be object-rich, audience-involving and suitable for Key Stage IV pupils.

Gallery 5: Disease in Retreat, where visitors are introduced to advances in medical science and treatments for disease over the last 150 years. Devised to change the 'pace' of the displays, with heavy use of interactive science 'experiments' and film, while also being object-rich.

Gallery 6: Live Long and Prosper, which examines key contemporary issues. This display includes considerable use of computer inter-actives.

B. First floor: Surgery

Gallery 7: Hannah Dyson's Ordeal, a film and reconstruction based on the amputation of the leg of a 12-year-old girl in 1842, that is before the invention of anaesthetics or the discovery of germ theory. Devised as an effective way of introducing the main issues affecting surgery in the 1840s, as an introduction to the first-floor galleries and as the second main marketing draw for the museum. Not for the queasy!

Gallery 8: Pain, Pus and Blood, exploring the main problems facing surgery in the nineteenth century and how these were overcome. Object-rich, with a variety of display techniques including archive film, audio and interactives.

Gallery 9: Childbirth, introducing the advances in the care of both mother and child since the 1840s. Again object-rich, with a variety of display techniques. It includes a quiet area where people can record their own experiences and read those of others.

C. Ground floor (right)

Gallery 10: Bodyworks, an interactive exhibition on how the body works, relating this to health care. This gallery is targeted particularly at 7–11-year-olds. It is the third main marketing draw for the museum and can be replaced entirely without affecting the remainder of the displays.

The visitor route around the museum is completed through a visit to the **cafeteria** and **shop**. These are both seen as essential features of the site, as a 'day-out' attraction, as well as earners of secondary income.

CONCLUSION

This article has attempted to outline the factors influencing the concept for the Thackray Medical Museum and to reflect their impact on the storyline and individual galleries.

The museum is a reflection of its time – of a need to combine a commitment to the integrity of its internationally important collections and a mission to act as a source of education and understanding with an ability both to ensure a positive experience for its audience and to remain financially viable in the long term.

Museums and other heritage sites are beginning to move beyond what has been a sustained conflict of views between 'traditionalists', who have felt that much modern display has reflected a debasement of the heritage, and 'modernizers', who have been faced with financial imperatives but have also claimed a greater commitment to audience needs. The Thackray Medical Museum is just one example of an exhibition that sets out to cross that divide.

Since opening, the museum has received considerable, very positive media coverage and has been heavily used, particularly by school groups. It has also won a number of awards, including the prestigious Interpret Britain Award 1998: Special Judges Prize; and the National Heritage/NPI Museum of the Year Award 1998: Best Museum of Industrial or Social History. Ticket sales will tell whether business plan requirements have been met. Evaluation, now under way, will explore the qualitative impact of the displays.

MODEL QUESTIONS

1. Define and illustrate two of the factors influencing the development of the concept for a major new heritage attraction.
   Range for question: basic grasp of and ability to define key concepts.

2. Provide a reasoned order of importance for the factors influencing the development of the concept for the Thackray Medical Museum.
   Range for question: ability to discriminate between and evaluate relevant key concepts.

3. What factors would you focus on in order to attract return visitors?
   Range for question: ability to deploy, use, illustrate and expand on a key relevant concept.

CHAPTER 18

Santa Trains at Bo'ness and Kinneil Railway

Jennifer J. Graham and David J. Morrison

INTRODUCTION

Santa Steam Trains at Bo'ness and Kinneil Railway have been a Christmas highlight for children and adults alike since 1981. Over the years, the Scottish Railway Preservation Society, operators of the heritage railway at Bo'ness in West Lothian, Scotland, have evolved and improved the product, so that it is now the most popular and well-known 'Santa' experience in Central Scotland.

The Scottish Railway Preservation Society (SRPS) was established in 1961, with the aim of preserving, restoring and displaying Scotland's railway heritage. The Society is a company limited by guarantee and is a charity registered in Scotland. Vigorous efforts in the 1960s and 1970s have resulted in a comprehensive collection of over 140 railway vehicles, including steam and diesel locomotives, carriages and wagons. Some of these date back to the last century. In addition there are numerous small items, documents, photographs, lamps, badges, nameplates etc. The collection is still being expanded, as and when noteworthy items become available. The current work of the Society may be categorized into six areas:

1. Operators of the Bo'ness and Kinneil Railway (B&KR).
2. Organizers of mainline Railtours through a subsidiary trading company.
3. Managers of a historic collection of railway artefacts owned by a subsidiary charitable trust, the Scottish Railway Museum Trust.
4. Providers of educational services through a series of winter lectures, bespoke talks to affinity groups, publications and schools' days on the B&KR.
5. Owners and operators of extensive engineering workshops, for the conservation, restoration and maintenance of the collection.
6. Providers of civil engineering resources to maintain the infrastructure, buildings, sidings and running lines of the B&KR, its workshops, storage and display facilities.

MANAGEMENT

The SRPS has nearly 1,300 members, who are encouraged to become active volunteers in the running of the Society and in its operations. About 250 are involved and undertake the wide range of duties necessary to run the services described above on a voluntary basis. These duties include not only such obvious tasks as driving and firing the engines on the Bo'ness and Kinneil Railway, but also the wide range of supporting duties such as restoring and maintaining the locomotives, carriages, and the railway line itself, front-of-house tasks in retail, catering and ticket sales, and administration, marketing, accountancy and legal work.

The Society is managed by unpaid directors, elected by the Society members. The Board of Directors, or Council, in turn appoints committees and individuals to take responsibility for various aspects of the Society's affairs.

FUNDING

Turnover for the year ending March 1997 was £354,792. Sources of income include members' subscriptions, grants and donations, operation of a public train service at Bo'ness, public Railtours on the Railtrack network using Society carriages, and associated retail sales and catering. Funds are wholly devoted to the development of the Society, through investments in better visitor and engineering facilities, adding to the collection, and the repair, restoration, display and interpretation of the existing artefacts. In addition, the Society's status as a charity results in it receiving many benefits in kind, including work done at non-commercial rates, and the loan or gift of equipment and services at no cost. The most valuable benefit in kind which does not show in the accounts however, is the work of the volunteers, estimated to be worth over £500,000 per annum. In the past few years the Society has had a substantial cash balance and has no long-term debt.

BO'NESS AND KINNEIL RAILWAY

The B&KR is located on the southern edge of the Firth of Forth approximately twenty miles west of Edinburgh and close to Falkirk and Linlithgow. Currently, scheduled train services are run over a 3.5 mile section to Birkhill where, in the summer season, passengers may disembark for a guided tour of the caverns of Birkhill Fireclay Mine.

THE SANTA STEAM TRAINS CONCEPT

Santa Steam Trains are not only exciting for children but they also bring back fond memories of steam trains for many of the adults. The package has developed over the years and in 1996 over 8,300 passengers were carried.

The unique selling points are:

- Santa coming to the children and spending time talking to them rather than having them queue, as in a department store.
- On-train entertainment in the form of participative carol singing.
- A festive atmosphere enhanced by each passenger, adult and child alike, being issued with a set of 'reindeer antlers'.

Timetable 1996

The special 'Santa's Polar Express' operates on the four weekends before Christmas. Each day the train makes four journeys at 11 a.m., 12.15 p.m., 1.15 p.m. and 3 p.m. Each return journey is scheduled to last 45 minutes. The one hour fifteen minute period between trains is required to load the 300 or so passengers, give Santa enough time with each child, allow passengers to disembark and have the train cleared of litter. The break of an additional 15 minutes in the middle of the day allows Santa, his elves and the train crew to have lunch!

Fares

The 1996 fare was £4.50 per person (infants 17 months and under are free). A 20 per cent discount is given for groups of sixteen paying passengers on the first two weekends. The price includes train fare, a mince pie and tea/coffee and a set of 'reindeer antlers' for adults. Children receive a gift from Santa, a balloon, a satsuma or an apple and a set of 'reindeer antlers'. Infants also receive a present.

Booking system

Eighty per cent of passengers book in advance by post, from mid-August onwards, although the first enquiry is often as early as April. Initial contact is often by telephone to one of several numbers manned by volunteers. These preliminary bookings are then followed up by a postal confirmation including payment by cheque or postal order. Unfortunately VISA or ACCESS cannot be accepted, and the inclusion of a SAE with the payment greatly reduces the administration effort which falls on a small number of volunteers. During the peak week, as many as 70 bookings a day are being processed by the volunteers after a full day's work.

The Santa Experience

Arrival

The site is near the centre of Bo'ness, but at the 'industrial' end of the town. Almost 100 per cent of visitors come by car and a few in mini-buses. The public bus service is very poor, particularly on Sundays. There are 50 spaces of paved car park, and although there is an overflow area next to the station for a further 250 cars, this is often wet and muddy. See Figure 18.1.

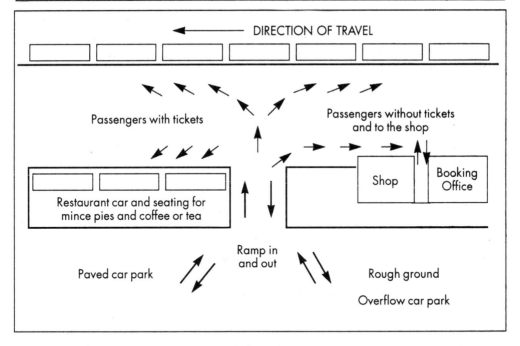

Figure 18.1: Diagram of the visitor flow at Bo'ness Station.

Boarding
Entrance to the platform is by way of a gate where the tickets are checked. The peak flow is approximately fifteen minutes before the departure of the train. Passengers with tickets may board as they arrive and are given help to find seats. Passengers without tickets also flow onto the platform and must double back to a small booking office in the station building. Advance ticket sales are essential to minimize queuing at the one-window ticket office. This old-style ticket window is not conducive to rapid selling or good communication. The seats are not numbered and are filled on a first-come basis. When all seats on the train are sold the station staff encounter difficulties in ensuring that family groups are seated together.

Santa's Polar Express
Near the scheduled departure time, a few passengers are usually still hurrying up the ramp and are guided to seats. The platform staff shout 'All aboard'. If there are some seats remaining, intending passengers who have not pre-booked will be swiftly dealt with, as the guard carries out his obligatory brake test. Observant passengers will see Santa and his three elves scurrying along the platform to board the train at a door held open by a station porter. The guard blows his whistle and the two engines acknowledge with a return whistle. The North Pole Express sets out, amid clouds of smoke and steam as the two engines struggle to get up speed pulling their 240–ton load of coaches and 15 tons of passengers.

Immediately after departure, Santa's helpers hand out inflated balloons to all the children, and a satsuma or apple. Adults and children alike are issued with 'reindeer antler' paper hats to make up. These are inscribed with the logo 'I've seen Santa at the Bo'ness and Kinneil Railway'.

Led by Santa's elves, the children sing Christmas songs and rhymes such as 'Rudolph the Red-Nosed Reindeer' and 'Santa's Coming to Town', with the adults joining in with gusto.

Santa makes his way up the train and spends time talking to each child. He skilfully ascertains the age and the helper hands him an appropriate present according to age and whether a boy or girl. The presents are wrapped in Christmas paper and include furry toys, magnetic games and jigsaw puzzles.

The train steams along the foreshore and then turns inland for the ascent to Birkhill. At Birkhill, the engines have to run round the coaches on a passing loop, to be placed at the head of the train for the return journey. Over 50 per cent of the passengers disembark to watch the proceedings from a nearby overbridge. Approximately fifteen minutes are allowed for this manoeuvre and re-boarding.

During the return journey Santa and the elves continue to visit the children who have not yet met Santa, and the carol singing starts up again in the coaches already visited by Santa.

The station

Once back at the station many passengers go to look at the steam engines, as they uncouple from the train, run to the water tower to refill, and then proceed past the train to once more take up their position ready for the next trip. Some passengers depart immediately, while others go to the shop or straight across the platform to the restaurant car to collect their cup of tea/coffee and mince pie. Many then look for a seat in one of the stationary carriages, although the more experienced know to arrive early, collect their tea/coffee and mince pie prior to departure, and take them on board for the journey.

The shop

The shop is relatively small being about twelve square metres in area. It stocks a range of merchandise with a railway theme, including badges, books, toys and small gift items. Soon after the arrival of a train, the shop rapidly fills up, but between trains, there is time to browse and purchase Christmas gifts.

Operational issues

The popularity of the Santa Steam Trains is such that most trains, and especially those in December, are fully booked and this gives rise to several capacity bottlenecks. Each train can theoretically carry 344 passengers. Almost 100 per cent of passengers come by car, so that, with one train unloading and people arriving for the next, considerable traffic builds up, and parking can become difficult to control. Mince pies, tea and coffee are dispensed from a static restaurant car and coaches in an adjoining platform. There are only 124 seats available in this area, and at times of peak demand serious logistical problems arise. The souvenir shop can only accommodate about fifteen people at a time. The single-window booking office is difficult to sell from and can only process 90 people per hour, assuming the median transaction is for three people and each transaction takes two minutes. For this reason, great emphasis is placed on postal purchase, since facilities for 'collect on the day' are limited.

Planning the 'Santas' begins in March with the selection of suitable gifts. Typical retail values are about £2.50, with a number of gifts covering both sexes, and all age ranges up to 12 years needing to be chosen. When making bookings, the ages of the children are noted, and from previous year's data, estimated numbers of each type of present are ordered. Where possible, gifts with some age flexibility are chosen, so that should the age or sex profile of the children not quite match that of previous years, the assigned present type can be moved up or down a year. Samples of the presents are reviewed by a small committee and informally 'focus group' tested on some unsuspecting schoolchildren. Excess presents from one year are held over for two years, so that children making a repeat visit in the following years do not receive the same gift twice.

The run-round loop length at Birkhill limits the train to a maximum of six coaches. Five of these are 'tourist open' coaches, each seating 64 in tables of four with a central aisle. The sixth coach is a brake van which has four compartments of six seats and a side corridor, a central guard's compartment, and a 'cage'. Historically the cage was used for carrying parcels and freight but in this context it is used as Santa's gift store and 'elf retreat'. The brake van is located in the centre of the train to service the coaches to the front and rear.

To give each child enough time with Santa, three Santas are required, one for each pair of coaches. Care is taken to ensure that the children never see more than one Santa at a time. On the return journey, a stop is made at Kinneil Halt, about 1½ miles from Bo'ness, depending on the progress of the three Santas through their allocated pair of coaches. Once each Santa has reached a pre-defined point in his carriage, the guard waves the train on.

The lighting on the train is provided by battery, with a limited life as the slow running speed does not allow it to recharge effectively. This restricts the running to daylight hours, which in winter means than the service is limited to four trains per day as it is dark by 4 p.m.

Toilets are provided on the train and therefore the water tanks on the coaches must be filled with water and drained at night in case of frost.

Over 60 volunteers are involved over the eight days, just to distribute the presents, balloons, fruit and antlers. Finding suitably extrovert volunteers can be difficult, since many potential candidates are busy with other Christmas festivities. On top of this each day requires five train crew, a minimum of four platform staff to man the doors, car park attendants, booking clerks and catering staff.

The SRPS must comply with all standard rail safety procedures and are subject to routine inspections from the Railway Inspectorate.

Income and expenditure

Santa Steam Trains attract about 1,300 people per day. Theoretically, the maximum income is 344 passengers times four trains per day times eight trains times £4.50 per passenger; that is £49,536. In practice, the following factors prevent this sum being realized.

- The first weekend, especially if it occurs in November, is relatively lightly loaded, to perhaps only 40 per cent of capacity.
- Seating is mostly in bays of four. A large number of bookings for two adults and one child results in spare single seats, which are unsaleable. In the worst case, a nominal 64-seat coach can be 'full' with just 48 passengers.
- The first two weekends are heavily booked by groups receiving a 20 per cent discount.

As a result of these restrictions, ticket income in 1996 was just under £35,000.

Over £3,500 is spent on advertising. Additional costs include the presents, consumables and operating expenses of coal, water and oil. Booking expenses include telephone calls to clarify bookings and postage for tickets if a SAE is not sent. This occurs in about 25 per cent of cases.

Without the huge investment of volunteer effort, the operation would not be profitable, but thanks to the entirely unpaid nature of the work, a healthy contribution to SRPS funds is generated.

Marketing and advertising

The site is thirty minutes from West Edinburgh via the M9 motorway and within one hour's drive for 2.2 million people. Some 40 per cent come from West Edinburgh and the Lothians. West Fife is also perceived as a major catchment area. A print run of 15,000, red ink on white paper 'Santa Leaflets' are distributed by volunteers to libraries, community centres, filling stations etc. Direct mail is used to previous customers and over 200 children's nurseries in central Scotland. Advertisements are placed in selected newspapers, 40 press releases sent out and 25–30 slots broadcast on local radio stations. A number of A4 posters are also distributed locally.

CONCLUSION

Santa Steam Trains on the Bo'ness and Kinneil Railway are very much a showpiece for the SRPS and one of its main marketing tools. It is difficult at times to know who is enjoying the experience more, the public or the volunteer workforce.

There is however, a serious side to the business. The SRPS needs the revenue from these trains to fund its educational and museum-related functions. The members are constantly aware of the need to deliver a high quality product which is widely perceived as good value for money.

As the final trains of the season are being put away, discussions are under way on the changes which would make the next year even better – new software to allow seat allocation – an earlier start to allow longer gaps between trains to relieve pressure on the car park – and so on.

The SRPS volunteers work hard for nine months of the year to make every Santa Train successful and an exciting, fun outing.

> If someone asks me to wrap another 'duck family bath toy' I'll scream – I've already done 600, and they are not even square!
>
> (Volunteer present wrapper)

MODEL QUESTIONS

1. Capacity management strategies includes the dimensions of visitor flow and revenue management.
   a) In what ways can visitor flow be improved?
   b) What opportunities are there for increasing revenue?

2. Within the Schmenner matrix of Service Factory, Service Shop, Mass Service and Professional Service where would you place the Santa Trains Experience at Bo'ness and Kinneil Railway? Discuss.

3. Following on from the Schmenner matrix, discuss the features of the service, process, customer-orientated, labour-related and management features of the Santa Trains Experience at Bo'ness and Kinneil Railway.

CHAPTER 19

Volunteer Management at Nugget Hill: A Case Study

Leo K. Jago and Margaret A. Deery

INTRODUCTION

This case study explores the management of a volunteer workforce within an award winning heritage visitor attraction. In particular, it examines strategic human resource management issues such as recruitment, training and development, and the reward system. Attention is also given to the relationship between the paid workforce and the volunteers. The data used in the case study were derived from interviews with management and key volunteers, together with quantitative survey information obtained from the volunteer workforce.

Nugget Hill is a re-created 1850s gold mining town set in Bendigo, a city with a strong gold mining tradition. Nugget Hill was opened to the public in 1970 and has been the recipient of numerous state and national tourism awards. It receives an annual visitation of over 600,000. Nugget Hill is renown for its authentic display of living history, and management goes to great lengths to preserve and develop this authenticity.

Funding for Nugget Hill was initially provided by several prominent Bendigo organizations, with further funding coming largely from four major public appeals. The State Government has also provided substantial support for Nugget Hill's major capital projects. The facility has no debt capital to support and all profits are invested in further developments at the site.

PHYSICAL SETTING AND FACILITIES

Nugget Hill is located on 60 acres in an original gold mining area some three kilometres from the centre of Bendigo. The City of Bendigo has a population of 80,000 and is a 1.5 hour drive to the north of Melbourne, the capital city of Victoria.

Being a re-created 1850s gold mining town, Nugget Hill has a comprehensive range of shops, industries, services and houses that one would expect to find in such a town. In order to add to the authenticity of the town and to increase the overall ambience of the attraction, all staff wear period costumes and are well versed in the behaviour and activities appropriate for the period.

Along with the regular maintenance program that is conducted at Nugget Hill, there is a continual expansion program that adds to the size of the town and provides an incentive for repeat visitation. Most of this expansion is incremental, but in 1994 a major project known as 'Eureka' opened. 'Eureka', which added a new dimension to the facility, is a sound and light show that operates each evening after dark and is a recreation of a rebellion known as the Eureka Uprising.

ORGANIZATION STRUCTURE

Nugget Hill is controlled by the Bendigo Historical Park Association which is a non-profit community-based organization. Membership is based on payment of an annual subscription, and the members elect a 21-member Board of Directors from which an eight-member Executive is appointed. The day-to-day operation of Nugget Hill is controlled by a professional staff led by an Executive Director who interacts closely with the Board.

There are over 300 people employed at Nugget Hill, with a full-time equivalent paid workforce of about 200. There are also 280 volunteers who offer their services on a regular basis in a variety of capacities. People in period costume are a fundamental component of the product at Nugget Hill and are essential to the delivery of an authentic experience. It is therefore necessary to have a team of volunteers to be able to fill this role and to help the visitor interpret the history on display. The main role of these volunteers is to act in the manner of 1850s townsfolk, including shopping in town, performing normal household duties or working in the mine. A simplified version of the organizational structure for Nugget Hill is represented diagrammatically in Figure 19.1. As illustrated by the chart, Nugget Hill has a relatively flat structure with most control resting with the three deputy directors.

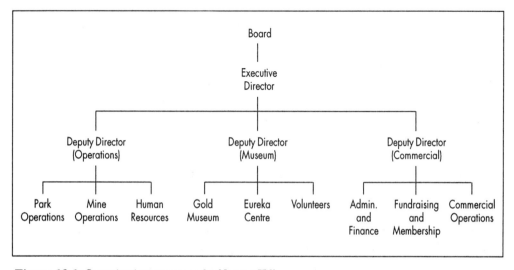

Figure 19.1: Organization structure for Nugget Hill.

The activities and rosters for the volunteers are co-ordinated by a member of the paid workforce. The person filling this position was herself a volunteer for some years and believes that this experience helps her empathise with the needs of the volunteers. The Volunteer Co-ordinator reports to the Deputy Director (Museum), placing this position on the same organizational level as important components of Nugget Hill, such as the Gold Museum and the Eureka Centre. However, it is interesting to note that the volunteers are not positioned with the Human Resources Department (HRD), but rather with the museum section. This suggests that the volunteers are viewed as an important addition to the historical dimension of the facility, but not an integrated component of the HRD.

ROLE OF VOLUNTEERS

In announcing Nugget Hill as the winner of Australia's leading Tourism Attraction category at the recent National Tourism Awards, the Minister for Tourism commented specifically on the importance of the volunteers in the tourist experience at Nugget Hill. As a result of this comment and the increasing importance of volunteers at other heritage attractions, the Board of Directors of Nugget Hill initiated a review of the volunteer program, with the aim of achieving best practice in the management of volunteers.

Volunteers were introduced to Nugget Hill in 1980, ten years after the attraction was officially opened. The volunteer program was initiated to add to the ambience and authenticity of Nugget Hill's historical product by helping to interpret the experience for the visitors. Each day there are usually between 15 and 20 volunteers who offer their services at the attraction. Their function is to role-play various characters from an 1850s gold mining town and to interact with the visitors. This interaction can include explaining why things were done in a particular fashion, explaining the significance of the clothing of the period, or even providing tourist information on other attractions in Bendigo.

For the first ten years of the volunteer programme there was substantial friction between the paid staff at Nugget Hill and the volunteers. The staff were concerned that their jobs would eventually be taken over by volunteers and staff would be made redundant. In order to ameliorate this perceived problem, management vowed that work done by a paid member of staff would never, under any circumstances, be carried out by a volunteer. Over time, paid staff came to recognize that volunteers were not a threat to their positions and the friction between the two groups dissipated. The situation was particularly assisted when some of the early protagonists left the organization.

Since the Board of Directors was unable to identify anyone within the Nugget Hill organization to implement the review of the volunteer programme objectively, it was decided to appoint an experienced HRM consultant, Anne Howley, to conduct the review.

Anne, having visited Nugget Hill as a tourist on a number of occasions, was aware that there was an extensive volunteer programme in place. Upon starting the consultancy, however, she was surprised to find that the volunteer programme was quite unstructured, little documentation about the programme existed, and there were virtually no records about the volunteers themselves. The volunteer programme was managed entirely by Jane Castle, the Volunteer Co-ordinator. Jane herself had been a volunteer for five years before being employed as Volunteer Co-ordinator eight years ago. Based on interviews with both Jane and many of the volunteers, Anne found that Jane played an enormous role in the overall success of the volunteer programme. Although few systems were in place to manage the volunteer programme, Jane had substantial empathy for the role of the volunteer and was greatly respected by all of the volunteers.

Following numerous interviews with both paid staff and volunteers at Nugget Hill, Anne confirmed the need to conduct a survey of the volunteers in order to evaluate the volunteer programme. The questionnaire that Anne designed and mailed to all of the volunteers at Nugget Hill sought information on a variety of topics including: volunteer motives, demographics, training needs, volunteer time commitment, and level of volunteer satisfaction. Despite comments from management that volunteers were notoriously poor in responding to questionnaires, over 50 per cent of the questionnaires were completed and returned. Even the range of open-ended questions that Anne had included in the questionnaire was completed in detail by most respondents. Anne's preliminary analysis of the questionnaire results indicated clearly that, despite the lack of structure associated with the volunteer programme, the volunteers themselves were generally satisfied with the experience; this was supported by the high average length of time that respondents had been volunteers. Table 19.1 (page 272) provides some of the details relating to volunteer demographics and volunteer work commitments that were obtained from this questionnaire.

Based on program reviews Anne had done elsewhere, she knew that the key issues in the evaluation of a volunteer program included recruitment, training and development, reward system, and the relationship between paid staff and volunteers.

RECRUITMENT

Recruitment of volunteers had been conducted, initially, through newspaper and radio advertisements in the local area. However, it was found that some of the people who responded to such advertisements were not suitable as volunteers but, as Jane Castle stated, it was extremely difficult to reject people who apply for volunteer positions.

Another problem was that some of the volunteers recruited in this manner did not deliver the desired level of service. As a consequence, advertisements for

Table 19.1: Volunteer demographics and volunteer involvement.

Gender	
Male	41%
Female	59%
Age	
18–24	4%
25–34	0%
35–44	19%
45–54	16%
55–64	22%
65 and above	39%
Duration of service	
Less than 1 year	6%
Between 1 and 3 years	24%
Between 3 and 5 years	15%
Between 5 and 10 years	25%
More than 10 years	30%
Hours of service per month	
Up to 5 hours	8%
5 to 10 hours	11%
10 to 20 hours	38%
20 to 40 hours	38%
More than 40 hours	5%

volunteers were abandoned and a system of recruitment through friends, family members and contacts of existing volunteers was implemented. As illustrated in Table 19.2, 67 per cent of volunteers were informed about the volunteering positions at Nugget Hill through a personal contact. Anne realized that this finding was consistent with volunteering organizations in general and she noted that Nugget Hill should do more to take greater advantage of personal contacts.

Nugget Hill had, traditionally, recruited volunteers twice per year, so that economies of scale could be achieved with the induction and training programmes. In between recruitments, Jane collected the names of prospective volunteers. Anne wondered whether this recruiting practice led to the loss of prospective volunteers

Table 19.2: Nugget Hill Volunteers' source of information about volunteer positions at Nugget Hill.

Newspaper	13%
Brochure	1%
Information session	5%
Friend or family member	26%
Another volunteer	41%
Other	14%

to other volunteer programs, especially since the results of her survey of volunteers indicated that 43 per cent of respondents also volunteered for other organizations besides Nugget Hill. This figure, which was above the national average for volunteer involvement, suggested that people who volunteered at Nugget Hill would be quite happy to offer their services elsewhere.

Anne also learnt that a number of people who offered Jane their services as volunteers at Nugget Hill, did so in the hope of eventually obtaining paid positions. Nugget Hill's management treated the volunteers and paid staff as quite separate entities and was against volunteers becoming paid staff. Only three people, including Jane herself, have made the transition from volunteer to a paid position at Nugget Hill during the 17 years that the volunteer programme has been operating. Having discovered management's opposition to fill paid positions at Nugget Hill from the volunteer force, Anne was surprised to learn that management actively sought to fill paid positions with friends and family of existing employees. Positions were advertised internally as well as externally to the organization. Management informed Anne that this form of recruitment led to a more contented workforce.

TRAINING AND DEVELOPMENT

Training at Nugget Hill, for both volunteers and paid staff, involved a two-day programme incorporating a comprehensive site inspection and lectures on the history of Nugget Hill and the period it represented. It was mandatory that no volunteer commenced work until the training programme had been attended. These programmes were run twice a year for volunteers to coincide with the biannual recruitments. Through the review survey, however, many of the volunteers stated that the large number of trainees, at least twenty people, tended to intimidate new volunteers and reduced their propensity to ask questions and participate.

Volunteers also received an information kit providing background details relating to the character they were to play, and they were encouraged to use the Nugget Hill library to source more information on the 1850s gold mining communities. No other ongoing training was organized for the volunteers by management.

In discussing the role of volunteer training, Jane Castle advised Anne that, although she felt some form of ongoing training would be of benefit to the volunteers, the volunteers themselves were not at all interested in extra training. The results of Anne's questionnaire supported this. However, it appeared that there was some confusion regarding the meaning of training. Through interviews with volunteers, it became clear to Anne that they believed training related only to additional historical information on the 1850s period. The questionnaire indicated that one of the most important motives for people volunteering their services at Nugget Hill was an interest in history and therefore many of the volunteers had read widely in their own time and had developed substantial expertise in this field. As a result, many considered that it would be a waste of their time to have even more training on this topic.

To compound this misunderstanding of training, the volunteer committee, a group of six volunteers elected by the volunteers on an annual basis to assist the Volunteer Co-ordinator, organized a guest speaker each month for the volunteers on a wide range of topics. Anne was surprised to find that neither the Volunteer Co-ordinator nor the volunteers themselves regarded these as training sessions.

Although there was no formal 'on-the-job' training system in place for volunteers at Nugget Hill, Anne discovered from her interviews that an informal mentoring system was an important part of the culture. Under this system, new volunteers would tend to associate with, and learn from, more experienced volunteers – even to the extent of 'recycling' their more popular anecdotes. This process was encouraged by the Volunteer Co-ordinator.

Anne also found that, until recently, the paid staff had received little training after their two-day induction period at the start of their employment. A newly appointed Deputy Director of Nugget Hill, Penny Jones, had embarked on a programme to ensure that all staff received on-going training in a wide variety of areas. Besides believing in the importance of on-going training, Penny informed Anne that such training was necessary to ensure that the organization complied with both health and safety legislation and anti-discrimination legislation. Penny hoped that volunteers would ultimately be encouraged to participate in these training programmes.

REWARD SYSTEM

The results of the questionnaire indicated clearly to Anne that the issue of rewards was the one causing most concern for volunteers. Although wages clearly do not apply in the case of volunteers, there are many other ways to reward volunteers. The rewards which volunteers at Nugget Hill received included discounted family entry to Nugget Hill, familiarization tours of other attractions, refreshments on hot days, and an invitation to a volunteer Christmas party. There was no formal recognition system of volunteer service at Nugget Hill and a large number of volunteers identified this as a major cause for concern. A few volunteers suggested that they should be entitled to travelling and meal allowances but these numbers were insignificant in comparison to the number of volunteers who wanted some type of formal recognition of their contribution.

When Anne raised this issue with Jane, she was told that the volunteer concerns were well known but that no records had been kept which would enable Jane to correctly document the hours of service provided by each of the volunteers over the years. Anne felt that to overcome this, awards for years of service should be given and all hours of service be documented from now on. Jane believed that this would cause problems with the volunteers as there were vast differences between the monthly contributions of various volunteers.

The reward systems for the paid staff of Nugget Hill were similar to those adopted in most other organizations. The main difference with Nugget Hill, however, was that management was determined to promote from within. Management informed Anne that the work environment at Nugget Hill was quite different from many other organizations and resulted in a very distinct work culture. To maintain this culture and to reduce employee turnover, management actively sought to promote internally. Management felt that the many tourism awards that Nugget Hill had won and the fact that it had a low employee turnover supported its policy in this area.

RELATIONSHIP BETWEEN VOLUNTEERS AND PAID STAFF

Despite the fact that the tourist experience offered by Nugget Hill was so cohesive, Anne was surprised to learn that paid staff and volunteers in the organization were treated as totally separate entities and there was virtually no interaction between the two groups. Figure 19.1 showed that human resources and volunteers were each managed by different Deputy Directors, demonstrating an organizational separation between the two groups. Anne was aware that there had been friction between the two groups in the early years of Nugget Hill because of the paid staff's suspicion that volunteers would replace them. Management had demonstrated, however, that this would not be the case although Anne felt that this had not been made clear to some of the volunteers who were keen to work with the paid staff in certain roles and did not understand management's concern about the precedent that it could set. In order to reinforce management's commitment to its paid workforce, management had allowed certain facilities at Nugget Hill to close temporarily due to absence of paid staff, rather than fill these positions in the short term with volunteer staff.

The formal reporting relationship between paid staff and volunteers was clearly understood and followed within the organization. Volunteers were managed by Jane Castle and no paid staff member, at any level, was able to direct volunteers; all such requests were to be directed through Jane. Anne noted that this system seemed to work well and both paid staff and volunteers were comfortable with it.

Even socially, Anne found that paid staff and volunteers operated as totally separate entities, with little intermingling. Both groups had their own kitchen and lounge facilities and operated their own social clubs. Jane Castle was the only person who seemed to have a strong relationship with both groups. Even though the two groups operated so independently, they both seemed aware of what the other group was doing. Anne discovered from the volunteers that the paid staff had just been given the opportunity to receive a 50 per cent discount on their meals at one of the restaurants within the facility. The volunteers were most irate that they too were not offered the same discount and reinforced in Anne's mind the fact that more should be done to treat these two groups as members of the same team. Anne knew that demographics was a key reason for the fact that the two groups did not intermingle. Most of the paid staff were aged below 40 whereas the results of the questionnaire, as presented in Table 19.1, showed that the average age of the volunteers was much higher, with 60 per cent being aged above 55 years. There was also a gender imbalance, with more of the paid staff being male and more of the volunteers being female.

CONCLUSION

After many interviews with both volunteers and paid staff and the analysis of the questionnaire that she had administered to the volunteers, Anne felt that she had quite a clear understanding of the position of the volunteers at Nugget Hill and felt comfortable in writing a report to the Board of Directors. Anne acknowledged that the volunteer programme had clearly worked well, despite the fact that it was so poorly documented and that there was a surprising gulf between volunteers and paid staff. She was confident, however, that the volunteer program would deliver even greater benefits all round if the recommendations that she would include in her report were adopted.

FURTHER READING

Go, F., Monachello, M. L. and Baum, T. (1996) *Human Resource Management in the Hospitality Industry*, New York: John Wiley & Sons.

Nankervis, A., Compton, R. and McCarthy, T. (1995) *Strategic Human Resource Management*, Melbourne: Pitman.

Pearce, J. (1993) *Volunteers. The Organisational Behaviour of Unpaid Workers*, London: Routledge.

Swarbrooke, J. (1995) *The Development and Management of Visitor Attractions*, Oxford: Butterworth-Heinemann.

MODEL QUESTIONS

1. What changes to the volunteer programme is Anne likely to recommend to Nugget Hill's Board of Directors? Include in your answer strategies that could be implemented to help volunteers and paid staff operate more cohesively.

2. What sort of training should be implemented for the volunteers and how should it be administered, given that volunteers are giving of their time freely? Should volunteers and paid staff be trained together?

3. Devise a recognition system for the volunteers.

CHAPTER 20

Visitor Satisfaction Management at Leeds Castle, Kent

Eric Laws

INTRODUCTION

This chapter presents a brief overview of the evolving fields of service and quality management theory as a context to a case study demonstrating service blueprinting methodology. It examines how blueprinting techniques can be used to gain an understanding of the issues confronting managers of an established service delivery system. Service design and resourcing decisions are crucial management responsibilities, because together they define the parameters for service encounters between staff and customers, and for customer satisfaction. Appropriate service design underpins successful service delivery, it minimizes dysfunction, and maximizes effective service transactions, providing satisfying experiences for customers and contributing to the organization's business objectives.

Castles and other historic buildings are amongst Europe's key tourist attractions, and they are also central to the cultural identity of European nations. The English Tourist Board has noted over 450,000 listed buildings, and 14,000 ancient monuments or structures of national importance (ETB 1996). Easthaugh and Weiss (1989) commented, 'As a tourist attraction, our heritage gives Great Britain a comparative advantage over other countries . . . our architectural and historic monuments are a major factor in making this country an attractive destination for overseas visitors.' Their striking external appearance and their often dominant siting, make them an almost inevitable feature of tourists' itineraries. Many are also treasure houses of medieval tapestry, furniture, portraits or armour, and some are still home to families who have owned them for many generations. Internally, their configurations are idiosyncratic, with steep narrow stairways, many passageways and tiny windows. Together, these conditions present contemporary managers in the visitor industry with a range of problems.

Leeds Castle, built on a small island in Kent and one of Britain's oldest historic houses, now epitomizes the appearance of a medieval Royal Castle and the enjoyment to be gained from visiting a well-managed historic building. This chapter concludes with a blueprinting study of visitor management at Leeds Castle.

MANAGING CASTLE VISITS

The visitor's experience of most castles is now highly structured by management decisions about how to control the flow of people in large numbers through a sequence of sights and activities determined by each castle's individual location, configuration and special features. Another aspect of visits to castles is that there is a variety of interaction between visitors and castle. In most historic buildings, visitors are either accompanied by a guide, or they encounter custodians in each major exhibit area. These points of contact are important in providing visitors with information to help them enjoy their visit, but are also essential in ensuring that every visitor follows the correct sequence through the castle. This minimizes congestion and ensures the safety both of visitors and of the artefacts on display. There are also additional points of contact with staff at the castle's point-of-ticket sale – and the catering and retail outlets. There are also occasional special events, and these include displays of traditional skills such as archery or falconry, crafts, walking in the castle's grounds or attending musical or other performances.

Another key problem is that although service managers may wish to specify precise standards consistent for all customers, just as a production manager in a factory setting would expect to, in reality each service transaction is itself a variable. The quality of the service experience for each visitor is dependent on his or her own interaction with staff, but this takes place in the context of the physical setting and the technical features of the visit (Gummesson 1988). Managers are responsible for the design and resourcing of the service, rather than the castle itself. In presenting it to tourists, they take decisions about the sequence of the visit, what information will be presented, and in what form, how the castle will be illuminated, internally and externally, where toilets and other visitor facilities will be located, how staff will be selected and trained in the various specialized roles needed for custodianship, how to maintain the structure and its surrounding grounds, and how the castle will be promoted to potential visitors. These decisions can be thought of as components in the design of the service which visitors experience, and as factors in the service organization's financial success (Kingman Brundage 1989). Therefore, these are significant factors in their overall satisfaction, and in the increasingly competitive tourism and heritage markets it is important to ensure that all components of a visit offer visitors the quality of experience which they desire (Reeves and Bednar 1994).

BLUEPRINTING A CASTLE VISIT

Many of the issues outlined above are inter-related, and the overall visit experience can be investigated by service blueprinting techniques. The concept of a service blueprint has been described as '. . . the process of defining the range of resources required for the performance of services, and of co-ordinating the various components' (Laws 1991). Berry (1995) noted that 'Dependability and accuracy can be designed into a service system, or designed out of it . . . (the real culprit for service mistakes) is often . . . a needlessly complicated and failure prone service system.'

An overview of service blueprinting

In essence, a service blueprint is a diagram which shows all the elements that go to make up the service being studied: its purpose is to enable the service to be analysed as objectively as possible. The sequence of steps in blueprinting a service is as follows:

1. Study the sequence of service elements experienced by a range of clients.
2. Arrange the clients' experience as a simplified flowchart.
3. Study the features of the service delivery system(s).
4. Flowchart the elements in the service delivery system.
5. Analyse customers' experience of the service delivery system to identify fail points.
6. Analyse the rationales for the crisis points in the existing service delivery system.
7. Assess the costs of service delivery system weaknesses.
8. Evaluate the opportunities for improvements, and assess the costs of implementation.

Blueprinting requires the researcher to generate two sets of information, and to compare them. One set of information can be presented as a flow chart showing the sequence of events which the customer experiences, this aspect of the methodology draws on observation and participant observation techniques as discussed in Gummesson (1993). The second set of information can also be presented as a flow chart, this shows the sequence of interlinked technical processes undertaken by the organization to prepare the service, and considers how they are resourced. This can be based on a combination of observation and interviews with managers and staff, including focus group work, thus eliciting the detail of the service delivery system lying below the line of customer visibility, a concept introduced by Shostack (1981) in her pioneering article on service blueprinting.

In more advanced applications, further detail can be mapped onto the diagram to show the dependency of the delivery system on articulation of the company's internal processes, managerial support and the physical constraints imposed, for example, by the architecture of the service setting (Fellows and Fellows 1990), or the equipment deployed. The data for both flow charts can be generated by a planned programme consisting of observation, participation and surveys, or a combination of these methodologies, as listed below. (The theoretical underpinnings of these procedures are not discussed further in this chapter.)

1.   Observation.
2.   Participant observation.
3.   Interviews.
4.   Focus groups.
5.   Analysis of customer correspondence.
6.   Study of company documents.

METHODOLOGIES IN STUDYING SERVICE DELIVERY SYSTEMS

Systems theory

The complexity of services can be appreciated using perspectives from systems theory. This concept argues that selected inputs are combined in a series of processes, with the intention of producing specified outputs, each process stage adding accumulating value to the service. Efficiency in the system's operation can therefore be evaluated by measuring outputs against the inputs required to produce them, by examining the quality of those outputs, and by considering the way each process contributes to the overall service. It has been noted that although systems thinking has mainly been applied to 'hard' engineering situations, where outcomes are unambiguous and highly predictable, the concept can be applied in situations where human behaviour is a significant factor in business activities combining social and technical processes (Checkland and Scholes 1990; Kirk 1995).

Service blueprinting theory

As with systems theory, blueprinting also has its origins in 'hard' applications. Traditionally, a blueprint is an ordered technical drawing in which the symbols represent instructions to technicians which they use as a template in manufacturing processes, or in wiring electrical circuitry. Shostack (1981) advocated the method and demonstrated its application to the analysis of quality and performance in service delivery systems.

Gummesson (1990) also advocated service blueprinting as a systematic way of describing a service in order to make sure that all elements are included, so that their cost and contribution to revenue in the composition of the service can be examined. Shostack (1985) herself suggested that a service blueprint should have three main features. Firstly, it must incorporate within the design a time dimension, enabling the researcher to follow the progression of the service delivery system which the customer experiences. Secondly, it should show the main functions which together comprise the service, and show their interconnectedness. Shostack argued that the third feature of a blueprint is that it should incorporate performance standards for each stage of the process. This introduces a further feature of service blueprints: they can be used to identify failpoints, the parts of a service which are most likely to cause errors (George and Gibson 1988), although the term 'crisis point' has been adopted in this chapter. It is this feature which provides the diagnostic capability of the service blueprinting method.

Several researchers have further developed the blueprinting concept. A significant refinement to blueprinting emphasises the significance of customers' perceptions of the service delivery system overall, or of selected elements in it (Senior and Akehurst 1992). This is particularly helpful, because it is widely accepted that customers' perceptions of service events differ, and that individual quality judgements are based on the divergence of the service experiences from the service anticipated by customers when purchasing it (Laws 1986).

Delivering quality services

Any service is composed of a series of events which the client experiences. The key points during the service are the customer's 'moments of truth' (Normann 1 991). Each of the moments of truth is an occurrence used by customers to judge the quality of the service, and Carlzon (1987) argued that these should be the focus of managers' attention.

The difficulty in achieving consistent service standards revolves around the two bases to services, termed Type A and Type B (Laws 1986). The technical 'Type A' aspects of managing any service are similar to the 'hard' systems elements discussed earlier, but contrast with the interactions between staff and clients which characterize the delivery of services. Type B aspects of service systems have much in common with the 'soft' features of systems theory. Differing, though connected implications flow from a recognition of these two factors in tourism management. While Type A factors (except for the actual structure of a historic building) are generally under the direct control of managers, the Type B factors are more complex. They include the skills and motivations of staff, their ability to interact effectively with clients, and the unpredictably variable expectations and behaviour which different clients bring to the service episode and its constituent elements.

Anticipating satisfaction from services

A key factor in managing services for quality is to understand the satisfaction which clients anticipate from the purchase of a service. Consumer decision-taking represents a choice between alternative allocations of time and funds, and these choices can cause anxiety about the correctness of the decision taken. One method by which consumers can reduce the potential risk of making an unsatisfactory purchase is to seek information beforehand, by informal word of mouth from friends or from formal marketing communication sources such as advertising, brochures or sales staff.

From a managerial perspective, the technique of service blueprinting can assist in locating any potential problems with a service delivery system (Leppard and Molyneux 1994). Implementing quality improvements requires investment in actions taken to get the service delivery system right, and continuous auditing to ensure that it is correctly delivered. These costs to the firm should be weighed against the expenses of responding to any failure (Lockyer and Oakland 1981). However, the advantages of enhancing service delivery through redesign or better use of resources include an improved rate of customer satisfaction.

Technical approaches to service quality

The challenge for service managers is to design a service delivery system which combines maximizing customers' judgements that the service experienced is satisfying, with technical efficiency in the use of resources used in delivering the service. Gronroos (1990) has distinguished between two approaches in analysing the quality of services: technology-driven and fitness for use, and customer-driven definitions.

One strategy which service managers often adopt in their search for consistent service is to eliminate employee discretion and judgement whenever possible (Sasser, Olsen and Wycoff 1978). This approach to service design relies on the specification of tasks to a standard of performance required by management, thereby providing a basis for measuring the effectiveness of staff performing services. Increased standardization implies a reduction in the discretion allowed to individual employees, although this contradicts clients' expectations of being treated as individuals, with needs which may vary during the many events of which a service is composed. Efficiency goals may clarify performance targets for staff, but can conflict with the customers' expectation of a warm and friendly service. Underlying this approach are the twin assumptions that consumers experience a service as a series of events, while managers see the service as a set of elements which require skilled co-ordination, and resource control, in delivering specified standards to clients.

The technical approach to quality is often expressed as performance criteria specified for elements in the service delivery system. Thus, transport companies publicize the proportion of their 'on-time' arrivals. Commenting on technical performance goals, Locke and Scweiger (1979) identified seven important characteristics of effective programmes. They suggested that the goals set must be specific, accepted, cover important job dimensions, be reviewed, with appropriate feedback, be measurable and challenging, but attainable. Hollins and Hollins (1991) also advocated a process of continuous improvements, relying on a view which underlies service blueprinting that the service is a chain of events which the customer experiences. The stage of designing the service is its managers' main opportunity to determine the characteristics of the service offered to customers.

Customer-oriented service quality

The second quality approach discussed by Gronroos (1990) was fitness for use. This can best be understood in terms of customers' expectations of satisfaction, against which they evaluate their subsequent individual experiences during the service. Marketing theory argues that customers' experiences with any purchase give rise to outcomes for them varying from satisfaction to dissatisfaction. This reflects a divergence from the standards of service which clients had anticipated, as the following abbreviated quotations indicate: 'The seeds of consumer satisfaction are planted during the pre-purchase phase of the consumer decision process' (Wilkie 1986). It is against this individual benchmark that tourists measure the quality of their service experiences. 'Satisfaction is defined as a postconsumption evaluation that the chosen alternative is consistent with prior beliefs and expectations (with respect to it). Dissatisfaction, of course, is the outcome when this confirmation does not take place' (Engel, Blackwell and Miniard 1986).

This type of quality is more difficult to measure and to manage than technical conformance to specification. Individuals confronted with any given situation experience varying degrees of satisfaction or dissatisfaction, for three reasons. Firstly, each individual approaches a service with his or her own set of expectations based on prior experience, immediate disposition and needs. Secondly, a guide leading a group around a historic building could, in explaining a particular feature, excite and inform one member of the group, but bore or antagonize another person with a different level of prior knowledge or understanding. Thirdly, the combination of these two factors, varying expectations and differing experiences, can result in unequal gaps between expectations and experience for customers. Managers who wish to provide services which fit their customers' needs must therefore incorporate flexibility into the design of their services so that staff can respond effectively to their clients' individual needs. This requires skilled staff, operating within an organizational culture focused on clients' needs, and empowered with (limited) discretion to make immediate judgements about the use of the company's resources to satisfy the clients they are serving.

Interactions between customers and staff

A key feature distinguishing services from the production of manufactured goods is that managerial decisions about the characteristics of the services offered are dependent to a greater extent on the way individual employees interpret service design and performance criteria. Furthermore, service delivery entails interaction with the customer, and its quality therefore depends partly on gaining their co-operation (Bitner, Booms and Tetreault 1990).

LEEDS CASTLE

Leeds Castle (illustrated on the cover of this book) is one of Britain's leading historic attractions, having featured prominently in many English Tourist Board and other high-profile international promotions. Its striking design and its location in a beautiful lake and country park provide a superb setting for many cultural and other events. The Castle entrance is adjacent to the main motorway linking London with the continent of Europe, and this provides easy access for day excursionists from a vast catchment area, as well as the potential of being a stopping-point for motorists travelling between Europe and Britain.

The origins of the Castle have been traced to Saxon times, when a wooden manor was built for the royal family near the village of Leeds in Kent. After the Norman conquest of England in 1066 – the country was subdued by the construction of stone castles, and Robert de Crevecoeur strated to build his castle on the present site around 1119. A century and a half later, his great-great grandson fought against Henry III at the Battle of Lewis (1246), and was later obliged to yield the Castle to Sir Roger de Leyburn, a supporter of the King. In 1287, his son conveyed Leeds Castle to 'the august prince and my most dear Lord Edward the noble King of England and my fair Lady Elinor Queen of England' (Leeds Castle Foundation 1994).

The Leeds Castle Foundation has documented the ownership of the Castle since the year 856, when it belonged to Ethelbert IV, until 1974 when the Honourable Olive Lady Baillie gave the castle in perpetuity to the Foundation 'for the British peoples' enjoyment for ever'. The Foundation was established as a charity with duties to preserve the Castle so that it is open and available to visitors, and if funds permitted, to promote the use of the Castle for significant national and international medical seminars and for artistic and cultural events, and to be used for important meetings of international statesmen. The Castle and its park were to be used for conferences and in other ways which could earn money to maintain the Castle, its parkland and their amenities, and to fulfil the other purposes of the charity (Leeds Castle Foundation 1994).

Although the main interest of this chapter is in visits to the Castle itself, it is important to note that Leeds Castle and its grounds serve a number of functions; in addition to being a major tourist attraction, the Castle houses a conference centre, the grounds include a golf course, gardens, greenhouses, a grotto, a maze, an aviary and vineyards. There are stable yards and a restored seventeenth-century barn, now operating as a restaurant. Other impressive buildings provide residential conference accommodation, shops and further catering facilities.

A major function of the Castle Trust is to host Board-level residential conferences, for which the standard 24-hour all-inclusive delegate rate is £245 compared to £8.50 maximum charge to day visitors (1997 rates). It is essential to maintain the privacy of conferences, and day visitors do not have access to the residential or the business accommodation in the Castle. Similarly, day visitors are at liberty to enjoy the extensive grounds of the castle, but the grounds also include a golf course with weekday rates of £9.50 and weekend charges of £10.50. These three operations – the Castle, conferences and golf course – are staffed separately, and co-ordination meetings are held regularly to ensure that staff are aware of the other operations at the Castle.

The Castle employs 110 full-time staff, and is open seven days per week, all year round. Fifty per cent of visitors are from overseas, and one-third come in groups. Leeds Castle produced a turnover of £6.5 million, two-thirds from day visitors, half this revenue was earned at the gate. Twenty-five per cent of revenue was derived from the conference and banqueting businesses, 10 per cent from open-air concerts, golf and the vineyard. In 1996, 600,000 people overall visited the Castle, half a million of them being day visitors.

Profile of a visit to Leeds Castle

After entering the grounds through the ticketing point, visitors are at liberty to undertake any of the activities available, in whatever sequence appeals to them. This chapter concentrates on the management of visitor experiences to the Castle itself, and discussion therefore does not deal with the other features enjoyed by typical visitors, such as the maze and grotto, the aviary, and the culpeper garden.

The basis of service blueprinting is to understand the customers' perspective: Table 20.1 (page 287) summarizes factors which influenced the satisfaction experienced during a recent visit to Leeds Castle by the researcher and his partner. It gives a brief account of each event, and notes whether it raised (+) or depressed (–) satisfaction. Overall, the two visitors were very pleased with their experiences, and it should be noted that overall satisfaction with the visit cannot be computed by merely comparing the number of positive and negative experiences; their significance is in assisting in the identification of actual or potential problem areas for managerial consideration. In a full service blueprinting exercise, the experiences of many visitors would be studied and evaluated.

Figure 20.1 (page 286) presents an outline blueprint of a visit to Leeds Castle,

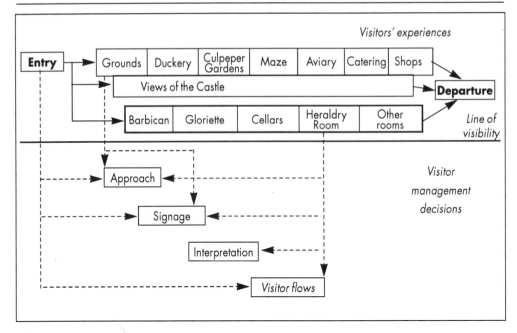

Figure 20.1: Blueprint of a visit to Leeds Castle.

drawing on the profile provided above, but it condenses the nineteen separate points affecting satisfaction into four factors in the service design. These are associated with the key management decisions regarding a visitor's approach to the Castle: signing, interpretation, and visitor flow management. The managerial rationales of these are discussed in the following section.

VISITOR SATISFACTION MANAGEMENT AT LEEDS CASTLE

1. The approach

(Points 2, 4, 6, 7, 11, in the visit profile, Table 20.1.) The Castle was opened to paying visitors in 1974, when Leeds Castle Foundation was established. At the outset, it was decided that views of the Castle and its lake, set in spacious lawns, were to be sacrosanct. From this, it followed that the car parks and most visitor amenities would be better located a considerable distance from the Castle. A notice is printed on entrance tickets, and the walk is well signposted. A duckery and attractive gardens were constructed to soften and enliven the walk, with strategically located benches, and special transport was provided in the grounds for the elderly or disabled. However, the use of wheelchairs inside the Castle itself is limited to three at any one time because of the many narrow staircases.

Table 20.1: Profile of satisfaction experienced during a visit to Leeds Castle.

Account of experience	Effect on satisfaction
After parking, we walk towards the entrance to the Castle grounds, but a barrier across the roadway, and buildings to each side, confuse us.	–
We queue behind a school group for tickets, before a steward indicates the ticket counter for individuals.	–
The shop is crowded.	–
The group of youngsters is now blocking the main entrance, and we feel concerned that we may be in for a noisy visit.	–
The group waits for all members to pass the entrance, so we walk ahead quickly.	+
The Castle comes into view across the lawn. The sun is shining and we are again glad that we decided to visit.	+
As we get nearer, a dark cloud obscures the sun. We begin to wonder if we should go back to the car for our coats, but decide not to.	–
The stonemason's plaque in the barbican catches our attention, and we look more closely at the old walls.	+
I want to take a photo of the Castle framed by the archway, and have to wait while a long stream of people are walking through it.	–
As we walk towards the Castle, two stewards jovially direct us away from what seems to be the main entrance.	–
At first we feel disappointment, but rounding the corner we see to our delight the gloriette rising from the lake. I cannot get far enough back to photograph it, having only brought a fixed focal-length lens.	+
A small group of people has congregated around a small doorway, wondering if that is the right way in to the Castle.	–
We all enter, and would like to know more about the cellars and barrels, and why an old stairway was walled off.	–
Everyone is delighted with the Heraldry Room. A couple are talking animatedly to one of the staff, asking about the Field of the Cloth of Gold. Another couple is asking about the hangings to be seen in the Queen's bedroom.	+
There are few visitors here, and we walk through the corridors and the first exhibits at our own pace.	+
We catch up with a party of about a dozen people, including some young children. They are noisy, and move very slowly.	–
We enjoy viewing the living accommodation, but can't ask questions as the guide is occupied in talking in detail to other visitors.	–
After leaving the Castle, we stroll to the restaurant and shops. There is a school group in the courtyard and the area is quite nosiy.	–
We are pleased with the visit, but are concerned that London is not signposted at the first roundabout after we leave.	–

Key: + a satisfying experience
      – a disappointing experience

2. Signing

(Points 1, 2, 10,12,19 in the visit profile, Table 20.1.) Signs in the grounds are kept to a minimum and are presented in a consistent style, using red or grey lettering on a cream background. However, as people often fail to read the information provided, there is a need for staff to be available to talk to visitors. At Leeds Castle, the ideal is for visitors to see a member of staff at every turning point. All staff are encouraged to interact with visitors, but for some gardeners, this may be less easy. They are primarily employed for their trade skills, although some enjoy talking about their skills with visitors who are often very interested in the carefully designed and tended gardens which are also home to the national collections of catmint and bergamot.

Leeds Castle has a higher staff-to-visitor ratio than most historic attractions: all contact staff are paid on one rate, £3.65 per hour in 1997, the rate being reviewed annually in September. There are about 200 part-time and casual staff, each working two to three days per week. A potential problem at the time this study was undertaken was the proposed introduction of a higher minimum wage, by the European Union. It was expected that they could result in higher entry charges.

3. Interpretation of Leeds Castle

(Points 8, 13, 14, 17 in the visit profle, Table 20.1.) There is very little signage within the Castle, as it is a policy that signs would intrude on the visitors' enjoyment of the building and its contents, giving the impression of being more of a museum than a lived-in house. During normal visiting hours, staff are stationed in each main room or area of the Castle and are expected to be proactive, responding to visitors' interests rather than reciting factual information by rote. This system enables people to move through the various parts of the Castle at a pace dictated by their own interests: some spend more time in the displays of the heraldry room, others are more attracted by other areas such as the furnishings of the drawing room or the Thorpe Hall room. The Castle is regularly opened early from 9.30 a.m. for pre-booked coach parties and for special-interest groups, and in these cases visitors are guided through the Castle by staff using their specialized knowledge and, if required, in a foreign language.

The Leeds Castle guide book is now available in nine languages as 50 per cent of visitors are from overseas. One in seven purchase a copy at the ticket box, the large print run means that it is profitable at £2.50 per copy, although £250,000 is tied up in three years' stock. The guide book is particularly useful when visiting the grounds where there are fewer staff, but also helps enhance visitor enjoyment and understanding of the Castle.

4. Flow of visitors through the Castle

(Points 2, 9, 10, 11, 15, 16 in the visit profile, Table 20.1.) The structure of old buildings such as Leeds Castle is not ideal for large numbers of visitors, and it was essential that they all followed one route through the building. From the first day of opening the Castle it was decided that visitors would enter through the Norman cellars, thus gaining pleasure from the unique exterior view of the gloriette rising from the lake. The visit then proceeds in chronological order through the Castle. Visitors have no choice but to follow the prescribed route through the Castle: unobtrusive rope barriers are placed to guide them.

CONCLUSION

Castles and other historic buildings are a major aspect of the heritage of European (and other) nations, being icons in tourist imagery, and they are an important feature on many tourists' itineraries. This chapter has reviewed some of the general issues in presenting them to visitors; they present many challenges to their managers, and it is imperative to develop appropriate ways to manage the large numbers of visitors they now attract. Leeds Castle is one of Europe's most striking and well-known Castles, and together with its grounds it offers a range of activities for its visitors, and supports a range of charitable causes.

This chapter has demonstrated how the service blueprinting technique can be applied to a well-managed historic building in order to examine how the design of the visit experience can enhance or detract from visitor satisfaction; in the case of Leeds Castle, most visitors are very satisfied. In other cases, a systematic blueprinting analysis of visitor experiences and of the way their visits are resourced and managed could result in the identification of ways to improve the quality of their experiences, and show how to enhance visitor satisfaction for this sector of the heritage tourism industry.

Note

The author acknowledges the courtesy of Mr Graham Jackson, Managing Director, Leeds Castle Enterprises Ltd, and the assistance of the Leeds Castle Foundation. The views expressed in this chapter are those of the author.

REFERENCES

Berry, L. (1995) *On Great Service. A Framework for Action*, New York: Free Press.
Bitner, M. J., Booms, B. H. and Tetreault, M. S. (1990) 'The service encounter: Diagnosing favorable and unfavorable incidents', *Journal of Marketing*, January, 54, 71–84.
Checkland, P. and Scholes, J. (1990) *Soft Systems Methodology in Action*, Chichester: John Wiley & Sons.

Carlzon, J. (1987) *Moments of Truth*, New York: Harper and Row.

Easthaugh, A. and Weiss, N. (1989) 'Broadening the market', in Uzzell, D. (ed.) *Heritage Interpretation*, London: Belhaven Press, 2, 58–67.

Engel, J. F., Blackwell, R. D. and Miniard, P. W. (1986) *Consumer Behaviour*, New York: Dryden Press.

ETB (1996) *National Heritage Monitor*, London: English Tourist Board.

Fellows, J. and Fellows, R. (1990) *Building for Hospitality. Principles of Care and Design for Accommodation Managers*, London: Pitman.

George, W. R. and Gibson, B. E. (1988) *Blueprinting: A Tool for Managing Quality in Organizations*, QUIS Symposium at the University of Karlstad, Sweden, August.

Gronroos, C. (1990) *Service Management and Marketing: Managing the Moments of Truth in Service Competition*, Mass.: Lexington Books.

Gummesson, E. (1988) 'Service quality and product quality combined', *Review of Business*, 9, 3.

Gummesson, E. (1990) 'Service design', *The Total Quality Magazine*, April, 2, 2, 97–101.

Gummesson, E. (1993) *Quality Management in Service Organization, an Interpretation of the Service Quality Phenomenon and a Synthesis of International Research*, Karlstadt, Sweden: ISQA.

Hollins, G. and Hollins, B. (1991) *Total Design, Managing The Design Process In The Service Sector*, London: Pitman.

Kingman-Brundage, J. (1989) 'Blueprinting for the bottom line', in *Service Excellence: Marketing's Impact on Performance*, Chicago: AMA.

Kirk, D. (1995) 'Hard and soft systems: A common paradigm for operations management?', *International Journal of Contemporary Hospitality Management*, 7, 5.

Laws, E. (1986) 'Identifying and managing the consumerist gap', *Service Industries Journal*.

Laws, E. (1991) *Tourism Marketing, Service and Quality Management Perspectives*, Cheltenham: Stanley Thornes.

Leeds Castle Foundation (1994) *Leeds Castle*, London: Philip Wilson Publishers.

Leppard, J. and Molyneux, L. (1994) *Auditing Your Customer Service*, London: Routledge.

Locke, E. A. and Scweiger, D. M. (1979) 'Participation in decision making, one more look', in Staw, B. M. (ed.) *Research in Organizational Behaviour*, Vol 1. Greenwich, Connecticut: JAI Press.

Lockyer, K. G. and Oakland, J. S. (1981) 'How to sample success', *Management Today*, July.

Normann, R. (1991) *Service Management: Strategy and Leadership In Service Businesses*, Chichester: John Wiley & Sons.

Reeves, C. A. and Bednar, D. A. (1994) 'Defining quality: alternatives and implications', *Academy of Management Review*, Spring, 19, 3, 419–445.

Sasser, E. W., Olsen, P. R. and Wycoff, D. D. (1978) *Management of Service Operations*, Boston: Allyn & Bacon.

Senior, M. and Akehurst, G. (1992) *The Perceptual Service Blueprinting Paradigm*, Proceedings of the Second QUIS Conference, St Johns University, New York, 177–192.

Shostack, G. L. (1981) 'How to design a service', in Donnelley, J. H. and George, W. R. *Marketing of Services*, American Marketing Association.

Shostack, L. (1985) 'Planning the service encounter', in Czepiel, J. A., Soloman, M. R. and Surprenant, C. F. (eds) *The Service Encounter, Managing Employee/Customer Interaction in Service Business*, Mass.: Lexington Books.

Wilkie, W. L. (1986) *Consumer Behaviour*, New York: John Wiley & Sons.

MODEL QUESTIONS

1. What special difficulties face the managers of historic buildings in opening them to paying visitors?

2. What do you consider to be the drawbacks of the interpretation system in use at Leeds Castle?

3. Surveys indicate that most visitors to Leeds Castle are very satisfied with their visit. How is this achieved?

CHAPTER 21

Coventry Museums and Galleries: A Case Study

Alf Hatton

This case study covers the period 1992 to 1994 and considers the strategy problem, reformulation process, and emergent strategy. While drawing conclusions specific to this case, they have general relevance for future strategy formulation in heritage organizations. Coventry Museums and Galleries at this time comprised:

- The Herbert Art Gallery & Museum ('the Herbert').
- The Lunt Roman Fort.
- Whitefriars.
- The Excavation Unit.
- St Mary's Mediaeval Guildhall Guides.
- The Exhibition Box.

The service had been amalgamated into cultural services, itself comprising libraries, arts, archives, and an arts and media studio, as a single division of Leisure Services. An immediate operational problem with strategic impact was the use of the Herbert as the common departmental, shorthand reference for the entire service. It implied a perception that all the service's outlets offered the same product to the same market: an undifferentiated product for a homogeneous market. The impact of this strategic myopia at an operational level was that each outlet was treated as identical: decisions about which would be closed (to achieve budget cuts) were even being seriously considered before the review. Leisure Services also financed and managed the Museum of British Road Transport, an independent museum, and sites of ecological interest. Other city departments were responsible for historic buildings. If a truly strategic approach was to have been taken, a council-wide review might have been expected.

Clearly, this lack of strategic thinking (Davies 1993) was not unique to the Herbert or leisure: '. . . research [which] reveals that less than 50 per cent of authorities currently possess any form of leisure and/or tourism strategy and many of these are ready for renewal' (Harniess 1991).

Everyone, including the museums and galleries staff, were of one mind: *the Herbert was under-performing*. No specific benchmark or comparator had been used to establish that view, but there was general agreement that much-needed change and improvements could and *should* be made.

THE STRATEGY 'PROBLEM'

There had been three previous internal reviews (1987, 1989 and 1990), centring solely on the Herbert and containing conflicting statements on the Herbert's mission. Thus, there was no clear agreement as to what the Herbert's purpose was, and no consideration of the product portfolio as a whole.

The reviews adhered to a formal, bureaucratic, strategic planning approach, significantly not even hinting at potential change blockers. This silence on *soft issues* in change management implied a belief that new systems alone would resolve the Herbert's inertia, that management could simply impose change.

What had amounted to strategy shoe-horned the Herbert into a narrow, community-oriented role and, laudable though this was, it ignored all other possible roles and economic impact. As a large civic museum and gallery, it seemed more reasonable to re-develop the Herbert with tourism and leisure as its primary mission, and clearly understood that, *en route*, enhanced facilities would benefit the various Coventry communities.

An implicit statement of the current museum priority from government was:

> Accustomed to high standards of display and communication through exposure to television, magazines, commercial exhibitions and shops, the public now demand similar standards in museums. They want to be entertained and informed in the manner to which they have become accustomed, and they expect access to information to be made easy for them.
>
> (Museums and Galleries Commission 1987)

This agenda was clearly moving museums away from an object-centred, curatorially-driven focus which favours collections and research. Some Herbert staff believed this shift in emphasis to be a major problem, as was shown later by the organizational culture research evidence.

Given previous review failures, it was essential that any new strategy be informed by investigating the Herbert's organizational culture, by a series of semi-structured interviews with the staff. Whilst the results clearly informed the concurrent, traditional strategic approaches, it would not be unreasonable to state that the research itself was responsible for eliciting much of the support for the later change agenda, by opening up discussion of change in a non-confrontational way. The strategy problem was that top management were focused almost exclusively on cost-cutting, there was no clearly defined primary role for any part of the service, and that a new gallery had been agreed on the basis of tourism without the full commitment of all the staff.

THE STRATEGY FORMULATION PROCESS

The allegation that the Herbert was a high spender appeared true when net expenditure/visitor (Audit Commission 1991) was calculated. Therefore the new strategy started with a traditional cost centre review of all six centres, complemented by an independently commissioned review by the council's external auditors, entitled *The Road to Wigan Pier?* (Audit Commission 1991).

This basic financial analysis showed that the Herbert was:

- a low earner: it did not realize average income of 13 per cent of gross expenditure (Audit Commission 1991);
- staff and overheads were being carried centrally, with income retained at cost centre;
- offices and even some office services for other parts of Leisure were being carried without charge or overhead recovery.

Although finance clearly was not insignificant, the problem was not previously analysed even to this level: where it had been posited as the problem, it was actually a symptom of much deeper problems.

At one extreme, the Herbert's need for a review was key to its survival both within the city council, itself struggling with decreasing resources and increasing demands, and also within Leisure, where the Herbert was not then perceived to be fulfilling any clearly articulated role.

The general justification for organizational reviews, and accompanying organizational change, is the need, or perceived need, to respond to the fact, or perceived fact, of the increasing rate of change (Toffler 1970, and museum-specific, Singleton 1979), and the by now universally cited dynamic and turbulent operating environment.

The imminent building of a major new gallery, significant cuts in budgets, and further predicted cuts, all added up to such an environment for the Herbert. In one sense, the decision to proceed with a new gallery before an overall strategy had been developed added to that complexity. Yet it also lent urgency to the strategy formulation process in a way that impressed even the most laggardly of resistors to change.

EMERGENT STRATEGY

The emergent strategy had three main aspects: 'learn little'; stop budget leakages; 'disinvest in bricks and mortar – reinvest in people and programmes'.

'Learn little' simply meant piloting new ideas, by taking the opportunity of the Lunt's relaunch during Year of the Romans (1993) a year earlier than the planned opening of the Herbert's new gallery. It meant, in relative terms, a smaller risk, and provided for experimentation and staff development in new ideas and approaches.

Stopping budget leakages reflected the fact that all but one cost centre – the Excavation Unit – actually drained the Herbert's budgets. Shifting overheads to appropriate cost centres *per se* did not resolve the Herbert's high spender/low earner conundrum. Indeed, it worsened the balance sheet for other cost centres. But it did begin to unpick the myth that all the service's problems were at the Herbert.

The service's aggregated net expenditure per visitor was actually below the national average (£4.50 for local authority museums: Audit Commission 1991). Three out of five cost centres recovered more income than the local authority average (13 per cent of gross expenditure: *ibid.*), and had lower-than-average net expenditure per visitor. The Lunt actually recovered more than the national average for independent museums (50 per cent of gross expenditure: *ibid.*). Though these figures were only a general guide, since user figures were estimates only where no admission charge applied, the objective had to be to concentrate resources on the main objective: the new gallery.

The guided tours service was to be made to pay for itself or close, if the proposed nominal charge turned out to be a barrier. The Lunt effectively made a small surplus during its 'closed' winter season from tours by school and other guided parties. However, this surplus was then fully consumed by losses on casual visitors in the 'open' summer season. It had never been marketed to casual visitors, and as a consequence its pricing (then £0.50p) had failed to keep up, the Heart of England Tourist Board regional average historic buildings admission price then being £1.94 (Eckstein 1992). The Lunt provided a useful model for admission charges while maintaining sensitivity to educational usage, and operating a thriving gift desk.

Its re-launch in Year of the Romans 1993 concentrated on casual visitors, a reduced 'open' season (thus reducing costs), augmenting the visitor experience with an audioguide, and repricing. At that time, three-quarters of schools' use was paid for directly by schools from outside the city, so city schools were brought into line. What evidence existed, showed city residents were neither frequent users, nor a high percentage of users. Nevertheless, a discount ticket scheme was floated to deflect accusations of an excessive price rise.

'Disinvest in bricks and mortar' was perhaps the most difficult aspect to address, both in terms of the consequent publicity and staff attachment: it closed Whitefriars as a visitor centre. Whitefriars had tried, and failed, to acquire and hold an audience three times in twenty years. However, a number of options were considered:

- a major annual exhibition of the calibre of the Royal Armouries Civil War Touring Exhibition;
- increasing income by charging for ecology advisory reports, replicating Archaeology Unit practice;
- an out-of-hours arts events programme;
- a programme of Living History events.

It was recognized that even a combination of these was unlikely to recover full annual operating costs. Any one of these scenarios would impact severely on the building through the increased numbers required to achieve self-financing status. As a prime objective was safeguarding heritage, in this case one of the most important buildings in the city, it seemed perverse even to pursue such usage models. Pursuing any one of these options also meant diverting limited resources available for investment in change: Whitefriars simply did not make top priority. This had already been decided by the city: a new gallery for the Herbert.

Each of these initiatives reinforced the new thinking that had been introduced, that the service's outlets actually had different products appropriate to different segments of the edutainment (Rodger 1987) market (see Table 21.1), and not, as had been the prior spurious assumption, a single product with universal appeal. This new strategic thinking also directly affected the shape of service at the operational level: if no casual visitors visit in winter, the outlet should not staff up to receive them!

The Herbert then needed to be re-positioned within city perceptions as a city-centre tourist attraction, rather than solely as a very costly and relatively ineffective community-oriented museum. This was underpinned by a major market research project to pinpoint existing audience characteristics.

The Herbert's new role would be to add its new gallery to the city's incoming tourism portfolio, and secondly to service the specific needs of disadvantaged groups most likely in outreach form, rather than attempting to cater for non-homogeneous audiences simultaneously with a single undifferentiated product. In its re-design, the Herbert would incorporate as many opportunities for disadvantaged groups as possible by removing both physical and intellectual barriers to participation.

Consistent with traditional strategic approaches, changes in external circumstances meant some changes in internal structures. The Herbert's staff structure had sections of no more than two, and frequently only one, and it was evident that the structure would not assist the planned changes in mission and markets.

Kovach's museum strategic planning model (1989) – a decentralized, divisional model with policy-making separated from operations – can be traced back to Alfred Sloan's reorganization of General Motors in the 1920s (Whittington 1993). It was introduced into the UK public sector with the Bains Report (1972) (Greenwood and Wilson 1989) and wholeheartedly adopted in 1974 Local Government Reorganization. As a model, it may be appropriate to larger UK museums, but, in emulating them, many smaller UK museums, such as the Herbert, have been generating their own problems.

Re-thinking staffing immediately raises questions of who are museum users, what do they want, and what 'products' or 'services' do museums provide? Effective market research can answer the first, but museums have been slow to undertake market research or absorb marketing models as a part of their overall thinking

(Prince and Higgins-McLoughlin 1987; Audit Commission 1994a). So museum staffing structures tend to be very traditional. Given a perceived shift toward greater customer focus added to increasingly varied demands on museums, alternative approaches deserve further consideration and experimentation. Diamond (1992) and Pheysey (1993) show alternatives to the usual approach.

So the staff structure was redesigned broadly with collections staff and visitor contact staff in two sections. Warding staff roles were also re-thought with the intention of achieving:

- a reduction in high security costs;
- more flexible front-of-house staffing.

This is another indication of the intimate link between strategy-building and operations: strategy predicates – in this case, structure; and structure shifts day-to-day operations from where they are at the outset of a new strategy, to where they have to be if the strategy is to be achieved.

THE ORGANIZATIONAL CULTURE RESEARCH

Fundamentally, where previous reviews had gone wrong was in tackling the concept of change from an entirely rational management perspective (Lenz and Lyles 1989). As Pugh states (1973): 'Organizations are organisms. They are not mechanisms which can be taken apart and reassembled differently as required.' Effective change is said to be a dynamic combination of structure, strategy, systems, style, skills, staff, and superordinate goals (Waterman, Peters and Phillips 1991), style and superordinate goals being another description of culture. Organizational culture is so powerful in organizations, that managing change is said to be about managing changes in culture (Johnson and Scholes 1989; Waterman, Peters and Phillips 1991).

Though there is much debate around organizational culture, it is clear that any new strategy would have had far less chance of implementation, without 'grass roots' involvement, engagement, and ownership. Thus, the semi-structured staff interviews, reflecting the manager's belief in a 'bottom up' approach, were pivotal in unblocking the organization.

In the specific context of the urgent need to develop a strategy to wrap around the primary objective of a new gallery, this could be seen as a mechanistic, classical management approach. In the context of the need to develop a self-sustaining organizational culture which actually addresses organizational challenges, it could equally validly be interpreted as being both thoroughly postmodern and strategic in that it engaged all staff in organizational developments which affected their future.

The imminent opening of the new gallery in June 1994 presented the city with a significant and once-only opportunity to:

- re-launch the Herbert with a new, upbeat identity reflecting its new role unequivocally in terms of incoming tourism, allowing the Herbert to develop outreach services, sensitive to need;
- introduce charges for some services;
- close for three months prior to opening, in order to conduct staff training and retraining; re-think the entrance, build new facilities – cafe, shop – and make a significant start on under-developed income-earning opportunities.

Delivering all this was of course just a matter of informing staff in a reasonable manner, and the staff, seeing the reasonableness of all of this, would simply fall into line, and enthusiastically engage with, and deliver, the desired outcomes!

Clearly also, there were subtexts:

- defining a new purpose by involving all staff in developing a new mission;
- a market-led, as opposed to product-led, strategy for each separate cost centre (Table 21.1), questioning outdated thinking in terms of a single undifferentiated product;

Table 21.1: A multi-level marketing strategy.

Cost centre	Lunt	The Herbert	Whitefriars	Exhibition Box	St Mary's Guides
Main 'products':	Tourism	Tourism	Lettings	Community Exhibitions	Tourism
	Education	Education Outreach	Training Events		
Targets:	Day trips in West Midlands	Family visits in West Midlands Outreach to communities and disadvantaged groups	Businesses Non-profits	All-comers	Those already in Coventry
	Schools	Schools			
UBP (Unique Buying Points):	Day out in Baginton	Quality of visitor experience, not just quality of exhibits	Exclusive ambience	Cheap and effective, accessible	Holding operation pending consultancy on Hall's longer-term use
	National Curriculum	National Curriculum Sense of identity for Coventry Owner ship of material remains of multiple Coventry 'identities'			

- market research to dispel the myth of a homogeneous audience;
- a flatter structure moving away from an academic basis, coupled with re-training – for some staff, their first ever.

CONCLUSIONS

Firstly, the very reliance of three previous reviews on a formal, rational approach may well have produced the very inertia they identified as the 'problem'. As prescriptive, deterministic approaches, they ignored the need to create awareness of the need for, and commitment to, change (Quinn 1989).

Thus this case study indicates that a dynamic combination of classical strategic management approaches with softer, phenomenological approaches does offer more guarantee of achieving desired outcomes. It also identifies the intimate link between strategy and operations, strategy predetermining the shape of operations, and operations to a very large extent determining the success or otherwise of strategy.

The crowning glory, as it were, is that the new gallery – Godiva City – was not only built and opened on time, but that it achieved wide recognition for the innovative way it dealt with both its content – a long and complex city social history – and the way it addressed the needs of disadvantaged groups, in particular visual impairment.

FURTHER READING

Anthony, P. (1994) *Managing Culture*, Buckingham: Open University Press.

Audit Commission (1994b) *The Quality Exchange. Museum Service, Section II, Detailed Findings of Survey*, London: Audit Commission.

Davies, S. (1994) *The Use and Value of Performance Indicators in the UK Museums Sector, Analysis of Responses to a Questionnaire*, London: Museums Association (Public Affairs Committee)/University of Leeds (School of Business and Economic Studies).

Hampden-Turner, C. (1990) *Corporate Culture: From Vicious to Virtuous Circles*, London: Hutchinson/Economist Books.

Handy, C. (1985) *Understanding Organizations*, Harmondsworth: Penguin.

Handy, C. (1988) *Understanding Voluntary Organizations*, Harmondsworth: Penguin.

Handy, C. (1989) *The Age of Unreason*, London: Random-Century.

Harrison, R. (1972) 'Understanding your organization's character', *Harvard Business Review*, 50, 3, 119–128.

Lorsch, J. (1986) 'Managing culture: the invisible barrier to change', *California Management Review*, 28, 2, 95–109.

Peters, T. J. and Waterman, R . H. (1982) *In Search of Excellence. Lessons from America's Best-Run Companies*, New York: Harper & Row.

Schein, E. (1985) *Organizational Culture and Leadership*, San Francisco: Jossey-Bass.

Schein, E. (1989) 'Organizational culture: What it is and how to change it', in Evans, P., Doz, T. and Laurent, A. (eds) *Human Resource Management in International Firms*, London: Macmillan, 56–81.

Schein, E. H. (1993) 'Coming to a new awareness of organizational culture', in Salaman, G. *et al.* (eds) *Human Resource Strategies*, London: Sage, 237–253.

Trice, H. and Beyer, J. (1984) 'Studying organizational cultures through rites and ceremonials', *Academy of Management Review*, 9, 4, 653–669.

Watson, T. J. (1994) *In Search of Management: Culture, Chaos and Control in Managerial Work*, London: Routledge.

REFERENCES

Audit Commission (1991) *The Road to Wigan Pier? Managing Local Authority Museums and Art Galleries*, London: HMSO.

Audit Commission (1994a) *The Quality Exchange, Museum Service. Section I, Overview of Findings*, London: Audit Commission.

Bains Report (1972) *The Local Authorities: Management and Structure*, London: HMSO.

Davies, S. (1993) 'Planning in a Crisis', *Museums Journal*, 93, 7, 31–33.

Diamond, M. (1992) 'Personnel management', in Thompson, J. M. A. *Manual of Curatorship, A Guide to Museum Practice*, 2nd edition, London: Butterworth-Heinemann, 159–166.

Eckstein, J. (ed.) (1992) *Cultural Trends 1992*, London: Policy Studies Institute.

Greenwood, J. and Wilson, D. (1989) *Public Administration in Britain Today*, London: Routledge.

Harniess, S. (1991) 'What's the Plan?', *Leisure Management*, 11, 10, 42–45.

Johnson, G. (1989) 'Rethinking incrementalism', in Asch, D. and Bowman, C. (eds) *Readings in Strategic Management*, London: Macmillan Educational Ltd., 37–56.

Johnson, G. and Scholes, K. (1989) *Exploring Corporate Strategy. Text and Cases*, London: Prentice-Hall.

Kovach, C. (1989) 'Strategic Management for Museums', *International Journal of Museum Management and Curatorship*, 8, 137–148.

Lenz, R. T. and Lyles, M. A. (1989) 'Paralysis by analysis: Is your planning system becoming too rational?', in Asch, D. and Bowman, C. *Readings in Strategic Management*, Basingstoke: Macmillan Educational Ltd, 57–70.

Museums and Galleries Commission (1987) *Museum Training and Career Structure*, London: HMSO.

Pheysey, D. C. (1993) *Organizational Cultures. Types and Transformations*, London: Routledge.

Prince, D. R. and Higgins-McLoughlin, B. (1987) *Museums UK: The Findings of the Museums Data-Base*, London: Museums Association.

Pugh, D. S. (1973) 'The measurement of organization structures: Does context determine form?', *Organization Dynamics*, Spring, 19–34, also in Pugh, D. S. (ed.) (1990) *Organization Theory. Selected Readings*, Harmondsworth: Penguin, 44–63.

Quinn, J. B. (1989) 'Managing strategic change', in Asch, D. and Bowman, C. (eds) *Readings in Strategic Management*, Basingstoke: Macmillan Educational Ltd, 20–36.

Rodger, L. (1987) 'Museums in education: seizing the market opportunities', in Ambrose, T. (ed.), *Education in Museums: Museums in Education*, Edinburgh: HMSO.

Singleton, H. R. (1979) 'Museums in a changing world', *Museums Journal*, 79, 1, June, 11–12.

Toffler, A. (1970) *Future Shock*, London: Pan Books Ltd.

Waterman, R. H., Peters, T. J., and Phillips, J. R. (1991) 'The 7-S framework' in Mintzberg, H. and Quinn, J. B. (eds) *The Strategy Process: Concepts, Contexts and Cases*, 2nd edition, London: Prentice-Hall, 308–314.

Whittington, R. (1993) *What is Strategy? and Does it Matter?* London: Routledge.

MODEL QUESTIONS

1. What can be determined from this case about local authority leisure department strategy-making? Can the very diverse services represented by leisure departments be strategically managed?

2. Approaches to strategy-making can be divided into hard and soft: which aspects of strategy-making in this case were hard, and which were soft? Which were critical in inducing so much change, where many previous change initiatives had failed?

3. Local authority museums tend to have traditional organizational structures based along the lines of the collections they look after. What other structures could they have, and what would be the implications of alternative structures?

Index